Fundamentals of
Game Design

Fundamentals of Game Design

Edited by
Zion Gibson

Larsen & Keller
www.larsen-keller.com

Fundamentals of Game Design
Edited by Zion Gibson
ISBN: 978-1-63549-130-2 (Hardback)

© 2017 Larsen & Keller

Published by Larsen and Keller Education,
5 Penn Plaza,
19th Floor,
New York, NY 10001, USA

Cataloging-in-Publication Data

Fundamentals of game design / edited by Zion Gibson.
        p. cm.
Includes bibliographical references and index.
ISBN 978-1-63549-130-2
1. Video games. 2. Video games--Design. 3. Games and technology. I. Gibson, Zion.
GV1469.3 .F86 2017
794.8--dc23

The publisher's policy is to use permanent paper from mills that operate a sustainable forestry policy. Furthermore, the publisher ensures that the text paper and cover boards used have met acceptable environmental accreditation standards.

Printed and bound in the United States of America.

For more information regarding Larsen and Keller Education and its products, please visit the publisher's website www.larsen-keller.com

Table of Contents

Preface

Game design is a fairly recent field. It deals with the creation of games by using the elements of design aesthetics. It is multidisciplinary, and uses the elements of optimization theory, probability, economics and artificial intelligence, etc. Different approaches, evaluations and methodologies on game design have been included in this book. Most of the topics introduced in it cover new techniques and the applications of this field. This textbook is meant for students who are looking for an elaborate reference text on game design.

To facilitate a deeper understanding of the contents of this book a short introduction of every chapter is written below:

Chapter 1- The designing and development of video and computer games for commercial and private use is known as game design. Game designers incorporate aesthetics, logic, strategy and popular culture into game designs to make them more appealing to the masses. Successful game franchises can run into several seasons and have earned their creators billions of dollars in sales revenue. This chapter provides a comprehensive overview of game design.

Chapter 2- When a video game design has been constructed by the designers, it is the programmers that convert the idea and images into the final game. This involves game programming which is the software side of game development. When the game is published internationally, it involves converting game language and content to the local language. Also, the gameplay content needs to be altered keeping in mind the sensitivities of the new target audience. This chapter deals with subjects like video game development, game programming, game testing, video game localization, game server, mod and independent video game development.

Chapter 3- The creation of a video game design requires input from designers and programmers. A video game starts from an idea that can be classified under one of the several genres. The whole game is planned out with consideration to game features, story, target audience, budget etc. This chapter illustrates the developmental course of a video game design from its inception till its final unveiling. The content informs the reader about topics like game mechanics, game art design, character creation, level design, field of view, dynamic game difficulty balancing etc.

Chapter 4- The earliest video games used text instead of vector graphics. This entailed players reading descriptions about the game setting, players and the actions that take place. But with the emergence of flash, vector graphics became popular. This was then replaced by 2D, 2.5D, 3D graphics and pixelated isometric graphics. In this chapter, the reader is introduced to the video game graphic styles chronologically to provide a timeline for the changing trends in video game graphic design.

Chapter 5- Based on the manner in which players interact with each other and the virtual environment through gameplay, video games are categorized into action, adventure, role-playing, simulation, strategy and massively multiplayer online video game. This chapter explains each type with suitable examples to aid in a better understanding of the different genres. A part of the chapter focuses on strategy video game and its sub-types. Game design is best understood in confluence with the major topics listed in the following chapter.

Chapter 6- This chapter introduces the reader to game design jargon like nonlinear gameplay, virtual world, virtual economy, free-to-play, gold sink, time sink, gamification, game engine and gameplay micromanagement. Some concepts have been in use for many decades while challenging narration and story-arcs have led to the development of newer concepts of game design. The aspects elucidated in this chapter are of vital importance, and provide a better understanding of this field.

I owe the completion of this book to the never-ending support of my family, who supported me throughout the project.

Editor

Introduction to Game Design

The designing and development of video and computer games for commercial and private use is known as game design. Game designers incorporate aesthetics, logic, strategy and popular culture into game designs to make them more appealing to the masses. Successful game franchises can run into several seasons and have earned their creators billions of dollars in sales revenue. This chapter provides a comprehensive overview of game design.

Game Design

Game design is the art of applying design and aesthetics to create a game to facilitate interaction between players for entertainment or for medical, educational, or experimental purposes. Game design can be applied both to games and, increasingly, to other interactions, particularly virtual ones.

Game design creates goals, rules, and challenges to define a sport, tabletop game, casino game, video game, role-playing game, or simulation that produces desirable interactions among its participants and, possibly, spectators.

Academically, game design is part of game studies, while game theory studies strategic decision making (primarily in non-game situations). Games have historically inspired seminal research in the fields of probability, artificial intelligence, economics, and optimization theory. Applying game design to itself is a current research topic in metadesign.

History

Sports, gambling, and board games are known, respectively, to have existed for at least ten thousand, six thousand, and five thousand years.

Folk Process

Tabletop games played today whose descent can be traced from ancient times include chess, go, pachisi, backgammon, mahjong, mancala, and pick-up sticks. The rules of these games were not codified until early modern times and their features gradually evolved and changed over time, through the folk process. Given this, these games are not considered to have had a designer or been the result of a design process in the modern sense.

After the rise of commercial game publishing in the late 19th century, many games which had formerly evolved via folk processes became commercial properties, often with custom scoring pads or preprepared material. For example, the similar public domain games Generala, Yacht, and Yatzy led to the commercial game Yahtzee in the mid-1950s.

Today, many commercial games, such as Taboo, Balderdash, Pictionary, or Time's Up!, are descended from traditional parlour games. Adapting traditional games to become commercial properties is an example of game design.

Similarly, many sports, such as soccer and baseball, are the result of folk processes, while others were designed, such as basketball, invented in 1891 by James Naismith.

New Media

Technological advances have provided new media for games throughout history. The printing press allowed packs of playing cards, adapted from Mahjong tiles, to be mass-produced, leading to many new card games. Accurate topographic maps produced as lithographs and provided free to Prussian officers helped popularize wargaming. Cheap bookbinding (printed labels wrapped around cardboard) led to mass-produced board games with custom boards. Inexpensive (hollow) lead figurine casting contributed to the development of miniature wargaming. Cheap custom dice led to poker dice. Flying discs led to disc golf and Ultimate. Personal computers contributed to the popularity of computer games, leading to the wide availability of video game consoles and video games. Smart phones have led to a proliferation of mobile games.

The first games in a new medium are frequently adaptations of older games. Pong, one of the first widely disseminated video games, adapted table tennis. Later games will often exploit distinctive properties of a new medium. Adapting older games and creating original games for new media are both examples of game design.

Theory

Game studies or gaming theory is a discipline that deals with the critical study of games, game design, players, and their role in society and culture. Prior to the late-twentieth century, the academic study of games was rare and limited to fields such as history and anthropology. As the video game revolution took off in the early 1980s, so did academic interest in games, resulting in a field that draws on diverse methodologies and schools of thought. These influences may be characterized broadly in three ways: the social science approach, the humanities approach, and the industry and engineering approach.

Broadly speaking, the social scientific approach has concerned itself with the question of "What do games do to people?" Using tools and methods such as surveys, controlled laboratory experiments, and ethnography researchers have investigated both the positive and negative impacts that playing games could have on people. More sociologically informed research has sought to move away from simplistic ideas of gaming as either 'negative' or 'positive', but rather seeking to understand its role and location in the complexities of everyday life.

In general terms, the humanities approach has concerned itself with the question of "What meanings are made through games?" Using tools and methods such as interviews, ethnographies and participant observation, researchers have investigated the various roles that videogames play in people's lives and activities together with the meaning they assign to their experiences.

From an industry perspective, a lot of game studies research can be seen as the academic response to the videogame industry's questions regarding the products it creates and sells. The main question this approach deals with can be summarized as "How can we create better games?" with the accompanying "What makes a game good?" "Good" can be taken to mean many different things, including providing an entertaining and an engaging experience, being easy to learn and play, and being innovative and having novel experiences. Different approaches to studying this problem have included looking at describing how to design games and extracting guidelines and rules of thumb for making better games

Strategic Decision Making

Game theory is a study of strategic decision making. Specifically, it is "the study of mathematical models of conflict and cooperation between intelligent rational decision-makers". An alternative term suggested "as a more descriptive name for the discipline" is *interactive decision theory*. The subject first addressed zero-sum games, such that one person's gains exactly equal net losses of the other participant or participants. Today, however, game theory applies to a wide range of behavioral relations, and has developed into an umbrella term for the logical side of decision science.

The games studied in game theory are well-defined mathematical objects. To be fully defined, a game must specify the following elements: the *players* of the game, the *information* and *actions* available to each player at each decision point, and the *payoffs* for each outcome. (Rasmusen refers to these four "essential elements" by the acronym "PAPI".) A game theorist typically uses these elements, along with a solution concept of their choosing, to deduce a set of equilibrium strategies for each player such that, when these strategies are employed, no player can profit by unilaterally deviating from their strategy. These equilibrium strategies determine an equilibrium to the game—a stable state in which either one outcome occurs or a set of outcomes occur with known probability.

Design Elements

Games can be characterized by "what the player does." This is often referred to as gameplay. Major key elements identified in this context are tools and rules that define the overall context of game.

Tools of Play

Games are often classified by the components required to play them (e.g. miniatures, a ball, cards, a board and pieces, or a computer). In places where the use of leather is well established, the ball has been a popular game piece throughout recorded history, resulting in a worldwide popularity of ball games such as rugby, basketball, football, cricket, tennis, and volleyball. Other tools are more idiosyncratic to a certain region. Many countries in Europe, for instance, have unique standard decks of playing cards. Other games such as chess may be traced primarily through the development and evolution of its game pieces.

Many game tools are tokens, meant to represent other things. A token may be a pawn on a board, play money, or an intangible item such as a point scored.

Games such as hide-and-seek or tag do not utilise any obvious tool; rather, their interactivity is defined by the environment. Games with the same or similar rules may have different gameplay if the environment is altered. For example, hide-and-seek in a school building differs from the same game in a park; an auto race can be radically different depending on the track or street course, even with the same cars.

Rule Development

Whereas games are often characterized by their tools, they are often defined by their rules. While rules are subject to variations and changes, enough change in the rules usually results in a "new" game. There are exceptions to this in that some games deliberately involve the changing of their own rules, but even then there are often immutable meta-rules.

Rules generally determine turn order, the rights and responsibilities of the players, and each player's goals. Player rights may include when they may spend resources or move tokens.

Victory Conditions

Common win conditions are being first to amass a certain quota of points or tokens (as in Settlers of Catan), having the greatest number of tokens at the end of the game (as in Monopoly), or some relationship of one's game tokens to those of one's opponent (as in chess's checkmate).

Single or Multiplayer

Most games require multiple players. However, single-player games are unique in respect to the type of challenges a player faces. Many games described as "single-player" may be termed actually puzzles or recreations. Unlike a game with multiple players competing with or against each other to reach the game's goal, a one-player game is a battle solely against an element of the environment (an artificial opponent), against one's own skills, against time, or against chance.

Storyline and Plot

Stories told in games may focus on narrative elements that can be communicated through the use of mechanics and player choice. Narrative plots in games generally have a clearly defined and simplistic structure. Mechanical choices on the part of the designer(s) often drastically effect narrative elements in the game. However, due to a lack of unified and standardized teaching and understanding of narrative elements in games, individual interpretations, methods, and terminology vary wildly. Because of this, most narrative elements in games are created unconsciously and intuitively. However, as a general rule, game narratives increase in complexity and scale as player choice or game mechanics increase in complexity and scale. One example of this is removing a players ability to directly affect the plot for a limited time. This lack of player choice necessitates an increase in mechanical complexity, and could be used as a metaphor to symbolize depression that is felt by a character in the narrative.

Luck and Strategy

A game's tools and rules will result in its requiring skill, strategy, luck, or a combination thereof, and are classified accordingly.

Games of skill include games of physical skill, such as wrestling, tug of war, hopscotch, target shooting, and stake, and games of mental skill such as checkers and chess. Games of strategy include checkers, chess, go, arimaa, and tic-tac-toe, and often require special equipment to play them. Games of chance include gambling games (blackjack, mah-jongg, roulette, etc.), as well as snakes and ladders and rock, paper, scissors; most require equipment such as cards or dice.

Most games contain two or all three of these elements. For example, American football and base-ball involve both physical skill and strategy while tiddlywinks, poker, and Monopoly combine strategy and chance. Many card and board games combine all three; most trick-taking games involve mental skill, strategy, and an element of chance, as do many strategic board games such as Risk, Settlers of Catan, and Carcassonne.

Use as Educational Tool

By learning through play children can develop social and cognitive skills, mature emotionally, and gain the self-confidence required to engage in new experiences and environments. Key ways that young children learn include playing, being with other people, being active, exploring and new experiences, talking to themselves, communication with others, meeting physical and mental challenges, being shown how to do new things, practicing and repeating skills and having fun.

Play develops children's content knowledge and provides children the opportunity to develop social skills, competences and disposition to learn. Play-based learning is based on a Vygotskian model of scaffolding where the teacher pays attention on specific elements of the play activity and provides encouragement and feedback on children's learning. When children engage in real-life and imaginary activities, play can be challenging in children's thinking. To extend the learning process, sensitive intervention can be provided with adult support when necessary during play-based learning.

Development Process

Game Artist

A game artist is an artist who creates art for one or more types of games. Game artists are responsible for all of the aspects of game development that call for visual art. Game artists are often noted in role-playing games, collectible card games and video games.

Testing

Game testing, a subset of game development, is a software testing process for quality control of video games. The primary function of game testing is the discovery and documentation of software defects (aka bugs). Interactive entertainment software testing is a highly technical field requiring computing expertise, analytic competence, critical evaluation skills, and endurance. In recent years the field of game testing has come under fire for being excessively strenuous and unrewarding, both financially and emotionally.

Strategies

Board Games

Board game design is the development of rules and presentational aspects of a board game. When a player takes part in a game, it is the player's self-subjection to the rules that creates a sense of purpose for the duration of the game. Maintaining the players' interest throughout the gameplay experience is the goal of board game design. To achieve this, board game designers emphasize different aspects such as social interaction, strategy, and competition, and target players of differing needs by providing for short versus long-play, and luck versus skill. Beyond this, board game design reflects the culture in which the board game is produced.

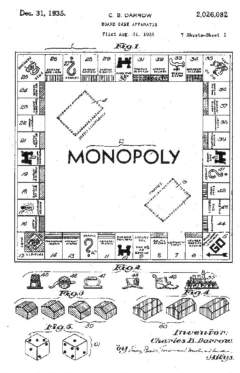

Charles Darrow's 1935 patent for *Monopoly* includes specific design elements developed during the prototype phase. Prototypes are very common in the later stages of board game design, and "prototype circles" in many cities today provide an opportunity for designers to play and critique each other's games.

The most ancient board games known today are over 5000 years old. They are frequently abstract in character and their design is primarily focused on a core set of simple rules. Of those that are still played today, games like go (c.400BC), mancala (c.700AD), and chess (c.600AD) have gone through many presentational and/or rule variations. In the case of chess, for example, new variants are developed constantly, to focus on certain aspects of the game, or just for variation's sake.

Traditional board games date from the nineteenth and early twentieth century. Whereas ancient board game design was primarily focused on rules alone, traditional board games were often influenced by Victorian mores. Academic (e.g. history and geography) and moral didacticism were important design features for traditional games, and Puritan associations between dice and the Devil meant that early American game designers eschewed their use in board games entirely. Even traditional games that did use dice, like *Monopoly* (based on the 1906 *The Landlord's Game*), were rooted in educational efforts to explain political concepts to the masses. By the 1930s and 1940s, board game design began to emphasize amusement over education, and characters from comic strips, radio programmes, and (in the 1950s) television shows began to be featured in board game adaptations.

Recent developments in modern board game design can be traced to the 1980s in Germany, and have led to increased popularity of "German-style board games" (also known as "Eurogames" or "designer games"). The design emphasis of these board games is to give players meaningful choices. This is manifested by eliminating elements like randomness and luck to be replaced by skill, strategy, and resource competition, by removing the potential for players to fall irreversibly behind in the early stages of a game, and by reducing the number of rules and possible player options to produce what Alan R. Moon has described as "elegant game design". The concept of elegant game design has been identified by *The Boston Globe*'s Leon Neyfakh as related to Mihaly Csikszentmihalyi's concept of "flow" from his 1990 book, "Flow: The Psychology of Optimal Experience".

Modern technological advances have had a democratizing effect on board game design, with services like Kickstarter providing designers with essential startup capital and tools like 3D printers facilitating the production of game pieces and board game prototypes. A modern adaptation of figure games are miniature wargames like *Warhammer 40,000*.

Card Games

The design of card games is constricted by the type of the deck of cards, like Tarot or the four-suited Latin decks. Card games can be played for fun, like Go Fish, or for profit like Poker.

In Asian cultures, special sets of tiles can serve the same function as cards, as in mahjong, a game similar to (and thought to be the distant ancestor of) the Western card game rummy. Western dominoes games are believed to have developed from Asian tile games in the 18th century.

Magic: The Gathering was the first collectible card game (or "trading card game") in 1993.]

The line between card and board games is not clear-cut, as many card games, such as solitaire, involve playing cards to form a "tableau", a spatial layout or board. Many board games, in turn, uses specialized decks of cards as randomization devices, such as a sub-type of wargames called card-driven wargames.

Dice Games

A set of poker dice and a dice cup

Dice games are among the oldest known games and have often been associated with gambling. The oldest known dice game is a backgammon set that was discovered by archaeologists excavating the site of the Burnt City, which was abandoned in 2100 BC. Non-gambling dice games, such as Yatzy, Poker dice, or Yahtzee became popular in the mid-20th century.

The line between dice and board games is not clear-cut, as dice are often used as randomization devices in board games, such as Monopoly or Risk, while serving as the central drivers of play in games such as Backgammon or Pachisi.

Casino Games

All casino games are designed to mathematically favor the house.
The house edge for a slot machine can range widely between 2 and 15 percent.

Casino game design can entail the creation of an entirely new casino game, the creation of a variation on an existing casino game, or the creation of a new side bet on an existing casino game. Casino game mathematician, Michael Shackleford has noted that it is much more common for casino game designers today to make successful variations than entirely new casino games. Gambling columnist John Grochowski points to the emergence of community-style slot machines in the mid-1990s, for example, as a successful variation on an existing casino game type. Unlike the majority of other games which are designed primarily in the interest of the player, one of the central aims of casino game design is to optimise the house advantage and maximise revenue from gamblers. Successful casino game design works to provide entertainment for the player and revenue for the gambling house. To maximise player entertainment, casino games are designed with simple easy-to-learn rules that emphasize winning (i.e. whose rules enumerate many victory conditions and few loss conditions), and that provide players with a variety of different gameplay postures (e.g. card hands). Player entertainment value is also enhanced by providing gamblers with familiar gaming elements (e.g. dice and cards) in new casino games. To maximise success for the gambling house, casino games are designed to be easy for croupiers to operate and for pit managers to oversee. The two most fundamental rules of casino game design is that the games must be non-fraudable (including being as nearly as possible immune from advantage gambling), and that they must mathematically favor the house winning. Shackleford suggests that the optimum casino game design should give the house an edge of smaller than 5%.

Role-playing Games

The design of role-playing games requires the establishment of setting, characters, and basic gameplay rules or mechanics. After a role-playing game is produced, additional design elements are often devised by the players themselves. In many instances, for example, character creation is left to the players. Likewise, the progression of a role-playing game is determined in large part by the gamemaster whose individual campaign design may be directed by one of several role-playing game theories.

There is no central core for tabletop role-playing game theory because different people want such different things out of the games. Probably the most famous category of RPG theory, GNS Theory assumes that people want one of three things out of the game – a better, more interestingly challenging game, to create a more interesting story, or a better simulation – in other words better rules to support worldbuilding. GNS Theory has been abandoned by its creator, partly because it neglects emotional investment, and partly because it just didn't work properly. There are techniques that people use (such as dice pools) to better create the game they want – but with no consistent goal or agreement for what makes for a good game there's no overarching theory generally agreed on.

Sports

Sports games are made with the same rules as the sport the game portrays.

Video Games

Video game prototypes created during the pre-production design phase are often used as a proof of concept for the implementation of new rules or gameplay features.

Video game design is a process that takes place in the pre-production phase of video game development. In the video game industry, game design describes the creation of the content and rules of a video game. The goal of this process for the game designer is to provide players with the opportunity to make meaningful decisions in relation to playing the game. Elements of video game design such as the establishment of fundamental gameplay rules provide a framework within which players will operate, while the addition of narrative structures provide players with a reason to care about playing the game. To establish the rules and narrative, an internally consistent game world is created, requiring visual, audio, and programming development for world, character, and level design. The amount of work that is required to accomplish this often demands the use of a design team which may be divided into smaller game design disciplines. In order to maintain internal consistency between the teams, a specialized software design document known as a "game design document" (and sometimes an even broader scope "game bible" document) provides overall contextual guidance on ambient mood, appropriate tone, and other less tangible aspects of the game world.

An important aspect of video game design is human-computer interaction and game feel.

War Games

H. G. Wells playing *Little Wars*

The first military war games, or Kriegsspiel, were designed in Prussia in the 19th century to train staff officers. They are also played as a hobby for entertainment.

Modern war games are designed to test doctrines, strategies and tactics in full scale exercises with opposing forces at venues like the NTC, JRTC and the JMRC, involving NATO countries.

References

- Leonard, Robert (2010), Von Neumann, Morgenstern, and the Creation of Game Theory, New York: Cambridge University Press, ISBN 9780521562669

- Human growth and the development of personality, Jack Kahn, Susan Elinor Wright, Pergamon Press, ISBN 978-1-59486-068-3

- Brathwaite, Brenda; Schreiber, Ian (2009). Challenges for Game Designers. Charles River Media. pp. 2–5. ISBN 158450580X.

- Dille, Flint; Platten, John Zuur (2007). The Ultimate Guide to Video Game Writing and Design. Lone Eagle. pp. 137–149. ISBN 158065066X.

- Rogers, Scott (2010). Level Up!: The Guide to Great Video Game Design. John Wiley & Sons. pp. 57–81. ISBN 0470970928.

- Whigfield, Nick. "Video Hasn't Killed Interest in Board Games ; New Technologies Have Contributed to Revival of Tabletop Entertainment". The Irish Times. 12 May 2014.

- Grochowski, John. "Gaming Guru: Tracing Back the Roots of Some Popular Gaming Machines at Casinos". The Press of Atlantic City. 28 August 2013.

- Griffiths, M. (1999). "Violent video games and aggression: A review of the literature" (PDF). Aggression and violent behavior. 4 (2): 203–212. Archived (PDF) from the original on 26 November 2013.

- Neyfakh, Leon. "Quest for fun; Sometimes the most addictive new technology comes in a simple cardboard box". Boston Globe. 11 March 2012

- Lischka, Konrad (22 June 2009). "Wie preußische Militärs den Rollenspiel-Ahnen erfanden". Der Spiegel (in German). Retrieved 15 February 2010.

2

Video Game Development: An Integrated Study

When a video game design has been constructed by the designers, it is the programmers that convert the idea and images into the final game. This involves game programming which is the software side of game development. When the game is published internationally, it involves converting game language and content to the local language. Also, the gameplay content needs to be altered keeping in mind the sensitivities of the new target audience. This chapter deals with subjects like video game development, game programming, game testing, video game localization, game server, mod and independent video game development.

Video Game Development

Video game development is the process of creating a video game. Development is undertaken by a game developer, which may range from one person to a large business. Traditional commercial PC and console are normally funded by a publisher and take several years to develop. Indie games can take less time and can be produced cheaply by individuals and small developers. The indie game industry has seen a rise in recent years with the growth of new online distribution systems and the mobile game market.

The first video games were developed in the 1960s, but required mainframe computers and were not available to the general public. Commercial game development began in the 1970s with the advent of first generation video game consoles and home computers. Due to low costs and low capabilities of computers, a lone programmer could develop a full game. However, approaching the 21st century, ever-increasing computer processing power and heightened consumer expectations made it difficult for a single developer to produce a mainstream console or PC game. The average cost of producing a video game slowly rose from US$1–4 million in 2000 to over $5 million in 2006, then to over $20 million by 2010. Mainstream PC and console games are generally developed in phases. First, in pre-production, pitches, prototypes, and game design documents are written. If the idea is approved and the developer receives funding, a full-scale development begins. This usually involves a 20–100 person team of various responsibilities, such as designers, artists, programmers, testers, etc.

Overview

Game development is the software development process by which a video game is produced. Games are developed as a creative outlet and to generate profit. Development is normally funded by a publisher. Well-made games bring profit more readily. However, it is important to estimate a game's financial requirements, such as development costs of individual features. Failing to provide clear implications of game's expectations may result in exceeding allocated budget. In fact, the majority of commercial games do not produce profit. Most developers cannot afford changing development schedule and require estimating their capabilities with available resources before production.

The game industry requires innovations, as publishers cannot profit from constant release of repetitive sequels and imitations. Every year new independent development companies open and some manage to develop hit titles. Similarly, many developers close down because they cannot find a publishing contract or their production is not profitable. It is difficult to start a new company due to high initial investment required. Nevertheless, growth of casual and mobile game market has allowed developers with smaller teams to enter the market. Once the companies become financially stable, they may expand to develop larger games. Most developers start small and gradually expand their business. A developer receiving profit from a successful title may store up a capital to expand and re-factor their company, as well as tolerate more failed deadlines.

An average development budget for a multiplatform game is US$18-28M, with high-profile games often exceeding $40M.

In the early era of home computers and video game consoles in the early 1980s, a single programmer could handle almost all the tasks of developing a game — programming, graphical design, sound effects, etc. It could take as little as six weeks to develop a game. However, the high user expectations and requirements of modern commercial games far exceed the capabilities of a single developer and require the splitting of responsibilities. A team of over a hundred people can be employed full-time for a single project.

Game development, production, or design is a process that starts from an idea or concept. Often the idea is based on a modification of an existing game concept. The game idea may fall within one or several genres. Designers often experiment with different combinations of genres. Game designer usually produces initial game proposal document, that contains the concept, gameplay, feature list, setting and story, target audience, requirements and schedule, staff and budget estimates. Different companies have different formal procedures and philosophies regarding game design and development. There is no standardized development method; however commonalities exist.

Game development is undertaken by a game developer—ranging from an individual to a large company. There can be independent or publisher-owned studios. Independent developers rely on financial support from a game publisher. They usually have to develop a game from concept to prototype without external funding. The formal game proposal is then submitted to publishers, who may finance the game development from several months to years. The publisher would retain exclusive rights to distribute and market the game and would often own the intellectual property rights for the game franchise. Publisher's company may also own the developer's company, or it may have internal development studio(s). Generally the publisher is the one who owns the game's intellectual property rights.

All but the smallest developer companies work on several titles at once. This is necessary because of the time taken between shipping a game and receiving royalty payments, which may be between 6 and 18 months. Small companies may structure contracts, ask for advances on royalties, use shareware distribution, employ part-time workers and use other methods to meet payroll demands.

Console manufacturers, such as Microsoft, Nintendo, or Sony, have a standard set of technical requirements that a game must conform to in order to be approved. Additionally, the game concept must be approved by the manufacturer, who may refuse to approve certain titles.

Most modern PC or console games take from one to three years to complete., where as a mobile game can be developed in a few months. The length of development is influenced by a number of factors, such as genre, scale, development platform and amount of assets.

Some games can take much longer than the average time frame to complete. An infamous example is 3D Realms' *Duke Nukem Forever*, announced to be in production in April 1997 and released fourteen years later in June 2011. Planning for Maxis' game *Spore* began in late 1999; the game was released nine years later in September 2008. The game *Prey* was briefly profiled in a 1997 issue of PC Gamer, but was not released until 2006, and only then in highly altered form. Finally, *Team Fortress 2* was in development from 1998 until its 2007 release, and emerged from a convoluted development process involving "probably three or four different games", according to Gabe Newell.

The game revenue from retails is divided among the parties along the distribution chain, such as — developer, publisher, retail, manufacturer and console royalty. Many developers fail to profit from this and go bankrupt. Many developers seek alternative economic models through Internet marketing and distribution channels to improve returns., as through a mobile distribution channel the share of a developer can be up to 70% of the total revenue and through an online distribution channel almost 100%.

History

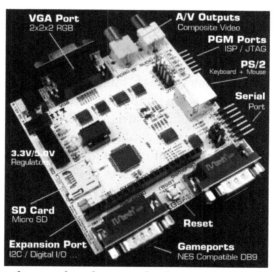

The XGS PIC 16-Bit game development board, a game development tool similar to those used in the 1990s.

The history of game making begins with the development of the first video games, although which video game is the first depends on the definition of *video game*. The first games created had little entertainment value, and their development focus was separate from user experience—in fact, these games required mainframe computers to play them. *OXO*, written by Alexander S. Douglas in 1952, was the first computer game to use a digital display. In 1958, a game called *Tennis for*

Two, which displayed its output on an oscilloscope, was made by Willy Higinbotham, a physicist working at the Brookhaven National Laboratory. In 1961, a mainframe computer game called *Spacewar!* was developed by a group of Massachusetts Institute of Technology students led by Steve Russell.

True commercial design and development of games began in the 1970s, when arcade video games and first-generation consoles were marketed. In 1971, *Computer Space* was the first commercially sold, coin-operated video game. It used a black-and-white television for its display, and the computer system was made of 74 series TTL chips. In 1972, the first home console system was released called Magnavox Odyssey, developed by Ralph H. Baer. That same year, Atari released *Pong*, an arcade game that increased video game popularity. The commercial success of *Pong* led other companies to develop *Pong* clones, spawning the video game industry.

Programmers worked within the big companies to produce games for these devices. The industry did not see huge innovation in game design and a large number of consoles had very similar games. Many of these early games were often *Pong* clones. Some games were different, however, such as *Gun Fight*, which was significant for several reasons: an early 1975 on-foot, multi-directional shooter, which depicted game characters, game violence, and human-to-human combat. Tomohiro Nishikado's original version was based on discrete logic, which Dave Nutting adapted using the Intel 8080, making it the first video game to use a microprocessor. Console manufacturers soon started to produce consoles that were able to play independently developed games, and ran on microprocessors, marking the beginning of second-generation consoles, beginning with the release of the Fairchild Channel F in 1976.

The flood of *Pong* clones led to the video game crash of 1977, which eventually came to an end with the mainstream success of Taito's 1978 arcade shooter game *Space Invaders*, marking the beginning of the golden age of arcade video games and inspiring dozens of manufacturers to enter the market. Its creator Nishikado not only designed and programmed the game, but also did the artwork, engineered the arcade hardware, and put together a microcomputer from scratch. It was soon ported to the Atari 2600, becoming the first "killer app" and quadrupling the console's sales. At the same time, home computers appeared on the market, allowing individual programmers and hobbyists to develop games. This allowed hardware manufacturer and software manufacturers to act separately. A very large amount of games could be produced by single individuals, as games were easy to make because graphical and memory limitation did not allow for much content. Larger companies developed, who focused selected teams to work on a title. The developers of many early home video games, such as *Zork*, *Baseball*, *Air Warrior*, and *Adventure*, later transitioned their work as products of the early video game industry.

> I wouldn't recommend [designing computer games] for someone with a weak heart or a large appetite
>
> — *Jon Freeman, 1984*

The industry expanded significantly at the time, with the arcade video game sector alone (representing the largest share of the gaming industry) generating higher revenues than both pop music and Hollywood films combined. The home video game industry, however, suffered major losses following the North American video game crash of 1983. In 1984 Jon Freeman warned in *Computer Gaming World*:

Q: Are computer games the way to fame and fortune?

A: No. Not unless your idea of fame is having your name recognized by one or two astute individuals at Origins ... I've been making a living (after a fashion) designing games for most of the last six years. I wouldn't recommend it for someone with a weak heart or a large appetite, though.

Chris Crawford and Don Daglow in 1987 similarly advised prospective designers to write games as a hobby first, and to not quit their existing jobs early. The home video game industry was revitalized soon after by the widespread success of the Nintendo Entertainment System.

By 1987 a video game required 12 months to develop and another six to plan marketing. Projects remained usually solo efforts, with single developers delivering finished games to their publishers. With the ever-increasing processing and graphical capabilities of arcade, console and computer products, along with an increase in user expectations, game design moved beyond the scope of a single developer to produce a marketable game in a reasonable time. This sparked the beginning of team-based development. In broad terms, during the 1980s, pre-production involved sketches and test routines of the only developer. In the 1990s, pre-production consisted mostly of game art previews. In the early 2000s, pre-production usually produced a playable demo.

In 2000 a 12 to 36 month development project was funded by a publisher for US$1M–3M. Additionally, $250k–1.5M were spent on marketing and sales development. In 2001, over 3000 games were released for PC; and from about 100 games turning profit only about 50 made significant profit. In the early 2000s it became increasingly common to use middleware game engines, such as Quake engine or Unreal engine.

In the early 2000s, also mobile games started to gain popularity. However, mobile games distributed by mobile operators remained a marginal form of gaming until the Apple App Store was launched in 2008.

In 2005, a mainstream console video game cost from US$3M to $6M to develop. Some games cost as much as $20M to develop. In 2006 the profit from a console game sold at retail was divided among parties of distribution chain as follows: developer (13%), publisher (32%), retail (32%), manufacturer (5%), console royalty (18%). In 2008 a developer would retain around 17% of retail price and around 85% if sold online.

Since the third generation of consoles, the home video game industry has constantly increased and expanded. The industry revenue has increased at least five-fold since the 1990s. In 2007, the software portion of video game revenue was $9.5 billion, exceeding that of the movie industry.

The Apple App Store, introduced in 2008, was the first mobile application store operated directly by the mobile platform holder. It significantly changed the consumer behaviour more favourable for downloading mobile content and quickly broadened the markets of mobile games.

In 2009 games market annual value was estimated between $7–30 billion, depending on which sales figures are included. This is on par with films box office market. A publisher would typically fund an independent developer for $500k–$5M for a development of a title. In 2012, the total value had already reached $66,3 billion and by then the video game markets were not anymore dominated by console games. According to Newzoo, the share of MMO's was 19.8%, PC/MAC's 9.8%, tablets' 3.2%, smartphones 10.6%, handhelds' 9.8%, consoles' only 36.7% and online casual games 10.2%. The fastest growing market segments being mobile games with an average annual rate of 19% for smartphones and 48% for tablets.

In the past several years, many developers opened and many closed down. Each year a number of developers are acquired by larger companies or merge with existing companies. For example, in 2007 Blizzard Entertainment's parent company, Vivendi Games merged with Activision. In 2008 Electronic Arts nearly acquired Take-Two Interactive. In 2009 Midway Games was acquired by Time-Warner and Eidos Interactive merged with Square Enix.

Roles

Q: What lessons had you learned from these ventures which you could share for the benefits of fans wanting to enter the game industry?

A: In the old days, when people asked me what they should study to become a game designer, I suggested literature, art and/or programming. Today, I recommend an undergraduate degree in professional management, followed by an MBA.

— Brian Moriarty, 2006

Producer

Development is overseen by internal and external producers. The producer working for the developer is known as the *internal producer* and manages the development team, schedules, reports progress, hires and assigns staff, and so on. The producer working for the publisher is known as the *external producer* and oversees developer progress and budget. Producer's responsibilities include PR, contract negotiation, liaising between the staff and stakeholders, schedule and budget maintenance, quality assurance, beta test management, and localization. This role may also be referred to as *project manager, project lead,* or *director*.

Publisher

A video game publisher is a company that publishes video games that they have either developed internally or have had developed by an external video game developer. As with book publishers or publishers of DVD movies, video game publishers are responsible for their product's manufacturing and marketing, including market research and all aspects of advertising.

They usually finance the development, sometimes by paying a video game developer (the publisher calls this external development) and sometimes by paying an internal staff of developers called a studio. Consequently, they also typically own the IP of the game. Large video game publishers also distribute the games they publish, while some smaller publishers instead hire distribution companies (or larger video game publishers) to distribute the games they publish.

Other functions usually performed by the publisher include deciding on and paying for any license that the game may utilize; paying for localization; layout, printing, and possibly the writing of the user manual; and the creation of graphic design elements such as the box design.

Large publishers may also attempt to boost efficiency across all internal and external development teams by providing services such as sound design and code packages for commonly needed functionality.

Because the publisher usually finances development, it usually tries to manage development risk with a staff of producers or project managers to monitor the progress of the developer, critique ongoing development, and assist as necessary. Most video games created by an external video game developer are paid for with periodic advances on royalties. These advances are paid when the developer reaches certain stages of development, called milestones.

Independent video game developers create games without a publisher and may choose to digitally distribute their games.

Development Team

Developers can range in size from small groups making casual games to housing hundreds of employees and producing several large titles. Companies divide their subtasks of game's development. Individual job titles may vary; however, roles are the same within the industry. The development team consists of several members. Some members of the team may handle more than one role; similarly more than one task may be handled by the same member. Team size can vary from 20 to 100 or more members, depending on the game's scope. The most represented are artists, followed by programmers, then designers, and finally, audio specialists, with two to three producers in management. These positions are employed full-time. Other positions, such as testers, may be employed only part-time. Salaries for these positions vary depending on both the experience and the location of the employee. An entry-level programmer can make, on average, around $70,000 annually and an experienced programmer can make, on average, around $125,000 annually.

A development team includes these roles or disciplines:

Designer

A game designer is a person who designs gameplay, conceiving and designing the rules and structure of a game. Development teams usually have a lead designer who coordinates the work of other designers. They are the main visionary of the game. One of the roles of a designer is being a writer, often employed part-time to conceive game's narrative, dialogue, commentary, cutscene narrative, journals, video game packaging content, hint system, etc. In larger projects, there are often separate designers for various parts of the game, such as, game mechanics, user interface, characters, dialogue, etc.

Artist

A game artist is a visual artist who creates video game art. The art production is usually overseen by an *art director* or *art lead*, making sure their vision is followed. The art director manages the art team, scheduling and coordinating within the development team.

The artist's job may be 2D oriented or 3D oriented. *2D artists* may produce concept art, sprites, textures, environmental backdrops or terrain images, and user interface. *3D artists* may produce models or meshes, animation, 3D environment, and cinematics. Artists sometimes occupy both roles.

Programmer

A game programmer is a software engineer who primarily develops video games or related software (such as game development tools). The game's codebase development is handled by programmers. There are usually one to several lead programmers, who implement the game's starting codebase and overview future development and programmer allocation on individual modules.

Individual programming disciplines roles include:

- Physics – the programming of the game engine, including simulating physics, collision, object movement, etc.;

- AI – producing computer agents using game AI techniques, such as scripting, planning, rule-based decisions, etc.

- Graphics – the managing of graphical content utilization and memory considerations; the production of graphics engine, integration of models, textures to work along the physics engine.

- Sound – integration of music, speech, effect sounds into the proper locations and times.

- Gameplay – implementation of various games rules and features (sometimes called a *generalist*);

- Scripting – development and maintenance of high-level command system for various in-game tasks, such as AI, level editor triggers, etc.

- UI – production of user interface elements, like option menus, HUDs, help and feedback systems, etc.

- Input processing – processing and compatibility correlation of various input devices, such as keyboard, mouse, gamepad, etc.

- Network communications – the managing of data inputs and outputs for local and internet gameplay.

- Game tools – the production of tools to accompany the development of the game, especially for designers and scripters.

Level Designer

A level designer is a person who creates levels, challenges or missions for computer and/or video games using a specific set of programs. These programs may be commonly available commercial 3D or 2D design programs, or specially designed and tailored level editors made for a specific game.

Level designers work with both incomplete and complete versions of the game. Game programmers usually produce level editors and design tools for the designers to use. This eliminates the need for designers to access or modify game code. Level editors may involve custom high-level scripting languages for interactive environments or AIs. As opposed to the level editing tools sometimes available to the community, level designers often work with placeholders and prototypes aiming for consistency and clear layout before required artwork is completed.

Sound Engineer

Sound engineers are technical professionals responsible for sound effects and sound positioning. They sometimes oversee voice acting and other sound asset creation. Composers who create a game's musical score also comprise a game's sound team, though often this work is outsourced.

Tester

The quality assurance is carried out by game testers. A game tester analyzes video games to document software defects as part of a quality control. Testing is a highly technical field requiring computing expertise, and analytic competence.

The testers ensure that the game falls within the proposed design: it both works and is entertaining.This involves testing of all features, compatibility, localization, etc. Although, necessary throughout the whole development process, testing is expensive and is often actively utilized only towards the completion of the project.

Development Process

Game development is a software development process, as a video game is software with art, audio, and gameplay. Formal software development methods are often overlooked. Games with poor development methodology are likely to run over budget and time estimates, as well as contain a large number of bugs. Planning is important for individual and group projects alike.

Overall game development is not suited for typical software life cycle methods, such as the waterfall model.

One method employed for game development is agile development. It is based on iterative prototyping, a subset of software prototyping. Agile development depends on feedback and refinement of game's iterations with gradually increasing feature set. This method is effective because most projects do not start with a clear requirement outline. A popular method of agile software development is Scrum.

Another successful method is Personal Software Process (PSP) requiring additional training for staff to increase awareness of project's planning. This method is more expensive and requires commitment of team members. PSP can be extended to Team Software Process, where the whole team is self-directing.

Game development usually involves an overlap of these methods. For example, asset creation may be done via waterfall model, because requirements and specification are clear, but gameplay design might be done using iterative prototyping.

Development of a commercial game usually includes the following stages:

Pre-production

Pre-production or *design phase* is a planning phase of the project focused on idea and concept development and production of initial design documents. The goal of concept development is to produce clear and easy to understand documentation, which describes all the tasks, schedules and estimates for the development team. The suite of documents produced in this phase is called production plan. This phase is usually not funded by a publisher, however good publishers may require developers to produce plans during pre-production.

The concept documentation can be separated into three stages or documents—high concept, pitch and concept; however, there is no industry standard naming convention, for example, both Bethke (2003) and Bates (2004) refer to *pitch document* as "game proposal", yet Moore, Novak (2010) refers to *concept document* as "game proposal".

The late stage of pre-production may also be referred to as *proof of concept*, or *technical review* when more detailed game documents are produced.

Publishers have started to expect broader game proposals even featuring playable prototypes.

High Concept

Pitch

A *pitch, concept document*, proposal document, or *game proposal* is a short summary document intended to present the game's selling points and detail why the game would be profitable to develop.

Verbal pitches may be made to management within the developer company, and then presented to publishers. A written document may need to be shown to publishers before funding is approved. A game proposal may undergo one to several *green-light meetings* with publisher executives who determine if the game is to be developed. The presentation of the project is often given by the game designers. Demos may be created for the pitch; however may be unnecessary for established developers with good track records.

If the developer acts as its own publisher, or both companies are subsidiaries of a single company, then only the upper management needs to give approval.

Concept

Concept document, game proposal, or *game plan* is a more detailed document than the pitch document. This includes all the information produced about the game. This includes the high concept, game's genre, gameplay description, features, setting, story, target audience, hardware platforms, estimated schedule, marketing analysis, team requirements, and risk analysis.

Before an approved design is completed, a skeleton crew of programmers and artists usually begins work. Programmers may develop quick-and-dirty prototypes showcasing one or more features that stakeholders would like to see incorporated in the final product. Artists may develop concept art and asset sketches as a springboard for developing real game assets. Producers may work part-time on the game at this point, scaling up for full-time commitment as development progresses. Game producers work during pre-production is related to planning the schedule, budget and estimating tasks with the team. The producer aims to create a solid production plan so that no delays are experienced at the start of the production.

Game Design Document

Before a full-scale production can begin, the development team produces the first version of a game design document incorporating all or most of the material from the initial pitch. The design document describes the game's concept and major gameplay elements in detail. It may also include preliminary sketches of various aspects of the game. Design document is sometimes accompanied by functional prototypes of some sections of the game. Design document remains a living document throughout the development—often changed weekly or even daily.

Compiling a list of game's needs is called "requirement capture".

Prototype

Writing prototypes of gameplay ideas and features is an important activity that allows programmers and game designers to experiment with different algorithms and usability scenarios for a game. A great deal of prototyping may take place during pre-production before the design document is complete and may, in fact, help determine what features the design specifies. When this happens the prototype is made physical and not on a computer, this is so it easier to test and make changes before wasting time and resources into what could be a canceled idea or project. Prototyping may also take place during active development to test new ideas as the game emerges.

Prototypes are often meant only to act as a proof of concept or to test ideas, by adding, modifying or removing some of the features. Most algorithms and features debuted in a prototype may be ported to the game once they have been completed.

Often prototypes need to be developed quickly with very little time for up-front design (around 15 to 20 minutes of testing). Therefore, usually very prolific programmers are called upon to quickly code these testbed tools. RAD tools may be used to aid in the quick development of these programs. In case the prototype it is in a physical form, programmers and designers alike will make the game with paper, dice, and other easy to access tools in order to make the prototype faster.

A successful development model is iterative prototyping, where design is refined based on current progress. There are various technology available for video game development

Production

Production is the main stage of development, when assets and source code for the game are produced.

Mainstream production is usually defined as the period of time when the project is fully staffed. Programmers write new source code, artists develop game assets, such as, sprites or 3D models. Sound engineers develop sound effects and composers develop music for the game. Level designers create levels, and writers write dialogue for cutscenes and NPCs. Game designers continue to develop the game's design throughout production.

Design

Game design is an essential and collaborative process of designing the content and rules of a game, requiring artistic and technical competence as well as writing skills. Creativity and an open mindness is vital for the completion of a successful video game.

During development, the game designer implements and modifies the game design to reflect the current vision of the game. Features and levels are often removed or added. The art treatment may evolve and the backstory may change. A new platform may be targeted as well as a new demographic. All these changes need to be documented and disseminated to the rest of the team. Most changes occur as updates to the design document.

Programming

The programming of the game is handled by one or more game programmers. They develop prototypes to test ideas, many of which may never make it into the final game. The programmers incorporate new features demanded by the game design and fix any bugs introduced during the development process. Even if an off-the-shelf game engine is used, a great deal of programming is required to customize almost every game.

Level Creation

From a time standpoint, the game's first level takes the longest to develop. As level designers and artists use the tools for level building, they request features and changes to the in-house tools that allow for quicker and higher quality development. Newly introduced features may cause old levels to become obsolete, so the levels developed early on may be repeatedly developed and discarded. Because of the dynamic environment of game development, the design of early levels may also change over time. It is not uncommon to spend upwards of twelve months on one level of a game developed over the course of three years. Later levels can be developed much more quickly as the feature set is more complete and the game vision is clearer and more stable.

Art Production

Audio Production

Game audio may be separated into three categories—sound effects, music, and voice-over.

Sound effect production is the production of sounds by either tweaking a sample to a desired effect or replicating it with real objects. Sound effects are important and impact the game's delivery.

Music may be synthesized or performed live.

There are several ways in which music is presented in a game.

- Music may be ambient, especially for slow periods of game, where the music aims to reinforce the aesthetic mood and game setting.

- Music may be triggered by in-game events. For example, in such games as Pac-Man or Mario, player picking up power-ups triggered respective musical scores.

- Action music, such as chase, battle or hunting sequences is fast-paced, hard-changing score.

- Menu music, similar to credits music, creates aural impact while relatively little action is taking place.

A game title with 20 hours of single-player gameplay may feature around 60 minutes of music.

Voice-overs and voice acting creates character gameplay interactivity. Voice acting adds personality to the game's characters.

Testing

At the end of the project, quality assurance plays a significant role. Testers start work once anything is playable. This may be one level or subset of the game software that can be used to any reasonable extent. Early on, testing a game occupies a relatively small amount of time. Testers may work on several games at once. As development draws to a close, a single game usually employs many testers full-time (and often with overtime). They strive to test new features and regression test existing ones. Testing is vital for modern, complex games as single changes may lead to catastrophic consequences.

At this time features and levels are being finished at the highest rate and there is more new material to be tested than during any other time in the project. Testers need to carry out regression testing to make sure that features that have been in place for months still operate correctly. Regression testing is one of the vital tasks required for effective software development. As new features are added, subtle changes to the codebase can produce unexpected changes in different portions of the game. This task is often overlooked, for several reasons. Sometimes, when a feature is implemented and tested, it is considered "working" for the rest of the project and little attention is given to repeated testing. Also, features that are added late in development are prioritized and existing features often receive insufficient testing time. Proper regression testing is also increasingly expensive as the number of features increases and is often not scheduled correctly.

Despite the dangers of overlooking regression testing, some game developers and publishers fail to test the full feature suite of the game and ship a game with bugs. This can result in customers dissatisfaction and failure to meet sales goals. When this does happen, most developers and publishers quickly release patches that fix the bugs and make the game fully playable again.

Milestones

Commercial game development projects may be required to meet milestones set by publisher. Milestones mark major events during game development and are used to track game's progress. Such milestones may be, for example, *first playable, alpha,* or *beta* game versions. Project milestones depend on the developer schedules.

There is no industry standard for defining milestones, and such vary depending on publisher, year, or project. Some common milestones for two-year development cycle are as follows:

First Playable

The *first playable* is the game version containing representative gameplay and assets, this is the first version with functional major gameplay elements. It is often based on the prototype created in pre-production. Alpha and first playable are sometimes used to refer to a single milestone, however large projects require first playable before feature complete alpha. First playable occurs 12 to 18 months before code release. It is sometimes referred to as the "Pre-Alpha" stage.

Alpha

Alpha is the stage when key gameplay functionality is implemented, and assets are partially finished. A game in alpha is *feature complete*, that is, game is playable and contains all the major features. These features may be further revised based on testing and feedback. Additional small, new features may be added, similarly planned, but unimplemented features may be dropped. Programmers focus mainly on finishing the codebase, rather than implementing additions. Alpha occurs eight to ten months before code release, but this can vary significantly based on the scope of content and assets any given game has.

Code Freeze

Code freeze is the stage when new code is no longer added to the game and only bugs are being corrected. Code freeze occurs three to four months before code release.

Beta

Beta is feature and asset complete version of the game, when only bugs are being fixed. This version contains no bugs that prevent the game from being shippable. No changes are made to the game features, assets, or code. Beta occurs two to three months before code release.

Code Release

Code release is the stage when many bugs are fixed and game is ready to be shipped or submitted for console manufacturer review. This version is tested against QA test plan. First code release candidate is usually ready three to four weeks before code release.

Gold Master

Gold master is the final game's build that is used as a master for production of the game.

Crunch Time

Overtime is expected in the games industry. Particularly, *crunch time* or *crunch mode* is unpaid overtime requested by many companies to meet project deadlines and milestones that negatively affects game developers. A team missing a deadline risks the danger of having the project cancelled or employees being laid off. Although many companies are reducing the amount of crunch time, it is still prominent in smaller companies.

Many companies offer time-off, called *comp time* or extra paid time off after product ships to compensate for crunch time's negative effects. Some companies offer bonuses and financial rewards for successful milestone reach. Sometimes on-site *crunch meals* are offered and delivered to the team during crunch time.

The International Game Developers Association (IGDA) surveyed nearly 1,000 game developers in 2004 and produced a report to highlight the many problems caused by bad practice.

Post-production

After the game goes gold and ships, some developers will give team members *comp time* (perhaps up to a week or two) to compensate for the overtime put in to complete the game, though this compensation is not standard.

Maintenance

Once a game ships, the maintenance phase for the video game begins.

Games developed for video game consoles have had almost no maintenance period in the past. The shipped game would forever house as many bugs and features as when released. This was common for consoles since all consoles had identical or nearly identical hardware; making incompatibility, the cause of many bugs, a non-issue. In this case, maintenance would only occur in the case of a port, sequel, or enhanced remake that reuses a large portion of the engine and assets.

In recent times popularity of online console games has grown, and online capable video game consoles and online services such as Xbox Live for the Xbox have developed. Developers can maintain their software through downloadable patches. These changes would not have been possible in the past without the widespread availability of the Internet.

PC development is different. Game developers try to account for majority of configurations and hardware. However, the number of possible configurations of hardware and software inevitably leads to discovery of game-breaking circumstances that the programmers and testers didn't account for.

Programmers wait for a period to get as many bug reports as possible. Once the developer thinks they've obtained enough feedback, the programmers start working on a patch. The patch may take weeks or months to develop, but it's intended to fix most accounted bugs and problems with the game that were overlooked past code release, or in rare cases, fix unintended problems caused by previous patches. Occasionally a patch may include extra features or content or may even alter gameplay.

In the case of a massively multiplayer online game (MMOG), such as a MMORPG or MMORTS, the shipment of the game is the starting phase of maintenance. Such online games are in continuous maintenance as the gameworld is continuously changed and iterated and new features are added. The maintenance staff for a popular MMOG can number in the dozens, sometimes including members of the original programming team.

Outsourcing

Several development disciplines, such as audio, dialogue, or motion capture, occur for relatively short periods of time. Efficient employment of these roles requires either large development house with multiple simultaneous title production or outsourcing from third-party vendors. Employing personnel for these tasks full-time is expensive, so a majority of developers outsource a portion of the work. Outsourcing plans are conceived during the pre-production stage; where the time and finances required for outsourced work are estimated.

- The music cost ranges based on length of composition, method of performance (live or synthesized), and composer experience. In 2003 a minute of high quality synthesized music cost between US$600-1.5k. A title with 20 hours of gameplay and 60 minutes of music may have cost $50k-60k for its musical score.

- Voice acting is well-suited for outsourcing as it requires a set of specialized skills. Only large publishers employ in-house voice actors.

- Sound effects can also be outsourced.

- Programming is generally outsourced less than other disciplines, such as art or music. However, outsourcing for extra programming work or savings in salaries has become more common in recent years.

Marketing

The game production has similar distribution methods to those of music and film industries.

The publisher's marketing team targets the game for a specific market and then advertises it. The team advises the developer on target demographics and market trends, as well as suggests specific features. The game is then advertised and the game's high concept is incorporated into the promotional material, ranging from magazine ads to TV spots. Communication between developer and marketing is important.

The length and purpose of a game demo depends on the purpose of the demo and target audience. A game's demo may range between a few seconds (such as clips or screenshots) to hours of gameplay. The demo is usually intended for journalists, buyers, trade shows, general public, or internal employees (who, for example, may need to familiarize with the game to promote it). Demos are produced with public relations, marketing and sales in mind, maximizing the presentation effectiveness.

Trade Show Demo

As a game nears completion, the publisher will want to showcase a demo of the title at trade shows. Many games have a "Trade Show demo" scheduled.

The major annual trade shows are, for example, Electronic Entertainment Expo (E3) or Penny Arcade Expo (PAX). E3 is the largest show in North America. E3 is hosted primarily for marketing and business deals. New games and platforms are announced at E3 and it received broad press coverage. Thousands of products are on display and press demonstration schedules are kept. In recent years E3 has become a more closed-door event and many advertisers have withdrawn, reducing E3's budget. PAX, created by authors of Penny Arcade blog and web-comic, is a mature and playful event with a player-centred philosophy.

Localization

A game created in one language may also be published in other countries which speak a different language. For that region, the game needs to be translated for the game to be playable. For example, some games created for Playstation Vita were initially published in Japanese language, like *Soul Sacrifice*. Non-native speakers of the game's original language may have to wait for translation of the game to their language. But most modern big-budget games take localization into account during the development process and the games are released for several different languages simultaneously.

Localization is the actual process of translating the language assets in a game into other languages. By localizing games, they increase their level of accessibility where games could help to expend the international markets effectively. Game localization is generally known as language translations yet a "full localization" of a game is a complex project. Different levels of translation range from: zero translation being that there is no translation to the product and all things are sent raw, basic translation where only a few text and subtitles are translated or even added, and a full translation where new voice overs and game material changes are added.

There are various essential elements on localizing a game including translating the language of the game to adjusting in-game assets for different cultures to reach more potential consumers in other geographies (or globalization for short). Translation seems to fall into scope of localization, which itself constitutes a substantially broader endeavor. These include the different levels of translation to the globalization of the game itself. However, certain developers seem to be divided on whether globalization falls under localization or not.

Moreover, in order to fit into the local markets, game production companies often change or redesign the graphic designs or the packaging of the game for marketing purposes. For example, the popular game *Assassin's Creed* has two different packaging designs for the Japanese and US market. By localizing the graphic and packaging designs, companies might arouse a better connections and attention from the consumers from various regions.

Indie Development

Independent games or *indie games* are produced by individuals and small teams with no large-scale developer or publisher affiliations. Indie developers generally rely on Internet distribution schemes. Many hobbyist indie developers create mods of existing games. Indie developers are credited for creative game ideas (for example, *Darwinia, Weird Worlds, World of Goo*). Current economic viability of indie development is questionable, however in recent years internet delivery platforms, such as, Xbox Live Arcade and Steam have improved indie game success. In fact, some indie games have become very successful, such as *Braid, World of Goo,* and *Minecraft*.

Game Industry

The video game industry (formally referred to as interactive entertainment) is the economic sector involved with the development, marketing and sale of video games. The industry sports several unique approaches.

Culture

Game development culture always has been and continues to be very casual by normal business standards. Many game developers are strongly individualistic and usually tolerant of divergent personalities. Despite the casual culture, game development is taken seriously by its practitioners, who may take offense if it is suggested that they don't have "a real job."

Locales

United States

In the United States, in the early history of video game development, the prominent locale for game development was the corridor from San Francisco to Silicon Valley in California. Most new developers in the US open near such "hot beds".

At present, many large publishers still operate there, such as: Activision Blizzard, Capcom Entertainment, Disney Interactive, Eidos Interactive, Electronic Arts, Foundation 9, LucasArts Entertainment, Namco Bandai Games, Sega of America, Sony Computer Entertainment America, THQ. However, due to the nature of game development, many publishers are present in other regions, such as Big Fish Games (Washington), GarageGames (Oregon), Majesco (New Jersey), Microsoft Corporation (Washington), Nintendo of America (Washington), Take-Two Interactive (New York), SouthPeak Interactive (Virginia).

Education

Many universities and design schools are offering classes specifically focused on game development. Some have built strategic alliances with major game development companies. These alliances ensure that students have access to the latest technologies and are provided the opportunity to find jobs within the gaming industry once qualified. Many innovative ideas are presented at conferences, such as Independent Games Festival (IGF) or Game Developers Conference (GDC).

Indie game development may motivate students who produce a game for their final projects or thesis and may open their own game company.

Universities offer Computer Science degrees which give you a strong basis of knowledge if you wish to become a programmer

Stability

Video game industry employment is fairly volatile, similar to other artistic industries including television, music, etc. Scores of game development studios crop up, work on one game, and then quickly go under. This may be one reason why game developers tend to congregate geographically; if their current studio goes under, developers can flock to an adjacent one or start another from the ground up.

In an industry where only the top 20% of products make a profit, it's easy to understand this fluctuation. Numerous games may start development and are cancelled, or perhaps even completed but never published. Experienced game developers may work for years and yet never ship a title: such is the nature of the business. This volatility is likely inherent to the artistic nature of games.

Game Programming

Game programming, a subset of game development, is the software development of video games. Game programming requires substantial skill in software engineering as well as specialization in one or more of the following areas, which overlap heavily to create a game: simulation, computer graphics, artificial intelligence, physics, audio programming, and input. For massively multiplayer online games, additional areas, such as network programming and database programming are often included. Though often engaged in by professional game programmers, many novices may program games as a hobby.

Development Process

Professional game development usually begins with a game design, which itself has several possible origins. Occasionally the game development process starts with no clear design in mind, but as a series of experimentation. For example, game designer Will Wright began development of *The Sims* by getting programmers to experiment with several ideas.

Prototyping

Programmers are often required to produce prototypes of gameplay ideas and features. A great deal of prototyping may take place during pre-production, before the design document is complete, and may help determine what features the design specifies.

Prototypes are developed quickly with very little time for up-front design and mostly act as a proof of concept or to test ideas. They are not expected to work flawlessly, but are developed to try out new, sometimes exotic, ideas.

Game Design

Though the programmer's main job is not to develop the game design, the programmers often contribute to the design, as do game artists. The game designer will solicit input from both the producer and the art and programming lead for ideas and strategies for the game design. Often individuals in non-lead positions also contribute, such as copywriters and other programmers and artists.

Programmers often closely follow the game design document. As the game development progresses, the design document changes as programming limitations and new capabilities are discovered and exploited.

Production

During production, programmers may create a great deal of source code to create the game described in the game's design document. Along the way, the design document is modified to meet limitations or expanded to exploit new features. The design document is very much a "living document", much of whose life is dictated by programmer's schedules, talent and resourcefulness.

While many programmers have some say in a game's content, most game producers solicit input from the lead programmer as to the status of a game programming development. The lead is responsible for knowing the status of all facets of the game's programming and for pointing out limitations. The lead programmer may also pass on suggestions from the programmers as to possible features they'd like to implement.

With today's visually rich content, the programmer must often interact with the art staff. This very much depends on the programmer's role, of course. For example, a 3D graphics programmer may need to work side by side with the game's 3D modelers discussing strategies and design considerations, while an AI programmer may need to interact very little, if at all, with the art staff. To help artists and level designers with their tasks, programmers may volunteer or be called upon to develop tools and utilities. Many of these may be for a specific purpose and can be buggy due to time constraints (time for development of such tools is often not included in a game's schedule) as well as because they are only for in-house use anyway. Many game tools are developed in RAD languages for quicker development and may be discarded after the completion of the game.

Testing

The formal quality assurance testing process, performed by professional game testers, begins well into game development. High-budget titles may begin testing with the first playable alpha, while low-budget and casual games might not enter testing until a release candidate is ready. The programmers' task is to fix errors and bugs as such are discovered by the QA teams.

Nearing Completion

Final tasks include "polishing" the game, such as programmers fixing occasional bugs—from minor to catastrophic—that may arise during the last phases of testing.

Game developers may have a beta testing period, but the definition of such varies from developer to developer. Often a beta contains all of the game's features, but may have a few bugs or incomplete content. Few games are given a public beta period, for example, to measure stress tolerance for game servers.

When the game is deemed complete, it is said to have "gone gold" and is shipped off to the publisher. Depending on circumstances, the publisher may then subject it to its own quality assurance or may begin pressing the game from the gold master.

Maintenance

Once a game ships, the maintenance phase for the video game begins. Programmers wait for a period to get as many bug reports as possible. Once the developer thinks they've obtained enough feedback, the programmers start working on a patch. The patch may take weeks or months to develop, but it's intended to fix most bugs and problems with the game. Occasionally a patch may include extra features or content or may even alter gameplay.

Duration

Most modern games take from one to three years to complete. The length of development depends on a number of factors, but programming is required throughout all phases of development except the very early stages of game design.

Tools

Like other software, game development programs are generated from source code to the actual program (called the *executable*) by a compiler. Source code can be developed with almost any text editor, but many professional game programmers use a full integrated development environment. Once again, which IDE one uses depends on the target platform.

In addition to IDEs, many game development companies create custom tools developed to be used in-house. Some of these include prototypes and asset conversion tools (programs that change artwork, for example, into the game's custom format). Some custom tools may even be delivered with the game, such as a level editor.

Game development companies are often very willing to spend thousands of dollars to make sure their programmers are well equipped with the best tools. A well outfitted programmer may have two to three development systems and multiple monitors dominating their office or cubicle.

Programming Languages

Language	Features
Assembly	Potentially minimal CPU overhead
C	Widely known, widely portable, numerous APIs, compiles to machine code
C++	Object-oriented, widely known, numerous APIs, compiles to machine code
Java	Object-oriented, garbage-collected, widely portable (via a virtual machine)
C#, Visual Basic .NET, etc.	Object-oriented, garbage-collected, interfaces with Microsoft products
Objective-C, Swift	Object-oriented, interfaces with Apple products
Lua, Python, JavaScript, Tcl, etc.	Familiar syntax, easily embedded in the above languages, often used for scripting
Lisp, Pascal, Perl, Smalltalk, etc.	Fringe game languages, although bindings to popular libraries are common

Once the game's initial design has been agreed upon, the development language must be decided upon. The choice depends upon many factors, such as language familiarity of the programming staff, target platforms, the execution speed requirements and the language of any game engines, APIs or libraries being used.

For personal computers, the language selected may be little more than a matter of preference. Language bindings for popular libraries such as SDL and Allegro are widespread, and the performance gap between idiomatic code written in modern compiled languages is negligible. The most popular languages are usually procedural/object-oriented and implemented via compilers; for example, C,

C++, and Java. However, developers may take into account domain-specific features, such as interfacing with the operating system, and resilience to reverse engineering for online video games. Many games are not written in one language exclusively, and may combine two or more languages; For example, Unity, a popular game engine, has different pieces written in C, C++, and C#.

For consoles, the support of the target platform is usually the most considered factor. In the past, video games for consoles were written almost exclusively in assembly due to limited resources in terms of both storage and processing speed. However, as technology has advanced, so have the options for game development on consoles. Nintendo, Microsoft, and Sony all have differing SDKs for their Wii U, Xbox One, and PlayStation 4 consoles, respectively.

High-level scripting languages are increasingly being used as embedded extensions to the underlying game written in a compiled programming language, for the convenience of both the original developer and anyone who would wish to mod the game. Lua is a very popular choice, as its API is written in ANSI C and the language is designed to be embedded into other applications. Many developers have created custom languages altogether for their games, such as id Software's QuakeC and Epic Games' UnrealScript.

APIs and Libraries

A key decision in game programming is which, if any, APIs and libraries to use. Today, there are numerous libraries available which take care of key tasks of game programming. Some libraries can handle sound processing, input, and graphics rendering. Some can even handle some AI tasks such as pathfinding. There are even entire game engines that handle most of the tasks of game programming and only require coding game logic.

Which APIs and libraries one chooses depends largely on the target platform. For example, libraries for PlayStation 2 development may not be available for Microsoft Windows and vice versa. However, there are game frameworks available that allow or ease cross-platform development, so programmers can program a game in a single language and have the game run on several platforms, such as the Wii, PlayStation 3, Xbox 360, PSP and Microsoft Windows.

Graphic Apis

Today, graphics are a key defining feature of most games. While 2D graphics used to be the norm for games released through the mid-1990s, most games now boast full 3D graphics. This is true even for games which are largely 2D in nature, such as *Civilization III*.

The most popular personal computer target platform is Microsoft Windows. Since it comes pre-installed on almost ninety percent of PCs sold, it has an extremely large user base. The two most popular 3D graphics APIs for Microsoft Windows are Direct3D and OpenGL. The benefits and weaknesses of each API are hotly debated among Windows game programmers.

DirectX is a collection of game APIs. Direct3D is DirectX's 3D API. Direct3D is freely available from Microsoft, as are the rest of the DirectX APIs. Microsoft developed DirectX for game programmers and continues to add features to the API. The DirectX specification is not controlled by an open arbitration committee and Microsoft is free to add, remove or change features. Direct3D is not portable; it is designed specifically for Microsoft Windows and no other platform (though a form of Direct3D is used on Microsoft's Xbox, Windows Phone 7.5 smartphones and mobile devices which run the Pocket PC operating system).

OpenGL is a portable API specification. Code written with OpenGL is easily ported between platforms with a compatible implementation. For example, *Quake II*, which uses OpenGL, was ported from Windows to Linux by a fan of the game. OpenGL is a standard maintained by the OpenGL Architecture Review Board (ARB). The ARB meets periodically to update the standard by adding emerging support for features of the latest 3D hardware. Since it is standards based and has been around the longest, OpenGL is used by and taught in colleges and universities around the world. In addition, the development tools provided by the manufacturers of some video game consoles (such as the Nintendo GameCube, the Nintendo DS, and the PSP) use graphic APIs that resemble OpenGL. OpenGL often lags behind on feature updates due to the lack of a permanent development team and the requirement that implementations begin development after the standard has been published. Programmers who choose to use it can access some hardware's latest 3D features, but only through non-standardized extensions. The situation may change in the future as the OpenGL architecture review board (ARB) has passed control of the specification to the Khronos Group in an attempt to counter the problem.

Other APIs

For development on Microsoft Windows, the various APIs of DirectX may be used for input, sound effects, music, networking and the playback of videos. Many commercial libraries are available to accomplish these tasks, but since DirectX is available for free, it is the most widely used.

For console programming, the console manufacturers provide facilities for rendering graphics and the other tasks of game development. The console manufacturers also provide complete development systems, without which one cannot legally market nor develop games for their system. Third-party developers also sell toolkits or libraries that ease the development on one or more of these tasks or provide special benefits, such as cross-platform development capabilities.

Game Structure

The central component of any game, from a programming standpoint, is the *game loop.* The game loop allows the game to run smoothly regardless of a user's input or lack thereof.

Most traditional software programs respond to user input and do nothing without it. For example, a word processor formats words and text as a user types. If the user doesn't type anything, the word processor does nothing. Some functions may take a long time to complete, but all are initiated by a user telling the program to do something.

Games, on the other hand, must continue to operate *regardless* of a user's input. The game loop allows this. A highly simplified game loop, in pseudocode, might look something like this :

```
while( user doesn't exit )
    check for user input
    run AI
    move enemies
```

    resolve collisions

    draw graphics

    play sounds

end while

The loop may be refined and modified as game development progresses, but most games are based on this basic idea.

Game loops differ depending on the platform they are developed for. For example, games written for DOS and many consoles can dominate and exploit available processing resources without restraint. However, games for a modern PC operating system such as Microsoft Windows must operate within the constraints of the process scheduler. Some modern games run multiple threads so that, for example, the computation of character AI can be decoupled from the generation of smooth motion within the game. This has the disadvantage of (slightly) increased overhead, but the game may run more smoothly and efficiently on hyper-threading or multicore processors and on multiprocessor platforms. With the computer industry's focus on CPUs with more cores that can execute more threads, this is becoming increasingly important. Consoles like the Xbox 360 and PlayStation 3 already have more than one core per processor, and execute more than one thread per core.

Hobbyists

The only platforms widely available for hobbyists to program are consumer operating systems. This is because development on game consoles requires special development systems that cost thousands of dollars. Often these must be obtained from the console manufacturer and are only sold or leased to professional game development studios. However, Microsoft used to distribute a game development framework, XNA, which runs on both Microsoft Windows and Xbox 360. XNA was discontinued, but other projects like MonoGame and SharpDX are trying to allow the same access for game coding. Games written for Windows often can be ported to Xbox with few changes. This allows individuals and small teams to develop games for consoles. Some hobbyists also develop homebrew games, especially for handheld systems or obsolete consoles.

Some software engineering students program games as exercises for learning a programming language or operating system.

Some hobbyists may use software packages that help with game development, such as Adobe Flash, Unity, pygame, Adventure Game Studio, GameMaker: Studio, Godot, UDK, or Construct.

Video Game Localization

Video game localization refers to the process of transforming video game software and hardware for preparation to be imported and sold in a new region, usually a different country. Although translating the text assets is a large part of localization, the process includes any changes made to a game, including altering art assets, creating new packaging and manuals, recording new audio, transforming hardware, cutting out whole portions of the game due to differing cultural sensitivities, and even adding sections to replace cut content.

The decision to localize a game relies heavily on economic factors, such as the potential profits that could be made in a new country. As such, the process is usually undertaken either by the game developers themselves or by a third-party translating company, though unauthorized fan localizations can occur if a translation is poor quality or if a game is not going to be released in a specific language. As an industrial field, localization is still in development and lacks consistency in terms of implementation and importance. Gathering information about industrial localization practices can often be difficult because of the lack of consistency between companies, as well as non-disclosure agreements many translators have to sign.

The goal of localization is to create an enjoyable, non-confusing play experience for the end user by paying heed to their specific cultural context. The suspension of disbelief is of utmost importance to the process; if a player feels as though the product was not meant for them, or if the localization creates confusion or difficulty in comprehension, this may break immersion and disrupt the player's ability to continue the game.

History

The founding concepts of game localization can be seen early in videogame history, as in the case of the localization of Pac-Man. The original transliteration of the Japanese title would be "Puck-Man," but the decision was made to change the name when the game was imported to the United States out of fear that the word 'Puck' would be vandalized into an obscenity. In addition, the names of the ghosts were originally based on colors - roughly translating to "Reddie," "Pinky," "Bluey," and "Slowly." Rather than translate these names exactly, they were renamed to Blinky, Pinky, Inky, and Clyde. This choice maintained the odd-man-out style of the original names without adhering to their exact meaning. The change in cultural context between the two countries provoked a change in the game text that was not a precise translation.

An important concern for early localization was the limited amount of processing space available to house text strings that were longer than the originals, as was often the case with the NES and SNES. Ted Woolsey, translator of Final Fantasy VI, recounts having to continually cut down the English text due to limit capacity.

Often the budgets and production times for localizations were short, resulting in translations that were either confusing or entirely re-written. Early translations were sometimes "literally done by a "programmer with a phrase book." For instance, the original translation for the Sega Genesis game Beyond Oasis (original Japanese title, Story of Thor) was discarded by the English editor because it was nonsensical. Instead, it was completely re-written without any input from the translator. Sometimes the poor quality of the translation helped make the game more notable, as in the case of the notoriously poor translation of Zero Wing, whose text "All Your Base Are Belong to Us" became an early Internet meme.

Technology in the early 2000s expanded to allow text to be stored in ASCII strings instead of in picture format, allowing for more efficient processing and more storage space for housing text. Better audio capabilities and reliance on voice acting created new challenges and avenues for translation, allowing the use of dubbing while also adding the burden of translating and recording new audio. As graphics improved and games relied more on cinematics, more attention had to be paid to lip-syncing as well as visual gestures that might be culturally-specific.

In present times, there has been significant uptake in the amount of text and dialogue in a game, especially for triple-A RPGs. For instance, the team in charge of localizing Fable II into five languages consisted of 270 actors and 130 personnel- a far cry from the lone programmer with a phrasebook. Likewise, the dialogue scripts for Star Wars: The Old Republic contained over 40 novels worth of text. Director of audio and localization Shauna Perry reports that SWTOR had as much audio as ten Knights of the Old Republic recorded back-to-back. The length and intensity of these projects presents never-before-seen complexity in the localization process.

Levels of Localization

Depending on the financial viability of importing a game to a new locale, a number of different levels of localization may be undertaken. The first level is no localization. A game may still be imported into a region in the original language if there is a potential market for it, but no efforts to localize the game will occur, to cut back on costs. The second level is box and documentation localization, in which the box and documentation or manuals for the game will be translated, but not the game itself. This tactic may be used if the game has little text or story, such as early arcade games, or if the target locale is expected to have a decent command of the original language, as in the importation of some English-language games such as *Secret of Mana* or *Terranigma* into Scandinavian countries. The third level of localization is partial localization, in which game text is translated but voiceover files aren't. This helps cut down on the cost of hiring actors and re-recording all of the dialogue, while still making the game comprehensible in another language. Voiceover dialogue that doesn't appear on screen may be subtitled. The final level of localization is full localization, where in all of a game's assets will be translated, including voiceover, game text, graphics, and manuals. This is the most expensive option, and is usually only undertaken by AAA game companies.

Production Models

Officially produced localizations generally fit into one of two shipping models: post-gold or sim-ship. The post-gold localization model is undertaken when the original game has already been completed, and usually has already been released. As a result, there is a lag between the release of the original and the release of the localized versions. The post-gold model allows localizers to access a completed game rather than working with incomplete bits and pieces, and generally allow for more time to complete translations, so fewer translation errors occur with this method. This model is used commonly by Japanese AAA producers, though these companies are starting to move towards a sim-ship method for marketing reasons.

The sim-ship model, short for simultaneous-shipment, allows a game to be released in multiple regions at the same time. Because games have a short shelf-life and are prone to be pirated, there is a profit incentive to release games simultaneously across the globe. However, with this method, a completed version of the game is unlikely to be made available for localization workers, resulting in a greater risk for translation errors, as crucial context and game information may be missing. Most Western games follow the sim-ship method of production.

In addition to these shipping models, different production methods may be used to create the localization, usually either outsourced or in-house production. Most game companies in North America and Europe rely on an outsourcing model of production, and this model is popular amongst emerging game development markets such as Chile, Russia, and China. In the outsourcing model, a company that specializes in game translation is hired to undertake the entire process. Oftentimes outsourced companies do not have the full game available to work with, and are dealing with only portions of the game's text or art, resulting in a "blind localization." In a blind localization, only a limited amount of information about the final game is available, resulting in a lack of context which can hinder productive localization. Sometimes, even if a game is incomplete, the developer may send a mostly-finished version of the game so that translators can play through the game and get a better sense of the text they're working with.

In the outsourcing model, developers and publishers will usually provide the translation company with a localization kit. A localization kit may contain elements such as general information about the project (including deadlines, contact information, software details), resources about the game itself (a walkthrough, plot or character descriptions, cheat codes), reference materials (glossaries of terms used in the game world or used for the specific hardware), software (such as computer-aided translation tools), code, and the assets to be translated (text files, graphics, audio, and so forth). An insufficient localization kit can severely hamper translation efforts.

Alternate to the outsourcing model, translators may control the localization in-house. This model is more common for Japanese developers, most notably Square Enix. In the in-house model, the localization process is completely controlled by the developer, though it is common for freelance translators to be hired on a project-basis. Translators working in this model still usually receive a localization kit, but also have greater access to the original game and to the original artists and authors. Because Japanese developers rely on the post-gold model, the in-house translators favored by these companies usually have full access to the completed game. This allows the translation to have fewer context mistakes and results in an overall smoother localization. The downside is the long delay between the game's release in the original country and the subsequent release of the localized version, which is of concern in a global market. Companies like Square Enix are beginning to move towards a simultaneous shipping model, with a shorter release time between different versions.

Finally, a game can be localized through the unauthorized efforts of fans. Fans may be willing to put forth a huge amount of unpaid labor in order to localize a game if it would be otherwise unavailable. If a game is not going to be released in a specific territory, for instance due to doubts about making sufficient profits, fans may take up the slack and release a translation on their own. For instance, the Game Boy Advance game Mother 3 (2004) was not going to be released in North America, possible due to poor sales of the previous installment of the series, Mother 2 (renamed EarthBound in North America). Fans petitioned Nintendo to localize the game, and when that failed, they undertook the process themselves, resulting in a fan-helmed English-language release of the game in 2008.

Inferior localization may also prompt fan action, as in the case of the fan community Clan DLAN. The group has undertaken the work of localizing many games, mods, cheats, guides, and more into Castilian Spanish when the official versions were of poor quality, such as with The Elder Scrolls IV: Oblivion.

Tasks and Challenges

The major types of localization are as follows.

- Linguistic and cultural: the translation of language and cultural references maintaining the feel of the game but making it more appealing for the receiving locale.

- Hardware and software: for example the change between PAL and NTSC, re-mapping of hotkeys, gameplay modifications.

- Legal: age ratings may differ depending on the country of release. They are controlled by national or international bodies like PEGI (for Europe), ESRB (for US and Canada), ACB (for Australia), or CERO (for Japan).

- Graphics and music: Some games may exhibit different characters, or the same ones with a slightly different appearance in order to facilitate players identification with their avatar. Music may also vary according to national trends or the preferences of major fan communities.

When games are more story- than action-driven, culturalising them can be challenging because of all the premises the designers are taking for granted in the development of the plot. Asian gamers seem to prefer more childlike characters, while Western countries might emphasize adult features. An example of the changes that are likely to happen during localization is Fatal Frame (known in Japan as *Zero* and known in Europe as *Project Zero*) (Tecmo 2001). In the original Japanese version the female protagonist, Miku, was a frightened seventeen-year-old girl looking for her brother Mafuyu who disappeared after entering a haunted mansion. In the US and European versions Miku is nineteen, has Western features, and is not wearing the original Japanese school uniform. Unfortunately, developers did not think necessary to change her brother's appearance, so when players do find Mafuyu at the end of the game they do not seem to be blood-related.

A similar thing happens with the depiction of blood, and real historical events; many things have to be readjusted to fit the country's tolerance and taste in order not to hurt sensibilities. This is probably one of the reasons why so many games take place in imaginary worlds. This customisation effort draws on the knowledge of geopolitical strategists, like Kate Edwards from Englobe. During the 2006 Game Developers Conference in California she explained the importance of being culturally aware when internationalising games in a presentation called "Fun vs. Offensive: Balancing the 'Cultural Edge' of Content for Global Games" (Edwards 2006). Both developers and publishers want to please their clients. Gamers are not particularly interested in where the game comes from, or who created it any more than someone buying a new car or DVD player. A product for mass consumption only keeps the branding features of the trademark; all the other characteristics might be subject to customisation due to the need to appeal to the local market. Therefore, the translation will be in some cases an actual recreation, or, to put it in the words of Mangiron & O'Hagan (2006), a "transcreation", where translators will be expected to produce a text with the right "feel" for the target market. It is important for translators to be aware of the logic behind this. Video games are a software product, and as such, they will have manuals and instructions, as well as interactive menus and help files. This will call for technical translation. On the other hand, we will also find narration and dialogue closer to literary texts or film scripts where a more creative translation would be expected. However, unlike most forms of translation, video games can adapt or even change the original script, as long as it is in the search of enhanced fun and playability of the target culture. We can only find a parallel of this type of practice in the translation of children's literature where professionals often adapt or alter the original text to improve children's understanding and enjoyment of the book.

SCEE David Reeves, has stated that the main reason that Europe is often affected by significant content delays is because of language localization. He stated "the problem is that there isn't enough incentive for developers to work on multiple language translations during development. Hence, Europeans suffer delays and may never see a particular title". He also commented on why the UK and Ireland which are English speaking countries, also experience the same delays as those in continental Europe with many different languages despite little or no modification. He stated "With PlayStation Store we could probably go in the UK almost day and date. But then what are the Germans and the French going to say to me? That I'm Anglo-centric" indicating that the reason that these countries also must wait is to avoid criticism from other large European gaming countries such as Germany and France.

Cultural Changes

Oftentimes localization changes include adjusting a game to consider specific cultural sensitivities. These changes may be self-enforced by the developers themselves, or enacted by national or regional rating boards (Video game content rating system). However, games are still sometimes released with controversial or insensitive material, which can lead to controversy or recall of the product.

Games localized for import into Germany often have significant changes made due to the Unterhaltungssoftware Selbstkontrolle's (USK) strict policies against blood and gore, profanity, and symbols associated with racial hatred, such as Nazi symbolism.

For instance, the German version of Team Fortress 2 (2007) has no blood or detached body parts as a result of this regulation, which can cause difficulty for players as it is hard to tell if an enemy has been hit or taken damage (218). As a result, mods known as "bloodpatches" have been created for this and many German games that allow the blood and gore of the original game to be unlocked. Despite a significant overhaul of the graphics, the German localization of the World War II game Wolfenstein (2009) contained a single visible swastika on an art asset. As a result, Raven Software recalled the game.

China also has strict censorship rules, and forbids content that endangers the "unity, sovereignty and territorial integrity of the state" or the "social moralities or fine national cultural traditions," amongst other qualifications. As a result, the Swedish PC game Hearts of Iron (2002), set during World War II, was banned because the historically accurate maps depicted Manchuria, West Xinjiang, and Tibet as independent states. Additionally, Taiwan was shown to be a territory of Japan, as was accurate for the time period. However, these inclusions were considered harmful to China's territorial integrity, so the game was forbidden from being legally imported. The localization of Football Manager (2005) was similarly banned because Tibet, Taiwan, Hong Kong, and China were all treated as separate teams, putting them on equal footing.

Linguistic Assets

Video games come accompanied by a variety of texts, for example manuals, dubbing scripts, and subtitles that need translating, but they also have other type of texts in a format only common to utility software, like a word processor, or an internet browser. All these programs have one thing in common: information and commands are readily available at the click of a button. It is what we call 'interactivity'. The interactive element of computer programs has serious consequences for translators because it means that access to texts and information is random, i.e., each user will activate a particular message or command at a different point, or not at all. An arbitrary sequence of events does not allow for linear texts and contextual information, therefore, translators lose two of the most important sources needed in the decision making process: co-text and context. When the program is still unfinished or no localization kit has been prepared, some information is still available, although difficult to obtain, from similar manuals, the localization manager, or the actual technical team responsible for the software. Esselink (2000) is probably one of the best references for the localization of utility software and web pages.

Unfortunately, the localization software industry has not been able to create a GUI (graphical user interface) localization tool for translators to use with video games, like the ones used in the translation of utility software and web pages. These programs (like Catalyst and Passolo) allow users to work directly but safely with the game code, generating a visual representation of the final product, which means that translators can see exactly what the end result will look like and adjust the text or the interface to suit the space available as well as the general look. The LRC (Localization Research Center) and LISA (The Localization Industry Standards Association) have ample information on these programs.

Linguistic assets will be utilised in a variety of ways at different times throughout the creation, development, and launch of the game, mainly: the game itself, which has a variety of texts in multiple formats, the official web site of the game, promotional articles, game patches and updates.

Textual Types and File Formats

Within these products there are different textual types, each of which has its own characteristics and purpose. Because we are dealing with a multimedia product, the challenges translators have to face are also multimedia. Within the same project they have to deal with a wide variety of issues like reproducing the oral quality of dialogue in writing, lip-synching for dubbing, space and time constraints for subtitling, number of characters for subtitle, UI, etc. The following paragraphs are an attempt to classify the several textual types that accompany the standard PC video game:

Manual

(Written form. May be a Pagemaker or a Word format) Although it always has some attractive and engaging creative writing, partly promotional partly literary, most of the manual would normally be filled with didactic texts when telling players the instructions to be followed to fully enjoy the game. Manuals would also include technical texts with the appropriate hardware and software specifications to be able to run the game application. In addition players will always find corporative and legal texts, informing users of their rights and responsibilities attached to the acquisition of an entertainment software product.

Packaging

(Written form. Pagemaker or Word format) Like manuals, game boxes and packaging present a mixture of textual types, the difference being the space provided, limited not only by the size of it but also by images of the game, logos of the companies involved and legal labelling requirements. It mixes an alluring promotional text, together with concise technical information and legal notices.

Readme File

(Written form. Wordpad format) This small .txt file is probably the last thing in the development process. It is used to inform users of all the last-minute adjustments and how to make sure that the product runs smoothly, as well as to correct mistakes and typos in the printed material, such as manual and packaging. It is mainly a technical text.

Official Website

(Written form. HTML or Java format) It mixes a promotional text with a journalistic one, but it will also have technical details like minimum requirements, etc. A lot of the information offered through the official web will be similar to the one that was shipped with the game. But websites tend to include previews and reviews of the product, notice boards, customer support and downloadable files to fix specific problems, or patches with new language versions, as well as screenshots, concept art, thematic screen savers, merchandising, and fan blogs.

Dialogue for Dubbing

(Spoken form. There will be a separate sound file per utterance. Written scripts will normally be in spreadsheets or Word tables.) Speech delivered by game characters where registers, accents, and idiosyncrasies have to be conveyed into other languages. Sometimes an extra column is included to add inflection comments for the dubbing director. A part of the dubbing script may include atmospheric utterances also in a spoken form. Many games might feature characters talking or reacting to players' actions. These characters may have little or no relevance to the plot, but their inclusion and to the immersion of the player in the virtual world. No synchronisation is normally required, but orality has to be maintained.

Dialogue for Subtitling

(Written form. Spreadsheets and tables are preferred for this although subtitles might be hard-coded in order to synchronize them with video and animations). Oral text in written form. The dubbing script may be applied directly in the subtitling of the game, which results in cluttered and fast subtitles with no character limit per line, nor lines per subtitle. In addition, translators may be faced with the fact that not all languages allow for the same freedom when writing subtitles. Often translators will have to apply techniques used in the translation of children's literature and comic-books to convey certain characteristics that would otherwise be lost. Time and space constraints are very relevant here.

User Interface (UI)

(Written form. Table format, sometimes hard-coded text file due to the interactivity of each item). Space in menus, pop-up windows and hint captions is at a premium and redesigning is rarely an option, so translators will have to maintain a similar number of characters to that of the original label. Similarly to what happens in software localization, video games may have very detailed and crowded menu options to control different features of the game such as difficulty level, as well as graphic display selection, mouse sensitivity, or feedback preferences.

Graphic Art with Words

(Written form. A multi-layered graphic format will be needed). Players will normally find this type of graphic-text in game names but they can often be seen throughout the game as part of the branding of the product, as well as in advertisements.

Controversy

In the 2010s there has been debate about how Japanese games are localized, particularly for Nintendo platforms. Some fans consider resulting changes to plot and characterization as marring the original artistic vision, and some object to sexual content being removed or bowlderized. Localization of Nintendo games is commonly handled by a Nintendo division called the Treehouse. In the face of Nintendo's unwillingness to communicate about localization, speculation and conspiracy theories circulated among enthusiasts, and several employees of the Treehouse were alleged to be responsible for unpopular changes.

Allison Rapp, a Treehouse employee not directly involved in localization, became a scapegoat due to her outspokenness on Twitter. Attention on Rapp was heightened as part of the Gamergate controversy by the circulation of an undergraduate essay by Rapp which favored cultural relativism regarding sexualization of minors in Japanese media. The essay argued against the sort of censorship that the Treehouse's critics decried. Some however interpreted the essay as defending the exploitation of children, and readers of The Daily Stormer organized a letter-writing campaign to have her fired. That initiative was controversial within the Gamergate movement, with some supporters considering it justifiable treatment of an ideological opponent, while others considered the campaign against Rapp to be unethical or not aligned with the movement's goals. Rapp was subsequently fired, though Nintendo issued a statement that the reason was that Rapp had held a second job against company policy. She maintains that her controversial online presence was the true cause.

Game Testing

Game testing, a subset of game development, is a software testing process for quality control of video games. The primary function of game testing is the discovery and documentation of software defects (aka bugs). Interactive entertainment software testing is a highly technical field requiring computing expertise, analytic competence, critical evaluation skills, and endurance. In recent years the field of game testing has come under fire for being excessively strenuous and unrewarding, both financially and emotionally.

History

In the early days of computer and video games, the developer was in charge of all the testing. No more than one or two testers were required due to the limited scope of the games. In some cases, the programmers could handle all the testing.

As games become more complex, a larger pool of QA resources, called "Quality Assessment" or "Quality Assurance" is necessary. Most publishers employ a large QA staff for testing various games from different developers. Despite the large QA infrastructure most publishers have, many developers retain a small group of testers to provide on-the-spot QA.

Now most game developers rely on their highly technical and game savvy testers to find glitches and 'bugs' in either the programming code or graphic layers. Game testers usually have a background playing a variety of different games on a multitude of platforms. They must be able to notate and reference any problems they find in detailed reports, meet deadlines with assignments and have the skill level to complete the game titles on their most difficult settings. Most of the time the position of game tester is a highly stressful and competitive position with little pay yet is highly sought after for it serves as a doorway into a rapidly growing industry.

A common misconception is that all game testers enjoy alpha or beta version of the game and report occasionally found bugs. In contrast, game testing is highly focused on finding bugs using established and often tedious methodologies before alpha version.

Overview

Quality assurance is a critical component in game development, though the video game industry does not have a standard methodology. Instead developers and publishers have their own methods. Small developers do not generally have QA staff; however, large companies may employ QA teams full-time. High-profile commercial games are professionally and efficiently tested by publisher QA department.

Testing starts as soon as first code is written and increases as the game progresses towards completion. The main QA team will monitor the game from its first submission to QA until as late as post-production. Early in the game development process the testing team is small and focuses on daily feedback for new code. As the game approaches *alpha* stage, more team members are employed and test plans are written. Sometimes features that are not bugs are reported as bugs and sometimes programming team fails to fix issues first time around. A good bug-reporting system may help the programmers work efficiently. As the projects enters *beta* stage, the testing team will have clear assignments for each day. Tester feedback may determine final decisions of exclusion or inclusion of final features. Introducing testers with fresh perspectives may help identify new bugs. At this point the lead tester communicates with the producer and department heads daily. If the developer has an external publisher, then coordination with publisher's QA team starts. For console games, a build for the console company QA team is sent. Beta testing may involve volunteers, for example, if the game is multiplayer.

Testers receive scheduled uniquely identifiable game builds from the developers. The game is play-tested and testers note any uncovered errors. These may range from bugs to art glitches to logic errors and level bugs. Testing requires creative gameplay to discover often subtle bugs. Some bugs are easy to document, but many require detailed description so a developer can replicate or find the bug. Testers implement concurrency control to avoid logging bugs multiple times. Many video game companies separate technical requirement testing from functionality testing altogether since a different testing skillset is required.

If a video game development enters crunch time before a deadline, the game-test team is required to test late-added features and content without delay. During this period staff from other departments may contribute to the testing—especially in multiplayer games.

Most companies rank bugs according to an estimate of their severity:

- *A bugs* are critical bugs that prevent the game from being shipped, for example, they may crash the game.

- *B bugs* are essential problems that require attention; however, the game may still be playable. Multiple B bugs are equally severe to an A bug.

- *C bugs* are small and obscure problems, often in form of recommendation rather than bugs.

Game Tester

A game tester is a member of a development team who performs game testing.

Roles

The organization of staff differs between organizations; a typical company may employ the following roles associated with testing disciplines:

- *Game producers* are responsible for setting testing deadlines in coordination with marketing and quality assurance. They also manage many items outside of game testing, relating to the overall production of a title. Their approval is typically required for final submission or "gold" status.

- *Lead tester, test lead* or *QA lead* is the person responsible for the game working correctly and managing bug lists. A lead tester manages the QA staff. The lead tester works closely with designers and programmers, especially towards the end of the project. The lead tester is responsible for tracking bug reports and ensuring that they are fixed. They are also responsible that QA teams produce formal and complete reports. This includes discarding duplicate and erroneous bug reports, as well as requesting clarifications. As the game nears alpha and beta stages, lead tester brings more testers into the team, coordinates with external testing teams and works with management and producers. Some companies may prevent the game going gold until lead tester approves it. Lead testers are also typically responsible for compiling representative samples of game footage for submission to regulatory bodies such as the ESRB and PEGI. A lead tester is often an aspiring designer or producer.

- *Testers* are responsible for checking that the game works, is easy to use, has actions that make sense, and contains fun gameplay. Testers need to write accurate and specific bug reports, and if possible providing descriptions of how the bug can be reproduced. Testers may be assigned to a single game during its entire production, or brought onto other projects as demanded by the department's schedule and specific needs.

- *SDET (Software Development Engineer in Test)* or *Technical Testers* are responsible for building automated test cases and frameworks as well as managing complex test problems such as overall game performance and security. These individuals usually have strong software development skills but with a focus on writing software which exposes defects in other applications. Specific roles and duties will vary between studios. Many games are developed without any Technical Testers.

Employment

Game QA is less technical than general software QA. Game testers most often require experience however occasionally only a high school diploma and no technical expertise will suffice. Game testing is normally a full-time job for experienced testers; however, many employees are hired as temporary staff, such as beta testers. In some cases, testers employed by a publisher may be sent to work at the developer's site. The most aggressive recruiting season is late summer/early autumn, as this is the start of the crunch period for games to be finished and shipped in time for the holiday season.

Some games studios are starting to take a more technical approach to game QA that is more inline with traditional software testing. Technical Test positions are still fairly rare throughout the industry but these jobs are often full-time positions with long term career paths and require a 4-year computer science degree and significant experience with test automation.

Some testers use the job as a stepping stone in the game industry. QA résumés, which display non-technical skill sets, tend towards management, than to marketing or production. Applicants for programming, art, or design positions need to demonstrate technical skills in these areas.

Compensation

Game testing personnel are usually paid hourly (around US$10–12 an hour). Testing management is usually more lucrative, and requires experience and often a college education. An annual survey found that testers earn an average of $39k annually. Testers with less than three years' experience earn an average of US$25k while testers with over three years' experience earn US$43k. Testing leads, with over six years' experience, earn on an average of US$71k a year. Typically, they will make $35–45k with less experience. Some employers offer bonuses for the number of bugs found.

Process

A typical bug report progression of testing process is seen below:

- *Identification.* Incorrect program behaviour is analyzed and identified as a bug.

- *Reporting.* The bug is reported to the developers using a defect tracking system. The circumstances of the bug and steps to reproduce are included in the report. Developers may request additional documentation such as a real-time video of the bug's manifestation.

- *Analysis.* The developer responsible for the bug, such as an artist, programmer or game designer checks the malfunction. This is outside the scope of game tester duties, although inconsistencies in the report may require more information or evidence from the tester.

- *Verification.* After the developer fixes the issue, the tester verifies that the bug no longer occurs. Not all bugs are addressed by the developer, for example, some bugs may be claimed as features (expressed as "NAB" or "not a bug"), and may also be "waived" (given permission to be ignored) by producers, game designers, or even lead testers, according to company policy.

Methodology

There is no standard method for game testing, and most methodologies are developed by individual video game developers and publishers. Methodologies are continuously refined and may differ for different types of games (for example, the methodology for testing an MMORPG will be different from testing a casual game). Many methods, such as unit testing, are borrowed directly from general software testing techniques. Outlined below are the most important methodologies, specific to video games.

- Functionality testing is most commonly associated with the phrase "game testing", as it entails playing the game in some form. Functionality testing does not require extensive technical knowledge. Functionality testers look for general problems within the game itself or its user interface, such as stability issues, game mechanic issues, and game asset integrity.

- Compliance testing is the reason for the existence of game testing labs. First-party licensors for console platforms have strict technical requirements titles licensed for their platforms. For example, Sony publishes a *Technical Requirements Checklist* (TRC), Microsoft publishes *Xbox Requirements* (XR), and Nintendo publishes a set of "guidelines" (Lotcheck). Some of these requirements are highly technical and fall outside the scope of game testing. Other parts, most notably the formatting of standard error messages, handling of memory card data, and handling of legally trademarked and copyrighted material, are the responsibility of the game testers. Even a single violation in submission for license approval may have the game rejected, possibly incurring additional costs in further testing and resubmission. In addition, the delay may cause the title to miss an important launch window, potentially costing the publisher even larger sums of money.

  The requirements are proprietary documents released to developers and publishers under confidentiality agreements. They are not available for the general public to review, although familiarity with these standards is considered a valuable skill to have as a tester.

  Compliance may also refer to regulatory bodies such as the ESRB and PEGI, if the game targets a particular content rating. Testers must report objectionable content that may be inappropriate for the desired rating. Similar to licensing, games that do not receive the desired rating must be re-edited, retested, and resubmitted at additional cost.

- Compatibility testing is normally required for PC titles, nearing the end of development as much of the compatibility depends on the final build of the game. Often two rounds of compatibility tests are done - early in beta to allow time for issue resolution, and late in beta or during release candidate. Compatibility testing team test major functionality of the game on various configurations of hardware. Usually a list of commercially important hardware is supplied by the publisher.

  Compatibility testing ensures that the game runs on different configurations of hardware and software. The hardware encompasses brands of different manufacturers and assorted input peripherals such as gamepads and joysticks.

  The testers also evaluate performance and results are used for game's advertised minimum system requirements. Compatibility or performance issues may be either fixed by the developer or, in case of legacy hardware and software, support may be dropped.

- Localization testing act as in-game text editors. Although general text issues are a part of functionality testing, QA departments may employ dedicated localization testers. In particular, early Japanese game translations were rife with errors, and in recent years localization testers are employed to make technical corrections and review translation work of game scripts - catalogued collections of all the in-game text. Testers native to the region where a game is marketed may be employed to ensure the accuracy and quality of a game's localization.

- Soak testing, in the context of video games, involves leaving the game running for prolonged periods time in various modes of operation, such as idling, paused, or at the title screen. This testing requires no user interaction beyond initial setup, and is usually managed by lead testers. Automated tools may be used for simulating repetitive actions, such mouse clicks. Soaking can detect memory leaks or rounding errors that manifest only over time. Soak tests are one of the compliance requirements.

- Beta testing is done during beta stage of development. Often this refers to the first publicly available version of a game. Public betas are effective because thousands of fans may find bugs that the developer's testers did not.

- Regression testing is performed once a bug has been fixed by the programmers. QA checks to see whether the bug is still there (regression) and then runs similar tests to see whether the fix broke something else. That second stage is often called "halo testing"; it involves testing all around a bug, looking for other bugs.

- Load testing tests the limits of a system, such as the number of players on an MMO server, the number of sprites active on the screen, or the number of threads running in a particular program. Load testing requires either a large group of testers or software that emulates heavy activity. Load testing also measures the capability of an application to function correctly under load.

- Multiplayer testing may involve separate multiplayer QA team if the game has significant multiplayer portions. This testing is more common with PC games. The testers ensure that all connectivity methods (modem, LAN, Internet) are working. This allows single player and multiplayer testing to occur in parallel.

- Mobile game testing is mainly done manually or as automated during the development. Mobile game testing typically includes all above testing types. Popular mobile game platforms are Android and iOS. Mobile game test automation with image recognition features can be found in Testdroid.

Test Automation

Implementing test automation for mobile application development process is the best way to gain agile, effective use of resources and time for testing.

Frameworks

The most popular test automation frameworks for Android testing:

- Appium
- Calabash
- Robotium
- uiautomator
- Espresso

The most popular test automation frameworks for iOS testing:

- Appium
- Calabash
- UI Automation
- Frank
- KIF

Console Hardware

For consoles, the majority of testing is not performed on a normal system or *consumer unit*. Special test equipment is provided to developers and publishers. The most significant tools are the *test* or *debug* kits, and the *dev* kits. The main difference between from consumer units is the ability to load games from a burned disc or from a hard drive, as well as being able to set the console for any publishing region. This allows game developers to produce copies for testing. This functionality is not present in consumer units to combat software piracy and grey-market imports.

- *Test kits* have the same hardware specifications and overall appearance as a consumer unit, though often with additional ports and connectors for other testing equipment. Test kits contain additional options, such as running automated compliance checks, especially with regard to save data. The system software also allows the user to capture memory dumps for aid in debugging.

- *Dev kits* are not normally used by game testers, but are used by programmers for lower-level testing. In addition to the features of a test kit, dev kits usually have higher hardware specifications, most notably increased system memory. This allows developers to estimate early game performance without worrying about optimizations. Dev kits are usually larger and look different from a test kit or consumer unit.

Game Server

A game server (sometimes host or shard) is a server which is the authoritative source of events in a multiplayer video game. The server transmits enough data about its internal state to allow its connected clients to maintain their own accurate version of the game world for display to players. They also receive and process each player's input.

Types

Dedicated Server

Dedicated servers simulate game worlds without supporting direct input or output, except that required for their administration. Players must connect to the server with separate client programs in order to see and interact with the game.

The foremost advantage of dedicated servers is their suitability for hosting in professional data centers, with all of the reliability and performance benefits that entails. Remote hosting also eliminates the low-latency advantage that would otherwise be held by any player who hosts and connects to a server from the same machine or local network.

Dedicated servers cost money to run, however. Cost are sometimes met by a game's developers (particularly on consoles) and sometimes by clan groups, but in either case, the public is reliant on third parties providing servers to connect to. For this reason, most games which use dedicated servers also provide listen server support.

Listen Server

Listen servers run in the same process as a game client. They otherwise function like dedicated servers, but typically have the disadvantage of having to communicate with remote players over the residential internet connection of the hosting player. Residential connections rarely support the upload requirements of games with many players; the typical limit is 16. Performance is also reduced by the simple fact that the machine running the server is also generating an output image. Furthermore, listen servers grant anyone playing on them directly a large latency advantage over other players ("host with most") and cease to exist when that player leaves the game.

But listen servers have the advantage of being essentially free and not requiring any special infrastructure or forward planning to set up, which makes them common at LAN parties where latency and bandwidth issues are not a concern. They are also common in console games.

Peer-to-Peer

In the client/server model outlined elsewhere in this article, clients receive processed data from the server and display it without much thought. In the alternative "peer-to-peer" model there is no server: each "peer" instead receives the raw input streams of each other player and determines the results itself.

Peer-to-peer is generally considered obsolete for action games, but it still common in the real-time strategy genre due to its suitability for games with large numbers of tokens and small numbers of players. Instead of constantly transmitting the positions of 1000 troops, the game can make a one-off transmission of the fact that 1000 troops are selected and that the player in command of them just issued a move order.

However, peer-to-peer has many disadvantages:

- It is very difficult to keep all peers synchronised. Minute differences between peers can escalate over time to game-breaking paradoxes.

- It is very difficult to support new peers joining part-way through a game.

- Each peer must communicate with all other peers, limiting the number of connected players.

- Each peer must wait for every other peer's message before simulating the next "network frame", resulting in all players experiencing the same latency as the player with the worst connection.

Tickrate

The rate at which a game server runs simulation steps is commonly referred to as its "tickrate". A "tick" is a number associated with each simulation step which is broadcast to clients to help them synchronise with the server.

There are three reasons to limit the frequency of server simulation steps to a predefined tickrate: to conserve server and client bandwidth, to conserve server CPU time, and to allow clients to be certain of how much time has elapsed between each tick. The last point is important for internet games, as network updates from the server can arrive at different intervals or even an incorrect order.

Customization

Servers, particularly those of PC games, can generally be customized in ways that still allow unaltered clients to connect to them. These customizations can include tweaks to built-in game settings, content that is downloaded by clients when they join the game, and new code which changes the way that the server behaves.

While server customization is popular with server administrators and players, it can be at odds with the desire of developers and other players for the game to be experienced as intended. It can also aggravate players by enabling abusive administrators to lie about what their server offers.

Mod (Video Gaming)

A mod, or modification, is the alteration of content from a video game in order to make it operate in a manner different from its original version. Mods can be created for any genre of game but are especially popular in first-person shooters, role-playing games and real-time strategy games. Mods are made by the general public or a developer and can be entirely new games in themselves, but mods are not stand-alone software and require the user to have the original release in order to run. They can include new items, modded weapons, characters, enemies, models, textures, levels, story lines, music, money, armor, life and game modes. They can be single-player or multiplayer. Mods that add new content to the underlying game are often called partial conversions, while mods that create an entirely new game are called total conversions and mods that fix bugs only are called unofficial patches.

Games running on a personal computer are often designed with change in mind, allowing modern

PC games to be modified by gamers without much difficulty. These mods can add extra replay value and interest.

The Internet provides an inexpensive medium to promote and distribute user created content like mods, an aspect commonly known as Web 2.0. Video game modding was described as remixing of games and can be therefore seen as part of the remix culture as described by Lawrence Lessig. The Mods have become an increasingly important factor in the commercial success of some games. Developers such as id Software, Valve Corporation, Mojang AB, Bethesda Softworks, Firaxis, Crytek, The Creative Assembly and Epic Games provide extensive tools and documentation to assist mod makers, leveraging the potential success brought in by a popular mod like *Counter-Strike*.

Mods can help to continue the success of the original game, even when the original game has become dated. In that case, players might have to clarify that they are referring to the unmodified game when talking about playing a game. The term *vanilla* is often used to make this distinction. "Vanilla *Battlefield 1942*", for example, refers to the original, unmodified game. For vanilla games, prefix "v" or "V" is commonly used together with the game title acronym, *e.g.*, VQ3 stands for "vanilla *Quake 3*".

As early as the 1980s, video game mods have been used for the sole purpose of creating art, as opposed to an actual game. They can include recording in-game action as a film, as well as attempting to reproduce real-life areas inside a game with no regard for game play value.

Popular websites dedicated to modding include *NexusMods* and *Mod DB*.

Types

Total Conversion

A *total conversion* is a mod of an existing game that replaces virtually all of the artistic assets in the original game, and sometimes core aspects of gameplay. Total conversions can result in a completely different genre from the original.

Often developers intend to sell their total conversion as a stand-alone product, which necessitates the need to replace any remaining original assets to avoid copyright infringement.

Since most total conversions only share the engine in common with the original game, if the engine becomes free software or freeware, the total conversion can be playable without having to own the original game. *Counter-Strike*, one of the most popular online games ever made, was originally a *Half-Life* total conversion. It was so popular that numerous official and unofficial *Counter-Strike* re-releases have been developed throughout the years.

Many mods for *Half-Life* such as *Earth's Special Forces* (fighting genre) or *Football Championship* (sports genre) are capable of changing gameplay while utilizing a modified engine.

Total Overhaul

A *total overhaul* mod changes or redefines the gameplay style of the original game, while keeping it in the original game's universe. This may include upgrading the graphics or adding new models, dialog and music to the original (while still respecting the plot), or changing the pace of how the game is played. Total overhauls are usually combined with significant add-on material as well. A prominent example is *Black Mesa*, which remakes the original *Half-Life* in Valve Corporation's Source game engine, or *Fallout: Project Brazil*, for Bethesda Softworks and Obsidian Entertainment's *Fallout: New Vegas*.

However, some overhauls also change the universe and background in itself in very extreme ways to the point where it no longer constitutes as the original, such as *Obscurum - Pandemic* also released for *Fallout: New Vegas*. This mod derails into an alternative history on its own, similar to the original Fallout storyline.

Add-on

An *add-on* or *addon* is a typically small mod which adds to the original content of a specific game. In most cases, an add-on will add one particular element to a game, such as a new weapon in a shooting game, a new vehicle or track in a racing game, or items in a game like *Minecraft*. This can be accomplished without changing any of the original game's existing content. Many games are flexible and allow this, however that is not always the case. Some add-ons occasionally have to replace in-game content, due to the nature of a peculiar game engine. It may be the case, for example, that in a game which does not give a player the option to choose their character, modders wishing to add another player model will simply have to overwrite the old one. A famous example of this type of mod can be found for the *Grand Theft Auto* series wherein modders may use downloadable tools to replace content (such as models) in the game's directory. The *Left 4 Dead* series can also be modded with individual add-ons which are stored in a .VPK format, so that a player may choose to activate a given mod or not.

Unofficial Patch

An *unofficial patch* can be a mod of an existing game that fixes bugs not fixed by an official patch or that unlocks content present in the released game's files but is inaccessible in official gameplay. Such patches are usually created by members of the game's fan base when the original developer is unwilling or unable to supply the functionality officially. Jazz Jackrabbit 2 has an unofficial patch which adds and fixes many of its features. One downside of this type of mod is that leaked content can be revealed. An example is the *Hot Coffee* mod for *Grand Theft Auto: San Andreas*, which was removed in version 1.01 because of lawsuits by parent associations. *Hot Coffee* was brought back to version 1.01 by a group of a modders in 2005 who found the animation files and scripts in the first version of the game. The scripts were re-added and the animations were re-hexed so the game would not have any conflict.

Art Mod

An *art mod* is a mod that is created for artistic effect. Art mods are most frequently associated with video game art, however modified games that retain their playability and are subject to more extensive mods (i.e. closer to total conversions) may also be classified as art games. Art mods are usually designed to subvert the original game experience. One example is the *Velvet-Strike* mod for *Counter Strike* in which the players spray-paint anti-violence messages in multiplayer games as a form of performance art. Another example is Robert Nideffer's *Tomb Raider I and II* patches which were designed to subvert the unofficial *Nude Raider* patch of the late 1990s by altering Lara Croft's sexual orientation. The origins of the art mod can be traced to the classic 1983 mod *Castle Smurfenstein* (a humorous subversion of *Castle Wolfenstein* which replaces the Nazi guards with Smurfs). The very first art mod, however, is generally considered to be Iimura Takahiko's 1993 *AIUEOUNN Six Features* (a modification of Sony's "System G").

Support Continuation by Mod

After EA lost the license and ended the support for the MVP Baseball 2005, the game's modding community continues the support and releases updated roster lists every year as also alternative leagues (e.g. MVP Caribe, a total conversion).

Official Status of Mods

Due to the increasing popularity and quality of modding, some developers, such as Firaxis, have included fan-made mods in official releases of expansion packs. A similar case is that of Valve Corporation, when they hired *Defense of the Ancients* author Icefrog in developing *Dota 2*.

For example, in the *Civilization IV* expansion *Beyond the Sword*: two existing mods, *Rhye's and Fall of Civilization* and *Fall from Heaven* made their way into the expansion (the latter through a spin-off called *Age of Ice*).

A number of fan-made maps, scenarios and mods, such as "Double Your Pleasure", were also included in the *Civilization III* expansion Play the World.

Development

Most mods do not progress very far and are abandoned without ever having a public release. Some are very limited and just include some gameplay changes or even a different loading screen, and others are total conversions and can modify content and gameplay extensively. A few mods become very popular and convert themselves into distinct games, with the rights getting bought and turning into an official modification.

A group of mod developers may join together to form a "mod team".

Mods are made for many first-person shooters and Real-Time-Strategies, such as the series based on *Quake, Doom, Chaos, Total Annihilation, Rise of Nations* and *Command and Conquer*.

The most well-known mod is the *Half-Life* multiplayer mod *Counter-Strike*, which was released shortly after the original game. Approximately one million games are hosted on dedicated servers per day. *Counter-Strike* is probably the best example of a modification that turns into a retail game. Another renowned mod is *Team Fortress*, which was based on the Quake engine and eventually became a whole series of games: *Team Fortress Classic, Team Fortress 2*, and an unofficial mod made originally as a fan-made sequel to *TFC, Fortress Forever*.

Tools

Mod-making tools are a variety of construction sets for creating mods for a game. Early commercial mod-making tools were the *Boulder Dash Construction Kit* (1986) and *The Bard's Tale Construction Set* (1991), which allowed users to create game designs in those series. Much more successful among early mod-making tools was the 1992 *Forgotten Realms: Unlimited Adventures* from Strategic Simulations, Inc., which allowed users to construct games based on the game world that was launched with the *Pool of Radiance* game.

Later mod-making tools include *The Elder Scrolls Construction Set* which shipped with *Morrowind*, the *World Editor* for *Warcraft III: Reign of Chaos*, the Aurora toolset which was included with *Neverwinter Nights*, FRED and FRED2, the mission editors for *Freespace* and *FreeSpace 2* respectively, the Obsidian tool set for *Neverwinter Nights 2*, the *Garden of Eden Creation Kit* SDK for *Fallout 3*, and the Valve Hammer Editor which is used to create maps for *Half-Life*, *Half-Life 2* and various other games based on the Source engine (older versions also supported the Quake engine).

There are also free content delivery tools available that make playing mods easier. They help manage downloads, updates, and mod installation in order to allow people who are less technically literate to play. Steam for *Half-Life 2* mods is an example.

Game Support for Modifications

The potential for end-user change in game varies greatly, though it can have little correlation on the number and quality of mods made for a game.

In general the most modification-friendly games will define gameplay variables in text or other non proprietary format files (for instance in the *Civilization* series one could alter the movement rate along roads and many other factors), and have graphics of a standard format such as bitmaps. Publishers can also determine mod-friendliness in the way important source files are available (some programs collect their source material into large proprietary archives, but others make the files available in folders).

Games have varying support from their publishers for modifications, but often require expensive professional software to make. One such example is *Homeworld 2*, which requires the program Maya to build new in-game objects. However, there is a free version available of Maya and other advanced modeling software. There are also free and even open-source modeling programs (such as Blender) that can be used as well.

For advanced mods such as *Desert Combat* that are total conversions, complicated modeling and texturing software is required to make original content. Advanced mods can rival the complexity and work of making the original game content (short of the engine itself), rendering the differences in ease of modding small in comparison to the total amount of work required. Having an engine that is for example easy to import models to, is of little help when doing research, modeling, and making a photorealistic texture for a game item. As a result, other game characteristics such as its popularity and capabilities have a dominating effect on the number of mods created for the game by users.

A game that allows modding is said to be "moddable". *The Elder Scrolls V: Skyrim* as well as its predecessors, *The Elder Scrolls III: Morrowind* and *The Elder Scrolls IV: Oblivion*, are examples of highly moddable games, with an official editor available for download from the developer. *Daggerfall* was much less moddable, but some people released their own modifications nevertheless.

Some modifications such as *Gunslingers Academy* have deliberately made the game more moddable by adding in scripting support or externalizing underlying code. An example of a widely seen mod of *The Elder Scrolls V: Skyrim* by a videogame designer by the name of Pastaspace exceeded 1.6 million views on December 10, 2013 as a YouTube video. The mod involved switching out the character of the terrifying dragon with what many commentators referred to as an equally terrifying, if humorous character: Thomas the Tank Engine.

Supreme Commander set out to be the 'most customisable game ever' and as such included a mod manager which allowed for modular modding, having several mods on at once.

The games industry is currently facing the question of how much it should embrace the players' contribution in creating new material for the game or mod-communities as part of their structure within the game. Some software companies openly accept and even encourage such communities. Others though have chosen to enclose their games in heavily policed copyright or Intellectual Property regimes(IPR) and close down sites that they see as infringing their ownership of a game.

Portability Issues

For cross-platform games, mods written for the Windows version have not always been compatible with the Mac OS X and/or Linux ports of the game. In large part, this is due to the publisher's concern with prioritizing the porting of the primary game itself, when allocating resources for fixing the porting of mod-specific functions may not be cost-effective for the smaller market share of alternate platforms. For example, *Battlefield 1942*, ported by Aspyr for Mac OS X, had file access issues specific to mods until the 1.61D patch. *Unreal Tournament 2004* does not have a working community mods menu for the Mac OS X version and, until the 3369 patch, had graphics incompatibilities with several mods such as *Red Orchestra* and *Metaball*.

Also, mods compiled into platform-specific libraries, such as those of *Doom 3*, are often only built for the Windows platform, leading to a lack of cross-platform compatibility even when the underlying game is highly portable. In the same line of reasoning, mod development tools are often available only on the Windows platform. id Software's Doom 3 Radiant tool and Epic Games' UnrealEd are examples of this.

Mod teams that lack either the resources or know-how to develop their mods for alternate platforms sometimes outsource their code and art assets to individuals or groups who are able to port the mod.

The mod specialist site for Macs, Macologist, has created GUI launchers and installers for many UT2004 mods, as well as solving cross-platform conversion issues for mods for other games.

Unforeseen Consequences or Benefits of Modding

In January 2005, it was reported that in *The Sims 2* modifications that changed item and game behavior were unexpectedly being transferred to other players through the official website's *exchange* feature, leading to changed game behavior without advance warning.

In July 2007, CNET News reported that a *Grand Theft Auto* mod video uploaded to YouTube contained a link to a malware website. When a viewer clicked on the link and downloaded the mod, it infected the computer.

In early 2012, the *DayZ* modification for *ARMA 2* was released and caused a massive increase in sales for the three-year-old game, putting it in the top spot for online game sales for a number of months and selling over 300,000 units for the game.

In 2015, reports of malware being circulated through modifications written using the .NET Framework were made on the *Grand Theft Auto* fan site GTAForums. Two of the modifications in question, namely "Angry Planes" and "No Clip", came with code for loading a remote access tool, and a keylogger for stealing Facebook and Steam account credentials. Instructions for removing the infected mods has since been posted on the forums. Gaming websites who have previously covered the said mods in their articles also followed suit, advising users to disinfect their computer and change their user credentials.

Mod Packs

Mod packs are groups of mods put into one package for download, often with an auto-installer. A mod pack's purpose is to make an easy download for downloading multiple mods, often with the goal of resolving cross-mod interactions that can happen, or to make the original game easier or more difficult.

Legal Status of Mod Packs

Mod packs have had legal issues in the past. Often mods are distributed without consent or consultation with the original mod author, which is believed by some of the *Minecraft* gaming community to be against copyright laws, while others believe the mod to be open and not copyrightable due to it being a modification for an already existing game. Some mod authors have included malicious code against mod pack authors to prevent distribution, often with other particular mods.

A small company named Micro Star was the subject of a 1997 court case, where in FormGen Inc., the distributor for 3D Realms' *Duke Nukem 3D*, sued the company for their unauthorised use of the *Duke Nukem* intellectual property in their *Nuke It* compilation of user-made levels for the game.

Controversy Surrounding Paid Mods

In April 2015, Valve Corporation implemented a "paid mod" feature onto Steam and the first game to implement this feature was *Skyrim*. This gave the developers of mods additional ways to charge for mods. There was a large uprising against this feature. There was a Change.org petition created which got over 133,000 signatures. When Gabe Newell did an AMA (ask me anything) on Reddit, he said "Our goal is to make modding better for the authors and gamers [...] if something doesn't help with that, it will get dumped. Right now I'm more optimistic that this will be a win for authors and gamers, but we are always going to be data driven."

The feature was implemented with the idea that there would be oversight from Valve or the third-party developer. This led to overpriced content, mods being improperly sold by a user that had not created the original mod, and copyright issues with content of such mods. After a large influx of complaints, Valve announced they would discontinue paid mods for *Skyrim* and refund those that spent money on the Workshop and re-evaluate the process. The removal of the system itself was also criticized.

Video Game Remake

A video game remake is a video game closely adapted from an earlier title, usually for the purpose of modernizing a game for newer hardware and contemporary audiences. Typically, a remake of such game software shares essentially the same title, fundamental gameplay concepts, and core story elements of the original game.

Pokémon Red and *Blue* for the Game Boy (top) were remade for the Game Boy Advance as *Pokémon FireRed* and *LeafGreen* (bottom).

A comparison of *Halo: Combat Evolved* (left) and *Halo: Combat Evolved Anniversary* (right) redrawn graphics.

A remake typically shares very little of the original assets and code with the original game, distinguishing it from an "enhanced port", partial remake, or remastering.

Remakes are often made by the original developer or copyright holder, sometimes by the fan community. If created by the community, video game remakes are sometimes also called fan game and can be seen as part of the retrogaming phenomena.

Definition

A remake offers a newer interpretation of an older work, characterized by updated or changed assets. A remake typically maintains the same story, genre, and fundamental gameplay ideas of the original work. The intent of a remake is usually to take an older game that has become outdated and update it for a new platform and audience. A remake may also include expanded stories, often to conform to the conventions of contemporary games or later titles in the same series in order to make a game marketable to a new audience. For example, Sierra's 1991 remake of *Space Quest*, the developers used the engine, point-and-click interface, and graphical style of *Space Quest IV: Roger Wilco and The Time Rippers*, replacing the dated graphics and text parser interface of the original. However, elements that had not become dated, like the narrative, puzzles, and sets, were largely preserved. Another example is Black Mesa, a Half-Life 2 mod that improves in-game textures, assets and models, and facial animations, while taking place in the events of the original Half-Life game.

Similar Concepts

Games that use an existing brand but are conceptually very different from the original, such as *Battlezone* (1998) and *Defender* (2002) or *Tomb Raider* (1996) and *Tomb Raider* (2013) are usually regarded as reboots rather than remakes.

A port is a conversion of a game to a new platform that relies heavily on existing work and assets. A port may include various enhancements like improved performance, resolution, and sometimes even additional content, but differs from a remake in that it still relies heavily on the original assets and engine of the source game. A port that contains a great deal of remade assets may sometimes be considered a remastering or partial remake.

History

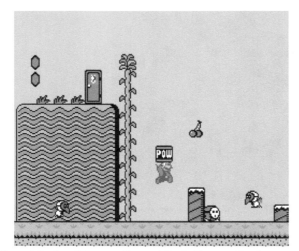 

The original 1988 game *Super Mario Bros. 2* (top) compared to the 1993 *Super Mario All-Stars* remake (bottom).

In the early history of video games, remakes were generally regarded as "conversions" and seldom associated with nostalgia. Due to limited and often highly divergent hardware, games appearing on multiple platforms usually had to be entirely remade. These conversions often included considerable changes to the graphics and gameplay, and could be regarded retroactively as remakes, but are distinguished from later remakes largely by intent. A conversion is created with the primary goal of tailoring a game to a specific piece of hardware, usually contemporaneous or nearly contemporaneous with the original release. An early example was *Gun Fight*, Midway's 1975 reprogrammed version of Taito's arcade game *Western Gun*, with the main difference being the use of a microprocessor in the reprogrammed version, which allowed improved graphics and smoother animation than the discrete logic of the original. In 1980, Atari released the first officially licensed home console game conversion of an arcade title, Taito's 1978 hit *Space Invaders*, for the Atari 2600. The game became the first "killer app" for a video game console by quadrupling the system's sales. Since then, it became a common trend to port arcade games to home systems since the second console generation, though at the time they were often more limited than the original arcade games due to the technical limitations of home consoles.

In 1985, Sega released a pair of arcade remakes of older home video games. *Pitfall II: Lost Caverns* was effectively a remake of both the original *Pitfall!* and its sequel with new level layouts and colorful, detailed graphics. That same year, Sega adapted the 1982 computer game *Choplifter* for the arcades, taking the fundamental gameplay of the original and greatly expanding it, adding new environments, enemies, and gameplay elements. This version was very successful, and later adapted to the Master System and Famicom. Both of these games were distinguished from most earlier conversions in that they took major liberties with the source material, attempting to modernize both the gameplay as well as the graphics.

Some of the earliest remakes to be recognized as such were attempts to modernize games to the standards of later games in the series. Some were even on the same platforms as the original, for example *Ultima I: The First Age of Darkness*, a 1986 remake of the original that appeared on multiple platforms, including the Apple II, the same platform the source game originated on. Other early remakes of this type include Sierra's early-'90s releases of *King's Quest*, *Space Quest* and *Leisure Suit Larry*. These games used the technology and interface of the most recent games in Sierra's series, and original assets in a dramatically different style. The intent was not simply to bring the game to a new platform, but to modernize older games which had in various ways become dated.

With the birth of the retrogaming phenomenon, remakes became a way for companies to revive nostalgic brands. *Galaga '88* and *Super Space Invaders '91* were both attempts to revitalize aging arcade franchises with modernized graphics and new gameplay elements, while preserving many signature aspects of the original games. The 16-bit generation of console games was marked by greatly enhanced graphics compared to the previous generation, but often relatively similar gameplay, which led to an increased interest in remakes of games from the previous generation. *Super Mario All-Stars* remade the entire NES *Mario* series, and was met with great commercial success. Remake compilations of the *Ninja Gaiden* and *Mega Man* series followed. As RPGs increased in popularity, *Dragon Quest*, *Ys* and *Kyūyaku Megami Tensei* were also remade. In the mid-'90s, Atari released a series of remakes with the *2000* brand, including *Tempest 2000*, *Battlezone 2000*, and *Defender 2000*. After Atari's demise, Hasbro continued the tradition, with 3D remakes of *Pong*, *Centipede*, and *Asteroids*.

With the rise of brand new genres and 3D gameplay, remakes became somewhat less common in the late 1990s, with notable exceptions like *Doom 64* and *Lunar: The Silver Star*. Emulation made perfect ports of older games possible, and compilations became a popular way for publishers to capitalize on older properties.

Budget pricing gave publishers the opportunity to match their game's price with the perceived lower value proposition of an older game, opening the door for newer remakes. In 2003, Sega launched the Sega Ages line for PlayStation 2, initially conceived as a series of modernized remakes of classic games, though the series later diversified to include emulated compilations. The series concluded with a release that combined the two approaches, and included a remake of *Fantasy Zone II* that ran, via emulation, on hardware dating to the time of the original release, one of the few attempts at an enhanced remake to make no attempts at modernization. The advent of downloadable game services like Xbox Live Arcade and PlayStation Network has further fueled the expanded market for remakes, as the platform allows companies to sell their games at a lower price, seen as more appropriate for the smaller size typical of retro games. Some XBLA and PSN remakes include *Bionic Commando Rearmed*, *Jetpac Refuelled*, *Wipeout HD* (a remake not of the original *Wipeout* but of the two PSP games), *Cyber Troopers Virtual-On Oratorio Tangram* and *Super Street Fighter II Turbo HD Remix*.

Games abandoned by the right holders often spark remakes created by hobbyist. An example is OpenRA which is a modernized remake of the classic Command & Conquer real-time-strategy games. Beyond cross-platform support it adds comfort functions and game-play functionality inspired by successors of the original games.

Some remakes may include the original game as a bonus feature. The 2009 remake of *The Secret of Monkey Island* took this a step further by allowing players to switch between the original and remade versions on the fly with a single button press. This trend was continued in the sequel, and is also a feature on the new remake *Halo: Combat Evolved Anniversary*.

The Nintendo 3DS's lineup has included numerous remasterings and remakes, including *The Legend of Zelda: Ocarina of Time*, *Star Fox 64*, *Cave Story*, *The Legend of Zelda: Majora's Mask* and *Pokémon Omega Ruby* and *Alpha Sapphire*.

Starting 2009, *Broken Sword: The Shadow of the Templars – Director's Cut* was released on PC, console and mobile platforms, with commercial success.

"Demakes"

Although remakes typically aim to adapt a game from a more limited platform to a more advanced one, a rising interest in older platforms has inspired some to do the opposite, adapting modern games to the standards of older platforms, sometimes even programming them for deprecated hardware.

Modern demakes often change the 3D gameplay to a 2D one. Popular demakes include *Quest: Brian's Journey*, an official Game Boy port of *Quest 64*; *Super Smash Land*, a Game Boy-style demake of *Super Smash Bros.*; a Flash version of *Portal*; *Rockman 7 Fc* and *Rockman 8 Fc*, NES-styled demakes of *Mega Man 7* and *8*, respectively; *Gang Garrison 2*, a pixelated demake of *Team Fortress 2*; and *Halo 2600*, an Atari 2600-style demake of Microsoft's *Halo* series. There is also a NES-style demake of Touhou Project game Embodiment of Scarlet Devil. Some demakes are created to show-case and push the abilities of older generation systems such as the Atari 2600. An example of this is the 2012 game *Princess Rescue* which is a demake of the NES title *Super Mario Bros.*.

For much of the 1990s in China and Hong Kong, black market developers would create unauthorized adaptations of modern games such as *Final Fantasy VII* or *Tekken* for the NES, which still enjoyed considerable popularity in the region because of the availability of low-cost black market systems.

Independent Video Game Development

Independent video game development is the video game development process of creating indie games; these are video games, commonly created by individual or small teams of video game de-velopers and usually without significant financial support of a video game publisher or other out-side source. These games may take years to be built from the ground up or can be completed in a matter of days or even hours depending on complexity, participants, and design goal.

Driven by digital distribution, the concept of independent video game development has spawned an "indie" movement. The increase in popularity of independent games has allowed increased dis-tribution on popular gaming platforms such as the PlayStation Network, Nintendo eShop, Xbox Live and Steam.

History

The origins of indie video games may be traced back to the 1970s, when there was virtually no established computer gaming industry. As video game firms developed they employed more pro-grammers. Nonetheless, independent programmers continued to make their own games. During the 1990s, indie games were most commonly distributed as shareware or shared from friend to friend and therefore known as "shareware games".

As the industry grew during the 1980s, publishing a game became more difficult. Chris Crawford said in late 1984,

I will point out the sad truth. We have pretty much passed the period where hobbyists could put together a game that would have commercial prospect. It's much more difficult to break in, much less stay in. Right now ... I would discourage anyone. If you want to do a game, do it for fun, but don't try to do game designs to make any money. The odds are so much against the individual that I would hate to wish that heartbreak on anyone.

Before the mid-1990s, commercial game distribution was controlled by big publishers and retail-ers, and developers of indie games were forced to either build their own publishing company, find one willing to distribute their game, or distribute it in some form of shareware (e.g. through BBSs). The increased production costs at the beginning of the 2000s made the video game publishers even more risk averse and let them reject all small-size and too innovative concepts of small game developers.

By the mid-2000s, some indie (computer) game developers have also taken the opportunity to make their games open source, thus rendering the group of possible participants much larger depending on the interest a project generates. Other developers decided to make their games open source on end of commercialization phase to prevent their work from becoming Abandonware. This approach allows the game community also to port the game to new platforms and to provide software support (community patches) by themselves, when the developer ends the official support. Several online communities have formed around independent game development, like TIGSource. Ludum Dare, and the indiegames.com blog.

The digital distribution available since the 2000s offers new possibilities for the whole video game industry, especially for independent video game developers who can now bypass the big publisher for game distribution. Gabe Newell, creator of the PC digital distribution service Steam, formulated the advantages over physical retail distribution for smaller game developers as:

The worst days [for game development] were the cartridge days for the NES. It was a huge risk – you had all this money tied up in silicon in a warehouse somewhere, and so you'd be conservative in the decisions you felt you could make, very conservative in the IPs you signed, your art direction would not change, and so on. Now it's the opposite extreme: we can put something up on Steam [a digital distributor], deliver it to people all around the world, make changes. We can take more interesting risks.[...] Retail doesn't know how to deal with those games. On Steam there's no shelf-space restriction.

—Gabe Newell, Rock, Paper, Shotgun

The creator of Oddworld, Lorne Lanning, expressed his desire to only make games independently instead of going through publishers. "I'd rather not make games than … be a slave for public companies who care more about their shareholders than they do about their customers.""

With the rise of online shopping and digital distribution like the Steam platform, gog.com, and the Humble Store), it has become possible to sell indie games to a worldwide market with little or no initial investment by using services such as XBLA, the PlayStation Network or PayPal.

Also since the 2000s, the new trend of crowdfunding platforms (like kickstarter.com or indiegogo) allows smaller developers to fund their work directly by their fans and customers, bypassing traditional and problematic financing methods.

Leading into 2015, there has been concern that with the number of easy-to-use tools to make independent games and avenues to commercially release such games through digital distribution, as well as a broader consumer market for games, that there is a potential for an "indiepocalypse", where the indie game market would become so large as to collapse under its weight similar to the dot-com bubble. The size of the indie game market is large, estimated in March 2016 to be at least $1 billion per year for just those games offered through Steam, using statistical sales estimates from Steam Spy. While no drastic event has happened as of December 2015, the indie market has seen shifts that are released to these factors, including the rise of publishers catering to indie developers to help on promotion, marketing and distribution, and improved storefronts like Steam that help consumers to find games more suited to their preferences. There still remains fear that such a collapse could happen in the future. There has been signs leading to potential issues but no dramatic event, according to indie developer Jeff Vogel; since 2008, where Steam and XBLA enabled for ease of distribution, there was a boom, a bust, and a recession within the indie game market, but not of the scale that some have worried the indiepocalypse would carry. Mike Wilson, Graeme Struthers and Harry Miller, the co-founders of indie publisher Devolver Digital, stated in April 2016 that the market in indie games is more competitive than ever but continues to appear healthy with no signs of faltering.

Definition

The definition of what qualifies for independent video game development is vague. The term itself bore out from the independent music arena, where "indie" refers to publishing music without using a major record label, such as using smaller independent labels or via self-publishing. One simple definition, described by Laura Parker for GameSpot, is "independent video game development is the business of making games without the support of publisher". However, this independent nature can be seen described from two broad directions.

- Financial independence: In such situations, the developers have paid for the development and/or publication of the game themselves or from other funding sources such as crowd funding, and specifically without financial support of a large publisher.

- Independence of thought: In this case, the developers crafted their game without any oversight or directional influence by a third party such as a publisher.

The term "indie development" has been broadly applied to small development teams, realizing small and non-traditional non-AAA game titles on small budgets without financial help of a larger publisher. Some notable instances of games that are generally considered "indie" but challenge this definition include:

- *Journey* was created by thatgamecompany, but had financial backing of Sony as well as publishing support. Kellee Santiago of thatgamecompany believes that because they were able to innovate on their game without Sony's involvement.

- *Bastion*, similarly, was developed by Supergiant Games, but with publishing by Warner Bros. Entertainment, primarily to avoid difficulties with the certification process on Xbox Live. Greg Kasavin of Supergiant notes they consider their studio indie as they lack any parent company.

- *The Witness* was developed by Jonathan Blow and his studio Thekla, Inc. Though self-funded and published, the game's development cost around $6 million and was priced at $40, in contrast to most indie games typically priced up to $20. Blow believed this type of game represented something between indie and AAA publishing.

- *No Man's Sky* is being developed by Hello Games, though with publishing but non-financial support from Sony; the game on release will also have a price equal to a typical AAA title. Sean Murray of Hello Games believes that because they are still a small team and the game is highly experimental that they consider themselves indie.

Distribution

During the 1980s, the common medium was cassette tape, which was the default software format for systems such as the ZX Spectrum, BBC Micro, Commodore VIC-20 and Commodore 64. This eventually gave way to floppy disk and then to CD-ROM in the 1990s.

Recently independent games have been released for big budget consoles like Xbox 360, PlayStation 3, and Wii. Many games that are being released for these consoles are ports of popular flash games and/or just plainly developed independent games that have received notice. Often indie games are completely programmer driven, due to lack of publisher funding for artwork.

On November 19, 2008, Microsoft launched *Xbox LIVE Community Games*, later renamed as *Xbox Live Indie Games*, which allowed independent developers to create games for the Xbox 360 using XNA development tools and sell them in an area of the Xbox Live Marketplace.

In May 2010, several independent developers organized the Humble Indie Bundle, which raised over $1.25 million in revenue (of which about $400,000 went to charity) and showed the value that community involvement and cross-platform development can have for independent developers.

The majority of the distribution of PC and Mac games comes via portals of digital distributors such as Steam, gog.com, Desura and several others.

With the advent of smartphones such as the iPhone and the relative ease of producing these titles many independent game developers solely develop games for various smart phone operating systems such as the iOS and the newer Android. This has also seen games being ported across to take advantage of this new revenue stream such as the successful game Minecraft.

There are also independent games distribution websites, such as IndieCity, springing up to cater exclusively for indie games, rather than including them alongside the mainstream games which are the main focus of most distribution portals. Before the launch of the PlayStation 4 Sony made it a priority to focus on getting independent de-velopers to create new games for the PlayStation 4.

Tools

C++ is a popular language of choice within the video game industry, partly due to its low-level efficient nature, but mostly because almost all popular 3D game engines are already written in C++. However, independent video games have seen use of a variety of other languages. Notably, C#, the language for XNA (Microsoft's toolkit that facilitates video game development on the Xbox 360, Windows Phone 7 and Windows PCs) and Objective-C, the language for the iPhone's Cocoa touch API, the popularity of which has grown greatly since 2008, due to the accessibility of the App Store to independent developers. Indie games written in Java are also prevalent, due to the wide compatibility for most operating systems and web browsers. Other dynamic languages, notably Python, Ruby, Lua and ActionScript have also found their way into the scene, lowering barriers of entry to game development.

Licensing Fees

Personal computer platforms (such as Linux, OS X, and Windows) are traditionally financially more accessible to independent game developers than video game consoles. Aside from basic development costs, console game developers are required to pay fees to license the required Software Development Kits (SDKs) from the console maker. Manufacturers often impose a strict approval process and take a percentage of the game's net profit in addition to yearly developer fees. To develop for Nintendo Wii, Xbox 360, or PlayStation 3 requires an SDK license fee of between US$2,000 and $10,000, in addition to yearly developer fees and profit cuts, although development for Xbox Live Indie Games only requires a $99/year Creators Club membership and Microsoft takes 30% of sales. Microsoft does provide a free membership to the Creators Club to students via the DreamSpark program. Indie game developers can also use homebrew development libraries, which are free of charge, and usually open source.

References

- Chris Kohler (2005), Power-Up: How Japanese Video Games Gave the World an Extra Life, BradyGames, p. 19, ISBN 0-7440-0424-1, retrieved 2011-03-27

- Shirley R. Steinberg (2010), Shirley R. Steinberg; Michael Kehler; Lindsay Cornish, eds., Boy Culture: An Encyclopedia, 1, ABC-CLIO, p. 451, ISBN 0-313-35080-9, retrieved 2011-04-02

- Steve L. Kent (2001), The ultimate history of video games: from Pong to Pokémon and beyond : the story behind the craze that touched our lives and changed the world, p. 64, Prima, ISBN 0-7615-3643-4

- Kent, Steven L. (2001). The Ultimate History of Video Games: From Pong to Pokémon. Three Rivers Press. p. 500. ISBN 0-7615-3643-4.

- Mangiron, Carmen; Orero, Pilar; O'Hagan, Minako (2014-01-01). Fun for all: translation and accessibility practices in video games. ISBN 9783034314503.

- Adams, Ernest; Rollings, Andrew (2003). Andrew Rollings and Ernest Adams on game design. New Riders Publishing. ISBN 1-59273-001-9.

- Cannon, Rebecca. "Meltdown" from Videogames and Art (Clarke, Andy and Grethe Mitchell, eds.). Bristol: Intellect Books. Pp.40-42. 2007. ISBN 978-1-84150-142-0

- Chris Kohler (2005), Power-up: how Japanese video games gave the world an extra life, BradyGames, p. 19, ISBN 0-7440-0424-1, retrieved 2011-03-27

- Wawro, Alex (March 15, 2016). "Devs share real talk about surviving the latest 'indiepocalypse'". Gamasutra. Retrieved March 15, 2016.

- Pearson, Dan (April 13, 2016). ""Every year has been better than the last. Thriving is the best way to put it."". GamesIndustry.biz. Retrieved April 13, 2016.

- Cook, Dave (May 13, 2014). "Why Supergiant ditched publishers for the release of Transistor – interview". VG247. Retrieved April 26, 2016.

- Conditt, Jessica (January 21, 2016). "Traveling through time with 'Braid' creator Jonathan Blow". Engadget. AOL Tech. Retrieved January 21, 2016.

3

Video Game Designing: An Overview

The creation of a video game design requires input from designers and programmers. A video game starts from an idea that can be classified under one of the several genres. The whole game is planned out with consideration to game features, story, target audience, budget etc. This chapter illustrates the developmental course of a video game design from its inception till its final unveiling. The content informs the reader about topics like game mechanics, game art design, character creation, level design, field of view, dynamic game difficulty balancing etc.

Video Game Design

Video game design is the process of designing the content and rules of a video game in the pre-production stage and designing the gameplay, environment, storyline, and characters in the production stage. The designer of a game is very much like the director of a film; the designer is the visionary of the game and controls the artistic and technical elements of the game in fulfillment of their vision. Video game design requires artistic and technical competence as well as writing skills. Within the video game industry, video game design is usually just referred to as "game design", which is a more general term elsewhere.

Video game programmers have also sometimes comprised the entire design team. This is the case of such noted designers as Sid Meier, John Romero, Chris Sawyer and Will Wright. A notable exception to this policy was Coleco, which from its very start separated the function of design and programming.

As games became more complex and computers and consoles became more powerful, the job of the game designer became separate from the lead programmer. Soon game complexity demanded team members focused on game design. Many early veterans chose the game design path eschewing programming and delegating those tasks to others.

With very complex games, such as MMORPGs, or a big budget action or sports title, designers may number in the dozens. In these cases, there are generally one or two principal designers and many junior designers who specify subsets or subsystems of the game. In larger companies like Electronic Arts, each aspect of the game (control, level design) may have a separate producer, lead designer and several general designers. They may also come up with a plot for the game.

Overview

Video game design starts with an idea, often a modification on an existing concept. The game idea may fall within one or several genres. Designers often experiment with mixing genres. The game designer usually produces an initial game proposal document containing the concept, gameplay, feature list, setting and story, target audience, requirements and schedule, staff and budget estimates.

Many decisions are made during the course of a game's development about the game's design; it is the responsibility of the designer to decide which elements will be implemented, based on, for example, consistency with the game's vision, budget or hardware limitations. Design changes may have a significant positive or negative impact on required resources.

The designer may use scripting languages to implement and preview design ideas without necessarily modifying the game's codebase.

A game designer often plays video games and demos to follow the game market development.

It is common for the game designer's name to misleadingly be given an undue amount of association to the game, neglecting the rest of the development team.

Funding game publishers must be taken into account, who may have specific expectations from a game as most video games are *market-driven* — developed to sell for profit. However, if financial issues do not influence designer's decisions, the game becomes *design-* or *designer-driven*; few games are designed this way because of lack of funding. Alternatively, a game may be *technology-driven*, such as Quake (1996), to show off a particular hardware achievement or to market the game engine. Finally, a game may be *art-driven*, such as *Myst* (1993), mainly to show off impressive visuals designed by artists.

In *The Study of Games* (1971), Brian Sutton-Smith writes:

> Each person defines games in his own way — the anthropologists and folklorists in terms of historical origins; the military men, businessmen, and educators in terms of usages; the social scientists in terms of psychological and social functions. There is overwhelming evidence in all this that the meaning of games is, in part, a function of the ideas of those who think about them. ...
>
> ... A game designer is a particular kind of designer, much like a graphic designer, industrial designer, or architect. A game designer is not necessarily a programmer, visual designer, or project manager, although sometimes he or she can also play these roles in the creation of a game. A game designer might work alone or as part of a larger team. A game designer might create card games, social games, video games, or any other kind of game. The focus of a game designer is designing game play, conceiving and designing rules and structures that result in an experience for players.
>
> Thus game design, as a discipline, requires a focus on games in and of themselves. Rather than placing games in the service of another field such as sociology, literary criticism, or computer science, our aim is to study games within their own disciplinary space. Because game design is an emerging discipline, we often borrow from other areas of knowledge — from mathematics and cognitive science; from semiotics and cultural studies. We may not borrow in the most orthodox manner, but we do so in the service of helping to establish a field of game design proper.

Game Designer

A game designer is a person who designs gameplay, conceiving and designing the rules and structure of a game. Many designers start their career in testing departments, other roles in game development or in classroom conditions, where mistakes by others can be seen first-hand.

- Lead designer coordinates the work of other designers and is the main visionary of the game. Lead designer ensures team communication, makes large design decisions, and presents design outside of the team. Often the lead designer is technically and artistically astute. Keeping well-presented documentation also falls within the lead designer responsibilities. Lead designer may be the founder of a game development company or a promoted employee.

- Game mechanics designer or systems designer designs and balances the game's rules.

- Level designer or environment designer is a position becoming prominent in the recent years. Level designer is the person responsible for creating game environment, levels, and missions.

Compensation

In 2010, a game designer with more than six years of experience earned an average of US$65,000 (GBP GB£44,761.22), $54,000 (GBP £37,186.24) with three to six years of experience and $44,000 (GBP £30,299.90) with less than 3 years of experience. Lead designers earned $75,000 (GBP £51,647.56) with three to six years of experience and $95,000(GBP £65,420.24) with more than six years of experience. In 2013, a game designer with less than 3 years of experience earned, on average, $55,000 (GBP £37,874.88). A game designer with more than 6 years of experience made, on average, $105,000 (GBP £72,306.58). The average salary of these designers varies depending on their region. As of 2015 the salary of experienced workers has shifted to approximately $87,000 USD (GBP £59,911.17)

Disciplines

World Design

World design is the creation of a backstory, setting, and theme for the game; often done by a lead designer.

System Design

System design is the creation of game rules and underlying mathematical patterns.

Content Design

Content design is the creation of characters, items, puzzles, and missions.

A secondary definition of Content design is the creation of any aspect of the game that is not required for the game to function properly and meet the minimum viable product standard. In essence, content is the complexity added to a minimum viable product to increase its value. An example of this is the item list from Final Fantasy. None of the items are necessary for the game to function, but they add value and complexity to the game as a whole.

Game Writing

Game writing involves writing dialogue, text, and story.

Writing in games also includes the elements in which the literature is presented. Voice acting, text, and music are all elements of game writing.

Level Design

Level design is the construction of world levels and its features.

Level design makes use of many different fields to create a game world. Lighting, space, framing, color and contrast are used to draw a player's attention. A designer can then use these elements to guide or direct the player in a specific direction through the game world, or mislead them

User Interface Design

User interface designer constructs the user interactions and feedback interface, like menus or heads-up displays.

The user interface also incorporates game mechanics design. Deciding how much information to give the player and in what way allows the designer to inform the player about the world, or perhaps leave them uninformed. These choices have a profound effect on the mood of the game, as it directly affects the player in clearly understood and noticeable ways.

Audio Design

Audio design involves the process of creating or incorporating all of the sounds that are in the game, like sound effects or voice acting.

Game Feel

The disciplines listed above all combine to form the discipline of game feel.

Game Elements

Narrative

Numerous games have narrative elements which give a context to an event in a game, making the activity of playing it less abstract and enhance its entertainment value, although narrative elements are not always clearly present or present at all. The original version of *Tetris* is an example of a game apparently without narrative. It should be noted that some narratologists claim that all games have a narrative element. Some go further and claim that games are essentially a form of narrative. Narrative in practice can be the starting point for the development of a game, or can be added to a design that started as a set of game mechanics.

Gameplay

Gameplay is the interactive aspects of video game design. Gameplay involves player interaction with the game, usually for the purpose of entertainment, education or training.

Design Process

The design process varies from designer to designer and companies have different formal procedures and philosophies.

The typical "textbook" approach is to start with a concept or a previously completed game and from there create a game design document. This document is intended to map out the complete game design and acts as a central resource for the development team. This document should ideally be updated as the game evolves throughout the production process.

Designers are frequently expected to adapt to multiple roles of widely varying nature: For example, concept prototyping can be assisted with the use of pre-existing engines and tools like Game Maker, Unity, Godot, or Construct. Level designs might be done first on paper and again for the game engine using a 3D modelling tool. Scripting languages are used for many elements—AI, cutscenes, GUI, environmental processes, and many other behaviours and effects—that designers would want to tune without a programmer's assistance. Setting, story and character concepts require a research and writing process. Designers may oversee focus testing, write up art and audio asset lists, and write game documentation. In addition to the skillset, designers are ideally clear communicators with attention to detail and ability to delegate responsibilities appropriately.

Design approval in the commercial setting is a continuous process from the earliest stages until the game ships.

When a new project is being discussed (either internally, or as a result of dialogue with potential publishers), the designer may be asked to write a sell-sheet of short concepts, followed by a one or two-page pitch of specific features, audience, platform, and other details. Designers will first meet with leads in other departments to establish agreement on the feasibility of the game given the available time, scope, and budget. If the pitch is approved, early milestones focus on the creation of a fleshed-out design document. Some developers advocate a prototyping phase before the design document is written to experiment with new ideas before they become part of the design.

As production progresses, designers are asked to make frequent decisions about elements missing from the design. The consequences of these decisions are hard to predict and often can only be determined after creating the full implementation. These are referred to as the *unknowns* of the design, and the faster they are uncovered, the less risk the team faces later in the production process. Outside factors such as budget cuts or changes in milestone expectations also result in cuts to the design, and while overly large cuts can take the heart out of a project, cuts can also result in a streamlined design with only the essential features, polished well.

Towards the end of production, designers take the brunt of responsibility for ensuring that the gameplay remains at a uniform standard throughout the game, even in very long games. This task is made more difficult under "crunch" conditions, as the entire team may begin to lose sight of the core gameplay once pressured to hit a date for a finished and bug-free game.

Game Mechanics

Game mechanics are constructs of rules or methods designed for interaction with the game state, thus providing gameplay. All games use mechanics; however, theories and styles differ as to their ultimate importance to the game. In general, the process and study of game design, or ludology, are efforts to come up with game mechanics that allow for people playing a game to have an engaging, but not necessarily fun, experience.

The interaction of various game mechanics in a game determines the complexity and level of player interaction in the game, and in conjunction with the game's environment and resources determine game balance. Some forms of game mechanics have been used in games for centuries, while others are relatively new, having been invented within the past decade.

Complexity in game mechanics should not be confused with depth or even realism. Go is perhaps one of the simplest of all games, yet exhibits extraordinary depth of play. Most computer or video games feature mechanics that are technically complex (in terms of making a human do all the calculations involved) even in relatively simple designs.

In general, commercial video games have gone from simple designs (such as *Space Invaders* and *Asteroids*) to extremely complex ones (such as *Gran Turismo 5* and *Crysis 2*) as processing power has increased. In contrast, casual games have generally featured a return to simple, puzzle-like designs, though some are getting more complex. In physical games, differences generally come down to style, and are somewhat determined by intended market.

Game Mechanics vs. Gameplay

Gameplay could be defined as the combination and interaction of many elements of a game. However, there is some confusion as to the difference between game mechanics and gameplay. For some, gameplay is nothing more than a set of game mechanics. For others, gameplay—especially when referenced in the term of "basic gameplay"—refers to certain core game mechanics which determine the overall characteristics of the game itself.

For example, the basic gameplay of a shooting or fighting video game is to hit while not being hit. In a graphic adventure game, the basic gameplay is usually to solve puzzles related to the context. The basic gameplay of poker is to produce certain numerical or categorical combinations. Golf's basic gameplay is to hit a ball and reach a designated spot.

The goal of these games is slightly different from the gameplay itself. For example, while reaching the end of a stage (in platform games), defeating the boss, advancing your characters' progress through the story (RPGs) or sinking the ball into a hole (golf) may be the *purpose* of playing a game, the *fun* is derived primarily by the means and the process in which such goal is achieved. Basic gameplay defines what a game is, to the player, while game mechanics determine the parts of which the entire game consists of.

In videogames, gamers have a well-defined notion of what is considered gameplay. This is:

- What the player can do

- What other entities can do, in response to player's actions

What a player and other entities can do within a game would also fall under the mechanics of a game.

However, from a programming or overall design perspective, basic gameplay can be deconstructed further to reveal constituent game mechanics. For example, the basic gameplay of fighting game can be deconstructed to attack and defense, or punch, kick, block, dodge and throw; which can be further deconstructed to strong/weak punch/kick. For this reason, game mechanics is more of an engineering concept while gameplay is more of a design concept.

Game Mechanics vs. Theme

Some games are 'abstract'—that is, the action is not intended to represent anything; Go is one famous example. Other games have a 'theme'—some element of representation. *Monopoly* is a famous example where the events of the game are intended to represent another activity, in this case the buying and selling of properties.

Games that are mechanically similar can vary widely in theme. Eurogames often feature relatively simple systems, and stress the mechanics, with the theme merely being a context to place the mechanics in.

Some wargames, at the other extreme, are known for complex rules and for attempts at detailed simulation.

Key Game Mechanism Categories

Game mechanics fall into several more or less well-defined categories, which (along with basic gameplay and theme) are sometimes used as a basis to classify games.

Turns

A game *turn* is an important fundamental concept to almost all non-computer games, and many video games as well (although in video games, various *real-time* genres have become much more popular). In general, a turn is a segment of the game set aside for certain actions to happen before moving on to the next turn, where the sequence of events can largely repeat. In a truly abstract game (*backgammon*) turns are nothing more than a means to regulate play. In less abstract games (*Risk*), turns obviously denote the passage of time, but the amount of time is not clear, nor important. In simulation games, time is generally more concrete. Wargames usually specify the amount of time each turn represents, and in sports games a turn is usually distinctly one 'play', although the amount of time a play takes can vary.

Some games use *player turns* where one player gets to perform his actions before another player can perform any on *his* turn (*Monopoly* and chess would be classic examples). Some use *game turns*, where all players contribute to the actions of a single turn (board-game simulations of American football tend to have both players pick plays and then determine the outcome; each 'play' or 'down' can be considered a turn). Some games have 'game turns' that consist of a round of player turns, possibly with other actions added in (*Civilization* plays with a series of player turns followed by a trading round in which all players participate).

In games that are meant to be some sort of simulation, the on/off nature of player turns can cause problems, and has led to a few extra variations on the theme. The semi-simultaneous turn allows for some reactions to be done during the *other* player's turn. The impulse-based turn divides the turn into smaller segments or *impulses* where everyone does *some* of their actions at one time, and then reacts to the current situation before moving on to the next impulse (as seen in *Star Fleet Battles* or *Car Wars*).

In some games, not all turns are alike. Usually, this is difference in what *phases* (or different portions of the turn) happen. *Imperium Romanum II* for instance, features a "Taxation and Mobilization

Phase" in every third turn (month), which does not occur in the other turns. *Napoleon* has an unusual variation on the idea, where every third *player* turn is 'night turn' where combat is not allowed.

Even in real-time computer games there are often certain periodic effects. For instance, a wounded character in *World of Warcraft* will gradually recover health while out of combat. The rate of recovery is calculated from the character's statistics and applied per "tick" as a lump sum, so a character would gain ten health per tick, instead of one every tenth of a tick. These periodic effects can be considered the vestigial remnants of the concept of turns.

Action Points

These control what players may do on their turns in the game by allocating each player a budget of "action points" each turn. These points may be spent on various actions according to the game rules, such as moving pieces, drawing cards, collecting money, etc. This type of mechanism is common in many "German-style board games".

Auction or Bidding

Some games use an auction or bidding system in which the players make competitive bids to determine which player gets the right to perform particular actions. Such an auction can be based on different forms of "payment":

- The winning bidder must pay for the won privilege with some form of game resource (game money, points, etc.) (e.g.: *Ra*).

- The winning bidder does not pay upon winning the auction, but the auction is a form of promise that the winner will achieve some outcome in the near future. If this outcome is not achieved, the bidder pays some form of penalty. Such a system is used in many trick-taking games, such as contract bridge.

In some games the auction determines a unique player who gains the privilege; in others the auction orders all players into a sequence, often the sequence in which they take turns during the current round of game play.

Cards

These involve the use of cards similar to playing cards to act as a randomizer and/or to act as tokens to keep track of states in the game.

A common use is for a deck of cards to be shuffled and placed face down on or near the game playing area. When a random result is called for, a player draws a card and what is printed on the card determines the outcome of the result.

Another use of cards occurs when players draw cards and retain them for later use in the game, without revealing them to other players. When used in this fashion, cards form a game resource.

Capture/Eliminate

In some games, the number of tokens a player has on the playing surface is related to his current strength in the game. In such games, it can be an important goal to *capture* opponent's tokens, meaning to remove them from the playing surface.

Captures can be achieved in a number of ways:

- Moving one of one's own tokens into a space occupied by an opposing token (e.g. chess, parchisi).

- Jumping a token over the space occupied by an opposing token (e.g. draughts).

- Declaring an "attack" on an opposing token, and then determining the outcome of the attack, either in a deterministic way by the game rules (e.g. *Stratego, Illuminati*), or by using a randomising method (e.g. *Illuminati: New World Order*).

- Surrounding a token or region with one's own tokens in some manner (e.g. go).

- Playing cards or other resources that the game allows to be used to capture tokens.

In some games, captured tokens are simply removed and play no further part in the game (e.g. chess). In others, captured tokens are removed but can return to play later in the game under various rules (e.g. backgammon, pachisi). Less common is the case in which the capturing player takes possession of the captured tokens and can use them himself later in the game (e.g. shogi, Reversi, Illuminati).

Many video games express the capture mechanism in the form of a kill count, (sometimes referred to as "frags"), reflecting the number of opposing pawns eliminated during the game.

Catch-up

Some games include a mechanism designed to make progress towards victory more difficult the closer a player gets to it. The idea behind this is to allow trailing players a chance to catch up and potentially still win the game, rather than suffer an inevitable loss once they fall behind. This may be desirable in games such as racing games that have a fixed finish line.

An example is from *The Settlers of Catan*. This game contains a neutral piece (the robber), which debilitates the resource generation of players whose territories it is near. Players occasionally get to move the robber, and frequently choose to position it where it will cause maximal disruption to the player currently winning the game.

Another example, often seen in racing games, such as *Chutes and Ladders* is by requiring rolling or spinning the exact number needed to reach the finish line; e.g., if a player is only four spaces from the finish line then he must roll a four on the die or land on the four with the spinner. If more than four is rolled, then the turn is forfeited to the next player.

Other games do the reverse, making the player in the lead more capable of winning, such as in *Monopoly*, and thus the game is drawn to an end sooner. This may be desirable in zero-sum games.

Dice

These involve the use of *dice*, usually as randomisers. Most dice used in games are the standard cubical dice numbered from 1 to 6, though games with polyhedral dice or those marked with symbols other than numbers exist.

The most common use of dice is to randomly determine the outcome of an interaction in a game. An example is a player rolling a die or dice to determine how many board spaces to move a game token.

Dice often determine the outcomes of in-game conflict between players, with different outcomes of the die/dice roll of different benefit (or adverse effect) to each player involved. This is useful in games that simulate direct conflicts of interest.

Movement

Many board games involve the movement of playing tokens. How these tokens are allowed to move, and when, is governed by movement mechanics.

Some game boards are divided into more or less equally-sized areas, each of which can be occupied by one or more game tokens. (Often such areas are called squares, even if not strictly square in shape.) Movement rules will specify how and when a token can be moved to another area. For example, a player may be allowed to move a token to an adjacent area, but not one further away. Dice are sometimes used to randomise the allowable movements.

Other games, particularly miniatures games are played on surfaces with no marked areas. A common movement mechanism in this case is to measure the distance which the miniatures are allowed to move with a ruler. Sometimes, generally in naval wargames, the *direction* of movement is restricted by use of a turning key.

Resource Management

Many games involve the management of *resources*. Examples of game resources include tokens, money, land, natural resources, human resources and game points. Resource management involves the players establishing relative values for various types of available resources, in the context of the current state of the game and the desired outcome (i.e. winning the game). The game will have rules that determine how players can increase, spend, or exchange their various resources. The skillful management of resources under such rules allows players to influence the outcome of the game.

Risk and Reward

Some games include situations where players can "press their luck" in optional actions where the danger of a risk must be weighed against the chance of reward. For example, in *Beowulf: The Legend*, players may elect to take a "Risk", with success yielding cards and failure weakening the player's ultimate chance of victory.

Role-playing

Role-playing games often rely on mechanics that determine the effectiveness of in-game actions by how well the player acts out the role of a fictional character. While early role-playing games such as *Dungeons & Dragons* relied heavily on either group consensus or the judgement of a single player (deemed the Dungeon Master or Game Master) or on randomizers such as dice, later generations of narrativist games use more structured and integrated systems to allow role-playing to influence the creative input and output of the players, so both acting out roles and employing rules take part in shaping the gameplay.

Tile-laying

Many games use tiles - flat, rigid pieces of a regular shape - that can be laid down on a flat surface to form a tessellation. Usually such tiles have patterns or symbols on their surfaces, that combine when tessellated to form game-mechanically significant combinations.

The tiles themselves are often drawn at random by the players, either immediately before placing them on the playing surface, or in groups to form a pool or hand of tiles from which the player may select one to play.

Tiles can be used in two distinct ways:

- The playing of a tile itself is directly significant to the outcome of the game, in that where and when it is played contributes points or resources to the player.

- Tiles are used to build a board upon which other game tokens are placed, and the interaction of those tokens with the tiles provides game points or resources.

Examples of tile mechanics include: *Scrabble*, in which tiles are letters and players lay them down to form words and score points; and *Tikal*, in which players lay tiles representing newly explored areas of jungle, through which archaeologists (represented by tokens) must move to score game points.

Worker Placement

Worker placement is a game mechanism where players allocate a limited number of tokens ("workers") to multiple stations that provide various defined actions. The worker placement mechanism originates with board games. Stewart Woods identifies *Keydom* (1998; later remade and updated as *Aladdin's Dragons*) as the first game to implement the mechanic. Worker placement was popularized by *Caylus* (2005) and became a staple of the Eurogame genre in the wake of the game's success. Other popular board games that use this mechanism include *Stone Age* and *Agricola*. Although the mechanism is chiefly associated with board games, the worker placement concept has been used in analysis of other game types. For instance, Adams and Dormans describe the assigning of tasks to SCV units in the real-time strategy game *StarCraft* as an example of the worker placement mechanic.

Game Modes

A *game mode* is a distinct configuration that varies gameplay and affects how other game mechanics behave. A game with several modes will present different settings in each one, changing how a particular element of the game is played. One of the most common examples of game mode is the single player versus multiplayer choice in video games, where multiplayer can further be cooperative or competitive.

Changing modes while the game is ongoing can be used as a means to increase difficulty and provide additional challenge, or as a reward for player success. Power-ups are modes that last for a few moments or that change only one or a few game rules; for example power pellets in Pac-Man give the temporary ability to eat the enemies for a few seconds.

Other examples include the availability of a sandbox mode without predefined goals or progression. The division of game content in stages or chapters, where each stage expands the rules that a player can use with respect to the previous stage, increases game complexity and variety. If the game advances through these stages by moving through different areas, these areas are called levels or maps; if the character unlocks new abilities through activities or rewards, they receive a currency called experience points. These points can be used to upgrade or augment various pre-determined abilities.

A game mode may restrict or change the behavior of the available tools (e.g. play with limited/ unlimited ammo, new weapons, obstacles or enemies, a timer, etc.), establish different rules and game mechanics (e.g. altered gravity; win at first touch in a fighting game; play with some cards face-up in a poker game) or even change the overall game goals (following a campaign, story or character's career vs. playing a limited deathmatch or capture the flag set).

Victory Condition Mechanics

These mechanics control how a player wins the game.

Goals

This is the most general sort of victory condition, which can be broad enough to encompass any method of winning, but here refers to game-specific goals that are usually not duplicated in other games. An example is the checkmate of a king in chess.

Quest

A quest in role-playing video games—including massively multiplayer online role-playing games (MMORPGs) and their predecessors, MUDs—is a task that a player-controlled character, "party" or group of characters may complete in order to gain a reward.

Loss Avoidance

Some games feature a losing condition, such as being checkmated (chess), running out of cards first (War), running out of hitpoints (Quake), or being tagged (tag). In such a game, the winner is the only remaining player to have avoided loss.

Piece Elimination

Some games with capture mechanics are won by the player who removes all, or a given number of, the opponents' playing pieces.

Puzzle Guessing

Some games end when a player guesses (or solves by logic) the answer to a puzzle or riddle posed by the game. The player who guesses successfully wins. Examples include hangman and zendo.

Races

Many simple games (and some complex ones) are effectively races. The first player to advance one or more tokens to or beyond a certain point on the board wins. Examples: backgammon, ludo.

Structure Building

The goal of a structure building game is to acquire and assemble a set of game resources into either a defined winning structure, or into a structure that is somehow better than those of other players. In some games, the acquisition is of primary importance (e.g. concentration), while in others the resources are readily available and the interactions between them form more or less useful structures (e.g. poker).

Territory Control

A winner may be decided by which player controls the most "territory" on the playing surface, or a specific piece of territory. This is common in wargames, but is also used in more abstract games such as go.

Victory Points

A player's progress is often measured by an abstract quantity of victory points or simply known as VP, which accumulate as the game develops. Victory points or similar quantities need not be restricted to development games, but are most common in that type as they ensure sufficient reward for all aspects of development. For example, in a game involving the development of civilizations, there is usually no need to reward investments such as trade and military expenditures, which yield their own strategic benefits. However, a victory point system may be used to reward more subjective aspects of civilization-building, such as the arts.

The winner can be decided either by:

- The first player to reach a set number of points.

- The player with the most points at a predetermined finishing time or state of the game.

This mechanism is often used explicitly in German-style board games, but many other games are played for points that form a winning condition. The electoral college of the United States political system is also a well-publicized example of this type of victory condition. Victory points may be partially disguised in the role of game resources, with play money being a common example.

Combination Conditions

Some games have multiple victory or loss conditions. For example, a round of *Pokémon Trading Card Game* can end in three ways:

- When one player has Knocked Out enough of the other's Pokémon to draw all his Prize Cards

- When one player is unable to play a Pokémon from his Bench to replace his Active Pokémon

- When one player has run out of cards in his Deck and is unable to draw at the beginning of his turn.

The first condition is a goal measured by victory points, while the other two are loss conditions.

Balance (Game Design)

In game design, balance is the concept and the practice of tuning a game's rules, usually with the goal of preventing any of its component systems from being ineffective or otherwise undesirable when compared to their peers. An unbalanced system represents wasted development resources at the very least, and at worst can undermine the game's entire ruleset by making important roles or tasks impossible to perform.

Balancing and Fairness

Balancing does not necessarily mean making a game fair. This is particularly true of action games: Jaime Griesemer, design lead at Bungie, said in a lecture to other designers that "every fight in *Halo* is unfair". This potential for unfairness creates uncertainty, leading to the tension and excitement that action games seek to deliver. In these cases balancing is instead the management of unfair scenarios, with the ultimate goal of ensuring that all of the strategies which the game intends to support are viable. The extent to which those strategies are equal to one another defines the character of the game in question.

Simulation games can be balanced unfairly in order to be true to life. A wargame may cast the player into the role of a general who was defeated by an overwhelming force, and it is common for the abilities of teams in sports games to mirror those of the real-world teams they represent regardless of the implications for players who pick them.

Player perception can also affect the appearance of fairness. Sid Meier stated that he omitted multiplayer alliances in *Civilization* because he found that the computer was almost as good as humans in exploiting them, which caused players to think that the computer was cheating.

Difficulty Level

Video games often allow players to influence their balance by offering a choice of "difficulty levels". These affect how challenging the game is to play.

In addition to altering the game's rules, difficulty levels can be used to alter what content is presented to the player. This usually takes the form of adding or removing challenging locations or events, but some games also change their narrative to reward players who play them on higher difficulty levels (*Max Payne 2*) or end early as punishment for playing on easy (*Castlevania*).

Difficulty selection is not always presented bluntly, particularly in competitive games where all players are affected equally and the standard "easy/hard" terminology no longer applies. Sometimes veiled language is used (*Mario Kart* offers "CC select"), while at other times there may be an array of granular settings instead of an overarching difficulty option.

An alternative approach to difficulty levels is catering to players of all abilities at the same time, a technique that has been called "subjective difficulty". This requires a game to provide multiple solutions or routes, each offering challenges appropriate to players of different skill levels (*Super Mario Galaxy*, *Sonic Generations*).

Pacing

Balancing goals shift dramatically when players are contending with the game's environment and/or non-player characters. Such player versus environment games are usually balanced to tread the fine line of regularly challenging players' abilities without ever producing insurmountable or unfair obstacles. This turns balancing into the management of dramatic structure, generally referred to by game designers as "pacing".

Pacing is also a consideration in competitive games, but the autonomy of players makes it harder to control.

Techniques

Symmetry

The simplest game balancing technique is giving each player identical resources. Most competitive games feature some level of symmetry; some (such as *Pong*) are completely symmetric, but those in which players alternate turns (such as chess) can never achieve total symmetry as one player will always have a first-move advantage.

Symmetry can be undone by human psychology. The advantage of players wearing red over players wearing blue is a well-documented example of this.

Statistical Analysis

The brute force approach to balancing is the mathematical analysis of game session results. With enough data, it is possible to identify unbalanced areas of a game and make corrections.

Randomization

Randomization of starting conditions is a technique common in board games, card games, and also experimental research which fights back against the human tendency to optimise patterns in one's favor.

The downside of randomization is that it takes control away from the player, potentially leading to frustration. Methods of overcoming this include giving the player a selection of random results within which they can optimise (*Scrabble*, *Magic: The Gathering*) and making each game session short enough to encourage multiple attempts in one play session (Klondike (solitaire), *Strange Adventures in Infinite Space*).

Feedback Loops

Many games become more challenging if the player is successful. For instance, real-time strategy games often feature "upkeep", a resource tax that scales with the number of units under a player's control. Team games which challenge players to invade their opponents' territory (football, capture the flag) have a feedback loop by default: the further a player pushes, the more opponents they are likely to face.

Feedback loops can lead to frequent ties if enforced too strictly.

Gamemaster

A game can be balanced dynamically by a gamemaster who observes players and adjusts the game in response to their emotional state

Although gamemasters have historically been humans, some videogames now feature AI systems that perform a similar role by monitoring player ability and inferring emotional state from input. Such systems are often referred to as having dynamic difficulty. One notable example is *Left 4 Dead* and its sequel *Left 4 Dead 2*, cooperative games that have the players fight through hoards of zombie-like creatures including unique creatures with special abilities. Both games use an AI Director which not only generates random events, but tries to create tension and fear by spawning in creatures to specific rule sets based on how players are progressing, specifically penalizing players through more difficult challenges for not working together. Research into biofeedback peripherals is set to greatly improve the accuracy of such systems.

Slang

Gimp

In role-playing game slang, a "gimp" is a character, character class or character ability that is underpowered in the context of the game (e.g., a close range warrior class equipping a full healing boosting armour set, despite having no healing abilities). Gimped characters lack effectiveness compared to other characters at a similar level of experience. A player may gimp a character by assigning skills and abilities that are inappropriate for the character class, or by developing the character inefficiently. However, this is not always the case, as some characters are purposely "gimped" by the game's developers in order to provide an incentive for raising their level, or, conversely, to give the player an early head-start. An example of this is Final Fantasy's Mystic Knight class, which starts out weak, but is able to become the most powerful class if brought to a very high level. Gimps may also be accidental on the part of the developer, and may require a software patch to rebalance.

Sometimes, especially in MMORPGs, gimp is used as a synonym for nerf to describe a rule modification that weakens the affected target. Unlike the connotatively neutral term nerf, gimp in this usage often implies that the rule change unfairly disadvantages the target.

Nerf

A "nerf" is a change to a game that reduces the desirability or effectiveness of a particular game element. The term is also used as a verb for the act of making such a change.

The first established use of the term was in Ultima Online, as a reference to the NERF brand of toys whose bullets are soft and less likely to cause serious injury.

Among game developers, MMORPG designers are especially likely to nerf aspects of a game in order to maintain game balance. Occasionally a new feature (such as an item, class, or skill) may be made too powerful, too cheap, or too easily obtained to the extent that it unbalances the game system. This is sometimes due to an unforeseen method of using or acquiring the object that was not considered by the developers. The frequency of nerfing and the scale of nerfing vary widely from game to game but almost all massively multiplayer games have engaged in nerfing at some point.

Nerfs in various online games, including Anarchy Online, have spurred in-world protests. Since many items in virtual worlds are sold or traded among players, a nerf may have an outsized impact on the virtual economy. As players respond, the nerf may cause prices to fluctuate before settling down in a different equilibrium. This impact on the economy, along with the original impact of the nerf, can cause large player resentment for even a small change. In particular, in the case of items or abilities which have been nerfed, players can become upset over the perceived wasted efforts in obtaining the now nerfed features.

A well-known instance in which a nerf has caused many protests, but much more praise, is when Infinity Ward nerfed the Model 1887s in its video game Call of Duty: Modern Warfare 2. Before the nerf, the Model 1887s were able to One Shot Kill from medium-long range when all other shotguns in game were limited to short-medium range. The nerfing of the Model 1887s reduced its range to short range. (The same thing occurred in Star Wars Battlefront 2015 [EA] where the DL-44 had its fire rate reduced from 250 RPM to 180 RPM, and was a 2 shot kill)

For games where avatars and items represent significant economic value, this may bring up legal issues over the lost value.

Buff

A buff (also a verb) is the opposite of a nerf: namely, a change to a game's rules which increases the desirability or effectiveness of a particular element.

Overpowered

Overpowered (often abbreviated to OP) is a common term referring to a perceived lack of game balance. It is often used when describing a specific class in an RPG, a specific faction in strategic games, or a specific tactic, ability, weapon or unit in various games. For something to be deemed overpowered, it is either the best choice in a disproportionate number of situations (marginalising other choices) and/or excessively hard to counter by the opponent compared to the effort required to use it. In the NBA, Stephen Curry is often referred to as OP, playing with an unfair advantage against the rest of the league.

Revamp

A revamp is a term for improving or modifying items, skills, abilities, or stats, as opposed to direct nerfing or gimping.

Underpowered

Underpowered, a common term, opposite of overpowered, is also a lack of game balance. However this weaker ability, item or skill shall need revamp.

Imba

Imbalanced, the opposite of balanced.

Dynamic Game Difficulty Balancing

Dynamic game difficulty balancing, also known as dynamic difficulty adjustment (DDA) or dynamic game balancing (DGB), is the process of automatically changing parameters, scenarios, and behaviors in a video game in real-time, based on the player's ability, in order to avoid making the player bored (if the game is too easy) or frustrated (if it is too hard). However, letting AI players break the rules to which players are bound can cause the AI to cheat—for example, AI players might be given unlimited speed in racing games to stay near the human player. The goal of dynamic difficulty balancing is to keep the user interested from the beginning to the end, providing a good level of challenge.

Traditionally, game difficulty increases steadily along the course of the game (either in a smooth linear fashion, or through steps represented by levels). The parameters of this increase (rate, frequency, starting levels) can only be modulated at the beginning of the experience by selecting a difficulty level. Still, this can lead to a frustrating experience for both experienced and inexperienced gamers, as they attempt to follow a preselected learning or difficulty curve. Dynamic difficulty balancing attempts to remedy this issue by creating a tailor-made experience for each gamer. As the users' skills improve through time (as they make progress via learning), the level of the challenges should also continually increase. However, implementing such elements poses many challenges to game developers; as a result, this method of gameplay is not widespread.

Dynamic Game Elements

Some elements of a game that might be changed via dynamic difficulty balancing include:

- Speed of enemies
- Health of enemies
- Frequency of enemies
- Frequency of powerups
- Power of player
- Power of enemies
- Duration of gameplay experience

Approaches

Different approaches are found in the literature to address dynamic game difficulty balancing. In all cases, it is necessary to measure, implicitly or explicitly, the difficulty the user is facing at a given moment. This measure can be performed by a heuristic function, which some authors call "challenge function". This function maps a given game state into a value that specifies how easy or difficult the game feels to the user at a specific moment. Examples of heuristics used are:

- The rate of successful shots or hits

- The numbers of won and lost pieces

- Life points

- Evolution

- Time to complete some task

... or any metric used to calculate a game score. Hunicke and Chapman's approach controls the game environment settings in order to make challenges easier or harder. For example, if the game is too hard, the player gets more weapons, recovers life points faster, or faces fewer opponents. Although this approach may be effective, its application can result in implausible situations. A straightforward approach is to combine such "parameters manipulation" to some mechanisms to modify the behavior of the non-player characters (NPCs) (characters controlled by the computer and usually modeled as intelligent agents). This adjustment, however, should be made with moderation, to avoid the 'rubber band' effect. One example of this effect in a racing game would involve the AI driver's vehicles becoming significantly faster when behind the player's vehicle, and significantly slower while in front, as if the two vehicles were connected by a large rubber band.

A traditional implementation of such an agent's intelligence is to use behavior rules, defined during game development. A typical rule in a fighting game would state "punch opponent if he is reachable, chase him otherwise". Extending such an approach to include opponent modeling can be made through Spronck *et al.*'s dynamic scripting, which assigns to each rule a probability of being picked. Rule weights can be dynamically updated throughout the game, accordingly to the opponent skills, leading to adaptation to the specific user. With a simple mechanism, rules can be picked that generate tactics that are neither too strong nor too weak for the current player.

Andrade *et al.* divides the DGB problem into two dimensions: competence (learn as well as possible) and performance (act just as well as necessary). This dichotomy between competence and performance is well known and studied in linguistics, as proposed by Noam Chomsky. Their approach faces both dimensions with reinforcement learning (RL). Offline training is used to bootstrap the learning process. This can be done by letting the agent play against itself (selflearning), other pre-programmed agents, or human players. Then, online learning is used to continually adapt this initially built-in intelligence to each specific human opponent, in order to discover the most suitable strategy to play against him or her. Concerning performance, their idea is to find an adequate policy for choosing actions that provide a good game balance, i.e., actions that keep both agent and human player at approximately the same performance level. According to the difficulty the player is facing, the agent chooses actions with high or low expected performance. For a given situation, if the game level is too hard, the agent does not choose the optimal action (provided by the RL framework), but chooses progressively less and less suboptimal actions until its performance is as good as the player's. Similarly, if the game level becomes too easy, it will choose actions whose values are higher, possibly until it reaches the optimal performance.

Demasi and Cruz built intelligent agents employing genetic algorithms techniques to keep alive agents that best fit the user level. Online coevolution is used in order to speed up the learning process. Online coevolution uses pre-defined models (agents with good genetic features) as parents in the genetic operations, so that the evolution is biased by them. These models are constructed by offline training or by hand, when the agent genetic encoding is simple enough.

Other work in the field of DGB is based on the hypothesis that the player-opponent interaction—rather than the audiovisual features, the context or the genre of the game—is the property that contributes the majority of the quality features of entertainment in a computer game. Based on this fundamental assumption, a metric for measuring the real time entertainment value of predator/prey games was introduced, and established as efficient and reliable by validation against human judgment.

Further studies by Yannakakis and Hallam have shown that artificial neural networks (ANN) and fuzzy neural networks can extract a better estimator of player satisfaction than a human-designed one, given appropriate estimators of the challenge and curiosity (intrinsic qualitative factors for engaging gameplay according to Malone) of the game and data on human players' preferences. The approach of constructing user models of the player of a game that can predict the answers to which variants of the game are more or less *fun* is defined as *Entertainment Modeling*. The model is usually constructed using machine learning techniques applied to game parameters derived from player-game interaction and/or statistical features of player's physiological signals recorded during play. This basic approach is applicable to a variety of games, both computer and physical.

Caveats

Andrew Rollings and Ernest Adams cite an example of a game that changed the difficulty of each level based on how the player performed in several preceding levels. Players noticed this and developed a strategy to overcome challenging levels by deliberately playing badly in the levels before the difficult one. The authors stress the importance of covering up the existence of difficulty adaptation so that players are not aware of it.

Uses in Recent Video Games

Archon's computer opponent slowly adapts over time to help players defeat it. Danielle Bunten designed both *M.U.L.E.* and *Global Conquest* to dynamically balance gameplay between players. Random events are adjusted so that the player in first place is never lucky and the last-place player is never unlucky.

The first *Crash Bandicoot* game and its sequels make use of a "Dynamic Difficulty Adjustement" system, slowing down obstacles and adding continue points according to the player's number of deaths. According to the game's lead designer Jason Rubin, the goal was to "help weaker players without changing the game for the better players".

The video game *Flow* was notable for popularizing the application of mental immersion (also called flow) to video games with its 2006 Flash version. The video game design was based on the master's thesis of one of its authors, and was later adapted to PlayStation 3.

SiN Episodes released in 2006 featured a "Personal Challenge System" where the numbers and toughness of enemies faced would vary based on the performance of the player to ensure the level of challenge and pace of progression through the game. The developer, Ritual Entertainment, claimed that players with widely different levels of ability could finish the game within a small range of time of each other.

In 2005, *Resident Evil 4* employed a system called the "Difficulty Scale", unknown to most players, as the only mention of it was in the Official Strategy Guide. This system grades the player's performance on a number scale from 1 to 10, and adjusts both enemy behavior/attacks used and enemy damage/resistance based on the player's performance (such as deaths, critical attacks, etc.). The selected difficulty levels lock players at a certain number; for example, on Normal difficulty, one starts at Grade 4, can move down to Grade 2 if doing poorly, or up to Grade 7 if doing well. The grades between difficulties can overlap.

God Hand, a 2006 video game developed by Clover Studio, directed by *Resident Evil 4* director Shinji Mikami, and published by Capcom for the PlayStation 2, features a meter during gameplay that regulates enemy intelligence and strength. This meter increases when the player successfully dodges and attacks opponents, and decreases when the player is hit. The meter is divided into four levels, with the hardest level called "Level DIE." The game also has three difficulties, with the easy difficulty only allowing the meter to ascend to level 2, while the hardest difficulty locks the meter to level DIE. This system also offers greater rewards when defeating enemies at higher levels.

The 2008 video game *Left 4 Dead* uses a new artificial intelligence technology dubbed "The AI Director". The AI Director is used to procedurally generate a different experience for the players each time the game is played. It monitors individual players' performance and how well they work together as a group to pace the game, determining the number of zombies that attack the player and the location of boss infected encounters based on information gathered. Besides pacing, the Director also controls some video and audio elements of the game to set a mood for a boss encounter or to draw the players' attention to a certain area. Valve calls the way the Director is working "procedural narrative" because instead of having a difficulty level which just ramps up to a constant level, the A.I. analyzes how the players fared in the game so far, and try to add subsequent events that would give them a sense of narrative.

Madden NFL 09 introduces "Madden IQ", which begins with an optional test of the players knowledge of the sport, and abilities in various situations. The score is then used to control the game's difficulty.

In the match-3 game *Fishdom*, the time limit is adjusted based on how well the player performs. The time limit is increased should the player fail a level, making it possible for any player to beat a level after a few tries.

In the 1999 video game *Homeworld*, the number of ships that the AI begins with in each mission will be set depending on how powerful the game deems the player's fleet to be. Successful players have larger fleets because they take fewer losses. In this way, a player who is successful over a number of missions will begin to be challenged more and more as the game progresses.

In *Fallout: New Vegas* and *Fallout 3*, as the player increases in level, tougher variants of enemies, enemies with higher statistics and better weapons, or new enemies will replace older ones to retain a constant difficulty, which can be raised, using a slider, with experience bonuses and vice versa in *Fallout 3*. This can also be done in *New Vegas*, but there is no bonus to increasing or decreasing the difficulty.

The *Mario Kart* series features items during races that help an individual driver get ahead of their opponents. These items are distributed based on a driver's position in a way that is an example of dynamic game difficulty balancing. For example, a driver near the bottom of the field is likely to get an item that will drastically increase their speed or sharply decrease the speed of their opponents, whereas a driver in first or second place can expect to get these kinds of items rarely (and will probably receive the game's weaker items). The *Mario Kart* series is also known for the aforementioned "rubber band effect"; it was tolerated in the earlier games in the series, because it compensated for an extremely unskilled AI, but as more sophisticated AIs are developed, players have begun to feel that it makes winning far too difficult for even skilled players.

An early example of difficulty balancing can be found in *Zanac*, developed in 1986 by Compile. The game featured a unique adaptive artificial intelligence, in which the game automatically adjusted the difficulty level according to the player's skill level, rate of fire, and the ship's current defensive status/capability. Earlier than this can be found in Midway's 1975 Gun Fight coin-op game. This head to head shoot-em-up would aid whichever player had just been shot, by placing a fresh additional object, such as a Cactus plant, on their half of the play-field making it easier for them to hide.

The recent *FIFA* series by EA has also started to introduce a difficulty balancing system. The Ultimate Team game mode has been known to lower the performance of players on the winning side's team. However, although the *Madden* developers has admitted to their handicapping system, the *FIFA* developers have yet to admit to it, raising question about their motives for it.

Level Design

Level design, environment design or game mapping is a discipline of game development involving creation of video game levels—locales, stages, or missions. This is commonly done using a level editor, a game development software designed for building levels; however, some games feature built-in level editing tools. Level design is both an artistic and technical process.

History

In early days of video games, a single programmer would create the maps and layouts for a game, and a discipline or profession dedicated solely to level design did not exist.

Early games often featured a level system of ascending difficulty as opposed to progression of story-line.

The first game genre that required significant amounts of time to design areas were text-based games, such as MUDs. Often, promoted users were assigned to create new paths, new rooms, new equipment, and new actions, often using the game interface itself. ZZT is another early game notable for its user-accessible mapping and event triggering/scripting

1983's *Lode Runner* was one of the first titles to ship with a level editor, and its designer, Douglas Smith, reputedly paid neighborhood children to design levels for the game.

Doom (1993) and *Doom II* (1994) were two of the first games to attract focused game modding activity, and many WAD level files were made for them. One of the reasons was a clear separation between the level files and game engine itself. Half-Life, Quake 3, and many other games have notable mapping tools and communities focusing on user-generated content.

In certain games, such as roguelike games, levels may be procedurally generated. In these cases, the original game programmer controls how the variations of rooms and tunnels are formed, by tweaking the randomly seeded algorithms.

Process

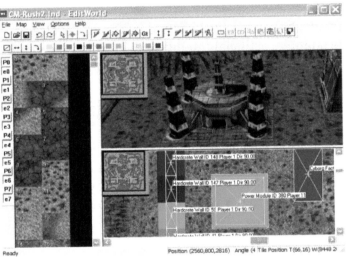

The level editor of *Warzone 2100*.

Level design for each individual level in a modern game typically starts with concept art, sketches, renderings, and physical models. Once completed, these concepts transform into extensive documentation, environment modeling, and the placing of game specific entities (actors), usually with the aid of a level editor.

A level editor may be distributed as a complete stand-alone package, at times, rivaling commercial 3D modelling software. There are various steps involved in laying out a map and these steps may vary dramatically across the many different game genres that exist today.

General steps include:

- Laying out the large-scale features of the map, such as hills, cities, rooms, tunnels, etc., for players and enemies to move around in;

- Determining environmental conditions and "ground rules" such as day/night, weather, scoring systems, allowable weapons or gameplay types, time limits, and starting resources.

- Specifying certain regions where certain gameplay activities or behaviors occur, such as resource harvesting, base building, water travelling, etc.;

- Specifying non-static parts of a level, such as doors, keys and buttons with associated mechanisms, teleporters, hidden passageways, etc.;

- Specifying locations of various entities, such as player units, enemies, monster spawn points, ladders, coins, resource nodes, weapons, save points, etc.;

- Specifying the start and exit locations for one or more players;

- Adding aesthetic details such as level-specific graphic textures, sounds, animation, lighting and music;

- Introducing scripted event locations, where certain actions by the player can trigger specified changes;

- Placing pathfinding nodes that non-player characters take as they walk around, the actions they will take in response to specific triggers, and any dialog they might have with the player.

The first level of the game usually designed to get players to explore the mechanics of the game, notably in World 1-1 of Super Mario Bros.

Cut scenes may be triggered by events in a level, but require distinctly different skills, and may be created by a different person or team.

The Level Design Process may be iterated several times before achieving the desired outcome.

Level designers and/or concept artists may also be required to provide a pre-rendered map of the level (or entire game world) for the player.

Level Bugs

There are many map bugs that level designers try to avoid, but sometimes go unnoticed for some time.

A player might get stuck in map geometry with no way to escape or to die. A player might be able to find a specific spot where they do not have to move to gain experience, because monsters are constantly spawned but can be easily and immediately killed. In multiplayer maps, a player may be able to reach areas of the map designed to be inaccessible, for example, reaching an advantageous rooftop position and camping other players. In the worst case, a player might be able to fall out-of-bounds of a map where other players cannot reach them. Invisible walls are cited to be level design bugs, and might be "left-over geometry" from an earlier version of the level or an object's improperly aligned "collision box".

In some cases, specific mapping tools can be designed to automatically detect problems such as falling "outside" a level, and reaching "stuck" areas. Careful level designers run these tools as the last step before releasing a new version of a level. In most cases, the best way to improve a map is by playtesting it with experienced players, and allowing them to try to exploit any problems.

Level Designer

A level designer is a game designer who creates environments and scenarios using a level editor and other tools. Level designers will usually work on a level from pre-production to completion; working with both incomplete and complete versions of the game. Game programmers usually produce level editors and design tools for the designers to use. This eliminates the need for designers to access or modify game code. As opposed to the level editing tools sometimes available to the community, level designers often work with placeholders and prototypes aiming for level consistency and clear layout before required artwork is produced by game artists. Many level designers have skills as both a visual artist and game designers, although in recent years the responsibility for visual, structural and gameplay related tasks has been increasingly divided among several specialists.

Notable Level Designers

A number of individuals have made significant contributions to the field of PC first person shooter levels. These level designers include: John Romero, responsible for a great deal of the level design for *Doom*, and Richard "Levelord" Gray, creator of a number of levels for *Duke Nukem 3D* and *SiN*.

Design Goals

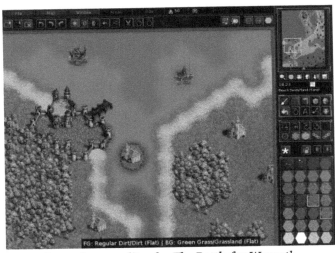

Example map editor for *The Battle for Wesnoth*.

Level design is necessary for two primary purposes - providing players with a goal and providing players with enjoyable play experience. Good level design strives to produce quality gameplay, provide an immersive experience, and sometimes, especially in story-based games, to advance the storyline. Skilled use of textures and audio is necessary to produce immersive player experience.

Gameplay Alteration

Maps' design can significantly impact the gameplay. For example, the gameplay may be shifted towards a platformer (by careful placement of platforms) or a puzzle game (by extensive use of buttons, keys, and doors). Some FPS maps may be designed to prevent sniping by not including any long hallways, while other maps may allow for a mix of sniping and closer combat.

Gimmick maps are sometimes created to explore selected features of gameplay, such as sniping or fist fighting. While they are briefly useful to level designers and interesting to experienced players, they are usually not included in final list of levels of the game because of their limited replay value.

Player Directing

Levels are generally constructed with flow control in mind, that is directing the player towards the goal of the level and preventing confusion and idling. This can be accomplished by various means.

Often the level layouts features power-ups and items aligned in path and combinations that collecting them inevitably progresses the game and advances the story-line. This is one of the basic player direction technique and is most often seen in platformers.

Lighting and illumination, as well as distinctly coloured objects are often used to unambiguously steer the player towards the correct path. Similarly, clearly marked choke-points can be introduced.

Another method is strategic placement of obstacles and aesthetic environment props, that direct the player's attention to "clear" paths instead. This is often used in closed, "stuffed" environments.

Levels may be designed to force the players to explore the map and advance. Most RTS maps give each player a starting base, but will have resource distribution and terrain features designed to draw players out of their base and engage each other. Teamplay maps can provide noticeable advantages to one team over another, when designed poorly.

Hidden Features

Level designers sometimes create hidden rooms and areas that usually require more effort for the player to reach or to notice. These usually give some additional rewards, such as ammo or powerups. Casual players usually do not discover these, but these areas are interesting enough to be discovered and documented by dedicated gamers. Sometimes, they serve as easter eggs, containing messages such as the level designers' names or pictures, or political or humorous messages. One of the first games with a 3D engine to feature hidden features was Wolfenstein 3D, where certain walls could be "pushed" to reveal hidden passages. For example, *Quake* has many secret areas that reward the player with ammo, weapons, quad damage powerups, and in one hard-to-reach secret area, Dopefish makes an appearance. In fact, the hardest difficulty level, titled "Nightmare", is only reachable through a secret portal in the fourth dimension's entrance hall.

Sometimes, a whole level may be designed as a secret level.

Tools

A wide variety of tools may be used by someone designing a level. Although it is faster to design models and textures with general purpose multimedia creation tools, games usually require the data to be in a unique format suited for that game's engine. For this, specific compilers and converters of models, textures, and audio data may be required to lay out a level.

Some level editors for games include

- Bethesda Softworks's Construction Set

- Valve Corporation's Hammer Editor

- Epic's UnrealEd and UDK

- BioWare's Aurora Toolset

- id Software's Q3Radiant

- Unity 3D

- Grome outdoor editor.

- Chukong Technologies's CocosStudio and Cocos Creator using cocos2d-x.

Multi engine, multi game editors include id Software's GtkRadiant, based on Q3Radiant, and the open source QuArK. Some games may have built-in level editors like

- *Battlezone 2*

- *Cube 2: Sauerbraten*

- *Doom 3.*

Example of console games with level editors are:

- *TimeSplitters*, developed by Free Radical Design.

- *Super Mario Maker*, developed by Nintendo.

Sometimes, professional 3D editing software, such as 3D Studio Max, Blender, AutoCAD, Lightwave, Maya, Softimage XSI or Grome is used, usually customized with a special plugin developed for the specific game.

Turns, Rounds and Time-keeping Systems in Games

In video and other games, the passage of time must be handled in a way that players find fair and easy to understand. This is usually done in one of two ways:

Real-time

In real-time games, game time progresses continuously according to the game clock. One example of such a game is the sandbox game Minecraft, where one day-night cycle is equal to 20 minutes in real time. Players perform actions simultaneously as opposed to in sequential units or turns. Players must perform actions with the consideration that their opponents are actively working against them in real time, and may act at any moment. This introduces time management considerations and additional challenges (such as physical coordination in the case of video games).

Real-time gameplay is the dominant form of time-keeping found in simulation video games, and has to a large degree supplanted turn-based systems in other video game genres as well (for instance real-time strategy). Time is an important factor in most sports; and many, such as soccer or basketball, are almost entirely simultaneous in nature, retaining only a very limited notion of turns in specific instances, such as the free kick in soccer and the free throw and shot clock in basketball. In the card games Nertz and *Ligretto,* players must compete to discard their cards as quickly as possible and do not take turns.

While game time in video games is in fact subdivided into discrete units due to the sequential nature of computing, these intervals or units are typically so small as to be imperceptible.

Turn-based

In turn-based games, game flow is partitioned into well-defined and visible parts, called turns. A player of a turn-based game is allowed a period of analysis (sometimes bounded, sometimes unbounded) before committing to a game action, ensuring a separation between the game flow and the thinking process, which in turn presumably leads to better choices. Once every player has taken his or her turn, that round of play is over, and any special shared processing is done. This is followed by the next round of play. In games where the game flow unit is time, turns may represent periods such as years, months, weeks or days.

Turn-based games come in two main forms depending on whether, within a turn, players play simultaneously or take their turns in sequence. The former games fall under the category of *simultaneously executed* games (also called *phase-based* or "We-Go"), with *Diplomacy* being a notable example of this style of game. The latter games fall into *player-alternated* games (also called "I-Go-You-Go", or "IGOUGO" for short), and are further subdivided into (A) ranked, (B) round-robin start and (C) random—the difference being the order under which players start within a turn: (A) the first player being the same every time, (B) the first player selection policy is round-robin, and (C) the first player is randomly selected. Some games also base the order of play on an "initiative" score that may in part be based on players' attributes or positions within the game or other, outside factors as well as dice rolls. *Wizard101* is an example of this style.

The term turn-based gaming is also used in Play-by-mail games and to refer to browser-based gaming sites that allow for gameplay to extend beyond a single session, over long periods of time— often taking months for complex games like Go or chess to finish.

Sub-types

Various adaptations of the real-time and turn-based systems have been implemented to address common or perceived shortcomings of these systems (though they often introduce new issues that did not exist before). These include:

Timed Turns and Time Compression

Timed turns are designed to resolve issues of fairness where one player uses a greater amount of time to complete his or her turn than another player. In chess, for instance, a pair of stop clocks may be used in order to place an upper limit on the game length.

In exchange chess, four players on two teams play on two boards with each team taking one white and one black side. Any taken piece is given to a teammate, and can be placed on his board as a standard move (in any position that does not put his opponent in check). A common strategy is to gain a temporary material advantage, pass it on to a teammate, and then stop playing on one's own board—thereby allowing the teammate to use the advantage for many future moves on his board. To avoid this, players are often limited to ten seconds per move—with their opponent being allowed to remove one of the player's pawns from the board for each additional ten seconds consumed.

The turn-based strategy game *Utopia* (1982) featured an early example of timed turns. The early *Ultima* role-playing video games were strictly turn-based, but starting with *Ultima III: Exodus* (1983), if the player waited too long to issue a command, the game would issue a "pass" command automatically, thereby allowing enemies to take their turns while the player character did nothing. Further, many browser-based games allocate a number of turns that can be played within a certain period of time, called a *tick*.

Time compression is a feature commonly found in real-time games such as flight simulators. It allows the player to speed up the game time by some (usually adjustable) factor. This permits the player to shorten the subjective duration of long and relatively uneventful periods of gameplay.

Ticks and Rounds

A *tick-based game* is a game that is played using *ticks*, or units of time. Not to be confused with a game *round*, a tick can be any measurement of real time, from seconds to days or even months, and is the basic unit upon which all important game actions take place. Players in tick-based games are allocated a certain number of turns per tick, which are subsequently refreshed at the beginning of each new tick. Predominantly found in browser-based MMORPGs, tick-based games differ from other turn-based games in that ticks always occur after the same amount of time has expired. Conversely, in a typical turn-based game, a turn would end only once every player has made all of his or her moves. In real-time games players are not limited, time-wise, in the number of actions they can take.

In some real-time games, a notion of *rounds* exists, whereby game actions are timed according to a common interval that is longer than 'real time'. For instance, units might only begin or cease to act at the beginning or end of a round. In video games such as the *Baldur's Gate* (1998–2001) and *Neverwinter Nights* (2002–2008) series, the notion of rounds is carried over in part from the pen-and-paper rule systems they are based upon; and a similar (but unrelated) example is when a game unit's ability to act is limited by the length of its combat animation, in which case the unit may become unresponsive until the animation has completed.

Online turn-based gaming uses the term *rounds* differently: in these games a round refers to when a new game begins following the completion of a previous one (i.e. after someone or some group of people has "won").

Active Time Battle

The "Active Time Battle" system was introduced by Hiroyuki Ito in *Final Fantasy IV* (1991). In this system, time-keeping does not stop at the end of a turn. Instead, each character has an ATB meter that gradually fills over time in real time, and players must think and act quickly lest they miss their chance to take their turn. Once filled, the player is allowed to issue a command for that character. The fact that enemies can attack or be attacked at any time is credited with injecting urgency and excitement into the combat system. The ATB system was fully developed in *Final Fantasy V* (1992), which improved it by introducing a time gauge to indicate to the player which character's turn is next. The ATB system has since been used in *Final Fantasy VI* (1994), *Final Fantasy VII* (1997), *Final Fantasy VIII* (1999), *Final Fantasy IX* (2000), and *Final Fantasy X-2* (2003). Both *Final Fantasy XII* (2006) and *Final Fantasy XIII* (2009) used heavily modified versions of the system. The ATB system was also used in *Chrono Trigger* (1995). On March 16, 1992 Square Co., Ltd. filed a United States patent application for the ATB system under the title, "Video game apparatus, method and device for controlling same", and was awarded the patent on February 21, 1995.

Games Featuring the ATB System

• *Chrono Trigger* (Various)	• *Final Fantasy VII* (Various)	• *Parasite Eve* (PlayStation)
• *Eien no Firēna* (Super Famicom)	• *Final Fantasy VIII* (Various)	• *Shí Kōng Zhī Lún* (Famicom)
• *Final Fantasy IV* (Various)	• *Final Fantasy IX* (PlayStation)	• *Sakura Taisen GB2* (Game Boy Color)
• *Final Fantasy IV: The After Years* (Various)	• *Final Fantasy X-2* (Various)	• *Surging Aura* (Mega Drive)
• *Final Fantasy V* (Various)	• *Lightning Returns: Final Fantasy XIII* (Various)	• *Tài Kōng Zhàn Shì* (Sega Genesis)
• *Final Fantasy VI* (Various)	• *Panzer Dragoon Saga* (Sega Saturn)	• *Tūn Shí Tiān Dì III* (Mega Drive)

Simultaneously Executed and Clock-based Turns

In *simultaneously executed* games (also called "phase-based" or "We-Go"), turns are separated into two distinct phases: *decision* and *execution*. During the decision phase each player plans and determines his units' actions. The decision phase occurs at the same time for everyone, so there is little wait for anyone to finish. In the execution phase, all players' decisions are put into action, and these actions are performed more or less automatically and at the same time. The execution phase is non-interactive, and there is no waiting for other players to complete their turns. Video game examples include *Laser Squad Nemesis* (2003), and the *Combat Mission* (2000+) and *Master of Orion* (1993–2003) series.

Clock-based games tie all unit actions directly to the game clock. Turns begin and end depending on the duration specified for each action, resulting in a sequence of turns that is highly variable and has no set order. This system is frequently cited for its realism when compared to other turn-based systems. It is also possible in this system for different players' actions to occur at the same time with respect to the game clock, as in real-time or simultaneously executed games. Examples of video games that use this type of system include *Typhoon of Steel* (1988) and *MechForce* (1991), both originally for the Amiga.

Unit Initiative and Acting Outside one's Turn

In some games the sequence of turns depends on the *initiative* statistic of each unit no matter which side the unit belongs to. Games of this type are still technically sequential (e.g. "I-Go-You-Go"), as only one unit can perform an action at a time, and the duration of actions is not tied to the game clock. Examples include the video games *The Temple of Elemental Evil* (2003) and *Final Fantasy Tactics* (1997).

Some games—notably, the *X-COM* series (1993–1998) of video games and the board wargame, *Advanced Squad Leader* (1985)—allow players to act outside of their normal turn by providing a means of *interrupting* an opponent's turn and executing additional actions. Typically, the number and type of actions a player may take during an *interrupt sequence* is limited by the amount of points remaining in the player's action point pool (or something similar) carried over from the previous turn.

The *Silent Storm* (2003–2004) video game series includes an "Interrupt" statistic for each character to determine the likelihood of out-of-turn action. In the video game *M.A.X.* (1996), defensive units may be set to fire out of turn at the expense of being able to fire in their own turn. In the board game *Tide of Iron*, the player may play a card that allows him to interrupt an opponent's turn and perform an action. In the *Mario & Luigi series*, the player often has the opportunity to "counterattack" on the enemy's turn, causing damage and often halting the attack.

Special Turns and Phases

In some turn-based games, not all turns are alike. The board game *Imperium Romanum II* (1985), for instance, features a "Taxation and Mobilization" phase in every third turn (month), which does not occur in the other turns. In the board game *Napoleon* (1974), every third *player* turn is "night turn" where combat is not allowed.

Other turn-based games feature several phases dedicated to different types of activities within each turn. In the *Battle Isle* (1991–2001) series of video games players issue movement orders for all units in one phase, and attack orders in a later phase. In the board game *Agricola* (2007) turns are divided into three phases: "Upkeep", "Replenishing" and "Work". A fourth phase, "Harvest", occurs every few turns.

Partially or Optionally Turn-based and Real-time

Many other games that are not generally turn-based retain the notion of turn-based play during specific sequences. For example, the role-playing video games *Fallout* (1997) and *Silent Storm* (2003) are turn-based during the combat phase, and real-time throughout the remainder of the game. This speeds up portions of the game (such as exploration) where the careful timing of actions is not crucial to player success. Some turn-based games have been criticized for omitting this feature.

Other video games, such as the *Total War* series (2000–2011), *X-COM* (1993) and *Jagged Alliance 2* (1999), combine a turn-based strategic layer with real-time tactical combat or vice versa.

Lastly, the video games *X-COM: Apocalypse* (1997), *Fallout Tactics* (2001) and *Arcanum: Of Steamworks and Magick Obscura* (2001) offered players the option to play in either turn-based or real-time mode via a configuration setting. The latter also offered a "fast turn-based" mode, though all three of the game's modes were criticized for being poorly balanced and oversimplified.

Pausable Real-time

In real-time games with an *active pause* system (also called "pausable real-time" or "real-time with pause"), players are able to pause the game and issue orders such that once a game is un-paused, orders are automatically put into effect. This type of system can offer additional tactical options, and can resolve issues that arise in other real-time games where orders must be given to multiple units at the same time (normally an impossibility in real-time games). It can also help players who desire extra time for analysis before issuing actions.

There are several variations of pausable real-time combat. Among mouse-driven party-based computer role-playing games, the pausable real-time system was popularized by the *Baldur's Gate* series (1998–2001), though the same mechanic was also present in the real-time strategy games, *Total Annihilation* (1997) and the pioneering *Homeworld* (1999) as well as earlier role-playing games such as *Knights of Xentar* (1991) and *Darklands* (1992). In *Baldur's Gate*, players also have the option to allow the artificial intelligence to take control during combat, though they can press the spacebar at any time to regain control of their characters. Further, in *Baldur's Gate*, players are able to configure the game to automatically pause when certain conditions are met, such as at the end of a *round* or upon the death of a non-player character. A variation of active pause, called "Smart Pause Mode" or SPM, is an advertised feature of Apeiron's *Brigade E5: New Jagged Union* (2006) and *7.62: High Calibre* (2007).

Among strategy video games, it is used exclusively in the slow-paced grand strategy games developed by Paradox Interactive, and was the originally intended mode of the *Civilization* series (1991-) before the developers decided to switch to turn-based. Among construction and management simulations, it has been present in the *SimCity* series since *SimCity* (1989).

In the *Growlanser* series of tactical RPGs, the player can attack enemies with various different attacks and status debuffs. In the single-character console RPGs, *Parasite Eve* (1995) and *Vagrant Story* (2000), the player can pause to take aim with a weapon. In *Vagrant Story's* case, this allows specific body parts to be targeted—a mechanic later used in *Fallout 3* (2008) and *Last Rebellion* (2010). *Final Fantasy XII* (2006) expanded on active pause combat with its "gambits" system, which allows players to collect and apply preferences to the artificial intelligence routines of partner characters, who will then perform certain actions in response to certain conditions. A similar "tactics" system later appeared in *Dragon Age: Origins* (2009) and *Dragon Age II* (2011). *Knights of Xentar* (1991) and *Secret of Mana* (1993) also allow an adjustable artificial intelligence to take control during combat.

Real-time vs. Turn-based Gameplay

A debate has emerged between fans of real-time and turn-based video games (usually some type of strategy or role-playing game) based on the merits of each system.

Various arguments are made by proponents. Arguments made in favor of turn-based systems include:

- The extra time available to players in turn-based systems allow them to plan their moves to a greater degree, and permit game designers to offer additional tactical and gameplay options. The same options when used in combination with the time-pressures of real-time games, on the other hand, can cause new players to feel overwhelmed.

- Games are fairer due to a lack of reliance upon player reflexes. A player with slower reflexes is not at a disadvantage compared to faster players; rather, only the ability to think through and solve the current problem is important.

- Games can in theory have better artificial intelligence due to the greater amount of computer processing power available to them.

- It is more realistic to control multiple units intelligently using this system, as players do not have to divide their attention among multiple independent units all moving simultaneously. Likewise, it is easier to keep track of what the enemy is doing at all times since the player is typically informed of every move in advance (not taking into account fog of war).

Arguments made in favor of real-time systems include:

- Armies pausing mid-combat to take turns and act in a sequential manner is unrealistic. Real-life combat occurs simultaneously with no side pausing to let the other side move; (However, this only pertains to sequential turn-based systems, not "we-go" systems.)

- Thinking (and acting) quickly is part of the strategy and constitutes an additional element of challenge.

- Real-time systems are viscerally exciting and add to players' sense of immersion. I.e. players feel more like they are really "there" and experiencing game events first-hand.

- Turn-based games have too many rules and are difficult to master.

- Real-time games are more multiplayer-friendly; sitting around and waiting while other players take their turns can become tiresome.

- The added element of a shared clock ensures that each situation cannot be reduced to an easily repeatable sequential series of steps. Rather, the reliance upon player timing ensures that outcomes are highly variable.

Character Creation

Character creation (also character generation or character design) is the process of defining a game character or other character. Typically, a character's individual strengths and weaknesses are represented by a set of statistics. Games with a largely fictional setting may include traits such as race and class. Games with a more contemporary or narrower setting may limit customization to physical and personality traits.

Role-playing Games

Character creation is typically the first step taken by the players (as opposed to the gamemaster) in preparation for a game. The result of character creation is a *direct characterization* that is recorded on a character sheet. In its most comprehensive form it includes not only a game-specific representation of the character's physical, mental, psychological and social properties in terms of statistics, but also often less formal descriptions of the character's physical appearance, personality, personal back-story ("background") and possessions. During play, only a character's appearance is usually described explicitly while other traits are *characterized indirectly*, with the exact statistics known to the character's player and the game master, but not necessarily to other players.

Character advancement refers to the improvement of a character's statistics later in the game. The player will modify existing stats and add new ones, usually by spending experience points or when gaining a new experience level. Character advancement typically uses similar rules as character creation. To avoid unrealistic sudden changes in character concept, though, character advancement is usually more restricted than the initial character creation. For example, attributes are almost always harder (if not impossible) to change during character advancement.

The term character development is, in some contexts, used interchangeably with *character advancement* (in a sense similar to *professional development* or *Human Development*), whereas elsewhere *character development* refers instead to the player's indirect characterization of the character through role-playing (in a sense similar to *film developing*).

Making Decisions

Character creation screen in S.C.O.U.R.G.E.: Heroes of Lesser Renown.

A character's initial attribute scores are usually either generated randomly or determined by distributing character points, and some systems use a combination of both possibilities. Some game systems allow attribute scores to be increased later in the game in a way similar to skills (but much less frequently), usually by some sort of point distribution system.

Characters can also gain a number of skills. What types of skills the characters can learn and how easily they can be learned usually depends on if the character creation system is "class based" or "skill based".

The process of creating a character for a given game involves a number of decisions: What advantages and disadvantages will the character have? What particular statistic will a certain value be assigned to? What values are there to assign anyway? For most of them, there will be a rule outlining by whom and how it can be made. Most of these rules can be classified into one of the three groups described below. They differ in several aspects, the most prominent being ease of use as well as game balance and diversity of the generated results.

So, most decisions in character creation are made according to the following principles:

Prescription: The decision is predetermined by the rules (often by a formula or a table that maps one or more already-established statistics to a specific choice for another), or it is made by the game master prior to character creation.

Examples would be the skill bonuses a character gets from his attributes in many games (which are usually determined by a table or a simple formula) or the amount of character points a player gets to use for character creation (in *GURPS*, for example, this is set by the game master).

This method facilitates fast and easy decisions that are likely to be balanced according to the judgement of the game's author and the game master, but doesn't allow for variation if not combined with other options. In an extreme case, characters are completely predesigned by the author of a scenario, but even then, players usually may choose their character from the selection provided. This technique is often used to save time for short games run on gaming conventions.

Random Choice: Random choices are usually made by rolling dice and either using the result directly or looking it up in a table, depending on the decision that is to be made.

For example, in *Dungeons & Dragons 3rd edition* the player rolls 4d6 and adds the highest three numbers to generate an ability score (attribute value) from 3 to 18. In the first editions of the *Stormbringer* roleplaying game, the character's race and class both are determined by rolling 1d100 and looking up the result in the appropriate table.

Usually, a random generation system allows the full (or at least a rather large) range of values to be generated for each stat, leading to a great diversity among newly generated characters. Thus, it is possible for a character to start the game with all-maximum scores (or nearly so). On the other hand, players have very little control over the scores, and rolling low scores can be very frustrating for some players. This method is generally less concerned with game balance than with ease of use.

Player's Choice: Another option is to let the player make decisions, normally within clearly defined restrictions. These restrictions often involve allowing players to distribute a number of *character points* among various statistics. In such a point distribution system, higher scores often cost more points per level than lower ones, and costs may vary between statistics even within a category. Usually, there is an upper and lower limit for each score. Additional constraints may apply, depending on the game system. How these points are spent will usually determine if the character will refer to himself as a warrior, a thief, or a scholar. If a player wants to be a fighter/mage/thief/cleric he can — as long as he spends his skill points in the right way.

Examples for systems that almost exclusively use point distribution to determine statistics are (in roughly chronological order) the *Hero System* (including its predecessor *Champions*), *GURPS*, the *World of Darkness* series, and the *Amber Diceless Roleplaying Game* with its unusual auction system. *Dungeons & Dragons 3rd edition* also has an optional *point buy* method for determining ability scores.

Point distribution gives the players much control over the character creation process and tends to make characters highly customizable. If the system is designed well, characters are usually more balanced than randomly created ones. On the other hand, this method is almost always more complicated and time-consuming than random generation.

Determining Numerical Values

Determining numerical values comprises several steps that are not always distinct:

1. (a) Obtain a set of values and (b) select the statistics to assign them to

2. Assign the values to the statistics

3. Possibly adjust statistics scores by "shifting around" (stat) levels.

Example: In *Castle Falkenstein*, *abilities* are the only type of statistic. Each player gets the same pre-defined set of *scores* (1a) and can freely choose (1b) which abilities he wants them to assign to (2). In addition, higher scores can be bought by balancing them with a number of low scores (3).

Obtaining and Assigning Values

Games that don't use point distribution to determine all statistics values typically use different methods for different types of statistic: In general, there are comparatively few *attributes*, and each one explicitly is assigned a value. Conversely, there are generally a rather large number of *skills*, and each character learns only some of them while the others are left at their respective default values. Here are some examples:

- To determine attribute values in Basic *Dungeons & Dragons*, *Marvel Super Heroes*, or *Stormbringer* 3rd edition, for example, the player rolls once (1a) for each attribute (1b) and must use whatever result occurred on the dice for that statistic (2). If for different attributes a different number of dice is used (as is the case for non-humans in *Palladium*, for instance), this is the most feasible option.

- *D&D 3.5*, on the other hand, allows the player to first randomly generate a number of values (1a) and then assign (2) each attribute one of them (1b).

- For determining skill values, *Stormbringer* 3rd edition combines two methods: Some of them (1b) are predetermined (1a, 2) by the character's randomly chosen profession (and race). The player then selects a randomly determined number of additional skills (1b) and rolls dice (1a) to determine starting values for them (2).

Adjusting Scores

Some creation systems use a mix of point-distribution and random generation; most common among these are variant rules that allow, for instance, the alteration of the initially random stats by taking a reduction of one trait in order to increase another. Often, such adjustments are made at a penalty, applying a two-for-one cost, for instance.

Another form of adjustment are racial or occupational ("class") modifiers. In many games, certain statistics are slightly increased or decreased depending on the character's race and sometimes profession. In *Dungeons & Dragons*, for example, non-human races typically increase one ability score by two (on a scale of 3 to 18) while another is lowered by the same amount. In *Stormbringer* 3rd edition, nearly all *nationalities* (subraces) cause adjustments of some or all attribute scores by an amount that is usually randomly determined and has a range of up to two third of an attribute's initial value. In point-distribution systems, these modifiers generally contribute to a race's "point cost", while in other systems, it is up to the race's designer to balance different races against each other (if this is desired).

Templates and Classes

Class selection screen in *Falcon's Eye*.

To speed up and ease the character creation process, many games use character templates of some sort: Sample characters representing genre-typical archetypes that are either completely ready-made or at least define the essential stats necessary for a character to be able to work in a given occupation or fill some dramatic role. For instance, a thief will probably know how to move quietly, pick locks, disarm traps, and climb walls. The use of character templates enables inexperienced players to easily create suitable characters as they won't be overwhelmed with having to select skills and abilities, and it still speeds up character creation for even the most experienced players.

In some games, these templates are only an optional character creation aid that has no prescribed effect on the rest of the game: They can be flexibly modified according to the game's character creation rules or can be ignored altogether. This is generally the case in games that try to give the player as much control over the character creation process as possible. (Examples are *Shadowrun* or *GURPS*.)

Other games use such a mechanism as a mandatory tool to provide direction and limitations to the character creation process as well as character development. This is the character class concept introduced by *Dungeons & Dragons* that is now used in all *d20 System* games and has been adopted by many others, such as Palladium Books' *Megaversal system*.

With a character class, most skills and abilities are predetermined, or must be chosen from a comparably narrow subset of all available traits, leaving the player to select only a few extra skills. Some people find this too limiting, while others like the fact that each character necessarily has to be specialized to fill a specific role in the group of player characters. In a class-based system, a fighter is often not allowed any magical abilities, while mages are typically poor fighters. When players are not required do adhere to a specific template, on the other hand, their characters might turn out very similar even if they started from different templates — a fighter with good spell casting abilities is not much different from a spell caster with good fighting abilities. Thus, the freedom of a class-less system requires extra caution on the side of the players to create a diverse group of characters.

There are games that aim to get the best of both worlds by using some kind of hybrid. One approach is to let the templates (called *careers* in *Classic Traveller* as well as in *Warhammer Fantasy Roleplay*) still restrict the choices available for character creation or development, but apply them only for a limited timespan:

During character creation in *Classic Traveller*, each character pursues one of six possible *careers* (professions) that decides which tables can be used to roll on, thus giving direction to the otherwise largely random process. When the character is ready to be played, he has ended this career, so it doesn't have a direct influence on character development during play.

Warhammer Fantasy Roleplay has a much more elaborate career system. Characters advance by entering a series of "Careers" that provide access to a set of new or improved skills, and bonuses to attributes (called "advances"). The menu of careers available to characters reflects the setting of the game world. Basic careers are those that might be filled by any individual with a modest amount of training or instruction. Advanced careers require greater preparation and training, and are often more appropriate for the lifestyle of an active adventurer. The career system gives both an idea of what a character might have been doing before embarking on a career as an adventurer (working as a baker, night watchman, rat catcher, or farmer), and how they changed and developed through their career (becoming a mercenary, explorer, ship's captain, etc.).

As another approach, some games (such as *Cyberpunk 2020*) use a hybrid skill-class system, in which each of the primary roles (classes) in the game has one skill that is absolutely unique to it and defines that role, but apart from that, characters are created and advance using a skill point system rather than a class-and-level system.

Sports Games

In sports games, creating players involves choosing features like skin color and vital stats. This may also be extended to creating entire teams of players. Common skills such as running and passing may be customized, as well as skills that are more specific to individual sports.

Game Art Design

Game art design is a subset of game development. It is the process of creating the artistic aspects for video games. Video game art design begins in the pre-production phase of creating a video game. The video game artists are visual artists involved from the conception of the game and they make rough sketches of the characters, setting, objects, etc. These starting concept designs can also be created by the game designers before the game is moved into actualization. Sometimes these are concept designs are called "programmer art". After the rough sketches are completed and the game is ready to be moved forward those artists or more artists are brought in to bring these sketches to life through graphic design.

The art design of a game can involve anywhere from two people and up. The larger the gaming company is the more people there are likely designing a game. Small gaming companies tend not to have as many artists meaning that their artist must be skilled in several types of art development, whereas the larger the company, although an artist can be skilled in several types of development, the roles each artist plays becomes more specialized.

Overview

A game's artwork included in media, such as demos and screenshots, has a significant impact on customers, because artwork can be judged from previews, while gameplay cannot.

Artists work closely with designers on what is needed for the game.

Tools used for art design and production are *art tools*. These can range from pen and paper to full software packages for both 2D and 3D art. A developer may employ a *tools team* responsible for art production applications. This includes using existing software packages and creating custom exporters and plug-ins for them.

History

Video game art development began when video games started to be created. When game development started the game artists were also the programmers, which is often why very old games like Pong lack any sort of creativity and were very minimalistic. It was not until the early 1980s that art began to become more developmentally intricate. One of the first video game artists who contributed more shape and two dimensional characters was Shigeru Miyamoto, who created Mario and Donkey Kong.

Starting in the early 1990s art requirements in video games were allowed to increase greatly because there was more room in the budget for art. Video game art began to be in 3D around 1994, before which it had mainly been 2D art design. This required the artist and programmer to work in congruence very carefully, in the beginning, due to the foreign nature of 3D in video games.

As the hardware of video games and technology on a whole advances the ability to develop art for video games increases exponentially. In more recent years many games have developed a much more realistic art design where some artists choose to have a more stylistic approach to the game. There are some games that aim for realism, modelling characters after real actors and using real film to create the back up the artistry to make it as real as possible like in Until Dawn.

Roles

There are several roles under the art development umbrella. Each role plays an important part in creating the art for the video game. Depending on the size of the game production company there may be anywhere from two people and up working on the game. The fewer the people working on the art design the more jobs the people will have to create the different facets of the game. The number of artists working on a game can also be dependent on the type of game being created. For most games there are many roles that must be filled to create characters, objects, setting, animation, and texturizing the game.

The video game artists must use the same design principles that any other kind of artists use. This adds to the aesthetic value of the art created for video games. The greater understanding of these techniques adds to games to make them have a unique experience.

- Lead Artist/Art Director

The art director/lead artist are people who monitor the progression of the other artists to make sure that the art for the game is staying on track. The art director is there to ensure that all the art created works cohesively. They manage their team of artists and distribute projects. The art director often works with other departments in the game and are involved from the conception of the game until the game is finished.

2D Artists

- Concept artist

A *concept artist* works with the game designers, producing character and environment sketches and story-board and influencing the "look of the game". A concept artist's job is to follow the art director's vision. The produced art may be in traditional media, such as drawings or clay molds, or 2D software, such as *Adobe Photoshop*. Concept art produced in the beginning of the production serves as a guide for the rest of development. Concept art is used for demonstration to the art director, producers and stakeholders. A *storyboarder* is a concept artist who designs and articulates scene sequences for review before main art production.

- Storyboard Artists

Storyboard Artists often work with the concept artists and designers of the game from conception. They develop the cinematics of the game. The storyboard artist creates an outline for the rest of the artists to follow. Sometimes this is passed on to other departments, like game writers and programmers, for a base of their work. The storyboards that are created breakdown scenes and how the camera will move.

- Texture/2D artist

A *texture/2D artist* adds texture to the work that has been created by the 3D modellers. Often the 2D/texture artists are the same people as the 3D modellers. The texture artist gives depth to the art in a video game. The artists apply shading, gradients, and other classic art techniques through art development software.

  o A *sprite artist* creates non-static characters and objects or sprites for 2D games. Each sprite may consist of several frames used for animation.

  o A *texture artist* creates textures or *skins* and applies them to 3D model meshes.

o   A *map artist* or *background modeller* creates static art assets for game levels and maps, such as environmental backdrops or terrain images for 2D games.

o   An *interface artist* works with the interface programmer and designer to produce game interface, such as game menus, HUDs, etc.

3D Artists

- 3D modeller

The *3D modellers* use digital software (Maya, Max, Blender) to create characters and environments. They create objects such as buildings, weapons, vehicles and characters. Any 3D component of a game is done by a 3D modeller.

- Environmental Artists

Environmental artists are 3D modellers who work specifically with the environment of a game. They also work with texturing and colours. They create the land that is featured in a video game. Environmental artists build the world, the layout, and the landscapes of the video game.

- Lighting artist

A *lighting artist* work on the light dynamics of a video game. Lighting artists adjust colours and brightness to add mood to the game. The lighting changes made in a video game depends on the type of game being created. The goal of the lighting artist is to create a mood that suits the scene and the game.

- The animator

The animator is responsible for bringing life to the characters, the environment, and anything that moves in a game. They use 3D programs to animate these components to make the game as real as possible. The animators often work with technical artists who aid in making the characters able to move in a realistic way.

Compensation

In 2010 an artist or animator with less than three years of experience on average earned US$45k a year. Artists with three to six years of experience earned US$61k. Artist with more than six years of experience earned $90k.

A lead artist or technical artist earned $66k with three to six years of experience; and $97k with more than six years of experience and an art director with six and more years of experience earned on average, $105k a year.

Game Design Document

A game design document (often abbreviated GDD) is a highly descriptive living design document of the design for a video game. A GDD is created and edited by the development team and it is primarily used in the video game industry to organize efforts within a development team. The document is created by the development team as result of collaboration between their designers, artists and programmers as a guiding vision which is used throughout the game development process. When a game is commissioned by a game publisher to the development team, the document must be created by the development team and it is often attached to the agreement between publisher and developer; the developer has to adhere to the GDD during game development process.

Life Cycle

Game developers may produce the game design document in the pre-production stage of game development—prior to or after a pitch. Before a pitch, the document may be conceptual and incomplete. Once the project has been approved, the document is expanded by the developer to a level where it can successfully guide the development team. Because of the dynamic environment of game development, the document is often changed, revised and expanded as development progresses and changes in scope and direction are explored. As such, a game design document is often referred to as a living document, that is, a piece of work which is continuously improved upon throughout the implementation of the project, sometimes as often as daily. A document may start off with only the basic concept outlines and become a complete, detailed list of every game aspect by the end of the project.

Content

A game design document may be made of text, images, diagrams, concept art, or any applicable media to better illustrate design decisions. Some design documents may include functional prototypes or a chosen game engine for some sections of the game.

Although considered a requirement by many companies, a GDD has no set industry standard form. For example, developers may choose to keep the document as a word processed document, or as an online collaboration tool.

Structure

The purpose of a game design document is to unambiguously describe the game's selling points, target audience, gameplay, art, level design, story, characters, UI, assets, etc. In short, every game part requiring development should be included by the developer in enough detail for the respective developers to implement the said part. The document is purposely sectioned and divided in a way that game developers can refer to and maintain the relevant parts.

The majority of video games should require an inclusion or variation of the following sections:

- Story
- Characters
- Level/environment design
- Gameplay
- Art

- Sound and Music

- User Interface, Game Controls

This list is by no means exhaustive or applicable to every game. Some of these sections might not appear in the GDD itself but instead would appear in supplemental documents.

Field of View in Video Games

A field of view.

In first person video games, the field of view or field of vision (abbreviated FOV) is the extent of the observable game world that is seen on the display at any given moment. It is typically measured as an angle, although whether this angle is the horizontal, vertical, or diagonal component of the field of view varies from game to game.

The FOV in a video game may change depending on the aspect ratio of the rendering resolution. In computer games and modern game consoles the FOV normally increases with a wider aspect ratio of the rendering resolution.

Field of View Calculations

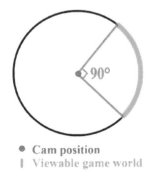

- Cam position
| Viewable game world

90 degrees FOV in a video game

The field of view is usually given as an angle for the horizontal or vertical component of the FOV. A larger angle indicates a larger field of view, however, depending on the FOV scaling method used by the game, it may only affect the horizontal or the vertical component of the field of view.

The horizontal and vertical FOV are calculated from the following equations:

$$r = \frac{w}{h} = \frac{\tan\left(\dfrac{H}{2}\right)}{\tan\left(\dfrac{V}{2}\right)}$$

$$H = 2\arctan\left(\tan\left(\frac{V}{2}\right) \times \frac{w}{h}\right)$$

$$V = 2\arctan\left(\tan\left(\frac{H}{2}\right) \times \frac{h}{w}\right)$$

where r is the aspect ratio, w and h are the width and height, and H and V are the horizontal and vertical FOV.

The different values for horizontal and vertical FOV may lead to confusion because the games often just mention FOV and not whether they mean the horizontal or vertical FOV.

Choice of field of View

Including peripheral vision, the visual field of the average person is approximately 170-180 degrees. Console games are usually played on a TV at a large distance from the viewer, while PC games are usually played on computer monitors close to the viewer. Therefore, a narrow FOV of around 60 degrees is used for console games as the screen subtends a small part of the viewer's visual field, and a larger FOV of 90 to 100 degrees is usually set for PC games as the screen occupies a larger amount of the viewer's vision.

Many PC games that are released after 2000 are ported from consoles, or developed for both console and PC platforms. Ideally, the developer will set a wider FOV in the PC release, or offer a setting to change the FOV to the player's preference. However, in many cases the narrow FOV of the console release is retained in the PC version. This results in an uncomfortable sensation likened to viewing the scene through binoculars, and may lead to disorientation, dizziness, or nausea.

Field of View Scaling Methods

The terms *Hor+, anamorphic, pixel-based, vert-* and *stretch* are widely used in gaming discussions to describe how different video games change field of view dependent on the aspect ratio of the rendering resolution. The terms were originally coined by members of the Widescreen Gaming Forum.

- *Hor+* (horizontal plus) is the most common scaling method for the majority of modern video games. In games with hor+ scaling the vertical FOV is fixed, while the horizontal FOV is expandable depending on the aspect ratio of the rendering resolution; a wider aspect ratio results in a larger FOV. Since the majority of screens used for gaming nowadays are widescreen, this scaling method is usually preferred as wider aspect ratios do not suffer from reduced FOV with it. This becomes especially important in more "exotic" setups like ultra-wide monitor or triple-monitor gaming.

| Field of view (FOV) in HOR+ video game in 16:9 resolution. | FOV in HOR+ video game in 16:10 resolution. | FOV in HOR+ video game in 4:3 resolution. |

- *Anamorphic* refers to when both the vertical and horizontal components of the FOV are fixed, typically to values comfortable on a widescreen picture, and when the resolution changes the picture is letterboxed to maintain the field of view and aspect ratio. Modern games using anamorphic scaling typically have a 16:9 aspect ratio. If this method is used by a game with a 4:3 aspect ratio, the image will be pillarboxed on widescreen resolutions.

| FOV in anamorphic video game in 16:9 resolution. | FOV in anamorphic video game in 16:10 resolution. | FOV in anamorphic video game in 4:3 resolution. |

- *Pixel-based* scaling is almost exclusively used in games with two-dimensional graphics. With pixel-based scaling, the amount of content displayed on screen is directly tied to the rendering resolution. A larger horizontal resolution directly increases the horizontal field of view, and a larger vertical resolution increases the vertical field of view.

- *Vert-* (vertical minus) is a scaling method used by some games that support a wide variety of resolutions. In vert- games, as the aspect ratio widens, the vertical component of the field of view is reduced to compensate. This avoids distortion of objects in the game world but results in a smaller field of view on widescreen resolutions, and may become especially problematic with extremely wide resolutions, such as those common on multiple-display setups.

- *Stretch* refers to a behaviour where the FOV is not adjusted at all, and the image is simply stretched to fill the screen. This method causes significant distortion if used on an aspect ratio different from the one the FOV was originally calibrated for, and is mostly found in games made when most displays had a 4:3 aspect ratio.

Field of View as an Effect

Temporary changes to the field of view can sometimes be used as a special effect in video games. Reducing the field of view is commonly used to convey focus, whereas widening it may indicate lack of control.

References

- Adams, Ernest; Rollings, Andrew (2003). Andrew Rollings and Ernest Adams on game design. New Riders Publishing. ISBN 1-59273-001-9.

- Moore, Michael E.; Novak, Jeannie (2010). Game Industry Career Guide. Delmar: Cengage Learning. ISBN 978-1-4283-7647-2.

- Woods, Stewart (2012). Eurogames: The Design, Culture and Play of Modern European Board Games. North Carolina: McFarland & Company. ISBN 978-0-7864-6797-6.

- Adams, Ernest; Dormans, Joris (2012). Game Mechanics: Advanced Game Design. California: New Riders Games, an imprint of Peachpit. ISBN 978-0-321-82027-3.

- Barton, Matt (2008). Dungeons & Desktops: The History of Computer Role-Playing Games. A K Peters, Ltd. ISBN 1-56881-411-9. Retrieved 2010-09-08.

- McGuire, Morgan; Jenkins, Odest Chadwicke (2009). Creating Games: Mechanics, Content, and Technology. Wellesley, Massachusetts: A K Peters. ISBN 978-1-56881-305-9.

- Adams, Ernest; Rollings, Andrew (2003). Andrew Rollings and Ernest Adams on game design. New Riders Publishing. ISBN 1-59273-001-9.

4

Understanding Video Game Graphics

The earliest video games used text instead of vector graphics. This entailed players reading descriptions about the game setting, players and the actions that take place. But with the emergence of flash, vector graphics became popular. This was then replaced by 2D, 2.5D, 3D graphics and pixelated isometric graphics. In this chapter, the reader is introduced to the video game graphic styles chronologically to provide a timeline for the changing trends in video game graphic design.

Video Game Graphics

A variety of computer graphic techniques have been used to display video game content throughout the history of video games. The predominance of individual techniques have evolved over time, primarily due to hardware advances and restrictions such as the processing power of central or graphics processing units.

Text-based

Some of the earliest video games were text games or text-based games that used text characters instead of bitmapped or vector graphics. Examples include MUDs (*Multi-User Dungeons*), where players could read or view depictions of rooms, objects, other players, and actions performed in the virtual world; and roguelikes, a subgenre of role-playing video games featuring many monsters, items, and environmental effects, as well as an emphasis on randomization, replayability and permanent death. Some of the earliest text games were developed for computer systems which had no video display at all.

Text games are typically easier to write and require less processing power than graphical games, and thus were more common from 1970 to 1990. However, terminal emulators are still in use today, and people continue to play MUDs and explore interactive fiction. Many beginning programmers still create these types of games to familiarize themselves with a programming language, and contests are held even today on who can finish programming a roguelike within a short time period, such as seven days.

Vector Graphics

Vector graphics refers to the use of geometrical primitives such as points, lines, and curves (i.e. shapes based on mathematical equations) instead of resolution-dependent bitmap graphics to represent images in computer graphics. In video games this type of projection is somewhat rare, but has become more common in recent years in browser-based gaming with the advent of Flash, since Flash supports vector graphics natively. An earlier example for the personal computer is *Starglider* (1986).

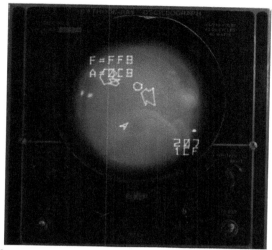

A free software Asteroids-like video game played on a vector monitor.

Vector game can also refer to a video game that uses a vector graphics display capable of projecting images using an electron beam to draw images instead of with pixels, much like a laser show. Many early arcade games used such displays, as they were capable of displaying more detailed images than raster displays on the hardware available at that time. Many vector-based arcade games used full-color overlays to complement the otherwise monochrome vector images. Other uses of these overlays were very detailed drawings of the static gaming environment, while the moving objects were drawn by the vector beam. Games of this type were produced mainly by Atari, Cinematronics, and Sega. Examples of vector games include *Armor Attack*, *Eliminator*, *Lunar Lander*, *Space Fury*, *Space Wars*, *Star Trek*, *Tac/Scan*, *Tempest* and *Zektor*. The Vectrex home console also used a vector display. After 1985, the use of vector graphics declined substantially due to improvements to sprite technology; rasterized 3D Filled Polygon Graphics returned to the arcades and were so popular that vector graphics could no longer compete.

Full Motion Video

Full motion video (FMV) games are video games that rely upon pre-recorded television- or movie-quality recordings and animations rather than sprites, vectors or 3D models to display action in the game. FMV-based games were popular during the early 1990s as CD-ROMs and Laserdiscs made their way into the living rooms, providing an alternative to the low-capacity ROM cartridges of most consoles at the time. Although FMV-based games did manage to look better than many contemporary sprite-based games, they occupied a niche market; and a vast majority of FMV games were panned at the time of their release, with many gamers citing their dislike for the lack of interaction inherent in these games. As a result, the format became a well-known failure in video gaming, and the popularity of FMV games declined substantially after 1995 as more advanced consoles started to become widely available.

A number of different types of games utilized this format. Some resembled modern music/dance games, where the player timely presses buttons according to a screen instruction. Others included early rail shooters such as *Tomcat Alley*, *Surgical Strike* and *Sewer Shark*. Full motion video was also used in several interactive movie adventure games, such as *The Beast Within: A Gabriel Knight Mystery* and *Phantasmagoria*.

2D

Parallel Projection

Games utilizing parallel projection typically make use of two-dimensional bitmap graphics as opposed to 3D-rendered triangle-based geometry, allowing developers to create large, complex gameworlds efficiently and with relatively few art assets by dividing the art into sprites or tiles and reusing them repeatedly (though some games use a mix of different techniques).

Top-down Perspective

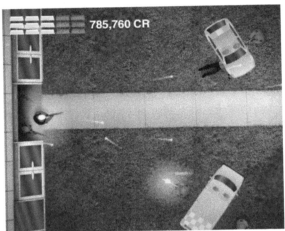

An example of a typical top-down, third-person view game, *The Heist 2*

Top-down perspective, also sometimes referred to as bird's-eye view, Overworld, overhead view or helicopter view, when used in video games refers to a camera angle that shows the player and the area around them from above. While not exclusive to video games that utilise parallel projection, it was at one time common in 2D role playing video games, wargames and construction and management simulation games such as *SimCity*, *Pokémon*, and *Railroad Tycoon*, as well as in action and action-adventure games such as the early *The Legend of Zelda* and *Grand Theft Auto* games.

Side-scrolling Game

Awesomenauts is a side scrolling MOBA game.

A side-scrolling game or side-scroller is a video game in which the viewpoint is taken from the side, and the onscreen characters generally move from the left side of the screen to the right. Games of this type make use of scrolling computer display technology, and sometimes parallax scrolling to suggest added depth.

In many games the screen follows the player character such that the player character is always positioned near the center of the screen. In other games the position of the screen will change according to the player character's movement, such that the player character is off-center and more space is shown in front of the character than behind. Sometimes, the screen will scroll not only forward in the speed and direction of the player character's movement, but also backwards to previously visited parts of a stage. In other games or stages, the screen will only scroll forwards, not backwards, so that once a stage has been passed it can no longer be visited. In games such as shoot 'em ups like *R-type*, the screen scrolls forward by itself at a steady rate, and the player must keep up with the screen, attempting to avoid obstacles and collect things before they pass off screen.

Examples of side-scrolling games include platform games such as *Sonic the Hedgehog*, beat 'em ups such as the popular *Double Dragon* and *Battletoads*, and shooters such as *R-type* and (more recently) *Jets'n'Guns*. The *Super Mario Bros.* series has used all three types of side-scrolling at some time in its history.

2.5D, 3/4 Perspective, and Pseudo-3D

2.5D ("two-and-a-half-dimensional"), 3/4 perspective and pseudo-3D are informal terms used to describe graphical projections and techniques that try to "fake" three-dimensionality, typically by using some form of parallel projection, wherein the point of view is from a fixed perspective, but also reveals multiple facets of an object. Examples of pseudo-3D techniques include isometric/axonometric projection, oblique projection, orthographic projection, billboarding, parallax scrolling, scaling, skyboxes, and skydomes. In addition, 3D graphical techniques such as bump mapping and parallax mapping are often used to extend the illusion of three-dimensionality without substantially increasing the resulting computational overhead introduced by increasing the polygon count.

The terms sometimes possess a second meaning, wherein the gameplay in an otherwise 3D game is forcibly restricted to a two-dimensional plane.

Examples of games that make use of pseudo-3D techniques include *Zaxxon*, *The Sims* and *Diablo* (isometric/axonometric projection); *Ultima VII* and *Paperboy* (oblique projection); *Sonic the Hedgehog* and *Street Fighter II* (parallax scrolling); *Fonz* and *Space Harrier* (scaling); and *Half-Life 2* (skyboxes). In addition to axonometric projection, games such as *The Sims* and *Final Fantasy Tactics* also make use of a combination of pre-drawn 2D sprites and real-time polygonal graphics instead of relying entirely on 2D sprites as is the norm.

3D

With the advent of 3D accelerated graphics, video games could expand beyond the typically sprite-based 2D graphics of older graphics technologies to describe a view frequently more true to reality and lifelike than their predecessors. Perspective projection has also been used in some earlier titles to present a 3D view from a fixed (and thus somewhat less hardware-intensive) perspective with a limited ability to move.

Fixed 3D

Fixed 3D refers to a three-dimensional representation of the game world where foreground objects (i.e. game characters) are typically rendered in real time against a static background. The principal advantage of this technique is its ability to display a high level of detail on minimal hardware. The main disadvantage is that the player's frame of reference remains fixed at all times, preventing players from examining or moving about the environment from multiple viewpoints.

Backgrounds in fixed 3D games tend to be pre-rendered two-dimensional images, but are sometimes rendered in real time (e.g. *Blade Runner*). The developers of *SimCity 4* took advantage of fixed perspective by not texturing the reverse sides of objects (and thereby speeding up rendering) which players could not see anyway. Fixed 3D is also sometimes used to "fake" areas which are inaccessible to players. *The Legend of Zelda: Ocarina of Time*, for instance, is nearly completely 3D, but uses fixed 3D to represent many of the building interiors as well as one entire town. (This technique was later dropped in favor of full-3D in the game's successor, *The Legend of Zelda: Majora's Mask*.) A similar technique, the skybox, is used in many 3D games to represent distant background objects that are not worth rendering in real time.

Used heavily in the survival horror genre, fixed 3D was first seen in Infogrames' *Alone in the Dark* series in the early 1990s and imitated by titles such as *Ecstatica*. It was later brought back by Capcom in the *Resident Evil* series. Gameplay-wise there is little difference between fixed 3D games and their 2D precursors. Players' ability to navigate within a scene still tends to be limited, and interaction with the gameworld remains mostly "point-and-click".

Further examples include the PlayStation-era titles in the *Final Fantasy* series (Square); the role-playing games *Parasite Eve* and *Parasite Eve II* (Square); the action-adventure games *Ecstatica* and *Ecstatica 2* (Andrew Spencer/Psygnosis), as well as *Little Big Adventure* (Adeline Software International); the graphic adventure *Grim Fandango* (LucasArts); and *3D Movie Maker* (Microsoft Kids).

Pre-rendered backgrounds are also found in some isometric video games, such as the role-playing game *The Temple of Elemental Evil* (Troika Games) and the *Baldur's Gate* series (BioWare); though in these cases the form of graphical projection used is not different.

First-person Perspective

First-person perspective as seen in *STALKER: Shadow of Chernobyl* (2007)

First person refers to a graphical perspective rendered from the viewpoint of the player character. In many cases, this may be the viewpoint from the cockpit of a vehicle. Many different genres have made use of first-person perspectives, ranging from adventure games to flight simulators. Perhaps the most notable genre to make use of this device is the first-person shooter genre, where the graphical perspective has an immense impact on game play.

Games with a first-person perspective are usually avatar-based, wherein the game displays what the player's avatar would see with the avatar's own eyes. Thus, players typically cannot see the avatar's body, though they may be able to see the avatar's weapons or hands. This viewpoint is also frequently used to represent the perspective of a driver within a vehicle, as in flight and racing simulators; and it is common to make use of positional audio, where the volume of ambient sounds varies depending on their position with respect to the player's avatar.

Games with a first-person perspective do not require sophisticated animations for the player's avatar, and do not need to implement a manual or automated camera-control scheme as in third-person perspective. A first person perspective allows for easier aiming, since there is no representation of the avatar to block the player's view. However, the absence of an avatar can make it difficult to master the timing and distances required to jump between platforms, and may cause motion sickness in some players.

Players have come to expect first-person games to accurately scale objects to appropriate sizes. However, key objects such as dropped items or levers may be exaggerated in order to improve their visibility.

Third-person Perspective

Third person refers to a graphical perspective rendered from a view that is some distance away (usually behind and slightly above) from the player's character. This viewpoint allows players to see a more strongly characterized avatar, and is most common in action and action-adventure games. This viewpoint poses some difficulties, however, in that when the player turns or stands with his back to a wall, the camera may jerk or end up in awkward positions. Developers have tried to alleviate this issue by implementing intelligent camera systems, or by giving the player control over the camera. There are three primary types of third-person camera systems: "fixed camera systems" in which the camera positions are set during the game creation; "tracking camera systems" in which the camera simply follows the player's character; and "interactive camera systems" that are under the player's control.

Examples of games utilizing third-person perspective include *Super Mario 64*, the *Tomb Raider* series, the 3D installments of the *Legend of Zelda* series, and *Crash Bandicoot*.

Stereo Graphics

Stereoscopic video games use stereoscopic technologies to create depth perception for the player by any form of stereo display. Such games should not to be confused with video games that use 3D computer graphics, which although they feature graphics on screen, do not give the illusion of depth beyond the screen.

Virtual Reality Headset

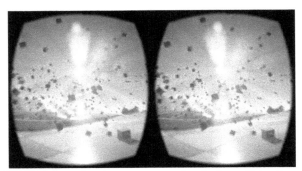

Image captured from Oculus Rift DK2, showing compensation for lens distortion and chromatic aberration.

The graphics for virtual reality gaming consist of a special kind of stereo 3D graphics to fit the up-close display. The requirements for latency are also higher to reduce the potential for virtual reality sickness.

Multi-monitor Setup

Many games can run multi-monitor setups to achieve very high display resolutions. Running games that way can create a better immersion, e.g. when playing a video racing game or flight simulator or give a tactical advantage due to the higher resolution.

Augmented/ Mixed Reality Graphics

Artist's illustration of *Minecraft* on Microsoft HoloLens

Augmented or Mixed reality game graphics use images that partial overlay the image of reality seen through partial transparent glasses or captured with a camera and seen with a head-mounted display or other displays such as smartphone or tablet displays.

Vector Graphics

Vector graphics is the use of polygons to represent images in computer graphics. Vector graphics are based on vectors, which lead through locations called control points or nodes. Each of these points has a definite position on the *x*- and *y*-axes of the work plane and determines the direction of the path; further, each path may be assigned various attributes, including such values as stroke color, shape, curve, thickness, and fill.

Example showing effect of vector graphics versus raster graphics.

Overview

One of the first uses of vector graphic displays was the US SAGE air defense system. Vector graphics systems were only retired from U.S. en route air traffic control in 1999, and are likely still in use in military and specialised systems. Vector graphics were also used on the TX-2 at the MIT Lincoln Laboratory by computer graphics pioneer Ivan Sutherland to run his program Sketchpad in 1963.

Subsequent vector graphics systems, most of which iterated through dynamically modifiable stored lists of drawing instructions, include the IBM 2250, Imlac PDS-1, and DEC GT40. There was a home gaming system that used vector graphics called Vectrex as well as various arcade games like *Asteroids*, *Space Wars* and many cinematronics titles such as *Rip-Off*, and *Tail Gunner* using vector monitors. Storage scope displays, such as the Tektronix 4014, could display vector images but not modify them without first erasing the display.

In computer typography, modern outline fonts describe printable characters (glyphs) by cubic or quadratic mathematical curves with control points. Nevertheless, bitmap fonts are still in use. Converting outlines requires filling them in; converting to bitmaps is not trivial, because bitmaps often don't have sufficient resolution to avoid "stairstepping" ("aliasing"), especially with smaller visible character sizes. Processing outline character data in sophisticated fashion to create satisfactory bitmaps for rendering is called "hinting". Although the term implies suggestion, the process is deterministic, and done by executable code, essentially a special-purpose computer language. While automatic hinting is possible, results can be inferior to that done by experts.

Modern vector graphics displays can sometimes be found at laser light shows, where two fast-moving X-Y mirrors position the beam to rapidly draw shapes and text as straight and curved strokes on a screen.

Vector graphics can be created in form using a pen plotter, a special type of printer that uses a series of ballpoint and felt-tip pens on a servo-driven mount that moves horizontally across the paper, with the plotter moving the paper back and forth through its paper path for vertical movement. Although a typical plot might easily require a few thousand paper motions, back and forth, the paper doesn't slip. In a tiny roll-fed plotter made by Alps in Japan, teeth on thin sprockets indented the paper near its edges on the first pass, and maintained registration on subsequent passes.

Some Hewlett-Packard pen plotters had two-axis pen carriers and stationery paper (plot size was limited). However, the moving-paper H-P plotters had grit wheels (akin to machine-shop grinding wheels) which, on the first pass, indented the paper surface, and collectively maintained registration.

Present-day vector graphic files such as engineering drawings are typically printed as bitmaps, after vector-to-raster conversion.

The term "vector graphics" is mainly used today in the context of two-dimensional computer graphics. It is one of several modes an artist can use to create an image on a raster display. Other modes include text, multimedia, and 3D rendering. Virtually all modern 3D rendering is done using extensions of 2D vector graphics techniques. Plotters used in technical drawing still draw vectors directly to paper.

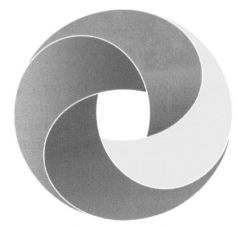

A vector-based image of a round four-color swirl.

Standards

The World Wide Web Consortium (W3C) standard for vector graphics is Scalable Vector Graphics (SVG). The standard is complex and has been relatively slow to be established at least in part owing to commercial interests. Many web browsers now have some support for rendering SVG data, but full implementations of the standard are still comparatively rare.

In recent years, SVG has become a significant format that is completely independent of the resolution of the rendering device, typically a printer or display monitor. SVG files are essentially printable text that describes both straight and curved paths, as well as other attributes. Wikipedia prefers SVG for images such as simple maps, line illustrations, coats of arms, and flags, which generally are not like photographs or other continuous-tone images. Rendering SVG requires conversion to raster format at a resolution appropriate for the current task. SVG is also a format for animated graphics.

There is also a version of SVG for mobile phones. In particular, the specific format for mobile phones is called SVGT (SVG Tiny version). These images can count links and also exploit anti-aliasing. They can also be displayed as wallpaper.

Conversion

The list of image file formats covers proprietary and public vector formats.

Original reference photo before vectorization

Detail can be added to or removed from vector art.

Modern displays and printers are raster devices; vector formats have to be converted to raster format (bitmaps – pixel arrays) before they can be rendered (displayed or printed). The size of the bitmap/raster-format file generated by the conversion will depend on the resolution required, but the size of the vector file generating the bitmap/raster file will always remain the same. Thus, it is easy to convert from a vector file to a range of bitmap/raster file formats but it is much more difficult to go in the opposite direction, especially if subsequent editing of the vector picture is required. It might be an advantage to save an image created from a vector source file as a bitmap/raster format, because different systems have different (and incompatible) vector formats, and some might not support vector graphics at all. However, once a file is converted from the vector format, it is likely to be bigger, and it loses the advantage of scalability without loss of resolution. It will also no longer be possible to edit individual parts of the image as discrete objects. The file size of a vector graphic image depends on the number of graphic elements it contains; it is a list of descriptions.

Printing

Vector art is ideal for printing since the art is made from a series of mathematical curves, it will print very crisply even when resized. For instance, one can print a vector logo on a small sheet of copy paper, and then enlarge the same vector logo to billboard size and keep the same crisp quality. A low-resolution raster graphic would blur or pixelate excessively if it were enlarged from business card size to billboard size. (The precise resolution of a raster graphic necessary for high-quality results depends on the viewing distance; e.g., a billboard may still appear to be of high quality even at low resolution if the viewing distance is great enough.)

If we regard typographic characters as images, then the same considerations that we have made for graphics apply even to composition of written text for printing (typesetting). Older character sets were stored as bitmaps. Therefore, to achieve maximum print quality they had to be used at a given resolution only; these font formats are said to be non-scalable. High quality typography is nowadays based on character drawings (fonts) which are typically stored as vector graphics, and as such are scalable to any size. Examples of these vector formats for characters are Postscript fonts and TrueType fonts.

Operation

Advantages to this style of drawing over raster graphics:

- This minimal amount of information translates to a much smaller file size compared to large raster images (the size of representation does not depend on the dimensions of the object), though a vector graphic with a small file size is often said to lack detail compared with a real world photo.

- Correspondingly, one can infinitely zoom in on e.g., a circle arc, and it remains smooth. On the other hand, a polygon representing a curve will reveal being not really curved.

- On zooming in, lines and curves need not get wider proportionally. Often the width is either not increased or less than proportional. On the other hand, irregular curves represented by simple geometric shapes may be made proportionally wider when zooming in, to keep them looking smooth and not like these geometric shapes.

- The parameters of objects are stored and can be later modified. This means that moving, scaling, rotating, filling etc. doesn't degrade the quality of a drawing. Moreover, it is usual to specify the dimensions in device-independent units, which results in the best possible rasterization on raster devices.

- From a 3-D perspective, rendering shadows is also much more realistic with vector graphics, as shadows can be abstracted into the rays of light from which they are formed. This allows for photo realistic images and renderings.

For example, consider a circle of radius r. The main pieces of information a program needs in order to draw this circle are

1. an indication that what is to be drawn is a circle

2. the radius r

3. the location of the center point of the circle

4. stroke line style and color (possibly transparent)

5. fill style and color (possibly transparent)

Vector formats are not always appropriate in graphics work and also have numerous disadvantages. For example, devices such as cameras and scanners produce essentially continuous-tone raster graphics that are impractical to convert into vectors, and so for this type of work, an image editor will operate on the pixels rather than on drawing objects defined by mathematical expressions. Comprehensive graphics tools will combine images from vector and raster sources, and may provide editing tools for both, since some parts of an image could come from a camera source, and others could have been drawn using vector tools.

Some authors have criticized the term *vector graphics* as being confusing. In particular, *vector graphics* does not simply refer to graphics described by Euclidean vectors. Some authors have proposed to use *object-oriented graphics* instead. However this term can also be confusing as it can be read as any kind of graphics implemented using object-oriented programming.

Typical Primitive Objects

Any particular vector file format supports only some kinds of primitive objects. Nearly all vector file formats support simple and fast-rendering primitive objects:

*   Lines, polylines and polygons

*   Bézier curves and bezigons

*   Circles and ellipses

Most vector file formats support

*   Text (in computer font formats such as TrueType where each letter is created from Bézier curves) or quadratics.

*   Color gradients

*   Often, a bitmap image is considered as a primitive object. From the conceptual view, it behaves as a rectangle.

A few vector file formats support more complex objects as primitives:

*   Many computer-aided design applications support splines and other curves, such as:

    o   Catmull–Rom splines

- o NURBS

- iterated function systems

- superellipses and superellipsoids

- metaballs

- etc.

If an image stored in one vector file format is converted to another file format that supports all the primitive objects used in that particular image, then the conversion can be lossless.

Vector Operations

Vector graphics editors typically allow rotation, movement (without rotation), mirroring, stretching, skewing, affine transformations, changing of z-order (loosely, what's in front of what) and combination of primitives into more complex objects.

More sophisticated transformations include set operations on closed shapes (union, difference, intersection, etc.).

Vector graphics are ideal for simple or composite drawings that need to be device-independent, or do not need to achieve photo-realism. For example, the PostScript and PDF page description languages use a vector graphics model.

2D Computer Graphics

2D computer graphics is the computer-based generation of digital images—mostly from two-dimensional models (such as 2D geometric models, text, and digital images) and by techniques specific to them. The word may stand for the branch of computer science that comprises such techniques, or for the models themselves.

Raster graphic sprites (left) and masks (right)

2D computer graphics are mainly used in applications that were originally developed upon traditional printing and drawing technologies, such as typography, cartography, technical drawing, advertising, etc. In those applications, the two-dimensional image is not just a representation of a real-world object, but an independent artifact with added semantic value; two-dimensional models are therefore preferred, because they give more direct control of the image than 3D computer graphics (whose approach is more akin to photography than to typography).

In many domains, such as desktop publishing, engineering, and business, a description of a document based on 2D computer graphics techniques can be much smaller than the corresponding digital image—often by a factor of 1/1000 or more. This representation is also more flexible since it can be rendered at different resolutions to suit different output devices. For these reasons, documents and illustrations are often stored or transmitted as 2D graphic files.

2D computer graphics started in the 1950s, based on vector graphics devices. These were largely supplanted by raster-based devices in the following decades. The PostScript language and the X Window System protocol were landmark developments in the field.

2D Graphics Techniques

2D graphics models may combine geometric models (also called vector graphics), digital images (also called raster graphics), text to be typeset (defined by content, font style and size, color, position, and orientation), mathematical functions and equations, and more. These components can be modified and manipulated by two-dimensional geometric transformations such as translation, rotation, scaling. In object-oriented graphics, the image is described indirectly by an object endowed with a self-rendering method—a procedure which assigns colors to the image pixels by an arbitrary algorithm. Complex models can be built by combining simpler objects, in the paradigms of object-oriented programming.

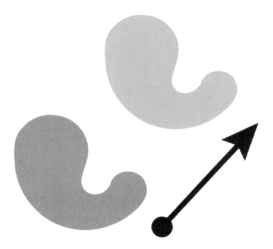

A translation moves every point of a figure or a space by the same amount in a given direction.

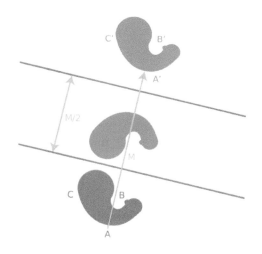

A reflection against an axis followed by a reflection against a second axis parallel to the first one results in a total motion which is a translation.

In Euclidean geometry, a translation moves every point a constant distance in a specified direction. A translation can be described as a rigid motion: other rigid motions include rotations and reflections. A translation can also be interpreted as the addition of a constant vector to every point, or as shifting the origin of the coordinate system. A translation operator is an operator T_δ such that

$$T_\delta f\,(\mathbf{v}) = f\,(\mathbf{v}+\delta)$$

If v is a fixed vector, then the translation T_v will work as $T_v(p) = p + v$.

If T is a translation, then the image of a subset A under the function T is the translate of A by T. The translate of A by T_v is often written $A + v$.

In a Euclidean space, any translation is an isometry. The set of all translations forms the translation group T, which is isomorphic to the space itself, and a normal subgroup of Euclidean group $E(n)$. The quotient group of $E(n)$ by T is isomorphic to the orthogonal group $O(n)$:

$$E(n\,)\,/\,T \cong O(n\,).$$

Translation

Since a translation is an affine transformation but not a linear transformation, homogeneous coordinates are normally used to represent the translation operator by a matrix and thus to make it linear. Thus we write the 3-dimensional vector $w = (w_x, w_y, w_z)$ using 4 homogeneous coordinates as $w = (w_x, w_y, w_z, 1)$.

To translate an object by a vector v, each homogeneous vector p (written in homogeneous coordinates) would need to be multiplied by this translation matrix:

$$T_\mathbf{v} = \begin{bmatrix} 1 & 0 & 0 & v_x \\ 0 & 1 & 0 & v_y \\ 0 & 0 & 1 & v_z \\ 0 & 0 & 0 & 1 \end{bmatrix}$$

As shown below, the multiplication will give the expected result:

$$T_\mathbf{v}\mathbf{p} = \begin{bmatrix} 1 & 0 & 0 & v_x \\ 0 & 1 & 0 & v_y \\ 0 & 0 & 1 & v_z \\ 0 & 0 & 0 & 1 \end{bmatrix}\begin{bmatrix} p_x \\ p_y \\ p_z \\ 1 \end{bmatrix} = \begin{bmatrix} p_x + v_x \\ p_y + v_y \\ p_z + v_z \\ 1 \end{bmatrix} = \mathbf{p} + \mathbf{v}$$

The inverse of a translation matrix can be obtained by reversing the direction of the vector:

$$T_\mathbf{v}^{-1} = T_{-\mathbf{v}}.$$

Similarly, the product of translation matrices is given by adding the vectors:

$$T_\mathbf{u}T_\mathbf{v} = T_{\mathbf{u}+\mathbf{v}}.$$

Because addition of vectors is commutative, multiplication of translation matrices is therefore also commutative (unlike multiplication of arbitrary matrices).

Rotation

In linear algebra, a rotation matrix is a matrix that is used to perform a rotation in Euclidean space.

$$R = \begin{bmatrix} \cos\theta & -\sin\theta \\ \sin\theta & \cos\theta \end{bmatrix}$$

rotates points in the xy-Cartesian plane counterclockwise through an angle θ about the origin of the Cartesian coordinate system. To perform the rotation using a rotation matrix R, the position of each point must be represented by a column vector v, containing the coordinates of the point. A rotated vector is obtained by using the matrix multiplication Rv. Since matrix multiplication has no effect on the zero vector (i.e., on the coordinates of the origin), rotation matrices can only be used to describe rotations about the origin of the coordinate system.

Rotation matrices provide a simple algebraic description of such rotations, and are used extensively for computations in geometry, physics, and computer graphics. In 2-dimensional space, a rotation can be simply described by an angle θ of rotation, but it can be also represented by the 4 entries of a rotation matrix with 2 rows and 2 columns. In 3-dimensional space, every rotation can be interpreted as a rotation by a given angle about a single fixed axis of rotation, and hence it can be simply described by an angle and a vector with 3 entries. However, it can also be represented by the 9 entries of a rotation matrix with 3 rows and 3 columns. The notion of rotation is not commonly used in dimensions higher than 3; there is a notion of a rotational displacement, which can be represented by a matrix, but no associated single axis or angle.

Rotation matrices are square matrices, with real entries. More specifically they can be characterized as orthogonal matrices with determinant 1:

$$R^T = R^{-1}, \det R = 1.$$

The set of all such matrices of size n forms a group, known as the special orthogonal group SO(n).

In Two Dimensions

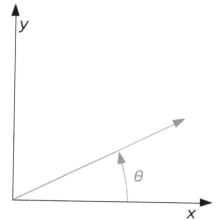

A counterclockwise rotation of a vector through angle θ. The vector is initially aligned with the x-axis.

In two dimensions every rotation matrix has the following form:

$$R(\theta) = \begin{bmatrix} \cos\theta & -\sin\theta \\ \sin\theta & \cos\theta \end{bmatrix}.$$

This rotates column vectors by means of the following matrix multiplication:

$$\begin{bmatrix} x' \\ y' \end{bmatrix} = \begin{bmatrix} \cos\theta & -\sin\theta \\ \sin\theta & \cos\theta \end{bmatrix} \begin{bmatrix} x \\ y \end{bmatrix}.$$

So the coordinates (x',y') of the point (x,y) after rotation are:

$$x' = x\cos\theta - y\sin\theta,$$

$$y' = x\sin\theta + y\cos\theta$$

The direction of vector rotation is counterclockwise if θ is positive (e.g. 90°), and clockwise if θ is negative (e.g. -90°).

$$R(-\theta) = \begin{bmatrix} \cos\theta & \sin\theta \\ -\sin\theta & \cos\theta \end{bmatrix}.$$

Non-standard Orientation of the Coordinate System

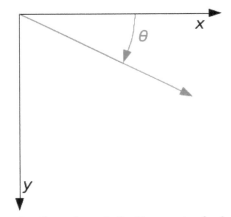

A rotation through angle θ with non-standard axes.

If a standard right-handed Cartesian coordinate system is used, with the x axis to the right and the y axis up, the rotation R(θ) is counterclockwise. If a left-handed Cartesian coordinate system is used, with x directed to the right but y directed down, R(θ) is clockwise. Such non-standard orientations are rarely used in mathematics but are common in 2D computer graphics, which often have the origin in the top left corner and the y-axis down the screen or page.

Common Rotations

Particularly useful are the matrices for 90° and 180° rotations:

$$R(90°) = \begin{bmatrix} 0 & -1 \\ 1 & 0 \end{bmatrix} \text{ (90° counterclockwise rotation)}$$

$$R(180°) = \begin{bmatrix} -1 & 0 \\ 0 & -1 \end{bmatrix} \text{ (180° rotation in either direction – a half-turn)}$$

$$R(270°) = \begin{bmatrix} 0 & 1 \\ -1 & 0 \end{bmatrix} \text{ (270° counterclockwise rotation, the same as a 90° clockwise rotation)}$$

In Euclidean geometry, uniform scaling (isotropic scaling, homogeneous dilation, homothety) is a linear transformation that enlarges (increases) or shrinks (diminishes) objects by a scale factor that is the same in all directions. The result of uniform scaling is similar (in the geometric sense) to the original. A scale factor of 1 is normally allowed, so that congruent shapes are also classed as similar. (Some school text books specifically exclude this possibility, just as some exclude squares from being rectangles or circles from being ellipses.)

More general is scaling with a separate scale factor for each axis direction. Non-uniform scaling (anisotropic scaling, inhomogeneous dilation) is obtained when at least one of the scaling factors is different from the others; a special case is directional scaling or stretching (in one direction). Non-uniform scaling changes the shape of the object; e.g. a square may change into a rectangle, or into a parallelogram if the sides of the square are not parallel to the scaling axes (the angles between lines parallel to the axes are preserved, but not all angles).

Scaling

A scaling can be represented by a scaling matrix. To scale an object by a vector $v = (v_x, v_y, v_z)$, each point $p = (p_x, p_y, p_z)$ would need to be multiplied with this scaling matrix:

$$S_v = \begin{bmatrix} v_x & 0 & 0 \\ 0 & v_y & 0 \\ 0 & 0 & v_z \end{bmatrix}.$$

As shown below, the multiplication will give the expected result:

$$S_v p = \begin{bmatrix} v_x & 0 & 0 \\ 0 & v_y & 0 \\ 0 & 0 & v_z \end{bmatrix} \begin{bmatrix} p_x \\ p_y \\ p_z \end{bmatrix} = \begin{bmatrix} v_x p_x \\ v_y p_y \\ v_z p_z \end{bmatrix}.$$

Such a scaling changes the diameter of an object by a factor between the scale factors, the area by a factor between the smallest and the largest product of two scale factors, and the volume by the product of all three.

The scaling is uniform if and only if the scaling factors are equal ($v_x = v_y = v_z$). If all except one of the scale factors are equal to 1, we have directional scaling.

In the case where $v_x = v_y = v_z = k$, the scaling is also called an enlargement or dilation by a factor k, increasing the area by a factor of k^2 and the volume by a factor of k^3.

A scaling in the most general sense is any affine transformation with a diagonalizable matrix. It includes the case that the three directions of scaling are not perpendicular. It includes also the case that one or more scale factors are equal to zero (projection), and the case of one or more negative scale factors. The latter corresponds to a combination of scaling proper and a kind of reflection: along lines in a particular direction we take the reflection in the point of intersection with a plane that need not be perpendicular; therefore it is more general than ordinary reflection in the plane.

Using Homogeneous Coordinates

In projective geometry, often used in computer graphics, points are represented using homogeneous coordinates. To scale an object by a vector $v = (v_x, v_y, v_z)$, each homogeneous coordinate vector $p = (p_x, p_y, p_z, 1)$ would need to be multiplied with this projective transformation matrix:

$$S_v = \begin{bmatrix} v_x & 0 & 0 & 0 \\ 0 & v_y & 0 & 0 \\ 0 & 0 & v_z & 0 \\ 0 & 0 & 0 & 1 \end{bmatrix}.$$

As shown below, the multiplication will give the expected result:

$$S_v p = \begin{bmatrix} v_x & 0 & 0 & 0 \\ 0 & v_y & 0 & 0 \\ 0 & 0 & v_z & 0 \\ 0 & 0 & 0 & 1 \end{bmatrix} \begin{bmatrix} p_x \\ p_y \\ p_z \\ 1 \end{bmatrix} = \begin{bmatrix} v_x p_x \\ v_y p_y \\ v_z p_z \\ 1 \end{bmatrix}.$$

Since the last component of a homogeneous coordinate can be viewed as the denominator of the other three components, a uniform scaling by a common factor s (uniform scaling) can be accomplished by using this scaling matrix:

$$S_v = \begin{bmatrix} 1 & 0 & 0 & 0 \\ 0 & 1 & 0 & 0 \\ 0 & 0 & 1 & 0 \\ 0 & 0 & 0 & \dfrac{1}{s} \end{bmatrix}.$$

For each vector $p = (p_x, p_y, p_z, 1)$ we would have

$$S_v p = \begin{bmatrix} 1 & 0 & 0 & 0 \\ 0 & 1 & 0 & 0 \\ 0 & 0 & 1 & 0 \\ 0 & 0 & 0 & \dfrac{1}{s} \end{bmatrix} \begin{bmatrix} p_x \\ p_y \\ p_z \\ 1 \end{bmatrix} = \begin{bmatrix} p_x \\ p_y \\ p_z \\ \dfrac{1}{s} \end{bmatrix}$$

which would be homogenized to

$$\begin{bmatrix} sp_x \\ sp_y \\ sp_z \\ 1 \end{bmatrix}.$$

Direct Painting

A convenient way to create a complex image is to start with a blank "canvas" raster map (an array of pixels, also known as a bitmap) filled with some uniform background color and then "draw", "paint" or "paste" simple patches of color onto it, in an appropriate order. In particular the canvas may be the frame buffer for a computer display.

Some programs will set the pixel colors directly, but most will rely on some 2D graphics library and/or the machine's graphics card, which usually implement the following operations:

- paste a given image at a specified offset onto the canvas;

- write a string of characters with a specified font, at a given position and angle;

- paint a simple geometric shape, such as a triangle defined by three corners, or a circle with given center and radius;

- draw a line segment, arc, or simple curve with a virtual pen of given width.

Extended Color Models

Text, shapes and lines are rendered with a client-specified color. Many libraries and cards provide color gradients, which are handy for the generation of smoothly-varying backgrounds, shadow effects, etc. The pixel colors can also be taken from a texture, e.g. a digital image (thus emulating rub-on screentones and the fabled "checker paint" which used to be available only in cartoons).

Painting a pixel with a given color usually replaces its previous color. However, many systems support painting with transparent and translucent colors, which only modify the previous pixel values. The two colors may also be combined in more complex ways, e.g. by computing their bitwise exclusive or. This technique is known as inverting color or color inversion, and is often used in graphical user interfaces for highlighting, rubber-band drawing, and other volatile painting—since re-painting the same shapes with the same color will restore the original pixel values.

Layers

A 2D animated character composited with 3D backgrounds using layers.

The models used in 2D computer graphics usually do not provide for three-dimensional shapes, or three-dimensional optical phenomena such as lighting, shadows, reflection, refraction, etc. However, they usually can model multiple *layers* (conceptually of ink, paper, or film; opaque, translucent, or transparent—stacked in a specific order. The ordering is usually defined by a single number (the layer's *depth*, or distance from the viewer).

Layered models are sometimes called *2½-D computer graphics*. They make it possible to mimic traditional drafting and printing techniques based on film and paper, such as cutting and pasting; and allow the user to edit any layer without affecting the others. For these reasons, they are used in most graphics editors. Layered models also allow better spatial anti-aliasing of complex drawings and provide a sound model for certain techniques such as mitered joints and the even-odd rule.

Layered models are also used to allow the user to suppress unwanted information when viewing or printing a document, e.g. roads and/or railways from a map, certain process layers from an integrated circuit diagram, or hand annotations from a business letter.

In a layer-based model, the target image is produced by "painting" or "pasting" each layer, in order of decreasing depth, on the virtual canvas. Conceptually, each layer is first rendered on its own, yielding a digital image with the desired resolution which is then painted over the canvas, pixel by pixel. Fully transparent parts of a layer need not be rendered, of course. The rendering and painting may be done in parallel, i.e., each layer pixel may be painted on the canvas as soon as it is produced by the rendering procedure.

Layers that consist of complex geometric objects (such as text or polylines) may be broken down into simpler elements (characters or line segments, respectively), which are then painted as separate layers, in some order. However, this solution may create undesirable aliasing artifacts wherever two elements overlap the same pixel.

2D Graphics Hardware

Modern computer graphics card displays almost overwhelmingly use raster techniques, dividing the screen into a rectangular grid of pixels, due to the relatively low cost of raster-based video hardware as compared with vector graphic hardware. Most graphic hardware has internal support for blitting operations and/or sprite drawing. A co-processor dedicated to blitting is known as a *Blitter chip*.

Classic 2D graphics chips and graphics processing units of the late 1970s to 1980s, used in 8-bit to early 16-bit, arcade games, video game consoles, and home computers, include:

- Atari's TIA, ANTIC, CTIA and GTIA

- Capcom's CPS-A and CPS-B

- Commodore's OCS

- MOS Technology's VIC and VIC-II

- Fujitsu's MB14241

- Hudson Soft's Cynthia and HuC6270

- NEC's µPD7220 and µPD72120

- Ricoh's PPU and S-PPU

- Sega's VDP, Super Scaler, 315-5011/315-5012 and 315-5196/315-5197

- Texas Instruments' TMS9918

- Yamaha's V9938, V9958 and YM7101 VDP

2D Graphics Software

Many graphical user interfaces (GUIs), including macOS, Microsoft Windows, or the X Window System, are primarily based on 2D graphical concepts. Such software provides a visual environment for interacting with the computer, and commonly includes some form of window manager to aid the user in conceptually distinguishing between different applications. The user interface within individual software applications is typically 2D in nature as well, due in part to the fact that most common input devices, such as the mouse, are constrained to two dimensions of movement.

2D graphics are very important in the control peripherals such as printers, plotters, sheet cutting machines, etc. They were also used in most early video games; and are still used for card and board games such as solitaire, chess, mahjongg, etc.

2D graphics editors or *drawing programs* are application-level software for the creation of images, diagrams and illustrations by direct manipulation (through the mouse, graphics tablet, or similar device) of 2D computer graphics primitives. These editors generally provide geometric primitives as well as digital images; and some even support procedural models. The illustration is usually represented internally as a layered model, often with a hierarchical structure to make editing more convenient. These editors generally output graphics files where the layers and primitives are separately preserved in their original form. MacDraw, introduced in 1984 with the Macintosh line of computers, was an early example of this class; recent examples are the commercial products Adobe Illustrator and CorelDRAW, and the free editors such as xfig or Inkscape. There are also many 2D graphics editors specialized for certain types of drawings such as electrical, electronic and VLSI diagrams, topographic maps, computer fonts, etc.

Image editors are specialized for the manipulation of digital images, mainly by means of free-hand drawing/painting and signal processing operations. They typically use a direct-painting paradigm, where the user controls virtual pens, brushes, and other free-hand artistic instruments to apply paint to a virtual canvas. Some image editors support a multiple-layer model; however, in order to support signal-processing operations like blurring each layer is normally represented as a digital image. Therefore, any geometric primitives that are provided by the editor are immediately converted to pixels and painted onto the canvas. The name *raster graphics editor* is sometimes used to contrast this approach to that of general editors which also handle *vector graphics*. One of the first popular image editors was Apple's MacPaint, companion to MacDraw. Modern examples are the free GIMP editor, and the commercial products Photoshop and Paint Shop Pro. This class too includes many specialized editors — for medicine, remote sensing, digital photography, etc.

Developmental Animation

With the resurgence of 2D animation, free and proprietary software packages have become widely available for amateurs and professional animators. The principal issue with 2D animation is labor requirements. With software like RETAS and Adobe After Effects, coloring and compositing can be done in less time.

Various approaches have been developed to aid and speed up the process of digital 2D animation. For example, by generating vector artwork in a tool like Adobe Flash an artist may employ software-driven automatic coloring and in-betweening.

2.5D

Two and a half dimensional (shortened to 2.5D, nicknamed three-quarter perspective and pseudo-3D) is a term used to describe either 2D graphical projections and similar techniques used to cause images or scenes to simulate the appearance of being three-dimensional (3D) when in fact they are not, or gameplay in an otherwise three-dimensional video game that is restricted to a two-dimensional plane or has a virtual camera with a fixed angle. By contrast, games using 3D computer graphics without such restrictions are said to use *true 3D*.

Common in video games, these projections have also been useful in geographic visualization (GVIS) to help understand visual-cognitive spatial representations or 3D visualization.

The terms three-quarter perspective and three-quarter view trace their origins to portraiture and facial recognition, where they are used to describe a view of a person's face which is partway between a frontal view and a side view.

Computer Graphics

Axonometric and Oblique Projection

In axonometric projection and oblique projection, two forms of parallel projection, the viewpoint is rotated slightly to reveal other facets of the environment than what are visible in a top-down perspective or side view, thereby producing a three-dimensional effect. An object is "considered to be in an inclined position resulting in foreshortening of all three axes", and the image is a "representation on a single plane (as a drawing surface) of a three-dimensional object placed at an angle to the plane of projection." Lines perpendicular to the plane become points, lines parallel to the plane have true length, and lines inclined to the plane are foreshortened.

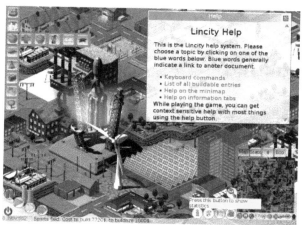

Lincity tiles 2D axonometric graphical elements to form a 2.5D game environment.

They are popular camera perspectives among 2D video games, most commonly those released for 16-bit or earlier and handheld consoles, as well as in later strategy and role-playing video games. The advantage of these perspectives are that they combine the visibility and mobility of a top-down game with the character recognizability of a side-scrolling game. Thus the player can be presented an overview of the game world in the ability to see it from above, more or less, and with additional details in artwork made possible by using an angle: Instead of showing a humanoid in top-down perspective, as a head and shoulders seen from above, the entire body can be drawn when using a slanted angle; Turning a character around would reveal how it looks from the sides, the front and the back, while the top-down perspective will display the same head and shoulders regardless.

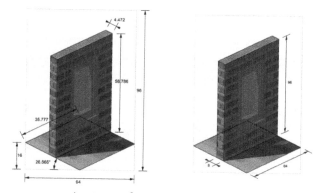

Anatomy of an axonometric sprite.

There are three main divisions of axonometric projection: *isometric* (equal measure), *dimetric* (symmetrical and unsymmetrical), and *trimetric* (single-view or only two sides). The most common of these drawing types in engineering drawing is isometric projection. This projection is tilted so that all three axes create equal angles at intervals of 120 degrees. The result is that all three axes are equally foreshortened. In video games, a form of dimetric projection with a 2:1 pixel ratio is more common due to the problems of anti-aliasing and square pixels found on most computer monitors.

In oblique projection typically all three axes are shown unforeshortened. All lines parallel to the axes are drawn to scale, and diagonals and curved lines are distorted. One tell-tale sign of oblique projection is that the face pointed toward the camera retains its right angles with respect to the image plane.

Two of the most consistent examples of oblique projection are the *The Legend of Zelda* series of games for the Game Boy, Game Boy Color, and Game Boy Advance; and the *Pokémon* series for the Nintendo DS. Examples of axonometric projection include the latter games in the *SimCity* series, and role-playing games such as *Diablo* and *Baldur's Gate*.

Billboarding

In three-dimensional scenes, the term billboarding is applied to a technique in which objects are sometimes represented by two-dimensional images applied to a single polygon which is typically kept perpendicular to the line of sight. The name refers to the fact that objects are seen as if drawn on a billboard. This technique was commonly used in early 1990s video games when consoles did not have the hardware power to render fully 3D objects. This is also known as a backdrop. This can be used to good effect for a significant performance boost when the geometry is sufficiently distant that it can be seamlessly replaced with a 2D sprite. In games, this technique is most frequently applied to objects such as particles (smoke, sparks, rain) and low-detail vegetation. A pioneer in the use of this technique was the game *Jurassic Park: Trespasser*. It has since become mainstream, and is found in many games such as *Rome: Total War*, where it is exploited to simultaneously display thousands of individual soldiers on a battlefield. Other examples include early first-person shooters like *Wolfenstein 3D*, *Doom*, *Hexen* and *Duke Nukem 3D* as well as racing games like Carmageddon and Super Mario Kart.

Skyboxes and Skydomes

Skyboxes and skydomes are methods used to easily create a background to make a game level look bigger than it really is. If the level is enclosed in a cube, the sky, distant mountains, distant buildings, and other unreachable objects are rendered onto the cube's faces using a technique called cube mapping, thus creating the illusion of distant three-dimensional surroundings. A *skydome* employs the same concept but uses a sphere or hemisphere instead of a cube.

As a viewer moves through a 3D scene, it is common for the skybox or skydome to remain stationary with respect to the viewer. This technique gives the skybox the illusion of being very far away since other objects in the scene appear to move, while the skybox does not. This imitates real life, where distant objects such as clouds, stars and even mountains appear to be stationary when the viewpoint is displaced by relatively small distances. Effectively, everything in a skybox will always appear to be infinitely distant from the viewer. This consequence of skyboxes dictates that designers should be careful not to carelessly include images of discrete objects in the textures of a skybox since the viewer may be able to perceive the inconsistencies of those objects' sizes as the scene is traversed.

Scaling Along the Z axis

In some games, sprites are scaled larger or smaller depending on its distance to the player, producing the illusion of motion along the Z (forward) axis. Sega's 1986 video game *Out Run*, which runs on the Sega OutRun arcade system board, is a good example of this technique.

In *Out Run*, the player drives a Ferrari into depth of the game window. The palms on the left and right side of the street are the same bitmap, but have been scaled to different sizes, creating the illusion that some are closer than others. The angles of movement are left and right and into the depth (while still capable of doing so technically, this game did not allow making a U-turn or going into reverse, therefore moving out of the depth, as this did not make sense to the high-speed game play and tense time limit). Notice the view is comparable to that which a driver would have in reality when driving a car. The position and size of any billboard is generated by a (complete 3D) perspective transformation as are the vertices of the poly-line representing the center of the street. Often the center of the street is stored as a spline and sampled in a way that on straight streets every sampling point corresponds to one scan-line on the screen. Hills and curves lead to multiple points on one line and one has to be chosen. Or one line is without any point and has to be interpolated lineary from the adjacent lines. Very memory intensive billboards are used in *Out Run* to draw corn-fields and water waves which are wider than the screen even at the largest viewing distance and also in *Test Drive* to draw trees and cliffs.

Drakkhen was notable for being among the first role-playing video games to feature a three-dimensional playing field. However, it did not employ a conventional 3D game engine, instead emulating one using character-scaling algorithms. The player's party travels overland on a flat terrain made up of vectors, on which 2D objects are zoomed. Drakkhen features an animated day-night cycle, and the ability to wander freely about the game world, both rarities for a game of its era. This type of engine was later used in the game *Eternam*.

Some mobile games, such as the mobile version of Asphalt: Urban GT 2 and Asphalt 3: Street Rules, used this method for rendering the scenery and the buildings. However, some objects (including the buildings and the tunnels) in the mobile phone versions of Asphalt series (except the first one) were polygonal (which are non-textured and mostly flat shaded). Except Asphalt 4: Elite Racing, Asphalt 6: Adrenaline and Asphalt Nitro, which are both textured for the buildings and the tunnel as well. However, both of these versions for the three Asphalt games are only available on some phones that are made by Sony Ericsson and they're both memory intensive and therefore it is quite slow. A basic version of these games for older mobile phones are available.

Parallax Scrolling

Parallaxing refers to when a collection of 2D sprites or layers of sprites are made to move independently of each other and/or the background to create a sense of added depth. The technique grew out of the multiplane camera technique used in traditional animation since the 1940s. This type of graphical effect was first used in the 1982 arcade game *Moon Patrol*. Examples include the skies in *Rise of the Triad*, the arcade version of *Rygar*, *Sonic the Hedgehog*, *Street Fighter II*, *Shadow of the Beast* and *Dracula X Chronicles*, as well as in a level near the Forest of Illusion's secret exit and an unused level in *Super Mario World*.

Mode 7

Mode 7, a display system effect that included rotation and scaling, allowed for a 3D effect while moving in any direction without any actual 3D models, and was used to simulate 3D graphics on the SNES.

Ray Casting

Ray casting is a technique in which a ray for every vertical slice of the screen is sent from the position of the camera. These rays shoot out until they hit an object or wall, and that part of the wall is rendered in that vertical screen slice. Early first-person shooters used ray casting as a technique to create a 3D effect from a 2D world. While the world appears 3D, the player cannot look up or down, nor actually move on the Y axis, because the playing field is 2D.

Bump, Normal and Parallax Mapping

Bump mapping, normal mapping and parallax mapping are techniques applied to textures in 3D rendering applications such as video games to simulate bumps and wrinkles on the surface of an object without using more polygons. To the end user, this means that textures such as stone walls will have more apparent depth and thus greater realism with less of an influence on the performance of the simulation.

Bump mapping is achieved by perturbing the surface normals of an object and using a grayscale image and the perturbed normal during illumination calculations. The result is an apparently bumpy surface rather than a perfectly smooth surface although the surface of the underlying object is not actually changed. Bump mapping was introduced by Blinn in 1978.

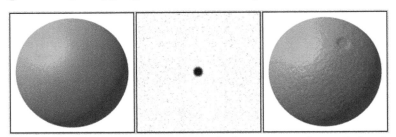

A sphere without bump mapping (left). The bump map to be applied to the sphere (middle). The sphere with the bump map applied (right).

In normal mapping, the unit vector from the shading point to the light source is dotted with the unit vector normal to that surface, and the dot product is the intensity of the light on that surface. Imagine a polygonal model of a sphere—you can only approximate the shape of the surface. By using a 3-channel bitmapped image textured across the model, more detailed normal vector information can be encoded. Each channel in the bitmap corresponds to a spatial dimension (X, Y and Z). These spatial dimensions are relative to a constant coordinate system for object-space normal maps, or to a smoothly varying coordinate system (based on the derivatives of position with respect to texture coordinates) in the case of tangent-space normal maps. This adds much more detail to the surface of a model, especially in conjunction with advanced lighting techniques.

Parallax mapping (also called offset mapping or virtual displacement mapping) is an enhancement of the bump mapping and normal mapping techniques implemented by displacing the texture coordinates at a point on the rendered polygon by a function of the view angle in tangent space (the angle relative to the surface normal) and the value of the height map at that point. At steeper view-angles, the texture coordinates are displaced more, giving the illusion of depth due to parallax effects as the view changes.

Film and Animation Techniques

The term is also used to describe an animation effect commonly used in music videos and, more frequently, title sequences. Brought to wide attention by the motion picture *The Kid Stays in the Picture* based on the book by film producer Robert Evans, it involves the layering and animating of two-dimensional pictures in three dimensional space. Earlier examples of this technique include Liz Phair's music video Down directed by Rodney Ascher and "A Special Tree" directed by musician Giorgio Moroder.

Graphic Design

Faux shading and reflections make these desktop icons appear three-dimensional.

The term also refers to an often-used effect in the design of icons and graphical user interfaces (GUIs), where a slight 3D illusion is created by the presence of a virtual light source to the left (or in some cases right) side, and above a person's computer monitor. The light source itself is always invisible, but its effects are seen in the lighter colors for the top and left side, simulating reflection, and the darker colours to the right and below of such objects, simulating shadow.

An advanced version of this technique can be found in some specialised graphic design software, such as Pixologic's ZBrush. The idea is that the program's canvas represents a normal 2D painting surface, but that the data structure that holds the pixel information is also able to store information with respect to a z-index, as well material settings, specularity, etc. Again, with this data it is thus possible to simulate lighting, shadows, and so forth.

2.5D Platform Games

The term "2.5D" is also applied to 3D games that use polygonal graphics to render the world and/or characters, but whose gameplay is restricted to a 2D plane. Examples include *Pandemonium!*, *Einhänder*, *Klonoa: Door to Phantomile*, *Kirby 64: The Crystal Shards* (although the scene moves towards and away from the camera), *LittleBigPlanet* (although it features a playing field three layers thick), *Nights into Dreams...* and *New Super Mario Bros. U*. The *Crash Bandicoot* series is sometimes referred to as 2.5D because the characters and scenery are rendered in 3D, yet most of its levels are not as free-roaming as "true" 3D platformers.

Trine 2 features 3D graphics, yet its gameplay is restricted to a 2D plane.

Some fighting games such as the *Super Smash Bros.* series, *Marvel vs. Capcom 3*, *Street Fighter IV*, *Mortal Kombat*, *BlazBlue*, *Guilty Gear Xrd* and *The King of Fighters XIV* also utilize 2.5D to showcase 3D backdrops and/or characters while limiting the action to a 2D plane. 2D scrolling shooters are another genre in which 3D graphics are often used in a 2D game, such as in *Ikaruga*.

In some games, such as *Goemon's Great Adventure* and *Pandemonium!*, the area of gameplay can be described as a two-dimensional surface twisting and bending in a three-dimensional space. Inside this surface, the character and physics behave like in a traditional sidescrolling platformer. There are, however, a number of twists that aren't possible with normal sidescroller platformers: it is common in such games to let the two-dimensional plane cross itself or other planes on certain points, thus creating "track switches" in the course. Players can explore different areas of the 3D world that way or can be brought back to previous points seamlessly. Interactions with the "background" (non-accessible points in the 3D landscape) are also used extensively. Other 2.5D games allow the character to interact with objects out of the primare 2D plane; for example in the platformer-shooter *Shadow Complex*, the player may need to target and fire at enemies that are in the background of the scene.

History

The first video games that used pseudo-3D were primarily arcade games, the earliest known examples dating back to the mid-1970s, when they began using microprocessors. In 1975, Taito released *Interceptor*, an early first-person shooter and combat flight simulator that involved piloting a jet fighter, using an eight-way joystick to aim with a crosshair and shoot at enemy aircraft that move in formations of two and increase/decrease in size depending on their distance to the player. In 1976, Sega released *Moto-Cross*, an early black-and-white motorbike racing video game, based on the motocross competition, that was most notable for introducing an early three-dimensional third-person perspective. Later that year, Sega-Gremlin re-branded the game as *Fonz*, as a tie-in for the popular sitcom, *Happy Days*. Both versions of the game displayed a constantly changing forward-scrolling road and the player's bike in a third-person perspective where objects nearer to the player are larger than those nearer to the horizon, and the aim was to steer the vehicle across the road, racing against the clock, while avoiding any on-coming motorcycles or driving off the road. That same year also saw the release of two arcade games that extended the car driving subgenre into three dimensions with a first-person perspective: Sega's *Road Race*, which displayed a constantly changing forward-scrolling S-shaped road with two obstacle race cars moving along the road that the player must avoid crashing while racing against the clock, and Atari's *Night Driver*, which presented a series of posts by the edge of the road though there was no view of the road or the player's car. Games using vector graphics had an advantage in creating pseudo-3D effects. 1979's *Speed Freak* recreated the perspective of *Night Driver* in greater detail.

In 1979, Nintendo debuted *Radar Scope*, a shoot 'em up that introduced a three-dimensional third-person perspective to the genre, imitated years later by shooters such as Konami's *Juno First* and Activision's *Beamrider*. In 1980, Atari's *Battlezone* was a breakthrough for pseudo-3D gaming, recreating a 3D perspective with unprecedented realism, though the gameplay was still planar. It was followed up that same year by *Red Baron*, which used scaling vector images to create a forward scrolling rail shooter.

Sega's arcade shooter *Space Tactics*, released in 1980, allowed players to take aim using crosshairs and shoot lasers into the screen at enemies coming towards them, creating an early 3D effect. It was followed by other arcade shooters with a first-person perspective during the early 1980s, including Taito's 1981 release *Space Seeker*, and Sega's *Star Trek* in 1982. Sega's *SubRoc-3D* in 1982 also featured a first-person perspective and introduced the use of stereoscopic 3-D through a special eyepiece. Sega's *Astron Belt* in 1983 was the first laserdisc video game, using full-motion video to display the graphics from a first-person perspective. Third-person rail shooters were also released in arcades at the time, including Sega's *Tac/Scan* in 1982, Nippon's *Ambush* in 1983, Nichibutsu's *Tube Panic* in 1983, and Sega's 1982 release *Buck Rogers: Planet of Zoom*, notable for its fast pseudo-3D scaling and detailed sprites.

In 1981, Sega's *Turbo* was the first racing game to feature a third-person perspective, rear view format. It was also the first racing game to use sprite scaling with full-colour graphics. *Pole Position* by Namco is one of the first racing games to use the trailing camera effect that is now so familiar. In this particular example, the effect was produced by linescroll—the practice of scrolling each line independently in order to warp an image. In this case, the warping would simulate curves and steering. To make the road appear to move towards the player, per-line color changes were used, though many console versions opted for palette animation instead.

Zaxxon, a shooter introduced by Sega in 1982, was the first game to use isometric axonometric projection, from which its name is derived. Though Zaxxon's playing field is semantically 3D, the game has many constraints which classify it as 2.5D: a fixed point of view, scene composition from sprites, and movements such as bullet shots restricted to straight lines along the axes. It was also one of the first video games to display shadows. The following year, Sega released the first pseudo-3D isometric platformer, *Congo Bongo*. Another early pseudo-3D platform game released that year was Konami's *Antarctic Adventure*, where the player controls a penguin in a forward-scrolling third-person perspective while having to jump over pits and obstacles. It was one of the earliest pseudo-3D games available on a computer, released for the MSX in 1983. That same year, Irem's *Moon Patrol* was a side-scrolling run & gun platform-shooter that introduced the use of layered parallax scrolling to give a pseudo-3D effect. In 1985, *Space Harrier* introduced Sega's "Super Scaler" technology that allowed pseudo-3D sprite-scaling at high frame rates, with the ability to scale 32,000 sprites and fill a moving landscape with them.

The first original home console game to use pseudo-3D, and also the first to use multiple camera angles mirrored on television sports broadcasts, was *Intellivision World Series Baseball* (1983) by Don Daglow and Eddie Dombrower, published by Mattel. Its television sports style of display was later adopted by 3D sports games and is now used by virtually all major team sports titles. In 1984, Sega ported several pseudo-3D arcade games to the Sega SG-1000 console, including a smooth conversion of the third-person pseudo-3D rail shooter *Buck Rogers: Planet of Zoom*.

With the advent of consoles and computer systems that were able to handle several thousands of polygons (the most basic element of *3D computer graphics*) per second and the usage of 3D specialized graphics processing unit, pseudo 3D became obsolete. But even today, there are computer systems in production, such as cellphones, which are often not powerful enough to display *true* 3D graphics, and therefore use pseudo-3D for that purpose. Interestingly, many games from the 1980s' *pseudo-3D arcade era* and *16-bit console era* are ported to these systems, giving the manufactures the possibility to earn revenues from games that are now nearly twenty years old.

By 1989, 2.5D representations were surfaces drawn with depth cues and a part of graphic libraries like GINO. 2.5D was also used in terrain modeling with software packages such as ISM from Dynamic Graphics, GEOPAK from Uniras and the Intergraph DTM system. 2.5D surface techniques gained popularity within the geography community because of its ability to visualize the normal thickness to area ratio used in many geographic models; this ratio was very small and reflected the thinness of the object in relation to its width, which made it the object realistic in a specific plane. These representations were axiomatic in that the entire subsurface domain was not used or the entire domain could not be reconstructed; therefore, it used only a surface and a surface is one aspect not the full 3D identity.

The resurgence of 2.5D or visual analysis, in natural and earth science, has increased the role of computer systems in the creation of spatial information in mapping. GVIS has made real the search for unknowns, real-time interaction with spatial data, and control over map display and has paid particular attention to three-dimensional representations. Efforts in GVIS have attempted to expand higher dimensions and make them more visible; most efforts have focused on "tricking" vision into seeing three dimensions in a 2D plane. Much like 2.5D displays where the surface of a three dimensional object is represented but locations within the solid are distorted or not accessible.

Technical Aspects and Generalizations

The reason for using pseudo-3D instead of "real" 3D computer graphics is that the system that has to simulate a three dimensional-looking graphic is not powerful enough to handle the calculation-intensive routines of 3D computer graphics, yet is capable of using tricks of modifying 2D graphics like bitmaps. One of these tricks is to stretch a bitmap more and more, therefore making it larger with each step, as to give the effect of an object coming closer and closer towards the player.

Even simple shading and size of an image could be considered pseudo-3D, as shading makes it look more realistic. If the light in a 2D game were 2D, it would only be visible on the outline, and because outlines are often dark, they would not be very clearly visible. However, any visible shading would indicate the usage of pseudo-3D lighting and that the image uses pseudo-3D graphics. Changing the size of an image can cause the image to appear to be moving closer or further away, which could be considered simulating a third dimension.

Dimensions are the variables of the data and can be mapped to specific locations in space; 2D data can be given 3D volume by adding a value to the x, y, or z plane. "Assigning height to 2D regions of a topographic map" associating every 2D location with a height/elevation value creates a 2.5D projection; this is not considered a "true 3D representation", however is used like 3D visual representation to "simplify visual processing of imagery and the resulting spatial cognition".

3D Computer Graphics

Three-dimensional computer graphics (3D computer graphics, in contrast to 2D computer graphics) are graphics that use a three-dimensional representation of geometric data (often Cartesian) that is stored in the computer for the purposes of performing calculations and rendering 2D images. Such images may be stored for viewing later or displayed in real-time.

3D computer graphics rely on many of the same algorithms as 2D computer vector graphics in the wire-frame model and 2D computer raster graphics in the final rendered display. In computer graphics software, the distinction between 2D and 3D is occasionally blurred; 2D applications may use 3D techniques to achieve effects such as lighting, and 3D may use 2D rendering techniques.

3D computer graphics are often referred to as 3D models. Apart from the rendered graphic, the model is contained within the graphical data file. However, there are differences: a 3D model is the mathematical representation of any three-dimensional object. A model is not technically a graphic until it is displayed. A model can be displayed visually as a two-dimensional image through a process called 3D rendering or used in non-graphical computer simulations and calculations. With 3D printing, 3D models are similarly rendered into a 3D physical representation of the model, with limitations to how accurate the rendering can match the virtual model.

History

William Fetter was credited with coining the term *computer graphics* in 1961 to describe his work at Boeing. One of the first displays of computer animation was *Futureworld* (1976), which included an animation of a human face and a hand that had originally appeared in the 1972 experimental short *A Computer Animated Hand*, created by University of Utah students Edwin Catmull and Fred Parke.

Overview

3D computer graphics creation falls into three basic phases:

- 3D modeling – the process of forming a computer model of an object's shape

- Layout and animation – the motion and placement of objects within a scene

- 3D rendering – the computer calculations that, based on light placement, surface types, and other qualities, generate the image

Modeling

The model describes the process of forming the shape of an object. The two most common sources of 3D models are those that an artist or engineer originates on the computer with some kind of 3D modeling tool, and models scanned into a computer from real-world objects. Models can also be produced procedurally or via physical simulation. Basically, a 3D model is formed from points called vertices (or vertexes) that define the shape and form polygons. A polygon is an area formed from at least three vertexes (a triangle). A polygon of n points is an n-gon. The overall integrity of the model and its suitability to use in animation depend on the structure of the polygons.

Layout and Animation

Before rendering into an image, objects must be laid out (place) in a scene. This defines spatial relationships between objects, including location and size. Animation refers to the temporal description of an object (i.e., how it moves and deforms over time. Popular methods include keyframing, inverse kinematics, and motion capture). These techniques are often used in combination. As with animation, physical simulation also specifies motion.

Rendering

Rendering converts a model into an image either by simulating light transport to get photo-realistic images, or by applying an art style as in non-photorealistic rendering. The two basic operations in realistic rendering are transport (how much light gets from one place to another) and scattering (how surfaces interact with light). This step is usually performed using 3D computer graphics software or a 3D graphics API. Altering the scene into a suitable form for rendering also involves 3D projection, which displays a three-dimensional image in two dimensions.

Examples of 3D Rendering

Left: A 3D rendering with ray tracing and ambient occlusion using Blender and YafaRay.
Center: A 3d model of a *Dunkerque*-class battleship rendered with flat shading.
2-nd Center: During the 3D rendering step, the number of reflections "light rays" can take, as well as various other attributes, can be tailored to achieve a desired visual effect. Rendered with Cobalt.
Right: Experience Curiosity, a real-time web application which leverages 3D rendering capabilities of browsers (WebGL).

Communities

There are a multitude of websites designed to help, educate and support 3D graphic artists. Some are managed by software developers and content providers, but there are standalone sites as well.

These communities allow for members to seek advice, post tutorials, provide product reviews or post examples of their own work.

Differences with other Types of Computer Graphics

Distinction from Photorealistic 2D Graphics

Not all computer graphics that appear 3D are based on a wireframe model. 2D computer graphics with 3D photorealistic effects are often achieved without wireframe modeling and are sometimes indistinguishable in the final form. Some graphic art software includes filters that can be applied to 2D vector graphics or 2D raster graphics on transparent layers. Visual artists may also copy or visualize 3D effects and manually render photorealistic effects without the use of filters.

Pseudo-3D and *true 3D*

Some video games use restricted projections of three-dimensional environments, such as isometric graphics or virtual cameras with fixed angles, either as a way to improve performance of the game engine, or for stylistic and gameplay concerns. Such games are said to use pseudo-3D graphics. By contrast, games using 3D computer graphics without such restrictions are said to use true 3D.

Virtual Camera System

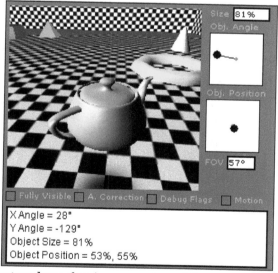

Virtual camera system demo showing parameters of the camera that can be adjusted.

In 3D video games, a virtual camera system aims at controlling a camera or a set of cameras to display a view of a 3D virtual world. Camera systems are used in videogames where their purpose is to show the action at the best possible angle; more generally, they are used in 3D virtual worlds when a third person view is required.

As opposed to film makers, virtual camera system creators have to deal with a world that is interactive and unpredictable. It is not possible to know where the player's character is going to be in the next few seconds; therefore, it is not possible to plan the shots as a film maker would do. To solve this issue, the system relies on certain rules or artificial intelligence to select the most appropriate shots.

There are mainly three types of camera systems. In *fixed camera systems*, the camera does not move at all and the system displays the player's character in a succession of still shots. *Tracking cameras*, on the other hand, follow the character's movements. Finally, *interactive camera systems* are partially automated and allow the player to directly change the view. To implement camera systems, video game developers use techniques such as constraint solvers, artificial intelligence scripts, or autonomous agents.

Third-person View

In video games, "third-person" refers to a graphical perspective rendered from a fixed distance behind and slightly above the player character. This viewpoint allows players to see a more strongly characterized avatar, and is most common in action games and action adventure games. Games with this perspective often make use of positional audio, where the volume of ambient sounds varies depending on the position of the avatar.

There are primarily three types of third-person camera systems: the "fixed camera systems" in which the camera positions are set during the game creation; the "tracking camera systems" in which the camera simply follows the player's character; and the "interactive camera systems" that are under the player's control.

Fixed

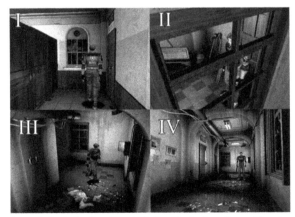
Selection of shots in *Resident Evil 2* that aim at creating tension.

In this kind of system, the developers set the properties of the camera, such as its position, orientation or field of view, during the game creation. The camera views will not change dynamically, so the same place will always be shown under the same set of views. An early example of this kind of camera system can be seen in *Alone in the Dark*. While the characters are in 3D, the background on which they evolve has been pre-rendered. The early *Resident Evil* games are notable examples of games that use fixed cameras. The God of War series of video games is also known for this technique. One advantage of this camera system is that it allows the game designers to use the language of film. Indeed, like filmmakers, they have the possibility to create a mood through camerawork and careful selection of shots. Games that use this kind of technique are often praised for their cinematic qualities.

Tracking

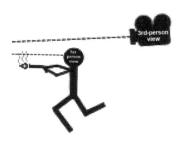

An illustration of a protagonist whom a player controls and a tracking camera just behind, slightly above, and slightly facing down towards that character.

As the name says, a tracking camera follows the characters from behind. The player does not control the camera in any way - he/she cannot for example rotate it or move it to a different position. This type of camera system was very common in early 3D games such as *Crash Bandicoot* or *Tomb Raider* since it is very simple to implement. However, there are a number of issues with it. In particular, if the current view is not suitable (either because it is occluded by an object, or because it is not showing what the player is interested in), it cannot be changed since the player does not control the camera. Sometimes this viewpoint causes difficulty when a character turns or stands face out against a wall. The camera may jerk or end up in awkward positions.

Interactive

Instead of staying behind Mario, the camera intelligently rotates to show the path (Super Mario 64).

This type of camera system is an improvement over the tracking camera system. While the camera is still tracking the character, some of its parameters, such as its orientation or distance to the character, can be changed. On videogame consoles, the camera is often controlled by an analog stick to provide a good accuracy; whereas on PC games it is usually controlled by the mouse. This is the case in games such as *Super Mario Sunshine* or *The Legend of Zelda: The Wind Waker*. Fully interactive camera systems are often difficult to implement in the right way. Thus Gamespot argues that much of the *Super Mario Sunshine'* difficulty comes from having to control the camera. *The Legend of Zelda: The Wind Waker* was more successful at it - IGN called the camera system "so smart that it rarely needs manual correction".

One of the first games to offer an interactive camera system was *Super Mario 64*. The game had two types of camera systems between which the player could switch at any time. The first one was a standard tracking camera system except that it was partly driven by artificial intelligence. Indeed, the system was "aware" of the structure of the level and therefore could anticipate certain shots. For example, in the first level, when the path to the hill is about to turn left, the camera automatically starts looking towards the left too, thus anticipating the player's movements. The second type allows the player to control the camera relatively to Mario's position. By pressing on the left or right buttons, the camera rotates around Mario, while pressing up or down moves the camera closer or away from Mario.

Implementation

There is a large body of research on how to implement a camera system. The role of a constraint solver software is to generate the best possible shot given a set of visual constraints. In other words, the constraint solver is given a requested shot composition such as "show this character and ensure that he covers at least 30 percent of the screen space". The solver will then use various methods to try creating a shot that would satisfy this request. Once a suitable shot is found, the solver outputs the coordinates and rotation of the camera, which can then be used by the graphic engine renderer to display the view.

In some camera systems, if no solution can be found, constraints are relaxed. For example, if the solver cannot generate a shot where the character occupies 30 percent of the screen space, it might ignore the screen space constraint and simply ensure that the character is visible at all. Such methods include zooming out.

Some camera systems use predefined scripts to decide how to select the current shot for commonly seen shot scenarios called film idioms. Typically, the script is going to be triggered as a result of an action. For instance, when the player's character initiates a conversation with another character, the "conversation" script is going to be triggered. This script will contain instructions on how to "shoot" a two-character conversation. Thus the shots will be a combination of, for instance, over the shoulder shots and close-up shots. Such script-based approaches may switch the camera between a set of predefined cameras or rely on a constraint solver to generate the camera coordinates to account for variability in scene layout. This scripted approach and the use of a constraint solver to compute virtual cameras was first proposed by Drucker. Subsequent research demonstrated how a script-based system could automatically switch cameras to view conversations between avatars in a realtime chat application.

Bill Tomlinson used a more original approach to the problem. He devised a system in which the camera is an autonomous agent with its own personality. The style of the shots and their rhythm will be affected by its mood. Thus a happy camera will "cut more frequently, spend more time in close-up shots, move with a bouncy, swooping motion, and brightly illuminate the scene".

While much of the prior work in automated virtual camera control systems has been directed towards reducing the need for a human to manually control the camera, the Director's Lens solution computes and proposes a palette of suggested virtual camera shots leaving the human operator to make the creative shot selection. In computing subsequent suggested virtual camera shots, the system analyzes the visual compositions and editing patterns of prior recorded shots to compute suggested camera shots that conform to continuity conventions such as not crossing the line of action, match placement of virtual characters so they appear to look at one another across cuts, and favors those shots which the human operator had previously used in sequence.

In Mixed-reality Applications

In 2010, the Kinect was released by Microsoft as a 3D scanner/webcam hybrid peripheral device which provides full-body detection of Xbox 360 players and hands-free control of the user interfaces of video games and other software on the console. This was later modified by Oliver Kreylos of University of California, Davis in a series of YouTube videos which showed him combining the Kinect with a PC-based virtual camera. Because the Kinect is capable of detecting a full range of depth (through computer stereo vision and Structured light) within a captured scene, Kreylos demonstrated the capacity of the Kinect and the virtual camera to allow free-viewpoint navigation of the range of depth, although the camera could only allow a video capture of the scene as shown to the front of the Kinect, resulting in fields of black, empty space where the camera was unable to capture video within the field of depth. Later, Kreylos demonstrated a further elaboration on the modification by combining the video streams of two Kinects in order to further enhance the video capture within the view of the virtual camera. Kreylos' developments using the Kinect were covered among the works of others in the Kinect hacking and homebrew community in a New York Times article.

Real-time Recording and Motion Tracking

Virtual cameras have been developed which allow a director to film motion capture and view the digital characters movements in real time in a pre-constructed digital environment, such as a house or spaceship. *Resident Evil 5* was the first video game to use the technology, which was developed for the 2009 film *Avatar*. The use of motion capture to control the position and orientation of a virtual camera enables the operator to intuitively move and aim the virtual camera by simply walking about and turning the virtual camera rig. A virtual camera rig consists of a portable monitor or tablet device, motion sensors, optional support framework, and optional joystick or button controls that are commonly used to start or stop recording and adjust lens properties. In 1992, Michael McKenna of MIT's Media Lab demonstrated the earliest documented virtual camera rig when he fixed a Polhemus magnetic motion sensor and a 3.2 inch portable LCD TV to a wooden ruler. The Walkthrough Project at the University of North Carolina at Chapel Hill produced a number of physical input devices for virtual camera view control including dual three-axis joysticks and a billiard-ball shaped prop known as the UNC Eyeball that featured an embedded six-degree of freedom motion tracker and a digital button.

Parallel Projection

Parallel projections have lines of projection that are parallel both in reality and in the projection plane.

Parallel corresponds to a projection with an infinite focal length (the distance from the image plane to the projection point), or "focal length".

Within parallel projection there is an ancillary category known as "pictorials". Pictorials show an image of an object as viewed from a skew direction in order to reveal all three directions of space in one picture. Because pictorial projections innately contain this distortion, in the rote, drawing instrument for pictorials, some liberties may be taken for economy of effort and best effect.

Orthographic Projection

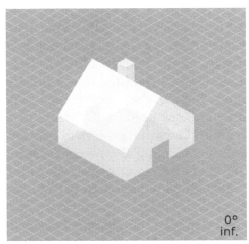

Parallel projection corresponds to a perspective projection with a hypothetical viewpoint; i.e. one where the camera lies an infinite distance away from the object and has an infinite focal length, or "zoom".

The orthographic projection is derived from the principles of descriptive geometry, and is a type of parallel projection where the projection rays are perpendicular to the projection plane. It is the projection type of choice for working drawings.

The term *orthographic* is also sometimes reserved specifically for depictions of objects where the axis or plane of the object is also parallel with the projection plane (paper on which the Orthographic or parallel projection is drawn.

In multiview orthographic projection, up to six pictures of an object are produced, with each projection plane parallel to one of the coordinate axes of the object.

Pictorials

Axonometric Projection

Axonometric projection is a type of parallel projection where the plane or axis of the object depicted is *not* parallel to the projection plane, such that multiple sides of an object are visible in the same image. It is further subdivided into three groups: *isometric, dimetric* and *trimetric projection*, depending on the exact angle at which the view deviates from the orthogonal. A typical characteristic of axonometric pictorials is that one axis of space is usually displayed as vertical.

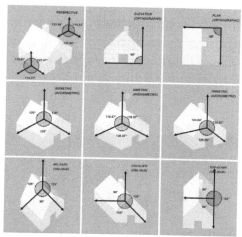

Comparison of several types of graphical projection. The presence of one or more 90° angles is usually a good indication that the perspective is oblique.

Isometric Projection

In isometric pictorials, the most common form of axonometric projection, the direction of viewing is such that the three axes of space appear equally foreshortened. There are two commonly used standards for creating scaled isometric drawings. An accurate drawing of a three-dimensional object projected isometrically would have its axis-parallel edges foreshortened by a factor of $\sqrt{2/3} \approx 81.65\%$, but for convenience this is usually approximated as $\frac{3}{4}$. That is, the length of an edge on a drawing of this type would be $\frac{3}{4}$ of its length on a three-dimensional object. Alternatively, "full-size" isometric drawings may be made in which no foreshortening is shown: the length of an edge on a drawing is the same as its three-dimensional length.

Dimetric Projection

In dimetric pictorials, the direction of viewing is such that two of the three axes of space appear equally foreshortened, of which the attendant scale and angles of presentation are determined according to the angle of viewing; the scale of the third direction (vertical) is determined separately. Approximations are common in dimetric drawings.

Trimetric Projection

In trimetric pictorials, the direction of viewing is such that all of the three axes of space appear unequally foreshortened. The scale along each of the three axes and the angles among them are determined separately as dictated by the angle of viewing. Approximations in trimetric drawings are common, and trimetric perspective is seldom used.

Oblique Projection

In oblique projections the parallel projection rays are not perpendicular to the viewing plane as with orthographic projection, but strike the projection plane at an angle other than ninety degrees. In both orthographic and oblique projection, parallel lines in space appear parallel on the projected image. Because of its simplicity, oblique projection is used exclusively for pictorial purposes rather than for formal, working drawings. In an oblique pictorial *drawing*, the displayed angles among the axes as well as the foreshortening factors (scale) are arbitrary. The distortion created thereby is usually attenuated by aligning one plane of the imaged object to be parallel with the plane of projection thereby creating a true shape, full-size image of the chosen plane. Special types of oblique projections are *military*, *cavalier* and *cabinet projection*.

Limitations

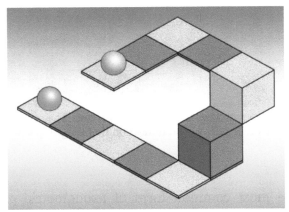

An example of the limitations of isometric projection. The height difference between the red and blue balls cannot be determined locally.

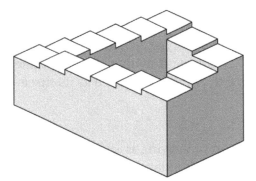

The Penrose stairs depicts a staircase which seems to ascend (anticlockwise) or descend (clockwise) yet forms a continuous loop.

Objects drawn with parallel projection do not appear larger or smaller as they extend closer to or away from the viewer. While advantageous for architectural drawings, where measurements must be taken directly from the image, the result is a perceived distortion, since unlike perspective projection, this is not how our eyes or photography normally work. It also can easily result in situations where depth and altitude are difficult to gauge, as is shown in the illustration to the right.

In this isometric drawing, the blue sphere is two units higher than the red one. However, this difference in elevation is not apparent if one covers the right half of the picture, as the boxes (which serve as clues suggesting height) are then obscured.

This visual ambiguity has been exploited in op art, As well as "impossible object" drawings. M. C. Escher's *Waterfall* (1961), while not strictly using parallel projection, is a well-known example, in which a channel of water seems to travel unaided along a downward path, only to then paradoxically fall once again as it returns to its source. The water thus appears to disobey the law of conservation of energy. An extreme example is depicted in the film *Inception*, where by a forced perspective trick an immobile stairway changes its connectivity.

Isometric Graphics in Video Games and Pixel Art

In video games and pixel art, "isometric" refers to some form of parallel projection (commonly, the form of dimetric projection with a 2:1 pixel ratio) where the viewpoint is rotated slightly to reveal other facets of the game environment than are typically visible from a top-down perspective or side view, thereby producing a three-dimensional effect. In almost all cases, however, the term "isometric" is misapplied; in true isometric projection, the representations of the x, y and z axes are strictly oriented 120° to each other, whereas in other views the angles may vary. The terms "3/4 perspective", "2.5D" and "pseudo-3D" are also commonly used, though these terms can possess alternate meanings as well.

With the advent of more powerful graphics systems, isometric projection is becoming less common, instead being replaced by perspective projection.

Overview

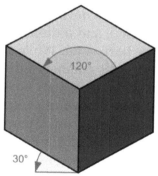

True isometric drawing of a cube. Note the 120° angles separating the x, y and z axes.

A television set drawn in near-isometric 2:1 pixel art. (Enlarged to show the pixel structure.)

In the fields of computer and video games and pixel art, the technique has become popular because of the ease with which 2D sprite- and tile-based graphics can be made to represent a 3D gaming environment. Because parallelly projected objects do not change size as they move about the game field, there is no need for the computer to scale sprites or do the complex calculations necessary to simulate visual perspective. This allowed older 8-bit and 16-bit game systems (and, more recently, handheld and mobile systems) to portray large 3D areas easily. And, while the depth confusion problems of parallel projection can sometimes be a problem, good game design can alleviate this.

Differences with "true" Isometric Projection

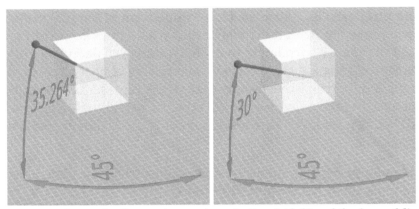

Corresponding camera rotation angles for true isometric projection (at left) and the form of dimetric perspective commonly found in video games and pixel art (at right). 35.264° is equivalent to arctan(sin(45°)).

The projection commonly used in videogames deviates slightly from "true" isometric due to the limitations of raster graphics. Lines in the x and y directions would not follow a neat pixel pattern if drawn in the required 30° to the horizontal. While modern computers can eliminate this problem using anti-aliasing, earlier computer graphics did not support enough colors or possess enough CPU power to accomplish this. So instead, a 2:1 pixel pattern ratio would be used to draw the x and y axis lines, resulting in these axes following a 26.565° (arctan 0.5) angle to the horizontal. (Game systems that do not use square pixels could, however, yield different angles, including true isometric.) Therefore, this form of projection is more accurately described as a variation of dimetric projection, since only two of the three angles between the axes are equal to each other (116.565°, 116.565°, 126.87°).

History of Isometric Video Games

While the history of computer games saw some true 3D games as soon as the early 1970s, the first video games to use the distinct visual style of isometric projection in the meaning described above were arcade games in the early 1980s.

1980s

The use of isometric graphics in video games began with the appearance of Sega's *Zaxxon*, released in January 1982. It is an isometric shooter where the player flies a space plane through scrolling levels. It is also one of the first video games to display shadows.

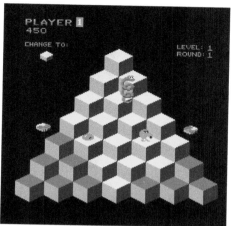

Q*bert from 1982 was one of the first games to use an isometric view.

Another early isometric game is *Q*bert*, which Warren Davis and Jeff Lee began programming in April 1982 and released in October/November 1982. *Q*bert* shows a static pyramid in an isometric perspective, with the player controlling a character which can jump around on the pyramid.

The following year in 1983, the isometric platformer arcade game *Congo Bongo* was released, running on the same hardware as *Zaxxon*. It allows the player character to move around in bigger isometric levels, including true three-dimensional climbing and falling. The same is possible in the 1984 arcade title *Marble Madness*.

At this time, isometric games were no longer exclusive to the arcade market and also entered home computers with the release of *Blue Max* for the Atari 8-bit family and *Ant Attack* for the ZX Spectrum in 1983. In *Ant Attack*, the player could move forward in any direction of the scrolling game, offering complete free movement rather than fixed to one axis as with *Zaxxon*. The views could also be changed around a 90 degrees axis. The *ZX Crash* magazine consequently awarded it 100% in the graphics category for this new technique, known as "Soft Solid 3-D".

A year later the ZX Spectrum saw the release of *Knight Lore*, which is generally regarded as a revolutionary title that defined the subsequent genre of isometric adventure games. Following *Knight Lore*, many isometric titles were seen on home computers – to an extent that it once was regarded as being the second most cloned piece of software after *WordStar*, according to researcher Jan Krikke. Other examples out of those were *Highway Encounter* (1985), *Batman* (1986), *Head Over Heels* (1987) and *La Abadía del Crimen* (1987). Isometric perspective was not limited to arcade/adventure games, though; for example, the 1989 strategy game *Populous* used isometric perspective.

1990s and Beyond

Throughout the 1990s some very successful games like *Civilization II*, *Diablo* and *Fallout* used a fixed isometric perspective. But with the advent of 3D acceleration on personal computers and gaming consoles, games previously using a 2D perspective generally started turning to true 3D instead. This can be seen in the successors to the above games: For instance *Civilization IV* and *Diablo III* both use full 3D; and while *Diablo II* used a fixed perspective like its predecessor, it optionally allowed for perspective scaling of the sprites in the distance to lend it a "pseudo-3D" appearance.

An example of a modern isometric game world.

POV-Ray render mimicking *Fallout*'s trimetric projection and hexagonal grid.

Also during the 1990s, isometric graphics began being used for role-playing video games on console systems, particularly tactical role-playing games, many of which still use isometric graphics today. Examples include *Front Mission* (1995), *Tactics Ogre* (1995) and *Final Fantasy Tactics* (1997)—the latter of which used 3D graphics to create an environment where the player could freely rotate the camera. Other titles such as *Vandal Hearts* (1996) and *Breath of Fire III* (1997) carefully emulated an isometric view, but actually used perspective projection.

Similar Projections

The term is often applied to any game with an—usually fixed—overhead projection that appears at first to be "isometric". These include games that utilize trimetric projection, such as *Fallout* (1997) and *SimCity 4* (2003); games that utilize oblique projection, such as *The Legend of Zelda: A Link to the Past* (1991) and *Ultima Online* (1997); and games that utilize a combination of perspective projection and a bird's eye view, such as *Silent Storm* (2003) and *Torchlight* (2009). There are also titles that utilize polygonal 3D graphics, but still render the graphics to the screen using parallel projection. These include *Syndicate Wars* (1996), *Dungeon Keeper* (1997) and *Depths of Peril* (2007).

Mapping Screen to World Coordinates

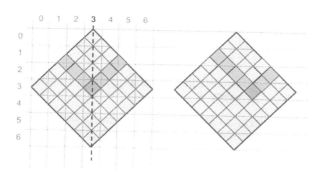

Finding world coordinates

One of the most common problems with programming games that use isometric (or more likely dimetric) projections is the ability to map between events that happen on the 2d plane of the screen and the actual location in the isometric space, called world space. A common example is picking the tile that lies right under the cursor when a user clicks. One such method is using the same rotation matrices that originally produced our isometric view in reverse to turn a point in screen coordinates into a point that would lie on the game board surface before it was rotated. Then, by dividing the x and y values by the tile width and height and rounding down we can derive the world-x and y values. Another way that is less computationally intensive and can have good results if our method is called on every frame, rests on the assumption that we have a square board that was rotated by 45 degrees and then squashed by 0.5 vertically as explained above. We first find the tile clicked on the a virtual grid that is laid on top of our projection as shown on the diagram, we call it virtual-x and virtual-y. As we can observe, clicking any tile on the central axis of the board where (x, y) = (tileMapWidth / 2, y), will produce the same tile value for both world-x and world-y which in our example is 3 (0 indexed). By selecting the tile that lies one position on the right on our virtual grid, we actually move one tile less on the world-y and one tile more on the world-x. We can then derive a formula that calculates world-x by taking the virtual-y and adding the virtual-x from the center of the board. Like wise we can derive world-y by taking virtual-y and subtracting virtual-x. These calculations measure virtual-x from the central axis, as shown, so we must subtract half the board. An example code in C can look like this (provided the variables have the correct values):

```
float virtualTileX = screenx / virtualTileWidth;

float virtualTileY = screeny / virtualTileHeight;

// some display systems have their origin at the bottom left while the tile map at the top left, so we need to reverse y

float inverseTileY = numberOfTilesInY - virtualTileY;

float isoTileX = inverseTileY + (virtualTileX - numberOfTilesInX / 2);

float isoTileY = inverseTileY - (virtualTileY - numberOfTilesInY / 2);
```

This method might seem counter intuitive at first since we are taking the coordinates of a virtual grid rather than the original isometric world and there is no one-to-one correspondence between virtual tiles and isometric tiles. A tile on the grid will contain more than one isometric tiles and depending on where it is clicked it should map to different coordinates. The key in this method is that the virtual coordinates are taken as floating point numbers rather than integers. A virtual-x and y value can be (3.5, 3.5) which means the center of the third tile. In the diagram on the left, we see the 3rd tile on the y in detail. As we can see, when the virtual-x and y can add up to 4 in which case the world x will also be 4.

References

- Arie Kaufman (1993). Rendering, Visualization and Rasterization Hardware. Springer Science & Business Media. pp. 86–87. ISBN 978-3-540-56787-5.

- Drucker, Steven M.; David Zeltzer (1995). "CamDroid: A System for Implementing Intelligent Camera Control" (PDF). Symposium on Interactive 3D Graphics. ISBN 0-89791-736-7. Retrieved 2009-03-22.

- Maynard, Patric (2005). Drawing distinctions: the varieties of graphic expression. Cornell University Press. p. 22. ISBN 0-8014-7280-6.

- Davis, Thomas B.; Nelson, Carl A. (2003), Audel Mechanical Trades Pocket Manual (4th ed.), John Wiley & Sons, p. 65, ISBN 9780764541704 .

- Bakalar, Jeff; Stein, Scott (August 21, 2009). "Shadow Complex: Classic gaming bliss in two-and-a-half dimensions". CNet. Retrieved August 26, 2016.

- Lewinski, John Scott (27 February 2009). "Resident Evil 5 Offers Sneak Peek at Avatar's 'Virtual Camera'". Wired. Retrieved 25 February 2015.

- Wrenn, Eddie (27 August 2009). "Avatar: How James Cameron's 3D film could change the face of cinema forever". Daily Mail. Retrieved 25 February 2015.

- Thompson, Anne (1 January 2010). "How James Cameron's Innovative New 3D Tech Created Avatar". Popular Mechanics. Retrieved 25 February 2015.

- Frederick Brooks, Jr. (June 1992). "Final Technical Report – Walkthrough Project" (PDF). TR92-026. University of North Carolina at Chapel Hill. Retrieved 2015-03-23.

5

Types of Video Games

Based on the manner in which players interact with each other and the virtual environment through gameplay, video games are categorized into action, adventure, role-playing, simulation, strategy and massively multiplayer online video game. This chapter explains each type with suitable examples to aid in a better understanding of the different genres. A part of the chapter focuses on strategy video game and its sub-types. Game design is best understood in confluence with the major topics listed in the following chapter.

Video Game Genre

A video game genre is a classification assigned to a video game based on its gameplay interaction rather than visual or narrative differences. A video game genre is defined by a set of gameplay challenges and are classified independent of their setting or game-world content, unlike other works of fiction such as films or books. For example, a shooter game is still a shooter game, regardless of whether it takes place in a fantasy world or in outer space.

As with nearly all varieties of genre classification, the matter of any individual video game's specific genre is open to personal interpretation. Moreover, each individual game may belong to several genres at once.

History

The first attempt to classify different genres of video games was made by Chris Crawford in his book *The Art of Computer Game Design* in 1984. In this book, Crawford primarily focused on the player's experience and activities required for gameplay. Here, he also stated that "the state of computer game design is changing quickly. We would therefore expect the taxonomy presented [in this book] to become obsolete or inadequate in a short time." Since then, among other genres, the platformer and 3D shooter genres, which hardly existed at the time, have gained a lot of popularity.

Though genres were mostly just interesting for game studies in the 1980s, more money was made in the video game industry in the 1990s and both smaller and independent publishers had little chance of surviving. Because of this, games settled more into set genres that larger publishers and retailers could use for marketing.

Definition

Due to "direct and active participation" of the player, video game genres differ from literary and film genres. Though one could state that *Space Invaders* is a science-fiction video game, such a classification "ignores the differences and similarities which are to be found in the player's experience of the game." In contrast to the visual aesthetics of games, which can vary greatly, it is argued that it is interactivity characteristics that are common to all games. Focusing on these characteristics would allow a more "nuanced, meaningful and critical vocabulary for discussing video games." Regardless, there is little agreement on how game genres are created or classified, resulting in multiple classification schemes.

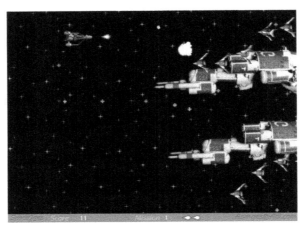

This space-themed video game is a shoot 'em up, or a "side-scrolling shooter."

Descriptive names of genres take into account the goals of the game, the protagonist and even the perspective offered to the player. For example, a first-person shooter is a game that is played from a first-person perspective and involves the practice of shooting. The term "subgenre" may be used to refer to a category within a genre to further specify the genre of the game under discussion. Whereas "shooter game" is a genre name, "first-person shooter" and "third-person shooter" are common subgenres of the shooter genre. Other examples of such prefixes are real-time, turn based, top-down and side-scrolling.

Video games may have aspects that don't fall within the genre the game is classified in. However, Aberrations are tolerated to some degree. For example, one of the weapons in a shooter game might be something other than a gun, which may be seen as a "breach" in the game's rules. If a shooter game *only* featured weapons that aren't guns, it would no longer be accepted as a representative of its genre and the game might fail commercially because of its misleading label.

The target audience, underlying theme or purpose of a game are sometimes used as a genre identifier, such as with "games for girls," "Christian game" and "Serious game" respectively. However, because these terms do not indicate anything about the gameplay of a video game, these are not considered genres.

In Practice

Video game genres vary in specificity, with popular video game reviews using genre names varying from "action" to "baseball." In this practice, basic themes and more fundamental characteristics are used alongside each other.

A game may combine aspects of multiple genres in such a way that it becomes hard to classify under existing genres. For example, because *Grand Theft Auto III* combined shooting, driving and roleplaying in an unusual way, it was hard to classify using existing terms. Since then, the term

Grand Theft Auto clone has been used to describe games mechanically similar to *Grand Theft Auto III*. Similarly, the term Roguelike has been developed for games that share similarities with *Rogue*.

Elements of the role-playing genre, which focuses on storytelling and character improvements, have been implemented in many different genres of video games. This is because the addition of a story to action, strategy or puzzle video games does not take away from the core gameplay, but adds an incentive other than survival to the experience.

Studies

Studying of video game genres as a discipline has only been done to some extent. As a "historical genre," video game genres developed naturally and are therefore uncategorized. According to Lars Konzack of the University of Copenhagen, "One should not expect that [a formal approach] may fully describe the field of video game genres," though "[t]hat is not to say, that no formal approach is unwelcome or discouraged." Furthermore, Konzack states that "with every new video game, video game genres slowly or radically transform," with most games having small changes, but once in a while, a new game comes along to radically change how a specific genre is perceived.

Richard van Eck argues that there are multiple ways for categorizing video game genres in use, one of them being the "popular" genre system used by game publishers and the mainstream gaming press. These are used by players as well to interpret the characteristics of individual games. Another way of defining genres are proposed by designers, who have extended and revised the "popular" genre system. Lastly, van Eck claims that academics in various disciplines have approached the topic in their own way and attempted to create a categorization of video games. Though all of these approaches share the objective of making meaningful distinctions, they differ somewhat in purpose. Where publishers and marketers use genres as a "buzzword" to attract sales, academics might attempt to understand "how the issue of genre fits into digital games as extended from a tradition of print-based writing ... film, and other forms of cultural production."

Action Game

The action game is a video game genre that emphasizes physical challenges, including hand–eye coordination and reaction-time. The genre includes diverse subgenres such as fighting games, shooter games and platform games which are widely considered the most important action games, though some real-time strategy games are also considered to be action games.

In an action game, the player typically controls the avatar of a protagonist. The avatar must navigate a level, collecting objects, avoiding obstacles, and battling enemies with various attacks. At the end of a level or group of levels, the player must often defeat a large boss enemy that is larger and more challenging than other enemies. Enemy attacks and obstacles deplete the avatar's health and lives, and the game is over when the player runs out of lives. Alternatively, the player wins the game by finishing a sequence of levels. But some action games, usually arcade games, are unbeatable and have an indefinite number of levels; and the player's only goal is to maximize their score by collecting objects and defeating enemies.

Defining Elements

The action genre includes any game where the majority of challenges are physical tests of skill. Action games can sometimes incorporate other challenges such as races, puzzles, or collecting objects, but they are not central to the genre. Players may also encounter tactical and exploration challenges, but these games first-and-foremost require high reaction speed and good hand–eye coordination. The player is often under time pressure, and there is not enough time for complex strategic planning. In general, faster action games are more challenging. Action games may sometimes involve puzzle solving, but they are usually quite simple because the player is under immense time pressure.

Game Design

Levels

Players advance through an action game by completing a series of levels. Levels are often grouped by theme, with similar graphics and enemies. Each level involves a variety of challenges, whether dancing in a dance game or shooting things in a shooter, which the player must overcome to win the game. Older games force players to restart a level after dying, although action games evolved to offer saved games and checkpoints to allow the player to restart partway through a level. Increasingly, though, some games allow for 'resurrection' or 'cloning' and the opportunity to regain lost items upon death for a certain sum of ingame currency, typically increasing exponentially the more times the player dies. The obstacles and enemies in a level do not usually vary between play sessions, allowing players to learn by trial and error. However, levels sometimes add an element of randomness, such as an enemy that randomly appears or that takes an unpredictable path.

Levels in an action game may be linear or nonlinear, and sometimes include shortcuts. For levels that require exploration, the player may need to search for a level exit that is hidden or guarded by enemies. Such levels can also contain secrets—hidden or hard-to-reach objects or places that con-tain something valuable. The prize can be a bonus or a non-standard exit that allows a player to access a hidden level, or jump ahead several levels. Action games sometimes offer a teleporter that will cause the player's avatar to re-appear somewhere else in the same level. Levels often make use of locked doors that can only be opened with a specific key found somewhere else in the level.

Action games sometimes make use of time restrictions to increase the challenge. However, game levels typically do not react to time passing, and day/night cycles are rare. When the timer expires, the player typically loses a life, although some games generate a difficult enemy or challenge. If the level is completed with time remaining, this usually adds to the player's score.

Character Abilities

In most action games, the player controls a single avatar as the protagonist. The avatar has the ability to navigate and maneuver, and often collects or manipulates objects. They have a range of defenses and attacks, such as shooting or punching. Many action games make use of a powerful attack that destroys all enemies within a limited range, but this attack is rare.

Players may find a power-up within the game world that grants temporary or permanent improvements to their abilities. For example, the avatar may gain an increase in speed, more powerful attacks, or a temporary shield from attacks. Some action games even allow players to spend upgrade points on the power ups of their choice. In action games, most of the avatar's character development comes from power-ups and new moves, and mental states do not usually change or progress.

Obstacles and Enemies

In action games that involve navigating a space, players will encounter obstacles, traps, and enemies. Enemies typically follow fixed patterns and attack the player, although newer action games may make use of more complex artificial intelligence to pursue the player. Enemies sometimes appears in groups or waves, with enemies increasing in strength and number until the end of the level. Enemies may also appear out of thin air. This can involve an invisible spawn point, or a visible generator which can be destroyed by the player. These points may generate enemies indefinitely, or only up to a certain number. At the end of a level or group of themed levels, players often encounter a boss. This boss enemy will often resemble a larger or more difficult version of a regular enemy. A boss may require a special weapon or attack method, such as striking when the boss opens their mouth or attacking particular part of the Boss.

Health and Lives

In many action games, the avatar has a certain amount of hitmarkers or health, which are depleted by enemy attacks and other hazards. Sometimes health can be replenished by collecting an in-game object. When the player runs out of health, the player dies. The player's avatar is often given a small number of chances to retry after death, typically referred to as lives. Upon beginning a new life, the player resumes the game either from the same location they died, a checkpoint, or the start of the level. Upon starting a new life, the avatar is typically invincible for a few seconds to allow the player to re-orient themselves. Players may earn extra lives by reaching a certain score or by finding an in-game object. Arcade games still limit the number of player lives, while home video games have shifted increasingly to unlimited lives.

Graphics and Interface

Action games take place in either 2D or 3D from a variety of perspectives. 2D action games typically use a side view or top-down view. The screen frequently scrolls as the player explores the level, although many games scroll through the level automatically to push the player forward. In 3D action games, the perspective is usually tied to the avatar from a first-person or third-person perspective. However, some 3D games offer a context-sensitive perspective that is controlled by an artificial intelligence camera. Most of what the player needs to know is contained within a single screen, although action games frequently make use of a heads-up display that display important information such as health or ammunition. Action games sometimes make use of maps which can be accessed during lulls in action, or a mini-map that is always visible.

Scoring and Victory

Action games tend to set simple goals, and reaching them is obvious. A common goal is to defeat the end-of-game boss. This is often presented in the form of a structured story, with a happy ending upon winning the game. In some games, the goal changes as the player reveals more of the story.

Many action games keep track of the player's score. Points are awarded for completing certain challenges, or defeating certain enemies. Skillful play is often rewarded with point multipliers, such as in *Pac-Man* where each ghost that the avatar eats will generate twice as many points as the last. Sometimes action games will offer bonus objects that increase the player's score. There is no penalty for failing to collect them, although these bonus objects may unlock hidden levels or special events. In many action games, achieving a high score is the only goal, and levels increase in difficulty until the player loses. Arcade games are more likely to be unbeatable, as they make their money by forcing the player to lose the game. On the other hand, games sold at home are more likely to have discrete victory conditions, since a publisher wants the player to purchase another game when they are done.

Subgenres

Action games have several major subgenres. However, there are many action games without any clear subgenre, such as *Frogger*, as well as other types of genres like Adventure or Strategy that have action elements.

Beat 'em ups are games that involve fighting through a side-scrolling stage of multiple adversaries, using martial arts or other close-range fighting techniques.

Fighting games feature combat between pairs of fighters, usually using martial arts moves. Actions are limited to various attacks and defenses, and matches end when a fighter's health is reduced to zero. They often make use of special moves and combos. There are both 2D and 3D fighting games, but most 3D fighting games largely take place in a 2D plane and occasionally include side-stepping. They are distinct from sports games such as boxing and wrestling games which attempt to model movements and techniques more realistically.

Maze games such as *Pac-Man* involve navigating a maze to avoid or chase adversaries.

Platform games involve jumping between platforms of different heights, while battling enemies and avoiding obstacles. Physics are often unrealistic, and game levels are often vertically exaggerated. They exist in both 2D and 3D forms.

Rhythm action games challenge the player's sense of rhythm, and award points for accurately pressing certain buttons in sync with a musical beat. This is a relatively new subgenre of action game. Rhythm games are sometimes classified as a type of music game.

Shooter games allow the player to take action at a distance using a ranged weapon, challenging them to aim with accuracy. Although shooting is usually a form of violence, non-violent shooters exist as well. This subgenre includes first-person shooters and third-person shooters, as well as a plethora of other shoot 'em up games taking place from a top-down or side-view perspective.

Physical Impact

Studies have shown that people can improve their eyesight by playing action video games. Tests by scientists at the University of Rochester on college students showed that over a period of a month, performance in eye examinations improved by about 20% in those playing *Unreal Tournament* compared to those playing *Tetris*. Most arcade games are action games, because they can be difficult for unskilled players, and thus make more money quickly.

Researchers from *Helsinki School of Economics* have shown that people playing a *first-person shooter* might secretly enjoy that their character gets killed in the game, although their expressions might show the contrary. The game used in the study was *James Bond 007: Nightfire*.

History

A major turning point for action games came with the 1978 release of the shoot 'em up game *Space Invaders*, which marked the beginning of the golden age of arcade video games. As a result of *Space Invaders'* mainstream success, the industry came to be dominated by action games, which have remained the most dominant genre in video arcades and on game consoles through to the present day. Along with *Space Invaders*, *Asteroids* from 1979 and *Pac-Man* from 1980 have also become iconic examples from the action genre. *Robotron: 2084*, released in arcades in 1982, also became a classic in the shooter subgenre.

In much the same way *Space Invaders* set the template for the shooter game subgenre, *Donkey Kong* did the same for the platform game subgenre when it released in 1981. 1984 saw the emergence of martial arts themed games, with *Karate Champ* establishing the one-on-one fighting game subgenre, and *Kung-Fu Master* laying the foundations for the side-scrolling beat 'em up subgenre.

Subgenres of Action Game

Beat 'em up

Beat 'em up (also known as brawler) is a video game genre featuring hand-to-hand combat between the protagonist and an improbably large number of opponents. These games typically take place in urban settings and feature crime-fighting and revenge-based plots, though some games may employ historical, sci-fi or fantasy themes. Traditional beat 'em ups take place in scrolling, two-dimensional (2D) levels, though some later games feature more open three-dimensional (3D) environments with yet larger numbers of enemies. These games are noted for their simple gameplay, a source of both critical acclaim and derision. Two-player cooperative gameplay and multiple player characters are also hallmarks of the genre.

The first influential beat 'em up was 1984's *Kung-Fu Master*, with 1986's *Renegade* introducing the urban settings and underworld revenge themes employed extensively by later games. The genre then saw a period of high popularity between the release of *Double Dragon* in 1987, which defined the two-player cooperative mode central to classic beat 'em ups, and 1991's *Street Fighter II*, which drew gamers towards one-on-one fighting games. Games such as *Streets of Rage, Final Fight* and *Golden Axe* are other classics to emerge from this period. The genre has been less popular since the emergence of 3D-based mass-market games, but still some beat 'em ups adapted the simple formula to utilize large-scale 3D environments.

Definition

A beat 'em up (sometimes also called "brawlers") is a type of action game where the player character must fight a large number of enemies in unarmed combat or with melee weapons. Gameplay consists of walking through a level, one section at a time, defeating a group of enemies before advancing to the next section; a boss fight normally occurs at the end of each level. However arcade versions of these games are often quite difficult to win, causing players to spend more money to try to win.

Beat 'em ups, such as *Streets of Rage 2*, feature combat against multiple antagonists, often taking place on city streets

Beat 'em ups are related to—but distinct from—fighting games, which are based around one-on-one matches rather than scrolling levels and multiple enemies. Such terminology is loosely applied, however, as some commentators prefer to conflate the two terms. At times, both one-on-one fighting games and scrolling beat 'em ups have influenced each other in terms of graphics and style and can appeal to fans of either genre. Occasionally, a game will feature both kinds of gameplay.

Game Design

Beat 'em up games usually employ vigilante crime fighting and revenge plots with the action taking place on city streets, though historical and fantasy themed games also exist. Players must walk from one end of the game world to the other, and thus each game level will usually scroll horizontally. Some later beat 'em ups dispense with 2D-based scrolling levels, instead allowing the player to roam around larger 3D environments, though they retain the same simple gameplay and control systems. Throughout the level, players may acquire weapons that they can use as well as power-ups that replenish the player's health.

As players walk through the level, they are stopped by groups of enemies who must be defeated before they can continue. The level ends when all the enemies are defeated. Each level contains many identical groups of enemies, making these games notable for their repetition. In beat 'em up games, players often fight a boss—an enemy much stronger than the other enemies—at the end of each level.

Beat 'em ups often allow the player to choose between a selection of protagonists—each with their own strengths, weaknesses, and set of moves. Attacks can include rapid combinations of basic attacks (combos) as well as jumping and grappling attacks. Characters often have their own special attacks, which leads to different strategies depending on which character the player selects. The control system is usually simple to learn, comprising as little as two buttons. These buttons can be combined to pull off combos, as well as jumping and grappling attacks. Since the release of *Double Dragon*, many beat 'em ups have allowed two players to play the game cooperatively—a central aspect to the appeal of these games. Beat 'em ups are more likely to feature cooperative play than other game genres.

History

Origin

The first game to feature fist fighting was Sega's boxing game *Heavyweight Champ* (1976), which is viewed from a side-view perspective like later fighting games. However, it was Data East's fighting game *Karate Champ* (1984) which popularized martial arts themed games. The same year, Irem's Hong Kong cinema-inspired *Kung-Fu Master* (known as *Spartan X* in Japan) laid the foundations for side-scrolling beat 'em ups with its simple gameplay and multiple enemies. Also in 1984, *Bruce Lee* combined multi-player, multi-character combat with traditional collecting, platform and puzzle gameplay. Later that year, *Karateka* combined the one-on-one fight sequences of *Karate Champ* with the freedom of movement in *Kung-Fu Master*, and it successfully experimented with adding plot to its fighting action. It was also among the first beat 'em ups to be successfully ported to home systems. *Nekketsu Kōha Kunio-kun*, released in 1986 in Japan, deviated from the martial arts themes of earlier games and introduced street brawling to the genre. The Western adaptation *Renegade* (released the same year) added an underworld revenge plot that proved more popular with gamers than the principled combat sport of other games. *Renegade* set the standard for future beat 'em up games as it introduced the ability to move both horizontally and vertically. It also introduced the use of combo attacks; in contrast to earlier games, the opponents in *Renegade* and *Double Dragon* could take much more punishment, requiring a succession of punches, with the first hit temporarily immobilizing the enemy, making him unable to defend himself against successive punches.

Golden Age

In 1987, the release of *Double Dragon* ushered in a "Golden Age" for the beat 'em up genre that lasted nearly five years. The game was designed as Technōs Japan's spiritual successor to *Renegade*, but it took the genre to new heights with its detailed set of martial arts attacks and its outstanding two-player cooperative gameplay. *Double Dragon*'s success resulted in a flood of beat 'em ups that came in the late 1980s, where acclaimed titles such as *Golden Axe* and *Final Fight* (both 1989) distinguished themselves from the others. *Final Fight* was Capcom's intended sequel to *Street Fighter* (provisionally titled *Street Fighter '89*), but the company ultimately gave it a new title. In contrast to the simple combo attacks in *Renegade* and *Double Dragon*, the combo attacks in *Final Fight* were much more dynamic. Acclaimed as the best game in the genre, *Final Fight* spawned two sequels and was later ported to other systems. *Final Fight* was also the cause for Capcom to be famous and for Technos Japan's bankruptcy. *Golden Axe* was acclaimed for its visceral hack and slash action and cooperative mode and was influential through its selection of multiple protagonists with distinct fighting styles. It is considered one of the strongest beat 'em up titles for its fantasy elements, distinguishing it from the urban settings seen in other beat 'em ups. Another beat 'em up—*River City Ransom* (1989), named *Street Gangs* in Europe—featured role-playing game elements with which the player's character could be upgraded, using money stolen from defeated enemies.

The *Streets of Rage* series was launched in the early 1990s and borrowed heavily from *Final Fight*. *Streets of Rage 2* for Sega's Mega Drive was notable for being one of the first console games to match the acclaim of arcade beat 'em ups. Its level design was praised for taking traditional beat 'em up settings and stringing them together in novel ways, and its success led to it being ported to arcades. The beat 'em up was also a popular genre for video games based on television series and movies, with *Teenage Mutant Ninja Turtles* a surprise success, and encouraged many more beat 'em up games based on the characters. However, the "golden age" of the genre ended in the wake of the success of Capcom's *Street Fighter II* (1991), which drew gamers back towards one-on-one fighting games, while the subsequent emerging popularity of 3D video games diminished the popularity of 2D-based pugilistic games in general. By the mid-1990s, the genre suffered from a lack of innovation.

32-bit Era Onward

Zeno Clash features beat 'em up gameplay from a first-person perspective

Core Design's *Fighting Force* (1997) was anticipated to redefine the genre for 32-bit consoles through its use of a 3D environment. However, it was met with a lukewarm reception. The *Dynasty Warriors* series, beginning with *Dynasty Warriors 2* in 2000, offered traditional beat 'em up action on large 3D battlefields, displaying dozens of characters on the screen at a time. The series to date spans 14 games (including expansions) which players in the West view as overly similar, although the games' creators claim their large audience in Japan appreciates the subtle differences between the titles. While critics saw *Dynasty Warriors 2* as innovative and technically impressive, they held a mixed opinion of later titles. These later games received praise for simple, enjoyable gameplay but were simultaneously derided as overly simplistic and repetitive. Another best-selling Japanese series, *Yakuza*, combined elaborate plots and detailed interactive environments with street brawling action. Despite these releases, game reviewers started to pronounce that the genre had died off. By 2002, there were virtually no new beat 'em ups being released in arcades.

Capcom's *Viewtiful Joe* (2003) used cel-shaded graphics and innovative gameplay features (such as the protagonist's special powers) to "reinvigorate" its traditional 2D scrolling formula. The Behemoth's *Castle Crashers* (2008) also featured cartoon graphics, quirky humor, and acclaimed cooperative gameplay. Rockstar Games' *The Warriors* (based on the 1979 movie of the same name), released in 2005, featured large scale brawling in 3D environments interspersed with other activities such as chase sequences. The game also featured a more traditional side-scrolling beat 'em up *Armies of the Night* as bonus content, which was acclaimed along with the main game and was later released on the PlayStation Portable. Releases such as *God Hand* in 2006 and *MadWorld* in 2009 were seen as parodies of violence in popular culture, earning both games praise for not taking themselves as seriously as early beat 'em up games. Classic beat 'em ups have been re-released on services such as the Virtual Console; critics reaffirmed the appeal of some, while the appeal of others has been deemed to have diminished with time. Although the genre lacks the same presence it did in the late 1980s, some titles such as *Viewtiful Joe* and *God Hand* kept the genre alive.

Guacamelee is a brawling-based game based on luchadors fashioned after a *Metroid*-style adventure game.

In recent years, the beat 'em up genre has seen a revival in the form of popular 3D hack and slash games in the style of *Devil May Cry* (2001 onwards), including *Ninja Gaiden* (2004 onwards), *God of War* (2005 onwards), *Heavenly Sword* (2007), *Afro Samurai* (2009), and *Bayonetta* (2009). Several traditional 2D scrolling beat 'em ups have also been released in recent years, including *Scott Pilgrim vs. the World: The Game* (2010). The popular *Grand Theft Auto* series also has elements of the beat 'em up genre.

Rhythm Game

Players using a dance mat to play *Dance Dance Revolution*, one of the most successful rhythm games

Rhythm game or rhythm action is a genre of music-themed action video game that challenges a player's sense of rhythm. Games in the genre typically focus on dance or the simulated performance of musical instruments, and require players to press buttons in a sequence dictated on the screen. Doing so causes the game's protagonist or avatar to dance or to play their instrument correctly, which increases the player's score. Many rhythm games include multiplayer modes in which players compete for the highest score or cooperate as a simulated musical ensemble. While conventional control pads may be used as input devices, rhythm games often feature novel game controllers that emulate musical instruments. Certain dance-based games require the player to physically dance on a mat, with pressure-sensitive pads acting as the input device.

The 1996 title *PaRappa the Rapper* has been deemed the first influential rhythm game, whose basic template formed the core of subsequent games in the genre. In 1997, Konami's *Beatmania* sparked an emergent market for rhythm games in Japan. The company's music division, Bemani, released a series of music-based games over the next several years. The most successful of these was the 1998 dance mat game *Dance Dance Revolution*, which was the only Bemani title to achieve large-scale success outside Japan, and would see numerous imitations of the game from other publishers.

Other Japanese games, particularly *Guitar Freaks*, led to development of *Guitar Hero* and *Rock Band* series that used instrument-shaped controllers to mimic the playing of actual instruments. Spurred by the inclusion of popular rock music, the two series revitalized the rhythm genre in the Western Market, significantly expanded the console video game market and its demographics. The games provided a new source of revenue for the artists whose music appeared on the soundtracks. The later release of *Rock Band 3* as well as the even later *Rocksmith* would allow players to play the songs using a real electric guitar. By 2008, rhythm games were considered to be one of the most popular video game genres, behind other action games. However, by 2009, the market was saturated by spin-offs from the core titles, which led to a nearly 50% drop in revenue for music game publishers; within a few years, both series announced they would be taking a hiatus from future titles.

Despite these setbacks, the rhythm game market continues to expand, introducing a number of danced-based games like *Just Dance* and *Dance Central* that incorporate the use of motion controllers and camera-based controls like the Kinect. Existing games also continue to thrive on new business models, such as the reliance on downloadable content to provide songs to players. The introduction of the new generation of console hardware has also spurred return of *Guitar Hero* and *Rock Band* titles in late 2015.

Definition and Game Design

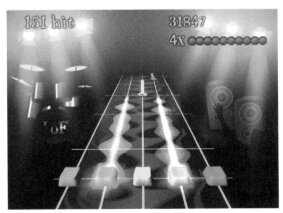

Many rhythm games, such as *Frets on Fire*, use a scrolling "note highway" to display what notes are to be played, along with a score and a performance meter.

Rhythm game, or rhythm action, is a subgenre of action game that challenges a player's sense of rhythm. The genre includes dance games such as *Dance Dance Revolution* and music-based games such as *Donkey Konga* and *Guitar Hero*. Games in the genre challenge the player to press buttons at precise times: the screen shows which button the player is required to press, and the game awards points both for accuracy and for synchronization with the beat. The genre also includes games that measure rhythm and pitch, in order to test a player's singing ability, and games that challenge the player to control their volume by measuring how hard they press each button. While songs can be sight read, players usually practice to master more difficult songs and settings. Certain rhythm games offer a challenge similar to that of Simon says, in that the player must watch, remember, and repeat complex sequences of button-presses. Rhythm-action can take a minigame format with some games blending rhythm with other genres or entirely comprising minigame collections.

In some rhythm games, the screen displays an avatar who performs in reaction to the player's controller inputs. However, these graphical responses are usually in the background, and the avatar is more important to spectators than it is to the player. In single-player modes, the player's avatar competes against a computer-controlled opponent, while multiplayer modes allow two player-controlled avatars to compete head-to-head. The popularity of rhythm games has created a market for speciality input devices. These include controllers that emulate musical instruments, such as guitars, drums, or maracas. A dance mat, for use in dancing games, requires the player to step on pressure-sensitive pads. However, most rhythm games also support more conventional input devices, such as control pads.

History

Origins and Popularity in Japan (1970s–2000)

The rhythm game genre has roots in the electronic game *Simon*, invented in 1978 by Ralph Baer (who created the Magnavox Odyssey) and Howard Morrison. The game originated the "call and response" mechanic used by later rhythm video games, in which players take turns repeating increasingly complicated sequences of button presses. Human Entertainment's *Dance Aerobics* was released in 1987, and allows players to create music by stepping on Nintendo's Power Pad peripheral for the NES video game console. The 1996 title *PaRappa the Rapper* has been credited as the first true rhythm game, and as one of the first music-based games in general. It requires players to press buttons in the order that they appear on the screen, a basic mechanic that formed the core of future rhythm games. The success of *PaRappa the Rapper* sparked the popularity of the music game genre. In 1997, Konami released the DJ-themed rhythm game *Beatmania* in Japanese arcades. Its arcade cabinet features buttons similar to those of a musical keyboard, and a rubber pad that emulates a vinyl record. *Beatmania* was a surprise hit, inspiring Konami's Games and Music Division to change its name to Bemani in honor of the game, and to begin experimenting with other rhythm game concepts. Its successes include *GuitarFreaks*, which features a guitar-shaped controller, and 1998's *Pop'n Music*, a game similar to *Beatmania* in which multiple colorful buttons must be pressed. While the *GuitarFreaks* franchise continues to receive new arcade releases in Japan, it was never strongly marketed outside of the country. This allowed Red Octane and Harmonix to capitalize on the formula in 2005 with the Western-targeted *Guitar Hero*. In general, few Japanese arcade rhythm games were exported abroad because of the cost of producing the peripherals and the resulting increases in retail prices. The 1999 Bemani title *DrumMania* featured a drum kit controller, and could be linked with *GuitarFreaks* for simulated jam sessions. Similarly, this concept was later appropriated by Harmonix for their game *Rock Band*.

Dance Dance Revolution, released in 1998, is a rhythm game in which players dance on pressure-sensitive pads in an order dictated by on-screen instructions. The game was highly successful both in and outside Japan, unlike games such as *GuitarFreaks*, *DrumMania* and *Beatmania*, though the latter had some success in Europe. Released the same year, Enix's *Bust a Groove* features a similar focus on dancing but employs a more conventional input method. The game contains competitive one-on-one battles, and grants the player more freedom than typical rhythm games.

NanaOn-Sha, the creators of *PaRappa the Rapper*, released *Vib-Ribbon* in 1999. It eschews instrument-shaped controllers; instead, players maneuver the protagonist through an obstacle course by pressing buttons at correct times. The game's levels are generated by the background music, which players may change by inserting audio CDs. While it was praised for its unique style and artistry, *Vib-Ribbon*'s simple vector graphics proved difficult to market, and the game was never released in North America. Sega's *Samba de Amigo*, released in arcades in 1999 and on the Dreamcast in 2000, features maraca-shaped, motion sensitive controllers. The game allows for two-player gameplay, provides a spectacle for onlookers and allows players to socialise while gaming. In 2000, *Taiko no Tatsujin* combined traditional Japanese drums with contemporary pop music, and became highly successful in Japanese arcades. The game was later released on consoles in the West as *Taiko Drum Master*, and the franchise continues to receive new installments in Japan. *Gitaroo Man* featured a guitar-playing protagonist four years before the release of *Guitar Hero*, though the game employed a conventional rather than guitar-shaped controller. *Gitaroo Man*'s creator, Keiichi Yano, later created *Osu! Tatakae! Ouendan*, a rhythm game for the Nintendo DS that utilizes the handheld's touchscreen features. It became a highly demanded import title, which led to the release of an altered version of the game in the West—*Elite Beat Agents*—and a sequel in Japan.

Popularity in the West (2001–2004)

Harmonix was formed in 1995 from a computer music group at MIT. Beginning in 1998, the company developed music games inspired by *PaRappa the Rapper*. In 2001, the company released *Frequency*, which puts the player in control of multiple instrument tracks. Ryan Davis of GameSpot wrote that the game provides a greater sense of creative freedom than earlier rhythm titles. *Frequency* was critically acclaimed; however, marketing was made difficult by the game's abstract style, which removed the player's ability to perform for onlookers. In 2003, Harmonix followed up *Frequency* with the similar *Amplitude*. The company later released more socially driven, karaoke-themed music games in *Karaoke Revolution* and *SingStar* (2003 and 2004, respectively). *Donkey Konga*, a GameCube title developed by Namco and released in 2003, achieved widespread success by leveraging Nintendo's *Donkey Kong* brand.

Peripheral-based Games (2005–2013)

In 2005, Harmonix and the small publisher RedOctane released *Guitar Hero*, a game inspired by Bemani's *GuitarFreaks*. However, instead of the Japanese pop that comprises the earlier title's soundtrack, *Guitar Hero* features Western rock music. The game reinvigorated the rhythm genre, which had stagnated because of a flood of *Dance Dance Revolution* sequels and imitations. *Guitar Hero* spawned several sequels, and the franchise overall earned more than $1 billion, with the third installment ranking as the best selling game in North America in 2007. Harmonix followed *Guitar Hero* with the *Rock Band* franchise, which also earned over $1 billion. *Rock Band* titles support multiple instrument controllers and cooperative multiplayer, allowing players to play as a full band. The *Guitar Hero* franchise followed suit with the band-oriented, Neversoft-developed *Guitar Hero World Tour*. *Guitar Hero* installments based on specific bands, such as Metallica and Aerosmith, were also published. Additional songs for *Guitar Hero* and *Rock Band* were made available for purchase via the Internet, which generated further revenue. Artists whose work is featured in the games receive royalties, and the increased publicity in turn generates further sales of their music. The success of the *Guitar Hero* and *Rock Band* franchises widened the console video game market and its demographics, and the popularity of the genre drove increased sales of consoles. In 2008, it was reported that music games had become the second most popular video game genre (behind action) in the United States, with 53% of players being female. At its height in 2008, music games represented about 18% of the video game market.

An impromptu group of *Rock Band 2* players

Video game industry analysts considered 2009 to be a critical year for rhythm games, and they believed that it would allow them to gauge the future success of the genre. Both the *Guitar Hero* and *Rock Band* franchises were expanded, and they received entries for handheld gaming devices and mobile phones. Specialized titles that targeted specific genres and demographics, such as *Band Hero* for pop music and *Lego Rock Band* for younger players, were released. Sales of music games were down in the first half of the year. This decline was attributed to fewer purchases of instrument controllers; it was assumed that players had already bought such controllers and were reusing them. While analysts had expected that United States sales of *Guitar Hero 5* and *The Beatles: Rock Band* would be high—close to or exceeding one million units each in the first month of their release—sales only reached roughly half of those projections. The failure to meet sales projections was partly attributed to the impact of the late-2000s recession on the video game industry; Harmonix's CEO Alex Rigopolis considered that at the time, both *Guitar Hero* and *Rock Band* were the most expensive video games on the market. Analysts also considered it to be a sign of market saturation. Further contributing to the decline was genre stagnation; the franchises retained the same basic gameplay over several iterations, giving consumers less incentive to buy additional titles.

Harmonix CEO Alex Rigopulos felt that the aggressive competition between the *Rock Band* and *Guitar Hero* brands on the belief that the market could only support one franchise also contributed to the decline of these games. As a result, analysts lowered their expectations for future music games; for example, projections of first quarter U.S. sales of *DJ Hero*, a *Guitar Hero* "spin-off", were reduced from 1.6 million units to only 600,000. Sales of rhythm games, which totalled $1.47 billion in 2008, reached only $700 million in 2009. Analysts predicted that the market would settle at the same "healthy" $500–600 million level of the *Call of Duty* series. Wedbush Securities analyst Michael Pachter concluded that the saturation of the rhythm game market accounted for one-third of the industry's 12% sales decline in 2009.

The fallout of the weakening rhythm game market affected game developers, publishers and distributors. Companies in the latter two categories believed that most consumers would own at least one set of instrument controllers by 2010, which would increase the importance of software and downloadable content sales. Activision scaled back its 2010 *Guitar Hero* release schedule to just two games, reducing the number of SKUs from 25 in 2009 to 10 in 2010. The company closed several in-house developers, including RedOctane, Neversoft's *Guitar Hero* division, and Underground Development. Viacom, which had paid Harmonix $150 million following the success of *Rock Band* in 2007, began seeking a "substantial" refund on that investment after weak sales in 2009. Viacom also sought to negotiate new deals with music publishers to reduce the costs of the *Rock Band* series' licensed music. Ultimately, the company began to seek a buyer for Harmonix during the third quarter of 2010.

In 2010, rhythm game developers included new features in their products. For example, *Rock Band 3* and *Power Gig: Rise of the SixString* support guitar controllers with strings, and both contain modes that teach players accurate fingering. Despite this new content, sales of music games faltered in 2010. *Guitar Hero: Warriors of Rock* and *DJ Hero 2* sold only 86,000 and 59,000 copies, respectively, in North America during their first week on the market. This was in sharp contrast to *Guitar Hero III*, which had sold nearly 1.4 million units in its first week in 2008. Through October 2010, music games achieved net sales of around $200 million, one-fifth of the genre's revenue during the same period in 2008. Analysts believed that the market likely would not break $400 million in revenue by the end of the year. End year sales were less than $300 million.

By the end of 2010, the rhythm market was considered "well past its prime", and developers shifted their focus to downloadable content and potential integration with motion control systems. In late 2010, Viacom sold Harmonix to an investment-backed group and allowed it to continue developing *Rock Band* and *Dance Central*. Citing the downturn in rhythm games, Activision shuttered their *Guitar Hero* division in February 2011. Analysts suggested that the market for peripheral-based rhythm games may remain stagnant for three to five years, after which sales could resurge because of digital distribution models or the release of new video game consoles. However, by 2013, the era of peripheral-based music games was considered at an end, as Harmonix announced that it would cease regular updates of *Rock Band* downloadable content on April 2, 2013 as the company shifts to newer games.

Future Directions (2010–present)

With the introduction of motion controllers for the Xbox 360 (Kinect) and the PlayStation 3 (PlayStation Move) in 2010 and 2011, some analysts stated that the rhythm market would resurge thanks to dance- and band-based games that use platform-agnostic controllers. Dance games such as *Just Dance, Dance Central* and *Michael Jackson: The Game* were based on the new motion sensing technology. Industry pundits believe that, because sales of peripheral-based music games are lagging and the popularity of pop music is surging, dance-based games will continue to thrive. Dance games such as *Just Dance* and *Dance Central* boosted the rhythm genre's late-2010 sales; the latter was the top-selling game for the Kinect in North America in November 2010. Both games helped the genre increase its sales by 38% over November 2009, according to NPD. Harmonix is expected to post more than $100 million in profit for 2011 buoyed by sales of *Dance Central* and downloadable content for the game, according to Bloomberg. *Just Dance* overcame a poor critical reception to topple *Call of Duty: Modern Warfare 2's* best-seller status, while *Just Dance 2* (2010) became the best selling non-Nintendo game for the Wii. The *Just Dance* series competed with top action franchises for sales. *Tap Tap Revenge,* the first installment of the iPhone rhythm series *Tap Tap,* was the platform's most downloaded game in 2008. The *Tap Tap* franchise ultimately generated 15 million downloads and received a Guinness World Record as the "most popular iPhone game series".

Over the course of 2014, the phenomenon of indie games produced several variations of the genre. The game Jungle Rumble uses a mechanic where players drum on a touch screen to control the game. Different rhythms correspond with different verbs to control entities in an RTS like environment. The game *Crypt of the NecroDancer* uses a mechanic where the player controls the main character in sync with the soundtrack's beat.

Harmonix returned to its core rhythm games in 2014. In 2014, it successfully funded a Kickstarter to produce a remake of the PS2 title, *Amplitude* for the PlayStation 3 and 4, with release expected in 2015. Further, in March 2015, the company announced *Rock Band 4* to be released later in the same year, with plans to keep the game as a platform with continued free and paid updates and downloadable content, while refocusing on the core social and music enjoyment of the game. Activision also announced *Guitar Hero Live,* slated for late 2015, which rebuilds the game from the ground up, keeping the core mechanics but using a 3-button with dual position controller, and using recorded footage of a rock concert taken from the lead guitarist's perspective to increase immersion.

Health and Education

Rhythm games have been used for health purposes. For example, research has found that dancing games dramatically increase energy expenditure over that of traditional video games, and that they burn more calories than walking on a treadmill. Scientists have further suggested that, due to the large amount of time children spend playing video games and watching television, games that involve physical activity could be used to combat obesity. Studies have found that playing *Dance Dance Revolution* can provide an aerobic workout, in terms of a sufficiently intense heart rate, but not the minimum levels of VO2 max. Based on successful preliminary studies, West Virginia, which has one of the highest rates of obesity and its attendant diseases in the US, introduced *Dance Dance Revolution* into its schools' physical education classes. According to *The New York Times,* more than "several hundred schools in at least 10 states" have used *Dance Dance Revolution* (along with *In the Groove*) in their curricula. Plans have been made to increase the number into the thousands in an effort to mitigate the country's obesity epidemic. Arnold Schwarzenegger, former Governor of California, was a noted proponent of the game's use in schools. In Japan, celebrities reported losing weight after playing *Dance Dance Revolution*, which drove sales of the game's home console version. Bemani's testers also found themselves losing weight while working on the game. There is further anecdotal evidence that these games aid weight loss, though the University of Michigan Health System has cautioned that dance games and other exergames should only be a starting point towards traditional sports, which are more effective. Dance games have also been used in rehabilitation and fall-prevention programs for elderly patients, using customised, slower versions of existing games and mats. Researchers have further experimented with prototypes of games allowing wider and more realistic stepping than the tapping actions found in commercial dance games.

Guitar Hero games have been used alongside physical therapy to help recovering stroke patients, because of the multiple limb coordination that the titles require. Blondie drummer Clem Burke has worked with researchers at the University of Chichester and the University of Gloucestershire to determine how games like *Guitar Hero* can address issues of "child and adult obesity, autism, stroke patients and health and mental well-being in the workplace". Researchers at Johns Hopkins University have used *Guitar Hero III* and its controller to help amputee patients, and to develop new prosthetic limbs for these patients. Researchers at University of Nevada, Reno modified a haptic feedback glove to work with the *Guitar Hero* freeware clone *Frets on Fire*, resulting in *Blind Hero*, a music game for visually impaired players that is played with only touch and audio. MIT students collaborated with the government of Singapore and a professor at the National University of Singapore to create *AudiOdyssey*, a game which allows both blind and sighted gamers to play together. *Guitar Hero* was used as part of a Trent University youth sleep study, which showed that, in general, players who played a song were better at it twelve hours later if that period included normal sleep.

Guitar Hero and *Rock Band* have introduced people to rock music and inspired them to learn how to play the guitar. A study by Youth Music found that 2.5 million out of 12 million children in the United Kingdom have begun learning how to play real instruments after playing music video games such as *Guitar Hero*. The group believes that these video games can be incorporated into music educational programs. Guitar teachers in the US have reported an increase in students who cite *Guitar Hero* as their inspiration to start learning. On the other hand, industry professionals, such the inventor of the Fretlight practice tool, have expressed scepticism over the game's educational value. There is anecdotal evidence that *Guitar Hero* aids rhythm and general hand-coordination, but also that it creates a false preconception of the difficulty of learning guitar, which can lead students to discontinue their studies. Guitar Center conducted a survey which found that a majority of instrument-based rhythm gamers intended to take up a real instrument in the future while a majority of those who were already musicians had been inspired to play their instruments more. Despite such popularity the guitar remains less popular than it was in the 1960s. Some musicians have been critical of *Guitar Hero*'s impact on music education. Jack White of The White Stripes stated that he was disappointed to learn that video games are the most likely venue where younger audiences will be exposed to new works, while Jimmy Page of Led Zeppelin does not believe that people can learn how to play real instruments from their video game counterparts. Similarly, Prince has turned down opportunities to have his music in the *Guitar Hero* series, stating that he felt that it was "more important that kids learn how to actually play the guitar". Other commentators have pointed to drum controllers (including the expanded, lifelike Drum Rocker kit) used in such games as potentially useful in learning and creating music with real drums.

Shooter Game

Shooter games are a subgenre of action game, which often test the player's speed and reaction time. It includes many subgenres that have the commonality of focusing on the actions of the avatar using some sort of weapon. Usually this weapon is a gun, or some other long-range weapon. A common resource found in many shooter games is ammunition. Most commonly, the purpose of a shooter game is to shoot opponents and proceed through missions without the player character being killed or dying.

Characteristics of Shooters

There are many criteria to determine the type of shooter; listed below are some of the major divisions. Using the following, it is possible to categorize almost all shooters developed.

Perspective

In a first-person shooter, the player usually views the events from a camera angle which simulates the character's point of view , while third-person shooters use a camera which follows the character and can often be controlled by the player. It is also possible for a game to have a fixed camera, especially shooting gallery games and some 2D overhead shooters such as *Robotron 2084*.

Realism

Tactical shooters are games that attempt to emulate lifelike ballistics and character damage, one example is *Rainbow Six*. Other shooter games range further away from realism and towards fantasy, like the Sci-Fi action shooting series titled Lost Planet.

Number of Characters

While most shooters are played as solo ventures, several offer the players the opportunity to control a squad of characters, usually directly controlling one, and giving orders to computer-controlled allies. Games which feature non-player characters fighting alongside the player, but which are not directly controllable (either by switching player control, or issuing orders to the character) are not considered squad-based games.

Multiplayer

If a shooter game is playable online, there are several other sharp divisions it can take. Many games will offer differing modes which allow players to choose from among various types, such as the following. In team modes, players are assigned to one of two (sometimes more, but very infrequently) factions which are competing for some goal. Co-op modes have several players on the same faction playing through either single-player or custom missions against computer-controlled enemies. Individual (often called deathmatch or free for all) has all players competing with each other.

Focus

This is often an optional way to categorize a shooter, but in some cases it's needed to help distinguish it. A game may quite often heavily rely on stealth as opposed to direct action. Others might have large horror elements to them. However, the one thing in common with all shooters is that combat with a gun or similar long range/projectile weapon is the primary focus of gameplay itself.

Subgenres

Shoot 'em up

Shoot 'em ups are a specific subgenre of shooters wherein the player may move up and down and left and right around the screen, typically firing straight forward.

Nuclear Throne (2015) is a roguelike shooter with a top-down perspective

Shoot 'em ups share common gameplay, but are often categorized by viewpoint. This includes fixed shooters on fixed screens, such as *Space Invaders* and *Galaxian*; scrolling shooters that mainly scroll in a single direction, such as *Xevious* and *Darius*; top-down shooters (sometimes referred to as twin-stick shooters) where the levels are controlled from an overhead viewpoint, such as *Bosconian* and *Time Pilot*; rail shooters where player movement is automatically guided down a fixed forward-scrolling "rail", such as *Buck Rogers: Planet of Zoom* and *Space Harrier*; and isometric shooters which use an isometric perspective, such as *Zaxxon* and *Viewpoint*. This genre also includes "run and gun" games which emphasize greater maneuvering or even jumping, such as *Thexder*, *Contra* and *Metal Slug*.

Shooting Gallery

Shooting gallery games include light gun games, although many can also be played using a regular joypad and an on-screen cursor to signify where the bullets are being aimed. When these debuted, they were typically played from a first-person perspective, with enemy fire that occurred anywhere on the screen damaging or killing the player. As they evolved away from the use of light guns, the player came to be represented by an on-screen avatar, usually someone on the bottom of the screen, who could move and avoid enemy attacks while returning fire. These sorts of shooters almost always utilize horizontal scrolling to the right to indicate level progression, with enemies appearing in waves from predestined locations in the background or from the sides. One of the earliest examples is the 1985 arcade game *Shootout* produced by Data East.

A specific subgenre of this type of game is the Cabal shooter, named for the game *Cabal*, in which the player controls an on-screen avatar that can run and often jump around the screen in addition to being able to aim their gun. Other games in this subgenre include *Blood Bros.*, *Dynamite Duke*, *NAM-1975*, *Wild Guns*, and *Sin and Punishment*.

As light gun games became more prevalent and started to make use of fully 3D backgrounds, such as the *Time Crisis* or *House of the Dead* series, these sorts of games fell out of popular production, but many like *Blood Bros.* still have their fanbase today. Other notable games of this category include *Operation Wolf* and *Laser Invasion*.

Light Gun Shooter

Light gun shooters are shooting gallery games that use a pointing device for computers and a control device for arcade and video games. The first light guns appeared in the 1930s, following the development of light-sensing vacuum tubes. It was not long before the technology began appearing in arcade shooting games, beginning with the Seeburg Ray-O-Lite in 1936. These early light gun games used small targets (usually moving) onto which a light-sensing tube was mounted; the player used a gun (usually a rifle) that emitted a beam of light when the trigger was pulled. If the beam struck the target, a "hit" was scored. Modern screen-based light guns work on the opposite principle—the sensor is built into the gun itself, and the on-screen target(s) emit light rather than the gun. The first light gun of this type was used on the MIT Whirlwind computer, which used a similar light pen. Like rail shooters, movement is typically limited in light-gun games.

Notable games of this category include the 1974 and 1984 versions of *Wild Gunman*, *Duck Hunt* for the NES, the *Virtua Cop* series, *Time Crisis* series, *House of the Dead* series, and *Resident Evil: The Umbrella Chronicles* & *Darkside Chronicles*.

First-person Shooters

Doom, one of the early games that defined the first-person shooter genre.

First-person shooters are characterized by an on-screen view that simulates the in-game character's point of view. While many rail shooters and light-gun shooters also use a first-person perspective, they are generally not included in this category.

Notable examples of the genre include *Doom*, *Quake*, *Half-Life*, *Counter-Strike*, *GoldenEye 007*, *Battlefield*, *Medal of Honor*, *Unreal*, *Call of Duty*, *Killzone*, *TimeSplitters*, *Team Fortress 2*, and *Halo*.

Third-person Shooters

Third-person shooters are characterized by a third-person camera view that fully displays the player character in his/her surroundings. Notable examples of the genre include the *Tomb Raider* series, *Syphon Filter*, *Max Payne*, *SOCOM*, *Star Wars: Battlefront*, *Resident Evil 4*, *Gears of War*, and *Splatoon*.

Hero Shooters

Hero shooters are a variation of multiplayer first- or third-person arena-based shooters, where players, split among two or more teams, select from pre-designed "hero" characters that each possess unique attributes, skills, weapons, and other activated abilities; players may gain abilities to customize the appearance of these characters, but these changes are cosmetic only and do not alter the game's balance. Hero shooters strongly encourage teamwork between players on a team, guiding players to select effective combinations of hero characters and coordinate the use of hero abilities during a match. Such games are inspired by multiplayer online battle arena games like *Dota 2* and *League of Legends*, and popular team-based shooters like *Team Fortress 2*, and are considered to have strong potential as eSports competitive titles. Examples of hero shooters include *Battleborn, Overwatch, Paladins* and *Quake Champions*.

Tactical Shooters

Tactical shooters are shooters that generally simulate realistic squad-based or man-to-man skirmishes. Notable examples of the genre include Ubisoft's *Tom Clancy's Rainbow Six* and *Ghost Recon* series and Bohemia Software's *Operation Flashpoint*.

Other

Additionally, artillery games have been described as a type of "shooting game", though they are more frequently classified as a type of strategy game.

Controversy

Shooter games have been accused of glorifying and promoting violence and several games have been the cause of notable video game controversies. After school shootings in Erfurt, Emsdetten and Winnenden, German conservative politicians accused violent shooter games, most notably *Counter Strike*, to incite young gamers to run amok. Several attempts were made to banish the so termed "Killerspiele" (killing games) in Germany and the European Union. Shooter games were further criticised when Anders Breivik claimed he used a Call of Duty game to gain target acquisition.

Fighting Game

A fighting game is a video game in which the player controls an on-screen character and engages in close combat with an opponent, which can be either an AI or controlled by another player. The fight matches typically consist of several rounds and take place in an arena, while each character has widely differing abilities but each is relatively viable to choose. Players must master techniques such as blocking, counter-attacking, and chaining attacks together into "combos". Since the early

1990s, most fighting games allow the player to execute special attacks by performing specific input combinations. The fighting game genre is related to but distinct from beat 'em ups, which involve large numbers of enemies against the human player.

The first video game to feature fist fighting was arcade game *Heavyweight Champ* in 1976, but it was *Karate Champ* which popularized one-on-one martial arts games in arcades in 1984. In 1985, *Yie Ar Kung-Fu* featured antagonists with differing fighting styles, while *The Way of the Exploding Fist* further popularized the genre on home systems. In 1987, *Street Fighter* introduced hidden special attacks. In 1991, Capcom's highly successful *Street Fighter II* refined and popularized many of the conventions of the genre. The fighting game subsequently became the preeminent genre for competitive video gaming in the early to mid-1990s, particularly in arcades. This period spawned dozens of other popular fighting games, including successful and long running franchises like *Mortal Kombat, Tekken, The King of Fighters, Virtua Fighter, Guilty Gear, Killer Instinct, Dead or Alive* and *SoulCalibur*.

Definition

Fighting games are a type of action game where on-screen characters fight each other. These games typically feature special moves that are triggered using rapid sequences of carefully timed button presses and joystick movements. Games traditionally show fighters from a side-view, even as the genre has progressed from two-dimensional (2D) to three-dimensional (3D) graphics. *Street Fighter II*, though not the first fighting game, popularized and standardized the conventions of the genre, and similar games released prior to *Street Fighter II* have since been more explicitly classified as fighting games. Fighting games typically involve hand-to-hand combat, but may also feature melee weapons.

This genre is distinct from beat 'em ups, another action genre involving combat, where the player character must fight many weaker enemies at the same time. During the 1980s publications used the terms "fighting game" and "beat 'em up" interchangeably, along with other terms such as "martial arts simulation" (or more specific terms such as "judo simulator"). With hindsight, critics have argued that the two types of game gradually became dichotomous as they evolved, though the two terms may still be conflated. Fighting games are sometimes grouped with games that feature boxing, UFC, or wrestling. Serious boxing games belong more to the sports game genre than the action game genre, as they aim for a more realistic model of boxing techniques, whereas moves in fighting games tend to be highly exaggerated models of Asian martial arts techniques. As such, boxing games, mixed martial arts games, and wrestling games are often described as distinct genres, without comparison to fighting games and belong more into the Sports game genre.

Game Design

Fighting games involve combat between pairs of fighters using highly exaggerated martial arts moves. They typically revolve around primarily brawling or combat sport, though some variations feature weaponry. Games usually display on-screen fighters from a side view, and even 3D fighting games play largely within a 2D plane of motion. Games usually confine characters to moving left and right and jumping, although some games such as *Fatal Fury: King of Fighters* allow players to move between parallel planes of movement. Recent games tend to be rendered in three dimensions and allow side-stepping, but otherwise play like those rendered in two dimensions.

Although *Street Fighter II* was not the first fighting game, it
popularized and established the gameplay conventions of the genre

Aside from moving around a restricted space, fighting games limit the player's actions to different offensive and defensive maneuvers. Players must learn which attacks and defenses are effective against each other, often by trial and error. Blocking is a basic technique that allows a player to defend against attacks. Some games feature more advanced blocking techniques: for example, Capcom's *Street Fighter III* features a move termed "parrying" which causes the attacker to become momentarily incapacitated (a similar state is termed "just defended" in SNK's *Garou: Mark of the Wolves*). In addition to blows such as punches and kicks, players can utilize throwing or "grappling" to circumvent "blocks". Predicting opponents' moves and counter-attacking, known as "countering", is a common element of gameplay. Fighting games also emphasize the difference between the height of blows, ranging from low to jumping attacks. Thus, strategy becomes important as players attempt to predict each other's moves, similar to rock–paper–scissors.

Special Attacks

The player's objective in a fighting game is to win a match by depleting their rival's health.
Mortal Kombat even allows the victor to perform a gruesome finishing maneuver called a "Fatality"

An integral feature of fighting games includes the use of "special attacks", also called "secret moves", that employ complex combinations of button presses to perform a particular move beyond basic punching and kicking. Combos, in which several attacks are chained together using basic punches and kicks, are another common feature in fighting games and have been fundamental to the genre since the release of *Street Fighter II*. Some fighting games display a "combo meter" that displays the player's progress through a combo. The effectiveness of such moves often relate to the difficulty of execution and the degree of risk. These moves are often beyond the ability of a casual gamer and require a player to have both a strong memory and excellent timing. Taunting is another feature of some fighting games and was originally introduced by Japanese company SNK in their game *Art of Fighting*. It is used to add humor to games, but can also have an effect on gameplay such as improving the strength of other attacks. Sometimes, a character can even be noted especially for taunting (for example, Dan Hibiki from *Street Fighter Alpha*).

Matches and Rounds

Fighting game matches generally consist of several rounds (typically "best of three"); the player who wins the most rounds wins the match. Fighting games widely feature life bars, which are depleted as characters sustain blows. Each successful attack will deplete a character's health, and the game continues until a fighter's energy reaches zero. Hence, the main goal is to completely deplete the life bar of one's opponent, thus achieving a "knockout". Beginning with Midway's *Mortal Kombat* released in 1992, the *Mortal Kombat* series introduced "Fatalities" in which the victor kills a knocked-out opponent in a gruesome manner. Games such as *Virtua Fighter* also allow a character to be defeated by forcing them outside of the fighting arena, awarding a "ring-out" to the victor. Round decisions can also be determined by time over (if a timer is present), which judges players based on remaining vitality to declare a winner. Fighting games often include a single player campaign or tournament, where the player must defeat a sequence of several computer-controlled opponents. Winning the tournament often reveals a special story–ending cutscene, and some games also grant access to hidden characters or special features upon victory.

Character Selection

In most fighting games, players may select from a variety of characters who have unique fighting styles and special moves. This became a strong convention for the genre with the release of *Street Fighter II*, and these character choices have led to deeper game strategy and replay value. Although fighting games offer female characters, their image tends to be hypersexualized, and they have even been featured as pin-up girls in game magazines. Male characters in fighting games tend to have extra-broad chests and shoulders, huge muscles, and prominent jaws. Custom creation, or "create–a–fighter", is a feature of some fighting games which allows a player to customize the appearance and move set of their own character. *Super Fire Pro Wrestling X Premium* was the first game to include such a feature, and later fighting games such as *Fighter Maker*, *Soulcalibur III*, *Mortal Kombat: Armageddon*, and *Dragon Ball Z: Budokai Tenkaichi 2* adopted the concept.

Multiplayer Modes

Fighting games may also offer a multiplayer mode in which players fight each other, sometimes by letting a second player challenge the first at any moment during a single player match. A few titles allow up to four players to compete simultaneously. Several games have also featured modes that involve teams of characters; players form "tag teams" to fight matches in which combat is one-on-one, but a character may leave the arena to be replaced by a team mate.

Some fighting games have also offered the challenge of fighting against multiple opponents in succession, testing the player's endurance. Newer titles take advantage of online gaming services, although lag created by slow data transmission can disrupt the split-second timing involved in fighting games. The impact of lag in some fighting games has been reduced by using technology such as GGPO, which keeps the players' games in sync by quickly rolling back to the most recent accurate game state, correcting errors, and then jumping back to the current frame. Games using this technology include *Skullgirls* and *Street Fighter III: 3rd Strike Online Edition*.

History

Late 1970s to 1980s

Fighting games find their origin in boxing games but evolved towards battles between characters with fantastic abilities and complex special maneuvers. Sega's black and white boxing game *Heavyweight Champ*, which was released in 1976, is considered the first video game to feature fist fighting. 1979's *Warrior* is another title sometimes credited as one of the first fighting games. In contrast to *Heavyweight Champ* and most later titles, *Warrior* was based on sword fighting duels and used a bird's eye view. In 1983, Sega released another boxing game *Champion Boxing*, which was Yu Suzuki's debut title at Sega. However, Data East and its related developer Technōs Japan's *Karate Champ* from 1984 is credited with establishing and popularizing the one-on-one fighting game genre. In it, a variety of moves could be performed using the dual-joystick controls, it used a best-of-three matches format like later fighting games, and it featured training bonus stages. It went on to influence Konami's *Yie Ar Kung Fu*, released in January 1985, which expanded on *Karate Champ* by pitting the player against a variety of opponents, each with a unique appearance and fighting style. The player could also perform up to sixteen different moves, including projectile attacks. The martial arts game *The Way of the Exploding Fist*, released in June 1985, achieved critical success and subsequently afforded the burgeoning genre further popularity on home systems. Numerous other game developers tried to imitate the financial successes of *Karate Champ, Yie Ar Kung-Fu* and *The Way of the Exploding Fist* with similar games; Data East took unsuccessful legal action against Epyx over the computer game *International Karate*. Also in 1985, Elite's *Frank Bruno's Boxing* introduced high and low guard, ducking, lateral dodging, and a meter which was built up with successful attacks, and when full enabled a special, more powerful punch, to be thrown.

Both *Karate Champ* and *Yie Ar Kung Fu* later provided a template for Capcom's *Street Fighter* in 1987. *Street Fighter* found its own niche in the gaming world, partially because many arcade game developers in the 1980s focused more on producing beat-em-ups and shoot 'em ups. Part of the game's appeal was the use of special moves that could only be discovered by experimenting with the game controls, which created a sense of mystique and invited players to practice the game, although similar controller motions used for grappling maneuvers in the earlier *Brian Jacks Uchi Mata* were deemed too difficult. Following *Street Fighter's* lead, the use of command-based hidden moves began to pervade other games in the rising fighting game genre. *Street Fighter* also introduced other staples of the genre, including the blocking technique as well as the ability for a challenger to jump in and initiate a match against a player at any time. The game also introduced pressure-sensitive controls that determine the strength of an attack, though due to causing damaged arcade cabinets, Capcom replaced it soon after with a six-button control scheme offering light, medium and hard punches and kicks, which became another staple of the genre. In 1988, Home Data released *Reikai Dōshi: Chinese Exorcist*, also known as *Last Apostle Puppet Show*, the first fighting game to use digitized sprites and motion capture animation. Meanwhile, home game consoles largely ignored the genre. *Budokan: The Martial Spirit* was one of few releases for the Sega Genesis but was not as popular as games in other genres. Technical challenges limited the popularity of early fighting games. Programmers had difficulty producing a game that could recognize the fast motions of a joystick, and so players had difficulty executing special moves with any accuracy.

Early 1990s

The release of *Street Fighter II* in 1991 is often considered a revolutionary moment in the fighting game genre. Yoshiki Okamoto's team developed the most accurate joystick and button scanning routine in the genre thus far. This allowed players to reliably execute multi-button special moves, which had previously required an element of luck. The game was also highly successful because its graphics took advantage of Capcom's CPS arcade chipset, with highly detailed characters and stages. Whereas previous games allowed players to combat a variety of computer-controlled fighters, *Street Fighter II* allowed players to play against each other. The popularity of *Street Fighter II* surprised the gaming industry, as arcade owners bought more machines to keep up with demand. *Street Fighter II* was also responsible for popularizing the combo mechanic, which came about when skilled players learned that they could combine several attacks that left no time for the opponent to recover if they timed them correctly.

SNK released *Fatal Fury* a few months before *Street Fighter II*. It was designed by Takashi Nishiyama, the creator of the original *Street Fighter*, which it was envisioned as a spiritual successor to. *Fatal Fury* placed more emphasis on storytelling and the timing of special moves, and added a two-plane system where characters could step into the foreground or background. Meanwhile, Sega experimented with *Dark Edge*, an early attempt at a 3D fighting game where characters could move in all directions. Sega however, never released the game outside Japan because it felt that "unrestrained" 3D fighting games were unenjoyable. Sega also attempted to introduced 3-D holographic technology to the genre with *Holosseum* in 1992, though it was unsuccessful. Several fighting games achieved greater commercial success, including SNK's *Art of Fighting* and *Samurai Shodown* as well as Sega's *Eternal Champions*. Nevertheless, *Street Fighter II* remained the most popular, spawning a special *Champion Edition* that improved game balance and allowed players to use additional characters. The popularity of *Street Fighter II* led it to be released for home game consoles and allowed it to define the template for fighting games. Fighting games soon became the dominant genre in the arcade game industry of the early 1990s.

Many American developers tried to capitalize on the template established by *Street Fighter II*, but it was Chicago's Midway Games who achieved unprecedented notoriety when they released *Mortal Kombat* in 1992. The game featured digital characters drawn from real actors, numerous secrets, and a "Fatality" system of finishing maneuvers with which the player's character kills their opponent. The game earned a reputation for its gratuitous violence, and was eventually adapted for home game consoles. The home version of *Mortal Kombat* was released on September 13, 1993, a day that was promoted as "Mortal Monday". The advertising resulted in line-ups to purchase the game and a subsequent backlash from politicians concerned about the game's violence. The *Mortal Kombat* franchise would ultimately achieve iconic status similar to that of *Street Fighter* with several sequels as well as movies, television series, and extensive merchandising. Numerous other game developers tried to imitate *Street Fighter II* and *Mortal Kombat*'s financial success with similar games; Capcom USA took unsuccessful legal action against Data East over the 1993 arcade game *Fighter's History*. Data East's largest objection in court was that their 1984 arcade game *Karate Champ* was the true originator of the competitive fighting game genre, which predated the original *Street Fighter* by three years.

Sega AM2's first attempt in the genre was the 1993 arcade game *Burning Rival*, but began to attract attention with the release of *Virtua Fighter* for the same platform the same year. It was the first fighting game with 3D polygon graphics and a viewpoint that zoomed and rotated with the action. Despite the graphics, players were confined to back and forth motion as seen in other fighting games. With only three buttons, it was easier to learn than *Street Fighter* and *Mortal Kombat*, having six and five buttons respectively. By the time the game was released for the Sega Saturn in Japan, the game and system were selling at almost a one-to-one ratio. Meanwhile, the 1993 title *Mortal Kombat II* captivated Western audiences, and a 2008 review considered the best *Mortal Kombat* game in retrospect.

Virtua Fighter is rendered in 3D, but is typical of most fighting games in
that most action takes place in a 2D plane of motion. Here, one player ducks the other's attack.

The 1994 PlayStation launch title *Battle Arena Toshinden* is credited for taking the genre into "true 3-D" due to its introduction of the sidestep maneuver, which IGN described as "one little move" that "changed the fighter forever." The same year, SNK released *The King of Fighters '94* in arcades, where players choose from teams of three characters to eliminate each other one by one. Eventually, Capcom released further updates to *Street Fighter II*, including *Super Street Fighter II* and *Super Street Fighter II Turbo*. These games featured more characters and new moves, some of which were a response to people who had hacked the original *Street Fighter II* game to add new features themselves. However, criticism of these updates grew as players demanded a true sequel. By 1995, the dominant franchises were the *Mortal Kombat* series in America and *Virtua Fighter* series in Japan, with *Street Fighter Alpha: Warriors' Dreams* unable to match the popularity of *Street Fighter II*. Throughout this period, the fighting game was the dominant genre in competitive video gaming, with enthusiasts popularly attending arcades in order to find human opponents.

Late 1990s

In the latter part of the 1990s, the fighting game genre began to decline in popularity, with specific franchises falling into difficulty. *Electronic Gaming Monthly* awarded the excess of fighting games the "Most Appalling Trend" award of 1995. Although the release of *Street Fighter EX* introduced 3D graphics to the series and continued the success of *Street Fighter II* and *Street Fighter Alpha*, the *Street Fighter: The Movie* arcade game was regarded as a failure. *Street Fighter: The Movie* used digitized images from the *Street Fighter* film. While a home video game also titled *Street Fighter: The Movie* was released for the PlayStation and Sega Saturn, it is not a port but a separately produced game based on the same premise. Capcom later released *Street Fighter III* in 1997 which featured improved visuals and character depth, but was also unable to match the impact of *Street Fighter II*. Despite excitement in Japan over *Virtua Fighter 3* in arcades, the limited hardware capabilities of the Sega Saturn led Sega to delay a console release. Sega eventually released the game for its Dreamcast console, but the company became unprofitable and was forced to discontinue the console. Meanwhile, SNK released several fighting games on their Neo-Geo platform, including *Samurai Shodown II* in 1994, *Real Bout Fatal Fury* in 1995, *The Last Blade* in 1997, and annual updates to their *The King of Fighters* franchise. *Garou: Mark of the Wolves* from 1999 was considered one of SNK's last great games, and the company announced that it would close its doors in 2001.

In retrospect, multiple developers attribute the decline of the fighting genre to its increasing complexity and specialization. This complexity shut out casual players, and the market for fighting games became smaller and more specialized. Furthermore, arcades gradually became less profitable throughout the 1990s due to the increased technical power and popularity of home consoles. Even as popularity dwindled, the fighting game genre continued to evolve; several strong 3D fighting games also emerged in the late 1990s. Namco's *Tekken* (released in arcades in 1994 and on the PlayStation in 1995) proved critical to the PlayStation's early success, with its sequels also becoming some of the console's most important titles. The *Soul* series of weapon-based fighting games also achieved considerable critical success, beginning with 1995's *Soul Edge* (known as *Soul Blade* outside Japan) to *Soulcalibur V* in 2012. Tecmo released *Dead or Alive* in Japanese arcades in 1996, porting it for the PlayStation in 1998. It spawned a long running franchise, known for its fast paced control system and innovative counterattacks. The series again included titles important to the success of their respective consoles, including *Dead or Alive 4* for the Xbox 360. In 1998, *Bushido Blade*, published by Square, introduced a realistic fighting engine that featured three-dimensional environments while abandoning time limits and health bars in favour of an innovative Body Damage System, where a sword strike to a certain body part can amputate a limb or decapitate the head.

Video game enthusiasts took an interest in gaming crossovers which feature characters from multiple franchises in a particular game. An early example of this type of fighting game was the 1998 arcade release *Marvel vs. Capcom: Clash of Super Heroes*, featuring comic book superheroes as well as characters from other Capcom games. In 1999, Nintendo released the first game in the *Super Smash Bros.* series, which allowed match-ups such as Pikachu versus Mario.

Early 2000s

The early part of the decade saw the rise of major international fighting game tournaments such as Tougeki – Super Battle Opera and Evolution Championship Series, and famous players such as Daigo Umehara. Several more fighting game crossovers were released in the new millennium. The two most prolific developers of 2D fighting games, Capcom and SNK, combined intellectual property to produce *SNK vs. Capcom* games. SNK released the first game of this type, *SNK vs. Capcom: The Match of the Millennium,* for its Neo Geo Pocket Color handheld at the end of 1999. GameSpot regarded the game as "perhaps the most highly anticipated fighter ever" and called it the best fighting game ever to be released for a handheld console. Capcom released *Capcom vs. SNK: Millennium Fight 2000* for arcades and the Dreamcast in 2000, followed by sequels in subsequent years. Though none matched the critical success of the handheld version, *Capcom vs. SNK 2 EO* was noted as the first game of the genre to successfully utilize internet competition. Other crossovers from 2008 included *Tatsunoko vs. Capcom* and *Mortal Kombat vs. DC Universe.* The most successful crossover, however, was *Super Smash Bros. Brawl,* also released in 2008 for the Wii. Featuring characters from Nintendo's various franchises, the game was a runaway commercial success in addition to being lavished with critical praise.

In the new millennium, fighting games became less popular and plentiful than in the mid-1990s, with multiplayer competition shifting towards other genres. However, SNK reappeared in 2003 as SNK Playmore and continued to release games. Arc System Works received critical acclaim for releasing *Guilty Gear X* in 2001, as well as its sequel *Guilty Gear XX*, as both were 2D fighting games featuring striking anime inspired graphics. The fighting game is currently a popular genre for amateur and doujin developers in Japan. The 2002 title *Melty Blood* was developed by then amateur developer French-Bread and achieved cult success on the PC. It became highly popular in arcades following its 2005 release, and a version was released for the PlayStation 2 the following year. While the genre became generally far less popular than it once was, arcades and their attendant fighting games remained reasonably popular in Japan in this time period, and still remain so even today. *Virtua Fighter 5* lacked an online mode but still achieved success both on home consoles and in arcades; players practiced at home and went to arcades to compete face-to-face with opponents. In addition to *Virtua Fighter* and *Tekken*, the *Soul* and *Dead or Alive* franchises continued to release installments. Classic *Street Fighter* and *Mortal Kombat* games were re-released on PlayStation Network and Xbox Live Arcade, allowing internet play, and in some cases, HD graphics.

Late 2000s to Present

Street Fighter IV, the series' first mainline title since *Street Fighter III: 3rd Strike* in 1999, was released in early 2009 to critical acclaim, having garnered praise since its release at Japanese arcades in 2008. The console versions of the game as well as *Super Street Fighter IV* sold more than 6 million copies in total. *Street Fighter's* successful revival sparked a renaissance for the genre, introducing new players to the genre and with the increased audience allowing other fighting game franchises to achieve successful revivals of their own, as well as increasing tournament participance. *Tekken 6* was positively received, selling more than 3 million copies worldwide as of August 6, 2010. Other successful titles that followed include *Mortal Kombat 9, Marvel vs. Capcom 3, The King of Fighters XIII, Dead or Alive 5, BlazBlue: Calamity Trig-*

ger, Persona 4 Arena, Street Fighter X Tekken, Tekken Tag Tournament 2, SoulCalibur V and *Guilty Gear Xrd.* Despite the critically acclaimed *Virtua Fighter 5* releasing to very little fanfare in 2007, its update *Virtua Fighter 5: Final Showdown* received much more attention due to the renewed interest in the genre. Numerous indie fighting games have also been crowdfunded on websites such as Kickstarter and Indiegogo, the most notable success being *Skullgirls* in 2012.

Visitors playing the crossover game *Street Fighter X Tekken* at the E3 2011

Platform Game

Platform game (or platformer) is a video game which involves guiding an avatar to jump between suspended platforms and/or over obstacles to advance the game. These challenges are known as jumping puzzles or freerunning. The player controls the jumps to avoid letting the avatar fall from platforms or miss necessary jumps. The most common unifying element of games of this genre is the jump button, but now there are other alternative like swiping in touchscreen. *Jumping*, in this genre, may include swinging from extendable arms, as in *Ristar* or *Bionic Commando*, or bouncing from springboards or trampolines, as in *Alpha Waves*. These mechanics, even in the context of other genres, are commonly called *platforming*, a verbification of *platform*. Games where jumping is automated completely, such as 3D games in *The Legend of Zelda* series, fall outside of the genre.

Platform games originated in the early 1980s, with 3D successors popularized in the mid-1990s. The term itself describes games where jumping on platforms is an integral part of the gameplay and came into use after the genre had been established, no later than 1983. It is not a pure genre; it is frequently coupled with elements of other genres, such as the shooter elements in *Contra*, the adventure elements of *Flashback*, or the role-playing game elements of *Castlevania: Symphony of the Night*.

While commonly associated with console gaming, there have been many important platform games released to video arcades, as well as for handheld game consoles and home computers. North

America, Europe and Japan have played major parts in the genre's evolution. Platform themes range from cartoon-like games to science fiction and fantasy epics.

At one point, platform games were the most popular genre of video game. At the peak of their popularity, it is estimated that between one-quarter and one-third of console games were platformers. No genre either before or since has been able to achieve a similar market share. As of 2006, the genre had become far less dominant, representing a two percentage market share as compared to fifteen percent in 1998, but is still commercially viable, with a number of games selling in the millions of units. Since 2010, a variety of endless running platformers for mobile devices have brought renewed popularity to the genre.

History

Single Screen Movement

Platform games originated in the early 1980s. Because of the technical limitations of the day, early examples were confined to a static playing field, generally viewed in profile. *Space Panic*, a 1980 arcade release by Universal, is sometimes credited as being the first platform game, though the distinction is contentious. While the player had the ability to fall, there was no ability to jump, swing, or bounce, so the game does not satisfy most modern definitions of the genre. However, it clearly influenced the genre, with gameplay centered on climbing ladders between different floors, a common element in many early platform games. Another precursor to the genre released that same year was Nichibutsu's *Crazy Climber*, which revolved around the concept of climbing buildings.

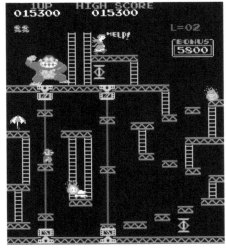

A *Donkey Kong* (1981) level demonstrates extensive jumping between platforms, the genre's defining trait.

Donkey Kong, an arcade game created by Nintendo and released in July 1981, was the first game that allowed players to jump over obstacles and across gaps, making it the first true platformer. *Donkey Kong* had a limited amount of platforming in its first two screens, but its last two screens had a more pronounced platform jumping component. This game also introduced Mario, a modern icon of the genre, under the name Jumpman. *Donkey Kong* was ported to many consoles and computers at the time, and the title helped to cement Nintendo's position as an important name in the video game industry internationally.

The following year, *Donkey Kong* received a sequel, *Donkey Kong Jr.*. The third game in the series, *Donkey Kong 3*, was not a platformer, but it was succeeded by *Mario Bros*, a platform game that offered two-player simultaneous cooperative play. This title laid the groundwork for other popular two-player cooperative platformers such as *Fairyland Story* and *Bubble Bobble*, which in turn influenced many of the single-screen platformers that would follow.

Beginning in 1982, transitional games emerged that did not feature scrolling graphics, but had levels that spanned several connected screens. *Pitfall!*, released for the Atari 2600, featured broad, horizontally extended levels. It became one of the best-selling games on the system and was a breakthrough for the genre. *Smurf: Rescue in Gargamel's Castle* was released on the ColecoVision that same year, adding uneven terrain and scrolling pans between static screens. *Manic Miner* (1983) and its sequel *Jet Set Willy* (1984) continued this style of multi-screen levels on home computers. *Wanted: Monty Mole* won the first ever award for Best Platform game in 1984. Later that same year, Epyx released *Impossible Mission*, which further expanded on the exploration aspect and laid the groundwork for such games as *Prince of Persia*.

Classification of Early Platformers

The term *platform game* is somewhat ambiguous, particularly when referring to games that pre-date the widespread, international use of the term. The concept of a platform game as it was defined in its earliest days is somewhat different from how the term is commonly used today.

Beginning with *Space Panic*, a genre of games emerged characterized by a profile view and a game field consisting of a number of tiers connected by ladders. These included *Donkey Kong*, *Canyon Climber*, *Miner 2049er*, and *Lode Runner*. The two most common gameplay goals were to get to the top of the screen, and to collect all of a particular item. By 1983 press in the UK began referring to these tiers as "platforms" and started calling these titles "platform games" not long after. The North American press, including Electronic Games Magazine, labeled the genre "climbing games."

The term "platform game" has since gained wide use in North America, and across Europe, and since the earliest uses the concept has evolved, particularly as the genre peaked in popularity during the latter half of the 1980s. Many of the games that were part of the early platform genre, such as *Donkey Kong* and *Miner 2049er*, are still regarded as platform games in the modern sense.

Scrolling Movement

The first platform game to use scrolling graphics came years before the genre became a trend. *Jump Bug* is a simple platform-shooter developed by Alpha Denshi under contract for Hoei/Core-land and released to arcades in 1981, only five months after *Donkey Kong*. Players control a bouncing car that jumps on various platforms such as buildings, clouds, and hills. As part of a nascent genre, its development was not strongly influenced by existing conventions, nor was it said to be a major influence on games immediately after it. *Jump Bug* offered an early glimpse of what was to come, with uneven, independently suspended platforms and levels that scroll both horizontally and vertically. This style of gameplay was further refined in the arcades by such games as 1983's Major Havoc.

Home consoles of US early 1980s generally lack hardware support for background scrolling — except for the Atari 2600 (with only vertical scrolling), Atari 5200 and Emerson Arcadia 2001, and notwithstanding Japan's Famicom. This makes it very difficult to produce a smooth scrolling effect on a console. Nevertheless, Sydney Development released *B.C.'s Quest For Tires* in 1983 on the ColecoVision and several home computer platforms. The game features large, smooth-scrolling levels and simplistic platform gameplay in which players jump over oncoming pitfalls and obstacles, much like *Moon Patrol*. Not long after this, a scrolling platform game appeared on the *Commodore 64* and Atari 800 computers called *Snokie*. It began to bridge the gap between these earlier scrolling arcade-style games and implements a more mature vision of the genre, with uneven terrain and an emphasis on precision jumping.

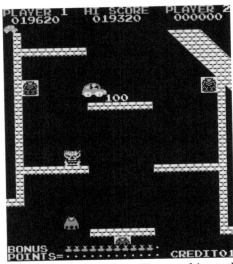

Jump Bug (1981) introduced scrolling graphics to the genre.

Namco took the scrolling platformer a step further with the 1984 release *Pac-Land*. *Pac-Land* was an evolution of earlier platform games that had more than simple hurdle jumping game like some of its predecessors. It was not only a very successful title that was later ported to many consoles, it resembled later scrolling platformers like *Wonder Boy* and *Super Mario Bros* and was probably a direct influence on them. It even had multi-layered parallax scrolling, an effect that would become much more common during the second generation of scrollers.

1984 continued to be a big year for scrolling platformers. Taito released *Legend of Kage*, which offered levels that extended both horizontally and vertically. Sega released *Flicky*, a simple platformer with horizontally scrolling levels that featured the company's first mascot character. Namco followed up *Pac-Land* with the fantasy-themed *Dragon Buster*, a game notable for introducing the hub level system similar to ones used in later two-dimensional (2D) *Super Mario* games. By the end of the year, the scrolling platform game was firmly established, but it was not until such games made their way to home consoles that the genre would be propelled to a new level of mainstream popularity.

Nintendo's platform game *Super Mario Bros.*, released for the Nintendo Entertainment System in 1985, became the archetype for many platformers to follow. The title was bundled with Nintendo systems in North America, Japan, and Europe, and went on to sell over 40 million copies, according to the 1999 Guinness Book of World Records. Its success as a pack-in led many companies to see platform games as vital to their success, and contributed greatly to popularizing the genre during the 8-bit console generation.

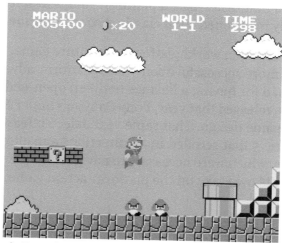

Super Mario Bros. (1985), one of the best selling video games of all time

Sega attempted to emulate this success with their *Alex Kidd* series, which began in 1986 on the Master System with *Alex Kidd in Miracle World*. It's a platformer that features horizontal and vertical scrolling levels, the ability to punch enemies and obstacles, and shops where the player can buy power-ups and vehicles. Some of the bosses are fought through a minigame of rock-paper-scissors where others you have to fight or crash the Sukopako "motorbike" into a pirate bear. The environments are varied, including mountains, caves, oceans, forests, and underwater segments. Another Sega platformer series that began that same year is *Wonder Boy*. The original *Wonder Boy* in 1986 was inspired more by *Pac-Land* than *Super Mario Bros*, and features skateboarding segments that gives the game a greater sense of speed than other platformers at the time, while its sequel, *Wonder Boy in Monster Land*, takes the series in a new direction by combining action-adventure and action role-playing elements with traditional platforming. *Wonder Boy* in turn inspired platformers such as *Adventure Island, Dynastic Hero, Popful Mail*, and *Shantae*.

Platformers went portable in the late 1980s with games such as *Super Mario Land*, and the genre continued to maintain its popularity, with many titles released for the handheld Game Boy and Game Gear systems. Because of their small size, technical constraints, and blurring associated with early LCD technology, fast paced action-based platformers are more difficult to develop for these handheld systems. Because of this, many handheld platformers lean toward slower-paced play styles and a greater emphasis on puzzles. After the transition of home consoles to three-dimensional (3D) displays, handhelds became a bastion for 2D platform games, where they remain popular. *New Super Mario Bros.* (2006) is a very successful traditional platform game, selling more than five million copies in Japan and North America during its first year of release.

On the stock Nintendo Entertainment System (NES), as well as on most 8-bit arcade hardware, platform games generally only scroll in one direction at a time, usually horizontally. This means designers must use a very narrow level progression, or break levels up into subareas that scrolled either horizontally or vertically, as was the case in *Metroid* and *Mega Man* — or effectively upgrade the system using memory management controller chips, embedded into each relevant cartridge. One of the first platform games to scroll in all four directions freely and follow the on-screen character's movement is in a vector game called *Major Havoc*, which comprises a number of mini-games, including a simple platformer, a shoot 'em up sequence, a landing sequence, and a *Breakout* clone. One of the first raster-based platform games to scroll fluidly in all directions in this manner is the previously mentioned 1984 classic, *Legend of Kage*.

In 1985, Enix released an early open world platform-adventure game, *Brain Breaker*. The following year saw the release of a more successful open-world platform-adventure, Nintendo's *Metroid*, which was critically acclaimed for having a balance between open-ended and guided exploration. Another platform-adventure released that year, Pony Canyon's *Super Pitfall*, was critically panned for its vagueness and weak game design. That same year Jaleco released *Esper Boukentai*, a plat-form-action sequel to *Psychic 5* that scrolled in all directions and allowed the player character to make huge multistory jumps, which were necessary to navigate the giant, vertically oriented levels. Telenet Japan also released its own take on the platform-action game, *Valis*, which contained an-ime-style cut scenes.

In 1987, Capcom's *Mega Man* introduced a non-linear option allowing the player to choose which part of the game to play next. This was a stark contrast to both linear games like *Super Mario Bros.* and open-world games like *Metroid*. GamesRadar credits the "level select" feature of *Mega Man* as the basis for the non-linear mission structure found in most open-world, multi-mission, sidequest-heavy games. Another Capcom platformer that year was *Bionic Commando*, a multi-directional-scrolling platform-action game known for introducing the grappling hook mechanic that has since appeared in dozens of later platform games, including *Earthworm Jim* and *Tomb Raider*. Though multidirectional scrolling did not seem important at the time, it would become a distinguishing feature of the next generation of platformers.

Second-generation Side-scrollers

The advent of 16-bit home consoles marked an evolutionary step for the genre. By the time the Genesis and Super NES launched, platform games were the most popular genre in home console gaming and were seen as vital for winning the console war. There was a particular emphasis on having a flagship platform title exclusive to a format, featuring a mascot character. In 1989, Sega released *Alex Kidd in the Enchanted Castle*. The title was only modestly successful, and Sega real-ized it needed a stronger mascot to move Genesis units. That same year, Capcom released the plat-former *Strider*, which scrolled in multiple directions and allowed the player to summon artificial intelligence (AI) partners, such as a droid, tiger, and hawk, to help fight enemies. Sega's *Shadow Dancer*, released the same year, also featured an AI partner, a dog who would follow the player around and aid in battle. In 1990, Hudson Soft released *Bonk's Adventure*, featuring a character that was positioned as NEC's mascot. The following year, Takeru's *Cocoron*, a late platformer for the Famicom, introduced true character customization, allowing players to build a character from a toy box filled with spare parts.

1990 marked the release of the Super NES, along with the eagerly anticipated *Super Mario World*. In order to fend off the new competition, Sega released *Sonic the Hedgehog*. Whereas Nintendo's offering featured a conservative design, true to the *Mario* tradition, *Sonic* show-cased a new style of design made possible by a new generation of hardware. *Sonic* featured large fields that scrolled effortlessly in all directions, as well as all manner of uneven terrain, curved hills, and a complex physics system that allowed players to rush through its levels with well-placed jumps and rolls. Lastly, there was the game's eponymous main character. Sega decided to give Sonic a rebellious personality in order to appeal to older gamers, and a super speed ability, in an attempt to make him appear "cooler" than Mario. The game proved to be a massive hit, was a successful pack-in with new systems, and cemented the view that platform games would make or break a console.

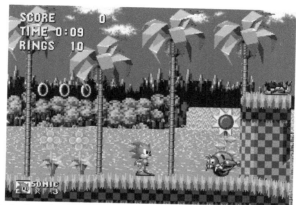

Sonic the Hedgehog (1991) showed what new technology could do for the genre.

The Sonic character was seen as a new model for mascots in the early 1990s, particularly for his perceived attitude, which characterized him as a rebel. This attitude would soon become the status quo, as companies attempted to duplicate Sonic's success with their own brightly colored anthropomorphisms. Very frequently these were characterized by impatience, sarcasm, and frequent quips. These mascots, which included the likes of Gex, Bug!, Aero the Acro-Bat, Awesome Possum, and Bubsy, have mostly faded from relevance.

Although there had long been important platform games on home computers, a second generation of platform games for computers appeared alongside the new wave of consoles. In the late 1980s and early 1990s, the Amiga was known as a stronger gaming platform than IBM-compatible PCs, thanks to its more powerful stock video hardware and sound hardware. The Atari ST was solidly supported as well. Games like *Shadow of the Beast* and *Turrican* showed that computer platform games could rival the graphics and sound of their console contemporaries, and *Prince of Persia* featured an unprecedented level of animation.

In 1990, DOS PC gaming made a breakthrough in the genre. *Commander Keen*, released by id Software, became the first IBM-compatible PC platformer to feature smooth scrolling graphics, thanks to a technique developed by programmer John Carmack called "adaptive tile refresh". The success of this game via the shareware distribution model prompted many others to attempt more console-styled scrolling platformers on the PC, including Todd Replogle's *Duke Nukem, Duke Nukem II, Cosmo's Cosmic Adventure* and *Dark Ages* by Apogee Software, and *Jill of the Jungle, Xargon* and *Jazz Jackrabbit* by Epic MegaGames. These games helped fuel the shareware model, which would drive PC gaming to greater relevance in the early to mid-1990s.

Decline of 2D

At the end of the 16-bit era, some very successful platform games were released, including *Sonic & Knuckles, Super Mario World 2: Yoshi's Island, Super Metroid* and *Donkey Kong Coun-*

try, but the release of new hardware caused players' attention to gradually shift away from traditional 2D genres. The Sega Saturn, PlayStation, and Nintendo 64 nevertheless featured a number of successful 2D platform games. *Rayman*, a traditional 2D platform game, was a big success on 32-bit consoles. *Mega Man 8* and *Mega Man X4* helped revitalize interest in Capcom's Mega Man character. *Castlevania: Symphony of the Night* revitalized its series and established a new foundation for later *Castlevania* games. *Oddworld* and *Heart of Darkness* kept the subgenre born from *Prince of Persia* alive. In a break from the past, the Nintendo 64 had the fewest 2D platformers—only *Yoshi's Story*, *Kirby 64: The Crystal Shards*, *Goemon's Great Adventure* and *Mischief Makers*—and both met with a tepid response from critics at the time. Despite this, *Yoshi's Story* sold over a million copies in the US, and *Mischief Makers* rode high on the charts in the months following its release.

The difficulties of adapting platform gameplay to three dimensions led some developers to compromise by pairing the visual flash of 3D with traditional 2D gameplay. These games are often referred to as "2.5D". The first such game was a Sega Saturn launch title, *Clockwork Knight* (1994). The game featured levels and boss characters rendered in 3D, but retained 2D gameplay and used pre-rendered 2D sprites for regular characters, similar to *Donkey Kong Country*. Its sequel improved upon its design, featuring some 3D effects such as hopping between the foreground and background, and the camera panning and curving around corners.

The formula has been repeated many times. *Pandemonium* and *Klonoa* brought the 2.5D style to the PlayStation.

The Third Dimension

The term *3D platformer* usually refers to games that feature gameplay in three dimensions and polygonal 3D graphics. Games that have 3D gameplay but 2D graphics are usually included under the umbrella of isometric platformers, while those that have 3D graphics but gameplay on a 2D plane are called 2.5D, as they are a blend of 2D and 3D.

The first attempts to bring platform games into 3D used 2D graphics and an isometric perspective. These games are nearly as old as the genre itself, one of the earliest examples being Sega's *Congo Bongo* in 1983. The first platformers to simulate a 3D perspective and moving camera emerged in the early-mid-1980s. An early example of this was Konami's platform game *Antarctic Adventure*, where the player controls a penguin in a forward-scrolling third-person perspective while having to jump over pits and obstacles. Originally released in 1983 for the MSX computer, it was subsequently ported to various platforms the following year, including an arcade version, NES, and ColecoVision. That same year, *I, Robot*, though not a platformer, featured filled 3D polygonal graphics, flat shading, and camera control options, which were not widely adopted by platformers until the 1990s.

1986 saw the release of the sequel to forward-scrolling platformer *Antarctic Adventure* called *Penguin Adventure*, which was designed by Hideo Kojima. It included more action game elements, a greater variety of levels, RPG elements such as upgrading equipment, and multiple endings. *Trailblazer*, released to various computer systems in 1986, used a simple line scroll effect to create a forward scrolling pseudo-3D play field where players manipulated a bouncing ball to leap over obstacles and pitfalls.

In early 1987, Square released *3-D WorldRunner*, designed by Hironobu Sakaguchi and Nasir Gebelli. Using a forward-scrolling effect similar to Sega's 1985 third-person rail shooter *Space Harrier*. *3-D WorldRunner* was an early forward-scrolling pseudo-3D third-person platform-action game where players were free to move in any forward-scrolling direction and could leap over obstacles and chasms. It was notable for being one of the first stereoscopic 3-D games. Square released its sequel, *JJ*, later that year. In 1990, an Estonian developer called Bluemoon released *Kosmonaut*, a forward-scrolling driving/action game similar to *Trailblazer*, which consisted almost entirely of platform-jumping obstacle courses. While the gameplay took place in three dimensions, and the graphics were polygonal, the game is considered pseudo-3D because it used a fixed viewpoint. The game was later remade in 1993 as *SkyRoads*, which experienced wider popularity.

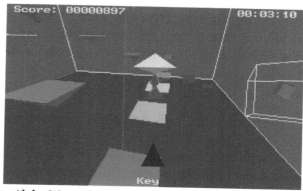

Alpha Waves (1990) was an early 3D platform game.

The earliest example of a true 3D platformer is a French computer game called *Alpha Waves*, created by Christophe de Dinechin and published by Infogrames in 1990 for the Atari ST, Amiga, and PC. It featured full-screen 3D graphics, true 3D movement, and a movable camera, all firsts for the genre. The environments were abstract, with simple gameplay focused on hopping from trampoline-like platforms. The game was released in North America by Data East` under the name *Continuum*. Much like *Jump Bug* before it, while it is believed to be the first of its kind, it is not widely recognized as especially influential, though it is sometimes regarded as a precursor to *Jumping Flash!*. Though its appearance was distinct from the popular 2D platformers of the day, it was billed as a platform game on its packaging.

Bug! (1995) extended traditional platform gameplay in all directions.

Bug!, a Sega Saturn game that was released in 1995, offered a more conservative approach to true 3D platforming. It allowed players to move in all directions, but it did not allow movement along more than one axis at once; the player could move orthogonally but not diagonally. Its characters were pre-rendered sprites, much like the earlier *Clockwork Knight*. The game played very similarly to 2D platformers, but it was considered a true 3D title, and let players walk up walls and on ceilings. It was a moderate success, and spawned a sequel called *Bug Too!*.

In 1995, Delphine Software released a 3D sequel to their popular 2D platformer *Flashback*. Entitled *Fade to Black*, it was the first attempt to bring a popular 2D platform game series into 3D. While it retained the puzzle-oriented level design style and step-based control, and bore a strong resemblance to its predecessor, it did not meet the criteria of a platform game, and was billed as an action adventure. It used true 3D characters and set pieces, but its environments were rendered using a rigid engine similar to the one used by *Wolfenstein 3D*, in that it could only render square, flat corridors, rather than suspended platforms that could be jumped between. *Fade to Black* would set the stage for other series, such as *Metroid* and *Duke Nukem*, that would gradually shift away from the traditional platform formula while retaining many of its gameplay conventions.

There was a great deal of pressure on Sony, Sega, and Nintendo to release mascot platformers before the 1996 holiday season. Sony chose to adopt an existing project by developers Naughty Dog, a small developer at the time, who had recently released the questionable *Way of the Warrior*. The move paid off; their game, *Crash Bandicoot*, beat Nintendo's new console to market in North America and was released in time for the holiday in Japan. Crash would remain Sony's unofficial mascot for the next several years before switching to multi-platform releases in the following console generation.

Sega did not fare as well. They had tasked their American studio, Sega Technical Institute, with bringing Sonic the Hedgehog into 3D. Their project, titled *Sonic Xtreme*, was to have featured a radically different approach for the series, with an exaggerated fisheye camera and multidirectional gameplay reminiscent of *Bug!*. Its development was rocky, due in part to conflicts with Sega Enterprises in Japan and a rushed schedule, and the game never made it to market.

Reshaping the Genre

In 1991, Nintendo's Shigeru Miyamoto had conceived of a 3D *Mario* game, *Super Mario FX*, while working on *Star Fox*. Miyamoto developed most of the concepts for the game during the era of the Super NES and considered using the Super FX chip to make it a SNES game, but decided to develop it for the Nintendo 64 due to the former system's technical limitations. The game was renamed *Super Mario 64* and went into development in 1994.

In 1994, a small developer called Exact released a game for the X68000 computer called *Geograph Seal*. The game was a fully 3D polygonal first-person shooter hybrid with a pronounced platform jumping component. Players piloted a frog-like mech that could jump and then double-jump or triple-jump high into the air, as the camera panned down to help players line up their landings. In addition to shooting, jumping on enemies was a primary means of attack. This was the first true 3D platform-action game with free-roaming environments, but it was never ported to another platform nor released outside Japan, so it remains relatively unknown in the West.

The following year, Exact released their follow-up to *Geograph Seal* as an early title for Sony's new PlayStation console. *Jumping Flash!*, released in April 1995, is generally regarded as a direct continuation of the gameplay concepts in *Geograph Seal*, and was likewise a mix of first-person shooting and platforming, with similar controls and camera-work, in free-roaming 3D environments. The frog-like mech was traded in for a more cartoony rabbit mech, called Robbit. Beyond this, the level design had an even greater focus on platform hopping, and it was released in Europe and North America as a launch title, helping it gain a much higher profile. The title was successful enough to receive two sequels, and is remembered as the first 3D platformer on a console. Rob Fahey of Eurogamer highlighted that the game was arguably one of the most important ancestors of any 3D platform game at the time. *Jumping Flash* holds the record of "First platform videogame in true 3D" according to *Guinness World Records*. Another early 3D platformer was *Floating Runner*, developed by Japanese company Xing and released for the PlayStation in early 1996, predating the release of *Super Mario 64*. *Floating Runner* used D-pad controls and a behind-the-character camera perspective.

Super Mario 64 (1996) replaced the linear obstacle courses of traditional platform games with vast worlds.

Nintendo released *Super Mario 64* in 1996. Before then, there was no established paradigm for bringing platform games into 3D. *Mario 64* set a new standard, and it was imitated by many subsequent 3D platformers. Its gameplay allowed players to explore open 3D environments with greater freedom than any previous attempt at a 3D platform game. To aid this, Nintendo added an analog control stick to its Nintendo 64 controller, something which had not been included in a standard console controller since the Vectrex, and which has since become standard on other controllers. This allowed for the finer precision needed for a free perspective. Players no longer followed a linear path to the ends of levels, either, with most levels providing objective-based goals. There were a handful of boss levels that offered more traditional platforming.

Super Mario 64 brought a change in the goals of some platformers. In most 2D platformers, the player only had to reach a single goal to complete a level, but in 3D platformers, each level had to be combed for collectible items such as puzzle pieces (*Banjo-Kazooie*) or stars (*Super Mario 64*). This allowed for more efficient use of large 3D areas and rewarded the player for thorough exploration, but they also often involved more elements of action-adventure games and less jumping.

As platform games settled into this new free-roaming model, it became necessary for developers to program a dynamic, intelligent camera. This was a non-issue with 2D platformers, which were able to maintain a fixed viewpoint. The addition of a free camera also made it more difficult for players to judge the exact height and distance of platforms, making jumping puzzles more difficult. Some of the more linear 3D platformers, like *Tork: Prehistoric Punk* and *Wario World* used scripted cameras that allowed for minimal player control. Others with more open environments, such as *Super Mario 64* and *Banjo Kazooie*, needed intelligent cameras that follow the players movements. These intelligent cameras were not perfect, and required the player to adjust the view at times when the view was obstructed, or simply not facing what the player needed to see.

RPGs, first person shooters, and more complex action-adventure games were all capturing more market share. Even so, *Tomb Raider* became one of the best selling series on the PlayStation, along with Insomniac Games' *Spyro* and Naughty Dog's *Crash Bandicoot*, one of the few 3D titles to retain the linear level design of 2D games. Also, many of the Nintendo 64's best sellers were first and second-party platformers like *Super Mario 64*, *Banjo-Kazooie*, and *Donkey Kong 64*.

Into the 21st Century

By the sixth generation era, platformers were no longer seen as hot system sellers. Sega finally produced a 3D Sonic game, *Sonic Adventure*, on its new Dreamcast console. It used a hub structure like *Mario 64* but featured more linear, action-oriented levels with an emphasis on speed. Although the game was a hit, it was not enough to save the Dreamcast from an early discontinuation in 2001.

Nintendo launched its GameCube console without a platform game, but in 2002, it released *Super Mario Sunshine*, the second 3D *Mario* game. While the title was well received at the time of its release, it has since received criticism regarding such factors as its short length, lack of location variety, and level design, which featured an abundance of open space, making for a much slower-paced game.

Other notable 3D platformers trickled out during this generation. *Maximo* was a spiritual heir to the *Ghosts'n Goblins* series. *Billy Hatcher and the Giant Egg* offered Yuji Naka's take on a *Mario 64*-influenced platformer, and *Psychonauts* became a critical darling based on its imaginative levels and colorful characters. *Rayman*'s popularity continued, though the franchise's third game was not as well received as the first two. Naughty Dog's deal with Universal was up, and they moved on from *Crash Bandicoot* to *Jak and Daxter*, a series that moved further away from traditional platforming with each sequel. A hybrid platformer/shooter game from Insomniac Games called *Ratchet & Clank* further pushed the genre away from such gameplay, as did Universal Interactive Studios' rebooted *Spyro* trilogy.

Platformers remained a vital genre, but they never recaptured the popularity they once held. In 1998, platform games had a 15% share of the market, and even higher during their heyday, but only four years later that figure had dropped to 2%. Even the much acclaimed *Psychonauts* experienced modest sales at first, leading publisher Majesco to withdraw from high budget console games, even though its sales in Europe were respectable, and franchises like *Tomb Raider* began to sag. Other forms of third-person action games have cut into the sales of platformers, while genres such as RPGs and first-person shooters have continued to grow in popularity. A broader and more diverse video game market has developed, and no single genre has managed to achieve the same kind of dominance that platform games did during the 8, 16, and 32/64-bit console eras.

Recent Developments

Despite a much smaller presence in the overall gaming market, some platform games continue to be successful into the seventh generation of consoles. 2007 saw the release of *Super Mario Galaxy* and *Ratchet & Clank Future: Tools of Destruction* to positive critical and fan reaction. *Super Mario Galaxy* was awarded the Best Game of 2007 on high-profile gaming websites including GameSpot, IGN, and GameTrailers, and was the most critically acclaimed game of all time according to GameRankings. In 2008, *LittleBigPlanet* paired traditional 2D platform game mechanics with physics simulation and user created content, earning strong sales and critical reaction. Electronic Arts released *Mirror's Edge*, which coupled platform gameplay with a first-person camera, but avoided marketing the game as a platformer because of the association the label had developed with games geared toward younger audiences. *Sonic Unleashed* featured stages containing both 2D and 3D styles of platform gameplay; this formula was also used in *Sonic Colors* and *Sonic Generations*. Two *Crash Bandicoot* platform games were also released 2007 and 2008.

Trine (2009) mixed traditional platform elements with more modern physics puzzles.

Freedom Planet (2014) is a more traditional, retro-style platformer: it draws heavy influence from early *Sonic the Hedgehog* games and features pixelated, sprite-based graphics.

Nintendo has revived the genre in recent years, releasing numerous platform games to high sales. *New Super Mario Bros.* was released in 2006 and has sold 18.45 million copies worldwide; it is the best-selling game for the Nintendo DS, and the fourth best-selling non-bundled video game of all time. *Super Mario Galaxy* has sold over eight million units, while *Super Paper Mario, Super Mario 64 DS, Sonic Rush, Yoshi's Island DS, Kirby Super Star Ultra*, and *Kirby: Squeak Squad* also have strong sales, and keep the genre active.

After the success of *New Super Mario Bros.*, consumers and publishers have shown renewed interest in 2D platformers, which can be attributed both to handheld consoles such as the Nintendo DS and PlayStation Portable, and low-risk downloadable services offered by WiiWare, Xbox Live Arcade, PlayStation Network, and Steam. These range from classic revivals such as *Bionic Commando: Rearmed, Contra ReBirth*, and *Sonic the Hedgehog 4*, to original titles like *Splosion Man* and *Henry Hatsworth in the Puzzling Adventure. Wario Land: The Shake Dimension*, released in 2008, was a platformer that featured completely two-dimensional graphics and a rich visual style. Subsequent games such as *Braid, A Boy and His Blob*, and The Behemoth's *BattleBlock Theater* also use completely 2D graphics. *New Super Mario Bros. Wii* is particularly notable, as unlike the majority of 2D platformers in the 21st century, it was a direct release for a non-portable console, and not restricted on a content delivery network. The success of *New Super Mario Bros. Wii* led to Nintendo releasing similar 2D platformer games for their classic franchises the following year: *Donkey Kong Country Returns* and *Kirby's Return to Dream Land*.

In 2009, independent developer Frozenbyte released *Trine*, a 2.5D platform game that mixed traditional elements with more modern physics puzzles. The game proved to be a commercial success, eventually selling more than 1.1 million copies. It spawned a sequel, *Trine 2*, which was released in 2011. The 2D platformer *Rayman Origins*, was also released in 2011 as a retail title on several platforms. In 2012, Nintendo released two more 2D platform games: *New Super Mario Bros. 2* for the 3DS and *New Super Mario Bros. U* for the Wii U. Nintendo has also released 3D platform games with gameplay elements of 2D platform games, namely "Super Mario 3D Land" for the 3DS in 2011 and "Super Mario 3D World" for the Wii U in 2013, the latter of which also included cooperative multiplayer gameplay. Each has achieved critical and commercial success.

Subgenres

There are many games that are platformers that do not adhere to any of the subgenres below, but the following are some of the more recognizable archetypes for different platform styles. There are many more vaguely defined subgenres that are not mentioned here because they are not as easily defined.

Puzzle-platform Game

Puzzle platformers are characterized by their use of a platform game structure to drive a game whose challenge is derived primarily from puzzles. Enix's 1983 release *Door Door* and Sega's 1985 release *Doki Doki Penguin Land* (for the SG-1000) are perhaps the first examples, though the genre is diverse, and classifications can vary. *Doki Doki Penguin Land* allowed players to run and jump in typical platform fashion, but they could also destroy blocks, and were tasked with guiding an egg to the bottom of the level without letting it break.

The Lost Vikings (1992) was one of the more popular titles in this genre, as well. It featured three characters players could switch between, each with different abilities. Players had to use all three characters to reach the level goals.

The puzzles in 2012 puzzle platformer *Fez* are based on a screen rotation mechanic.

This subgenre has a strong presence on handheld platforms. *Wario Land 2* moved the Wario series into the puzzle-platformer genre by eliminating the element of death and adding temporary injuries, such as being squashed or lit on fire, and specialized powers. *Wario Land 3* continued this tradition, while *Wario Land 4* was more of a mix of puzzle and traditional platform elements. The Game Boy update of *Donkey Kong* was also a successful portable puzzle-platformer, and saw a sequel on Game Boy Advance called *Mario vs Donkey Kong*. *Klonoa: Empire of Dreams*, the first handheld title in its series, was also a puzzle-platformer.

In more recent years, the genre has experienced some revival, especially in independent game development. *Braid* uses time manipulation for its puzzles, and *And Yet It Moves* uses frame of reference rotation. In contrast to these side-scrollers, *Narbacular Drop* and its successor, *Portal* are first-person camera games that use portals to solve puzzles in 3D. Since the release of *Portal*, there have been more puzzle platformers that use a first-person camera, including *Purity* and *Tag: The Power of Paint*.

Run-and-gun Platform Game

The run and gun platformer genre was popularized by Konami's classic *Contra*. *Gunstar Heroes* and *Metal Slug* are also among the most popular examples of this style. Side-scrolling run and gun games are an attempt to marry platform games with shoot 'em ups, characterized by a minimal focus on precise platform jumping and a major emphasis on multi-directional shooting. These games are sometimes called platform shooters. This genre has strong arcade roots, and as such, these games are generally known for being very difficult, and having very linear, one-way game progression.

There are games which feature a heavy degree of shooting but do not fall into this subgenre. *Mega Man*, *Metroid*, *Vectorman*, *Jazz Jackrabbit*, *Earthworm Jim* and *Turrican* are all platformers with a heavy focus on action and shooting, but unlike *Contra* or *Metal Slug*, platform jumping elements, as well as exploration and back-tracking, still figure prominently. Run and guns are generally very pure, and while they may have vehicular sequences or other changes in style, they stay focused on shooting throughout.

Cinematic Platform Game

Cinematic platformers are a small but distinct subgenre of platform games, usually distinguished by their relative realism compared to traditional platformers. These games focus on fluid, lifelike movements, without the unnatural physics found in nearly all other platform games. To achieve this realism, many cinematic platformers, beginning with *Prince of Persia*, have employed rotoscoping techniques to animate their characters based on video footage of live actors performing the same stunts. Jumping abilities are typically roughly within the confines of an athletic human's capacity. To expand vertical exploration, many cinematic platformers feature the ability to grab onto ledges, or make extensive use of elevator platforms. Other distinguishing characteristics include step-based control, in which an action is performed after the character completes his current animation, rather than the instant the button is pressed, and multi-screen stages that do not scroll.

Another World, like other cinematic platformers, features a realistically proportioned character and rotoscoped animation.

As these games tend to feature vulnerable characters who may die as the result of a single enemy attack or by falling a relatively short distance, they almost never have limited lives or continues. Challenge is derived from trial and error problem solving, forcing the player to find the right way to overcome a particular obstacle.

Prince of Persia was the first cinematic platformer and perhaps the most influential. *Impossible Mission* pioneered many of the defining elements of cinematic platformers and is an important precursor to this genre. Other games in the genre include *Flashback* (and its 2013 remake), *Another World*, *Heart of Darkness*, the first two *Oddworld* games, *Blackthorne*, *Bermuda Syndrome*, *Generations Lost*, *Heart of the Alien*, *Weird Dreams*, *LIMBO*, *INSIDE*, *onEscapee*, *Deadlight*.

Comical Action Game

This genre lacks a commonly agreed upon name in the West, but games in the genre are most commonly called "comical action games" (CAGs) in Japan. The original arcade *Mario Bros* is generally recognized as the originator of this genre, though *Bubble Bobble* is also highly influential. These games are characterized by single screen, non-scrolling levels and cooperative two-player action. A level is cleared when all enemies on the screen have been defeated, and vanquished foes usually drop score bonuses in the form of fruit or other items. CAGs are almost exclusively developed in Japan and are either arcade games, or sequels to arcade games, though they are also a common genre among amateur *doujinshi* games. Other examples include *Don Doko Don*, *Snow Bros* and *Nightmare in the Dark*.

Isometric Platform Game

Arguably a subgenre of both 3D and 2D platformers, isometric platformers present a three-dimensional environment using two-dimensional graphics in isometric projection. Although not the first isometric games, the earliest examples of isometric platform games are the arcade game *Congo Bongo* and *Ant Attack* for the Sinclair ZX Spectrum, both released in 1983.

Knight Lore, an example of three-dimensional space represented on low-end hardware

Knight Lore, an isometric sequel to *Sabre Wulf*, helped to establish the conventions of early isometric platformers. This formula would be repeated in later games like *Head Over Heels*, and *Monster Max*. These games were generally heavily focused on exploring indoor environments, usually a series of small rooms connected by doors, and have distinct adventure and puzzle elements. Japanese developers blended this gameplay style with that of Japanese action-adventure games like *The Legend of Zelda* to create games like *Land Stalker* and *Light Crusader*. While these games are more generally classified as action adventures, they are also isometric platformers and an evolution of earlier conventions in the genre. This influence would later travel to Europe with Adeline Software's sprawling epic *Little Big Adventure*, which blended RPG, adventure, and isometric platforming elements.

Before consoles were able to display true polygonal 3D graphics, the ¾ isometric perspective was used to move some popular 2D platformers into three-dimensional gameplay. *Spot Goes To Hollywood* was a sequel to the popular *Cool Spot*, and *Sonic 3D Blast* was Sonic's outing into the isometric subgenre.

Platform-adventure Game

Many games fuse platform game fundamentals with elements of action-adventure games, such as *The Legend of Zelda*, or with elements of RPGs. Typically these elements include the ability to explore an area freely, with access to new areas granted by either gaining new abilities or using inventory items. Many 2D games in the *Metroid* and *Castlevania* franchises are among the most popular games of this sort, and so games that take this type of approach are often labeled as "Metroidvania" games. *Castlevania: Symphony of the Night* popularized this approach in the *Castlevania* series. Other examples of such games include *Wonder Boy III: The Dragon's Trap, Tails Adventure, Cave Story, Mega Man ZX, Shadow Complex*, and the recent *DuckTales: Remastered*.

Early examples of free-roaming, side-scrolling, 2D platform-adventures in the vein of "Metroidvania" include Nintendo's original *Metroid* in 1986 and Konami's *Castlevania* games: *Vampire Killer* in 1986 and *Simon's Quest* in 1987, as well as Enix's sci-fi Sharp X1 computer game *Brain*

Breaker in 1985, Pony Canyon's *Super Pitfall* in 1986, System Sacom's *Euphory* in 1987, Bothtec's *The Scheme* in 1988, and several *Dragon Slayer* action RPGs by Nihon Falcom such as the 1985 release *Xanadu* and 1987 releases *Faxanadu* and *Legacy of the Wizard*.

Endless Running Game

"Endless running" or "infinite running" games are platform games in which the player character is continuously moving forward through a usually procedurally generated, theoretically endless game world. Game controls are limited to making the character jump, attack, or perform special actions. The object of these games is to get as far as possible before the character dies. Endless running games have found particular success on mobile platforms. They are well-suited to the small set of controls these games require, often limited to a single screen tap for jumping.

Game designer Scott Rogers named side-scrolling shooters like *Scramble* (1981) and *Moon Patrol* (1982) and chase-style game play in platform games like *Disney's Aladdin* (1994) and *Crash Bandicoot* (1996) as forerunners of the genre.

In February 2003, Gamevil published *Nom* for mobile phones in Korea. The game's designer Sin Bong-gu, stated that he wanted to create a game that was only possible on mobile phones, therefore he made the player character walk up walls and ceilings, requiring players to turn around their mobile phones while playing. To compensate for this complication, he limited the game's controls to a single button and let the character run automatically and indefinitely, "like the people in modern society, who must alway look forward and keep running".

While the concept thus was long known in Korea, Eurogamer credits *Canabalt* as "the title that single-handedly invented the smartphone-friendly single-button running genre" in 2009 and spawned a wave of clones. Fotonica (2011), a one-button endless runner viewed from the first person, was described by The Sixth Axis as a "hybrid of Canabalt's running, Mirror's Edge's perspective (and hands) and Rez's visual style".

Temple Run (2011) and its successor *Temple Run 2* have become especially popular endless running games. The latter became the world's fastest-spreading mobile game in January 2013, with 50 million installations within thirteen days. Other successful "endless runners" include *Subway Surfers*, *Sonic Dash*, *Rayman Jungle Run*, *Stampede Run*, *Flappy Bird*, and *Snowden Run 3D*.

Adventure Game

An adventure game is a video game in which the player assumes the role of protagonist in an interactive story driven by exploration and puzzle-solving. The genre's focus on story allows it to draw heavily from other narrative-based media, literature and film, encompassing a wide variety of literary genres. Many adventure games (text and graphic) are designed for a single player, since this emphasis on story and character makes multi-player design difficult. *Colossal Cave Adventure* is identified as the first such adventure game, first released in 1976, while other notable adventure game series include *Zork*, *King's Quest*, *The Secret of Monkey Island*, and *Myst*.

Initial adventure games developed in the 1970s and early 1980s were text-based, using text parsers to translate the player's input into commands. As personal computers became more powerful with the ability to show graphics, the graphic adventure game format became popular, initially by augmenting player's text commands with graphics, but soon moving towards point and click interfaces. Further computer advancements led to adventure games with more immersive graphics using real-time or pre-rendered three-dimensional scenes or full-motion video taken from the first- or third-person perspective.

For markets in the Western hemisphere, the genre's popularity peaked during the late 1980s to mid-1990s when many considered it to be among the most technically advanced genres, but had become a niche genre in the early 2000s due to the popularity of first-person shooters and became difficult to find publishers to support such ventures. Since then, a resurgence in the genre has occurred spurred on by success of independent video game development, particularly from crowd-funding efforts, the wide availability of digital distribution enabling episodic approaches, and the proliferation of new gaming platforms including portable consoles and mobile devices; *The Walking Dead* is considered to be a key title that rejuvenated the genre.

Within the Asian markets, adventure games continue to be popular in the form of visual novels, which make up nearly 70% of PC games released in Japan. The Asian markets have also found markets for adventure games for portable and mobile gaming devices.

Definition

Components of an adventure game
Puzzle solving, or problem solving.
Narrative, or interactive story.
Exploration.
Player assumes the role of a character/hero.
Collection or manipulation of objects.

The term "Adventure game" originated from the 1970s text computer game *Colossal Cave Adventure*, or as it was often referred to simply as *Adventure*, which pioneered a style of gameplay that was widely imitated and became a genre in its own right. The video game genre is therefore defined by its gameplay, unlike the literary genre, which is defined by the subject it addresses, the activity of adventure.

Essential elements of the genre include storytelling, exploration, and puzzle solving. Adventure games have been described as puzzles embedded in a narrative framework, where games involve "narrative content that a player unlocks piece by piece over time". While the puzzles that players encounter through the story can be arbitrary, those that do not pull the player out of the narrative are considered examples of good design.

Relationship to other Genres

Combat and action challenges are limited or absent in adventure games, thus distinguishing them from action games. In the book *Andrew Rollings and Ernest Adams on Game Design*, the authors state that "this [reduced emphasis on combat] doesn't mean that there is no conflict in adventure games ... only that combat is not the primary activity." Some adventure games will include a minigame from another video game genre, which are not always appreciated by adventure game purists. Hybrid action-adventure games blend action and adventure games throughout the game experience, incorporating more physical challenges than pure adventure games and at a faster pace. This definition is hard to apply, however, with some debate among designers about which games are action games and which involve enough non-physical challenges to be considered action-adventures.

Adventure games are also distinct from role-playing video games that involve action, team-building, and points management. Adventure games lack the numeric rules or relationships seen in role-playing games, and seldom have an internal economy. These games lack any skill system, combat, or "an opponent to be defeated through strategy and tactics." However, some hybrid games exist here, where role-playing games with strong narrative and puzzle elements are considered RPG-adventures. Finally, adventure games are classified separately from puzzle video games. Although an adventure game may involve puzzle-solving, they typically involve a player-controlled avatar in an interactive story.

Game Design

Puzzle-solving

Adventure games contain a variety of puzzles, decoding messages, finding and using items, opening locked doors, or finding and exploring new locations. Solving a puzzle will unlock access to new areas in the game world, and reveal more of the game story. Logic puzzles, where mechanical devices are designed with abstract interfaces to test a player's deductive reasoning skills, are common.

Some puzzles are criticized for the obscurity of their solutions, for example, the combination of a clothes line, clamp, and deflated rubber duck used to gather a key stuck between the subway tracks in *The Longest Journey*, which exists outside of the game's narrative and serves only as an obstacle to the player. Others have been criticized for requiring players to blindly guess, either by clicking on the right pixel, or by guessing the right verb in games that use a text interface. Games that require players to navigate mazes have also become less popular, although the earliest text-adventure games usually required players to draw a map if they wanted to navigate the abstract space.

Gathering and Using Items

Many adventure games make use of an inventory management screen as a distinct gameplay mode. Players are only able to pick up some objects in the game, so the player usually knows that only objects that can be picked up are important. Because it can be difficult for a player to know if they missed an important item, they will often scour every scene for items. For games that utilize a point and click device, players will sometimes engage in a systematic search known as a pixel hunt. Games try to avoid this by highlighting the item, or by snapping the player's cursor to the item.

Many puzzles in these games involve gathering and using items from their inventory. Players must apply lateral thinking techniques where they apply real-world extrinsic knowledge about objects in unexpected ways. For example, by putting a deflated inner tube on a cactus to create a slingshot, which requires a player to realize that an inner tube is stretchy. They may need to carry items in their inventory for a long duration before they prove useful, and thus it is normal for adventure games to test a player's memory where a challenge can only be overcome by recalling a piece of information from earlier in the game. There is seldom any time pressure for these puzzles, focusing more on the player's ability to reason than on quick-thinking.

Story, Setting, and Themes

Adventure games are single-player experiences that are largely story-driven. More than any other genre, adventure games depend upon their story and setting to create a compelling single-player experience. They are typically set in an immersive environment, often a fantasy world, and try to vary the setting from chapter to chapter to add novelty and interest to the experience. Comedy is a common theme, and games often script comedic responses when players attempt actions or combinations that are "ridiculous or impossible".

Since adventure games are driven by storytelling, character development usually follows literary conventions of personal and emotional growth, rather than new powers or abilities that affect gameplay. The player often embarks upon a quest, or is required to unravel a mystery or situation about which little is known. These types of mysterious stories allow designers to get around what Ernest W. Adams calls the "Problem of Amnesia", where the player controls the protagonist but must start the game without their knowledge and experience. Story-events typically unfold as the player completes new challenges or puzzles, but in order to make such storytelling less mechanical new elements in the story may also be triggered by player movement.

Dialogue and Conversation Trees

Adventure games have strong storylines with significant dialog, and sometimes make effective use of recorded dialog or narration from voice actors. This genre of game is known for representing dialog as a conversation tree. Players are able to engage a non-player character by choosing a line of pre-written dialog from a menu, which triggers a response from the game character. These conversations are often designed as a tree structure, with players deciding between each branch of dialog to pursue. However, there are always a finite number of branches to pursue, and some adventure games devolve into selecting each option one-by-one. Conversing with characters can reveal clues about how to solve puzzles, including hints about what that character would want before they will cooperate with the player. Other conversations will have far-reaching consequences, deciding to disclose a valuable secret that has been entrusted to the player. Characters may also be convinced to reveal their own secrets, either through conversation or by giving them something that will benefit them.

Goals, Success and Failure

The primary goal in adventure games is the completion of the assigned quest. Early adventure games often had high scores and some, *Zork*, also assigned the player a rank, a text description based on their score. High scores provide the player with a secondary goal, and serve as an indicator of progression. While high scores are now less common, external reward systems, Xbox Live's Achievements perform a similar role.

The primary failure condition in adventure games, inherited from more action-oriented games, is player death. Without the clearly identified enemies of other genres, its inclusion in adventure games is controversial, and many developers now either avoid it or take extra steps to foreshadow death. Some early adventure games trapped the players in unwinnable situations without ending the game. Infocom's text adventure *The Hitchhiker's Guide to the Galaxy* has been criticized for a scenario where failing to pick up a pile of junk mail at the beginning of the game prevented the player, much later, from completing the game. The adventure games developed by LucasArts purposely avoided creating a dead-end situation for the player due to the negative reactions to such situations.

Subgenres

Text Adventures and Interactive Fiction

A computer terminal running *Zork* (1977), one of the first commercially successful text adventure games.

Text adventures convey the game's story through passages of text, revealed to the player in response to typed instructions. Early text adventures, *Colossal Cave Adventure*, "Hugo's House of Horrors" and Scott Adams' games, used a simple verb-noun parser to interpret these instructions, allowing the player to interact with objects at a basic level, for example by typing "get key". Later text adventures, and modern interactive fiction, use natural language processing to enable more complex player commands like "take the key from the desk". Notable examples of advanced text adventures include most games developed by Infocom, including *Zork* and *The Hitchhiker's Guide to the Galaxy*. With the onset of graphic adventures, the text adventure fell to the wayside, though the medium remains popular as a means of writing Interactive Fiction (IF), which tend to be focused more on the narrative through player exploration and discovery rather than puzzle solving. Interactive fiction may include puzzles, but these tend to be incorporated as part of the narrative in comparison to being specifically added as gameplay that must be solved to continue within adventure games.

Graphic Adventure

Graphic adventures are adventure games that use graphics to convey the environment to the player. Games under the graphic adventure banner may have a variety of input types, from text parsers to touch screen interfaces. Graphic adventure games will vary in how they present the avatar. Some games will utilize a first-person or third-person perspective where the camera follows the player's movements, whereas many adventure games use drawn or pre-rendered backgrounds, or a context-sensitive camera that is positioned to show off each location to the best effect.

Point-and-click Adventure Games

Point-and-click adventure games are those where the player typically controls their character through a point-and-click interface using a computer mouse or similar pointing device, though additional control schemes may also be available. The player clicks to move their character around, interact with non-player characters, often initiating conversation trees with them, examine objects in the game's settings or with their character's item inventory. Many point-and-click games would include a list of on-screen verbs to describe specific actions in the manner of a text adventure, but newer games have used more context-sensitive user interface elements to reduce or eliminate this approach. Often, these games come down to collecting items for the character's inventory, and figuring where is the right time to use that item; the player would need to use clues from the visual elements of the game, descriptions of the various items, and dialogue from other characters to figure this out. Later games developed by Sierra Online including the *King's Quest* games, and nearly all of the LucasArts adventure games, are point-and-click based games.

The Whispered World (2009) is an example of a context-based point-and-click adventure game using high-definition graphics and animation.

Escape the Room Games

Escape the room games are a further specialization of point-and-click adventure games; these games are typically short and confined to a small space to explore, with almost no interaction with non-player characters. Most games of this type require the player to figure out how to escape a room using the limited resources within it and through the solving of logic puzzles. Other variants include games that require the player to manipulate a complex object to achieve a certain end in the fashion of a puzzle box. These games are often delivered in Adobe Flash format and are also popular on mobile devices. Examples of the subgenre include the *Submachine*-series, *MOTAS* (*Mystery of Time and Space*) and *The Room*.

Puzzle Adventure Games

Puzzle adventure games are adventure games that put a strong emphasis on logic puzzles. They typically emphasize self-contained puzzle challenges with logic puzzle toys or games. Completing each puzzle opens more of the game's world to explore, additional puzzles to solve, and can expand on the game's story. There are often few to none non-playable characters in such games, and lack the type of inventory puzzles that typical point-and-click adventure games have. Puzzle adventure games were popularized by *Myst* and *The 7th Guest*. These both used mixed media consisting of pre-rendered images and movie clips, but since then, puzzle adventure games have taken advantage of modern game engines to present the games in full 3D settings, such as *The Talos Principle*. *Myst* itself has been recreated in such a fashion in the title *realMyst*. Other puzzle adventure games are casual adventure games made up series of puzzles used to explore and progress the story, exemplified by *The Witness* and the *Professor Layton* series of games.

Exploration Games

The Stanley Parable (2014) is a first-person exploration game set in an office building.

Exploration games are narrative-focused adventures that allow players to experience their story through exploration and discovery. They are story-focused and feature fewer puzzles or even no puzzles at all. They allow players to roam around a garden-like environment freely and often tell their story through discovering elements like books, journals, or clues rather than through dialog and cutscenes as in more traditional adventure games. As win/lose conditions are de-emphasized, story and atmosphere are placed at the forefront. The term walking simulators has been used, though sometimes pejoratively in contrast with the systems-heavy genre immersive sims. Some examples of exploration games include *Gone Home*, *Dear Esther*, *The Stanley Parable*, *Jazzpunk*, and *Thirty Flights of Loving*.

Visual Novel

A visual novel (ビジュアルノベル *bijuaru noberu*?) is a hybrid of text and graphical adventure games, typically featuring text-based story and interactivity aided by static or sprite-based visuals. They resemble mixed-media novels or tableau vivant stage plays. The format has its primary origins in Japanese and other Asian video game markets, typically for personal computers and more recently on handheld consoles or mobile devices. The format has not gained much traction in Western markets. A common type of visual novel are dating sims, which has the player attempt to improve a relationship with one or more other characters, such as *Hatoful Boyfriend*.

A common layout for a visual novel game

Interactive Movie

Some adventure games have been presented as interactive movies; these are games where most of the graphics are either fully pre-rendered or use full motion video from live actors on a set, stored on a media that allows fast random access such as laserdisc or CD-ROM. The game's software would present a scene and then display options for the player to continue on, the choice leading to the game playing a new scene from the media. The video may be augmented by additional computer graphics; *Under a Killing Moon* used a combination of full motion video and 3D graphics. Because these games are limited by what has been pre-rendered or recorded, there is a lack of player interactivity in these titles, with wrong choices or decisions leading quickly to an ending scene. Interactive movies have seen a larger growth with the advancement of computing power that can render pre-scripted scenes in real-time, thus providing for more depth of gameplay that is reactive to the player (often including the use of quick time events for more interactivity), but still following a pre-written story. Such games include Quantic Dream's *Fahrenheit* and *Heavy Rain*, and many of Telltale Games' episodic adventure series such as *The Walking Dead*.

Hybrids

There are a number of hybrid graphical adventure games, borrowing from two or more of the above classifications. For example, the *Ace Attorney* series of games, while presenting itself as a visual novel, includes elements of point-and-click adventure games. The *Zero Escape* series wraps several escape-the-room puzzles within the context of a visual novel. The *Adventures of Sherlock Holmes* series has the player use point-and-click type interfaces to locate clues, and minigame-type mechanics to manipulate those clues to find more relevant information.

While most adventure games typically do not include any time-based interactivity by the player, action-adventure games are a hybrid of action games with adventure games that often require to the player to react quickly to events as they occur on screen. The action-adventure genre is broad, spanning many different subgenres, but typically these games utilize strong storytelling and puzzle-solving mechanics of adventure games among the action-oriented gameplay concepts. The foremost title in this genre was *Adventure*, a graphic home console game developed based on the text-based *Colossal Cave Adventure*, while the first *The Legend of Zelda* brought the action-adventure concept to a broader audience.

History

Text Adventures (1976–1989)

The origins of text adventure games is difficult to trace as records of computing around the 1970s were not as well documented. Text-based games had existed prior to 1976 that featured elements of exploring maps or solving puzzles, such as *Hunt the Wumpus* (1975), but lacked a narrative element, a feature essential for adventure games. *Colossal Cave Adventure* (1976), written by William Crowther and Don Woods, is widely considered to be the first game in the adventure genre, and a significant influence on the genre's early development, as well as influencing core games in other genres such as *Adventure* (1979) for the action-adventure video game and *Rogue* (1980) for roguelikes. Crowther was an employee at Bolt, Beranek and Newman, a Boston company involved with ARPANET routers, in the mid-1970s. As an avid caver and role-playing game enthusiast, he wrote a text adventure based on his own knowledge of the Mammoth Cave system in Kentucky. The program, which he named *Adventure*, was written on the company's PDP-10 and used 300 kilobytes of memory. The program was disseminated through ARPANET, which led to Woods, working at the Stanford Artificial Intelligence Laboratory at Stanford at the time, to modify and expand the game, eventually becoming *Colossal Cave Adventure*.

```
.RUN ADV11

WELCOME TO ADVENTURE!!  WOULD YOU LIKE INSTRUCTIONS?

YES
SOMEWHERE NEARBY IS COLOSSAL CAVE, WHERE OTHERS HAVE FOUND
FORTUNES IN TREASURE AND GOLD, THOUGH IT IS RUMORED
THAT SOME WHO ENTER ARE NEVER SEEN AGAIN. MAGIC IS SAID
TO WORK IN THE CAVE.  I WILL BE YOUR EYES AND HANDS. DIRECT
ME WITH COMMANDS OF 1 OR 2 WORDS.
(ERRORS, SUGGESTIONS, COMPLAINTS TO CROWTHER)
(IF STUCK TYPE HELP FOR SOME HINTS)

YOU ARE STANDING AT THE END OF A ROAD BEFORE A SMALL BRICK
BUILDING . AROUND YOU IS A FOREST. A SMALL
STREAM FLOWS OUT OF THE BUILDING AND DOWN A GULLY.

GO IN
YOU ARE INSIDE A BUILDING, A WELL HOUSE FOR A LARGE SPRING.

THERE ARE SOME KEYS ON THE GROUND HERE.

THERE IS A SHINY BRASS LAMP NEARBY.

THERE IS FOOD HERE.

THERE IS A BOTTLE OF WATER HERE.
```

Telechrome^type output of Will Crowther's original version of *Colossal Cave Adventure*.

Colossal Cave Adventure set concepts and gameplay approaches that would become staples of text adventures and interactive fiction. Following its release on ARPANET, numerous variations of *Colossal Cave Adventure* appeared throughout the late 1970s and early 1980s, with some of these later versions being re-christened *Colossal Adventure* or *Colossal Caves*. These variations were enabled by the increase in microcomputing that allowed programmers to work on home computers rather than mainframe systems. The genre gained commercial success with titles designed for home computers. Scott Adams launched Adventure International to publish text adventures including an adaptation of *Colossal Cave Adventure*, while a number of MIT students formed Infocom to bring their game *Zork* from mainframe to home computers and was a commercial success. Other companies in this field included Level 9 Computing, Magnetic Scrolls and Melbourne House.

When personal computers gained the ability to display graphics, the text adventure genre began to wane, and by 1990 there were few if any commercial releases. Non-commercial text adventure games are still developed today, as the genre of interactive fiction.

Early Graphical Development (1980–1990)

The first known graphical adventure game was *Mystery House* (1980), by Sierra On-Line, then at the time known as On-Line System. The game featured static vector graphics atop a simple command line interface, building on the text adventure model. Sierra would continue to produce similar games under the title *Hi-Res Adventure*. Vector graphics would give way to bitmap graphics which also enabled for simple animations to show the player-character moving in response to typed commands. Here, Sierra's *King's Quest* (1984), though not the first game of its type, is recognized as a commercially successful graphical adventure game, enabling Sierra to expand on more titles. Other examples of early games include Koei's *Night Life* and *Danchi Tsuma no Yuwaku* (1982), *Sherwood Forest* (1982), Yuji Horii's *Portopia Serial Murder Case* (1983), *The Return of Heracles* (which faithfully portrayed Greek mythology) by Stuart Smith (1983), Dale Johnson's *Masquerade* (1983), Antonio Antiochia's *Transylvania* (1982, re-released in 1984), and *Adventure Construction Set* (1985), one of the early hits of Electronic Arts.

Mystery House for the Apple II was the first adventure game to use graphics in the early home computer era.

As computers gained the ability to use pointing devices and point-and-click interfaces, graphical adventure games moved away from including the text interface and simply provided appropriate commands the player could interact with on-screen. The first known game with such an interface was *Enchanted Scepters* (1984) from Silicon Beach Software, which used drop-down menus for the player to select actions from while using a text window to describe results of those actions. In 1985, ICOM Simulations released *Déjà Vu*, the first of its MacVenture series, utilized a more complete point-and-click interface, including the ability to drag objects around on the current scene, and was a commercial success. The point-and-click system also worked well for game consoles, with games like Chunsoft's *Portopia Serial Murder Case* (1985) and Square's *Suishō no Dragon* (1986), both on the Nintendo Entertainment System using the controller input instead of text-based actions. LucasArts started developing their own point-and-click adventures, starting with *Maniac Mansion* in 1987, and continuing a line of highly successful titles based on their SCUMM game engine.

Graphical adventure games were considered to have spurred the gaming market for personal computers from 1985 through the next decade, as they were able to offer narratives and storytelling that could not readily be told by the state of graphical hardware at the time.

Expansion (1990–2000)

Graphical adventure games would continue to improve with advances in graphic systems for home computers, providing more detailed and colorful scenes and characters. With the adoption of CD-ROM in the early 1990s, it became possible to include higher quality graphics, video, and audio in adventure games. This saw the addition of voice acting to adventure games, the rise of Interactive movies, *The Beast Within: A Gabriel Knight Mystery*, and the gradual adoption of three-dimensional graphics in adventure games, the critically acclaimed *Grim Fandango*, Lucasarts' first 3D adventure.

Myst used high-quality 3D rendered graphics to deliver images that were unparalleled at the time of its release.

Myst, released in 1993 by Cyan Worlds, is considered one of the genre's more influential titles. *Myst* included pre-rendered 3D graphics, video, and audio. *Myst* was an atypical game for the time, with no clear goals, little personal or object interaction, and a greater emphasis on exploration, and on scientific and mechanical puzzles. Part of the game's success was because it did not appear to be aimed at an adolescent male audience, but instead a mainstream adult audience. *Myst* held the record for computer game sales for seven years—it sold over nine million copies on all platforms, a feat not surpassed until the release of *The Sims* in 2000. In addition, *Myst* is considered to be the "killer app" that drove mainstream adoption of CD-ROM drives, as the game was one of the first to be distributed solely on CD-ROM, forgoing the option of floppy disks. *Myst*'s successful use of mixed-media would lead to its own sequels, and other puzzle-based adventure games using mixed-media such as *The 7th Guest*. With many companies attempting to capitalize on the success of *Myst*, a glut of similar games followed its release, which contributed towards the start of the decline of the adventure game market in 2000.

Sega's ambitious *Shenmue* (1999) attempted to redefine the adventure game genre with its realistic 3D graphics, third-person perspective, direct character control interface, sandbox open-world gameplay, quick time events, and fighting game elements. Its creator Yu Suzuki originally touted it as a new kind of adventure game, "FREE" ("Full Reactive Eyes Entertainment"), offering an unparalleled level of player freedom, giving them full reign to explore expansive interactive city environments with its own day-night cycles and changing weather, and interact with fully voiced non-player characters going about their daily routines. Despite being a commercial failure, the game was critically acclaimed and has remained influential.

Decline (2000–2010)

Whereas once adventure games were one of the most popular genres for computer games, by the mid-1990s the market share started to drastically decline. The forementioned saturation of *Myst*-like games on the market led to little innovation in the field and a drop in consumer confidence in the genre. *Computer Gaming World* reported that a "respected designer" felt it was impossible to design new and more difficult adventure puzzles as fans demanded, because Scott Adams had already created them all in his early games. Another factor that led to the decline of the adventure game market was the advent of first person shooters, *Doom* and *Half-Life*. These games, taking further advantage of computer advancement, were able to offer strong, story-driven games within an action setting.

This slump in popularity led many publishers and developers to see adventure games as financially unfeasible in comparison. Notably, Sierra was sold to CUC International in 1998, and while still a separate studio, attempted to recreate an adventure game using 3D graphics, *King's Quest: Mask of Eternity*, as well as *Gabriel Knight 3*, both of which fared poorly; the studio was subsequently closed in 1999. Similarly, LucasArts released *Grim Fandango* to many positive reviews but poor sales; it released one more title, *Escape from Monkey Island* in 2000, but subsequently stopped development of *Sam & Max: Freelance Police* and had no further plans for adventure games. Many of those developers for LucasArts, including Grossman and Schafer, left the company during this time. Sierra developer Lori Ann Cole stated in 2003 her belief that the high cost of development hurt adventure games: "They are just too art intensive, and art is expensive to produce and to show. Some of the best of the Adventure Games were criticized they were just too short. Action-adventure or Adventure Role-playing games can get away with re-using a lot of the art, and stretching the game play."

Traditional adventure games became difficult to propose as new commercial titles. Gilbert wrote in 2005, "From first-hand experience, I can tell you that if you even utter the words 'adventure game' in a meeting with a publisher you can just pack up your spiffy concept art and leave. You'd get a better reaction by announcing that you have the plague." In 2012 Schaefer said "If I were to go to a publisher right now and pitch an adventure game, they'd laugh in my face." Though most commercial adventure game publication had stopped in the United States by the early 2000s, the genre was still popular in Europe. Games such as *The Longest Journey* by Funcom as well as *Amerzone* and *Syberia*, both conceived by Benoît Sokal and developed by Microïds, with rich classical elements of the genre still garnered high critical acclaims.

Similar to the fate of interactive fiction, conventional graphical adventure games have continued to thrive in the amateur scene. This has been most prolific with the tool Adventure Game Studio. Some notable AGS games include those by Ben Croshaw (namely the *Chzo Mythos*), *Ben Jordan: Paranormal Investigator*, *Time Gentlemen, Please!*, *Soviet Unterzoegersdorf*, *Metal Dead*, and AGD Interactive's Sierra adventure remakes. Adobe Flash is also a popular tool known for adventures such as *MOTAS* and the escape the room genre entries.

New Platforms and Rebirth (2005–onward)

Following the demise of the adventure genre in the early 2000s, a number of events have occurred that have led to a revitalization of the adventure game genre as commercially viable: the introduction of new computing and gaming hardware and software delivery formats, and the use of crowdfunding as a means of achieving funding.

The 2000s saw the growth of digital distribution and the arrival of smart phones and tablet computers, with touch-screen interfaces well-suited to point-and-click adventure games. The introduction of larger and more powerful touch screen devices like the iPad allowed for more detailed graphics, more precise controls, and a better sense of immersion and interactivity compared to personal computer or console versions. In gaming hardware, the handheld Nintendo DS and subsequent units included a touch-screen, and the Nintendo Wii console with its Wii Remote allowed players to control a cursor through motion control. These new platforms helped decrease the cost of bringing an adventure game to market, providing an avenue to re-release older, less graphically advanced games *The Secret of Monkey Island*, *King's Quest* and *Space Quest* and attracting a new audience to adventure games.

The Nintendo DS in particular helped spark a resurgence in the genre's popularity through the introduction of otherwise unknown Japanese adventure games, typically visual novels localized for Western audiences. In 2005, Capcom re-released the courtroom-based visual novel game *Phoenix Wright: Ace Attorney*, originally a 2001 Game Boy Advance game released only in Japan, for the Nintendo DS in both Asian and Western markets. The game and its sequels proved popular with Western audiences, and are credited for revitalizing the adventure game genre. Following on *Ace Attorney*'s success, Level-5 and Nintendo published the *Professor Layton* series worldwide starting in 2007. Both have since become some of the best-selling adventure game franchises, with *Ace Attorney* selling more than 4 million units worldwide and *Professor Layton* selling nearly 12 million units worldwide. Other successful Japanese adventure games for the DS in Western markets include Cing's *Another Code: Two Memories* (2005) and *Hotel Dusk: Room 215* (2006). and Chunsoft's *Zero Escape* series, which includes *Nine Hours, Nine Persons, Nine Doors* and *Zero Escape: Virtue's Last Reward*.

Further, the improvements in digital distribution led to the concept of episodic adventure games, delivering between three and five "chapters" of a full game over a course of several months via online storefronts, Steam, Xbox Live Marketplace, PlayStation Store, and Nintendo eShop. Modeled off the idea of televisions episodes, episodic adventure games break the story into several parts, giving players a chance to digest and discuss the current story with others before the next episode is available, and further can enhance the narrative by creating cliffhangers or other dramatic elements to be resolved in later episodes. The first major successful episodic adventure games were those of Telltale Games, a developer founded by former LucasArts employees following the cancellation of *Sam & Max: Freelance Police*. Telltale found critical success in *The Walking Dead* series released in 2012, which eschewed traditional adventure game elements and puzzles for a strong story and character-driven game, forcing the player to make on-the-spot decisions that would become determinants and affect not only elements in the current episode but future episodes and in sequels. The game also eschewed the typical dialog tree with a more natural language progression, which created a more believable experience. Its success was considered a revitalization of the genre, and would lead Telltale to produce more licensed games driven by story rather than puzzles. The episodic format would become popular with other adventure games *Life Is Strange*.

Online distribution has also helped lower the costs of brings niche Japanese titles to consumers, which has enabled another outlet for visual novels and dating sims to be localized and released for Western markets. Localization and distribution can be performed by small teams, removing financial barriers to bringing these games, often released as dōjin soft or hobbist titles, to Western countries. A noted example of this is *Hatoful Boyfriend*, a comedy dating sim in which the player attempts to date pigeons in a high school setting. The game was originally released in Japan in 2011, but received significant attention on its remake and localization in 2014, in part due to its humorous concept, and its distribution was supported by Western publisher Devolver Digital.

Meanwhile, another avenue for adventure game rebirth came from the discovery of the influence of crowdfunding. Tim Schafer had founded Double Fine Productions after leaving LucasArts in 2000. He had tried to find funding support for an adventure game, but publishers refused to consider his proposals for fear of the genre being unpopular. In 2012, Schafer turned to Kickstarter to raise $400,000 to develop an adventure game; the month-long campaign ended with over $3.4 million raised, making it, at the time, one of the largest Kickstarter projects, enabling Double Fine to expand the scope of their project and completing the game as *Broken Age*, released over two parts in 2014 and 2015. The success led many other developers to consider the crowd funding approach, including those in the adventure game genre who saw the Double Fine Kickstarter as a sign that players wanted adventure games. Many sequels, remakes, and spiritual successors to classic adventure games emerged on Kickstarter, leading to a significant increase in traditional adventure game development during this time. Some of these include:

- *Armikrog*

- *Broken Sword: The Serpent's Curse*

- *Dreamfall Chapters*

- *Gabriel Knight*

- *Leisure Suit Larry: Reloaded*

- *Moebius: Empire Rising*

- *Obduction*

- *SpaceVenture*

- *Tesla Effect: A Tex Murphy Adventure*

- *Thimbleweed Park*

Japanese Adventures

Due to the differences in computer hardware, language and culture, development of adventure games took a different course in Japan compared to Western markets, generally focusing on visual novels and its subgenres in comparison to point-and-click and other graphical adventures.

Early Japanese Adventures (1982–1986)

In the early 1980s, adventure games began gaining popularity in Japan. The country's computer market was largely dominated by NEC's 8-bit PC-8801 (1981) and 16-bit PC-9801 (1982) platforms, which could display 8 simultaneous colors and had a resolution of 640×400, higher than Western computers at the time, in order to accommodate Japanese text. This in turn influenced game design, as NEC PCs became known for adventure games with detailed color graphics, which would eventually evolve into visual novels. NEC soon had several competitors such as the FM-7 (1982), the AV (1985) version of which could display more than 4000 colors in addition to featuring FM synthesis sound. Its 16-bit successor, the FM Towns (1989), could display 24-bit color (16.8 million colors) and featured a CD-ROM drive.

Japan's first domestic adventure games were ASCII's *Omotesando Adventure* (表参道アドベンチャー) and *Minami Aoyama Adventure* (南青山アドベンチャー), released for the PC-9801 in 1982. Another early Japanese adventure that same year was MicroCabin's *Mystery House*, which was unrelated to (but inspired by) the On-Line Systems game of the same name. MicroCabin released a sequel, *Mystery House II*, for the MSX that same year. The following year, the Japanese company Starcraft released an enhanced remake of On-Line Systems' *Mystery House* with more realistic art work and depiction of blood.

Due to a lack of content restrictions, some of Japan's earliest adventure games were also bishoujo games with *eroge* content. In 1982, Koei released *Night Life*, the first commercial erotic computer game. It was a graphic adventure, with sexually explicit images. That same year, they released another *eroge* title, *Danchi Tsuma no Yuwaku* (*Seduction of the Condominium Wife*), which was an early adventure game with color graphics, owing to the eight-color palette of the NEC PC-8001 computer, and role-playing video game elements. It became a hit, helping Koei become a major software company. Other now-famous companies such as Enix, Square and Nihon Falcom also produced similar *eroge* in the early 1980s before they became famous for their mainstream role-playing games. In some of their early *eroge*, the adult content is meaningfully integrated into a thoughtful and mature storyline, though others often used it as a flimsy excuse for pornography.

Meanwhile, in the arcades, Japanese developers also began producing early interactive movie laserdisc video games, the first being Sega's *Astron Belt*, unveiled in 1982 and released in 1983, though it was more of a shooter game presented as an action movie using full-motion video. A more story-driven interactive movie game was *Bega's Battle*, released in 1983, which combined shooting stages with interactive anime cutscenes, where player input had an effect on the game's branching storyline. *Time Gal* (1985), in addition to featuring quick time events, added a time-stopping feature where specific moments in the game involve Reika stopping time; during these moments, players are presented with a list of three options and have seven seconds to choose one.

The most famous early Japanese adventure game was the 1983 murder mystery game *Portopia Serial Murder Case*, developed by Yūji Horii (of *Dragon Quest* fame) and published by Enix. The game was viewed in a first-person perspective, followed a first-person narrative, and featured color graphics. Originally released for the PC-6001, the player interacts with the game using a verb-noun parser which requires typing precise commands with the keyboard; finding the exact words to type is considered part of the riddles that must be solved. The game featured non-linear elements, which includes travelling between different areas in a generally open world, a branching dialogue conversation system where the story develops through entering commands and receiving responses from other characters, and making choices that determine the dialogues and order of events as well as alternative outcomes, though there is only one true culprit while the others are red herrings. It also features a phone that could be used to dial any number to contact several non-player characters. The game was well received in Japan for its well-told storyline and surprising twist ending, and for allowing multiple ways to achieve objectives. Hideo Kojima praised the game for its mystery, drama, humor, 3D dungeons, for providing a proper background and explanation behind the murderer's motives, and expanding the potential of video games. The game has also been compared to the later-released *Shadowgate* where the player must examine and collect objects, and find their true purpose later on. According to Square Enix, *Portopia* was "the first real detective adventure" game.

The command selection menu input system, where the player chooses from a menu list of commands either through keyboard shortcuts or scrolling down the menu, was introduced in 1983, and would largely replace the verb-noun parser input method over the years. The earliest known title to use the command selection menu system was the Japanese adventure game *Spy 007* (スパイ00.7), published in April 1983, and it was followed soon after by several other Japanese adventure games in 1983. These included the *eroge* title *Joshiryo Panic*, authored by Tadashi Makimura and published by Enix for the FM-7 in June and slightly earlier for the FM-8; *Atami Onsen Adventure* (熱海温泉アドベンチャー), released by Basic System (ベーシックシステム) in July for the FM-7 and slightly earlier for the PC-8001; *Planet Mephius*, released in July; and *Tri-Dantal* (トリダンタル), authored by Y. Takeshita and published by Pax Softnica for the FM-7 in August. The game that popularized the command selection system was the 1984 adventure game *Okhotsk ni Kiyu: Hokkaido Rensa Satsujin Jiken* (*Okhotsk ni Kiyu: Hokkaido Chain Murders*), designed by Yuji Horii (his second mystery adventure game after *Portopia*) and published by ASCII for the PC-8801 and PC-9801. Its replacement of the traditional verb-noun text parser interface with the command selection menu system would lead to the latter becoming a staple of adventure games as well as role-playing games (through Horii's 1986 hit *Dragon Quest* in the latter case).

Another notable adventure game released in 1983 was *Planet Mephius*, authored by Eiji Yokoyama and published by T&E Soft for the FM-7 in July 1983. In addition to being one of the earliest titles to use a command menu system, its key innovation was the introduction of a point-and-click interface to the genre, utilizing a cursor to interact with objects displayed on the screen. A similar point-and-click cursor interface was later used in the adventure game *Wingman*, released for the PC-8801 in 1984.

The NES version of *Portopia Serial Murder Case* was released in 1985 and became a major hit in Japan, where it sold over 700,000 copies. With no keyboard, the NES version, developed by Chunsoft, replaced the verb-noun parser of the original with a command selection menu list, which included fourteen set commands selectable with the gamepad. It also featured a cursor that can be moved on the screen using the D-pad to look for clues and hotspots, like a point-and-click interface. Horii's second adventure game *Hokkaido Chain Murders* was later also ported to the NES in 1987. Yuji Horii's third mystery adventure game *Karuizawa Yūkai Annai* (*The Karuizawa Kidnapping Guide*) was released for the PC-8801 in early 1985 and for the FM-7 in June that same year. It utilized the command menu system and point-and-click cursor interface of both *Portopia Serial Murder Case* and *Hokkaido Chain Murders*, in addition to introducing its own innovation: an overhead map. This gave the player direct control over the player character, who can be moved around in a top-down view to explore the area. That same year, Square's *Will: The Death Trap II* was one of the first animated computer games.

In 1986, Square released the science fiction adventure game *Suishō no Dragon* for the NES console. The game featured several innovations, including the use of animation in many of the scenes rather than still images, and an interface resembling that of a point-and-click interface for a console, like *Portopia*, but making use of visual icons rather than text-based ones to represent various actions. Like the NES version of *Portopia*, it featured a cursor that could be moved around the screen using the D-pad to examine the scenery, though the cursor in *Suishō no Dragon* was also used to click on the action icons. That same year saw the release of *J.B. Harold Murder Club*, a point-and-click graphic adventure, for the PC-98. It featured character interaction as the major gameplay element and has a similar type of multiple phrase response to more recent titles such as the adventures *Shenmue* and *Shadow of Memories* as well as the role-playing game *Star Wars: Knights of the Old Republic*. The TurboGrafx-CD port of *J.B. Harold Murder Club* was one of the first Japanese adventure games released in the United States. The *J.B. Harold* series went on to sell 20 million copies on various platforms as of 2011.

Japanese Adventures (1987–present)

Sega's *Anmitsu Hime: From Amakara Castle*, released in 1987, was an adventure game with some platform game segments. The adventure game segments were puzzle-oriented and played in a side-scrolling view where the player has direct control over the character. Originally based on the *Anmitsu Hime* anime, an edited version based on *Alex Kidd* was later released in 1989 as *Alex Kidd in High-Tech World*. *The Goonies II*, also released in 1987, was a first-person adventure game with some side-scrolling action game segments. The game featured a non-linear open world environment similar to *Metroid*. The same year, Jiro Ishii (later known for *428: Fūsa Sareta Shibuya de* and *Time Travelers*) released *Imitation City*, an adventure game with a similar cyberpunk theme to Kojima's later hit *Snatcher*. Another notable 1987 adventure game was Arsys Software's *Reviver: The Real-Time Adventure*, which introduced a real-time persistent world, where time continues to elapse, day-night cycles adjust the brightness of the screen to indicate the time of day, and certain stores and non-player characters would only be available at certain times of the day. The game also gives players direct control over the player character.

A distinct form of Japanese adventure game that eventually emerged is the visual novel, a genre that was largely inspired by *Portopia Serial Murder Case*, and uses many conventions that are distinct from Western adventures. They are almost universally first-person, and driven primarily by dialog. They also tend to use menu-based interactions and navigation, with point and click implementations that are quite different from Western adventure games. Inventory-based puzzles of the sort that form the basis of classic Western adventures, are quite rare. Logic puzzles like those found in *Myst* are likewise unusual. Because of this, Japanese visual novels tend to be streamlined, and often quite easy, relying more on storytelling than challenge to keep players interested.

Hideo Kojima (of *Metal Gear* fame) was inspired by *Portopia* to enter the video game industry, and produce his own adventure games. After completing the stealth game *Metal Gear*, his first graphic adventure was released by Konami the following year: *Snatcher* (1988), an ambitious cyberpunk detective novel graphic adventure that was highly regarded at the time for pushing the boundaries of video game storytelling, cinematic cut scenes, and mature content. It also featured a post-apocalyptic science fiction setting, an amnesiac protagonist, and some light gun shooter segments. It was praised for its graphics, soundtrack, high quality writing comparable to a novel, voice acting comparable to a film or radio drama, and in-game computer database with optional documents that flesh out the game world. The Sega CD version of *Snatcher* was for a long time the only major visual novel game to be released in America, where it, despite a Mature rating limiting its accessibility, gained a cult following.

Following *Metal Gear 2: Solid Snake*, Kojima produced his next graphic adventure, *Policenauts* (1994), a point-and-click adventure notable for being an early example of extensive voice recording in video games. It also featured a hard science fiction setting, a theme revolving around space exploration, a plot inspired by the ancient Japanese tale of *Urashima Taro*, and some occasional full-motion video cut scenes. The gameplay was largely similar to *Snatcher*, but with the addition of a point-and-click interface and some first-person shooter segments. *Policenauts* also introduced summary screens, which act to refresh the player's memory of the plot upon reloading a save, an element Kojima would later use in *Metal Gear Solid*. The PlayStation version of *Policenauts* could also read the memory card and give some easter egg dialogues if a save file of Konami's dating sim *Tokimeki Memorial* is present, a technique Kojima would also later use in *Metal Gear Solid*. From 1997 to 1999, Kojima developed the three *Tokimeki Memorial Drama Series* titles, which were adaptations of *Tokimeki Memorial* in a visual novel adventure game format.

Mirrors, released by Soft Studio Wing for the PC-8801 and FM Towns computers in 1990, featured a branching narrative, multiple endings, and audio CD music. In 1995, Human Entertainment's *Clock Tower: The First Fear* was a hybrid between a point-and-click graphic adventure and a survival horror game, revolving around survival against a deadly stalker known as Scissorman that chased players throughout the game. The success of *Resident Evil* in 1996 was followed by the release of the survival horror graphic adventures *Clock Tower (Clock Tower 2)* and *Clock Tower II: The Struggle Within* for the PlayStation. The *Clock Tower* games proved to be hits, capitalizing on the success of *Resident Evil*, though both games stayed true to the graphic-adventure gameplay of the original *Clock Tower* rather than following the lead of *Resident Evil*.

From the early 1990s, Chunsoft, the developer for the NES version of *Portopia*, began producing a series of acclaimed visual novels known as the *Sound Novels* series, which include *Otogirisō* (1992), *Kamaitachi no Yoru* (1994), *Machi* (1998), *428: Fūsa Sareta Shibuya de* (2008), and *999: Nine Hours, Nine Persons, Nine Doors* (2010). From the late 1990s, a number of Japanese adventure games began using a 3D third-person direct control format, particularly on consoles like the Dreamcast and PlayStation 2. Examples include Sega's *Shenmue* series (since 1999), Konami's *Shadow of Memories* (2001), Irem's *Disaster Report* series (since 2002), and Cing's *Glass Rose* (2003).

In recent years, Japanese visual novel games have been released in the West more frequently, particularly on the Nintendo DS handheld following the success of mystery-solving titles such as Capcom's *Ace Attorney* series (which began on the Game Boy Advance in 2001), Cing's *Hotel Dusk* series (beginning in 2006), and Level-5's *Professor Layton* series (beginning in 2007). English fan translations of visual novels such as Square's *Radical Dreamers* (a 1996 side story to the *Chrono* series of role-playing video games) and Key's *Clannad* (2004) have also been made available in recent years.

Notable Developers

Within the adventure game genre, several developers and studios became instrumental in the direction that the genre has taken.

Adventure International (1978–1985)

Adventure International is a development company founded by programmer Scott Adams alongside his wife Alexis. Adams was a fan of *Colossal Cave Adventure*, and had spent days to run through the game to achieve the highest score possible, "Adventure Grandmaster". From this, he was inspired to write a similar game for the home computer system TRS-80, which lacked the memory capacity of the mainframes that *Colossal Cave Adventure* ran on. To get around this, he wrote a reusable high-level language and an interpreter written in BASIC. Adventure International was founded to sell the title, becoming the first commercially-sold adventure game. Adams' second title, *Pirate Adventure*, was an original game in a similar style to *Colossal Cave Adventure*, and its source code, written in BASIC, was published in the December 1980 issue of *Byte*. In his subsequent games, starting with *Mission Impossible*, Adams reworked his interpreter in assembly language that improved the speed of his software. Adventure International went on to produce a total of twelve adventure games before a downturn in the industry led to the company's bankruptcy in 1985. Several adventure game designers and writers cite Adams' games as an influence on their own creations.

Infocom (1979–1989)

Infocom was a game development company formed in June 1979 by, among others, Dave Lebling, Marc Blank, Tim Anderson, Bruce Daniels, and Albert Vezza. Lebling and Blank were students at MIT's Laboratory for Computer Science at the time of *Colossal Cave Adventure*'s release. Desiring to create a similar game, they worked alongside fellow students Anderson and Daniels to create the text adventure *Zork* for the PDP-10 minicomputer, distributed via ARPANET. On graduation the students, together with their group leader Albert Vezza, decided to form Inforcom to port *Zork* for home computers, As with Adams, Infocom was also limited by the size of memory on home computers at the time like the Apple II and TRS-80. They broke up *Zork* into three episodes to manage the size, and then created the Zork Implementation Language (ZIL) and the Z-machine to run ZIL programs, the first virtual machine used in a commercial product. *Zork* was very successful, with the first episode *Zork I* released in 1980 and selling nearly 380,000 copies by 1986.

The company continued to develop new text adventure games, expanding in size to over 100 employees at its peak; by 1984, they had sold over $10 million in game software. Their success drew writer Douglas Adams, who had loved *Zork*, to help produce two games through them: the first based on Douglas Adams' popular *Hitchhiker's Guide to the Galaxy*, and an original work called *Bureaucracy*. The company also attempted to expand into business software, writing the relational database program *Cornerstone*, released in 1985; though *Cornerstone* was well-received, its release was at a time of a slump in software sales, and the company lost a significant amount of money on the title, as well as divided the company internally on progress going forward. Struggling for funding, Infocom was bought by Activision in 1986 and returned to adventure game development, but following that, the increased power of home microcomputers and graphic-driven games saw the demand for Infocom titles decline. Infocom was late to add graphics to its games as to be able to compete with other titles until 1987. By 1989, the Infocom division at Activision had been reduced to 10 employees, and was ultimately shuttered; Activision would continue to develop some text adventure games inhouse using the Infocom brand but with no connection to the original team. The demise of Infocom is considered to be the end of the commercial age for interactive fiction, but its legacy would remain; the Z-machine remains a popular source for running non-commercial interactive fiction games developed in more modern tools such as Inform.

Sierra (1979–1999)

Sierra On-Line was founded by Roberta and Ken Williams in 1980. Roberta had also been inspired by *Colossal Cave Adventure*, and unable to find similar games of that type, wrote her own detective story based loosely on Agatha Christie's novel *And Then There Were None* and the board game *Clue*. Once she had completed its design, she had convinced Ken to stop work on a FORTRAN compiler he had been developing as to bring her game to light on the Apple II home computer. The game, initially titled *Hi-Res Adventure*, was ultimately released as *Mystery House*; *Mystery House* was the first adventure game to feature graphics, using vector graphics atop a simple two-word command parser. The Williamses initially sold the game on their own, achieving reasonable sales. Though Ken wanted to continue developing business software, they ultimately decided to continue to develop games, forming On-Line Systems in 1980, which they would eventually rename as Sierra On-Line.

Sierra's initial games, labeled as part of the *Hi-Res Adventure* series, followed the same approach as *Mystery House*, using a first-person perspective graphical view along with text commands; Roberta would design each game's story and puzzles, while Ken would program it. In 1983, IBM contacted Sierra to develop a game for their new system, the PCjr, which featured more advanced graphics at the time as well as a more advanced sound system. Roberta designed a fairy-tale style adventure that would better visualized by the PCjr's graphics, and Ken developed software to allow animations include the player's character to occur on-screen in response to the player's typed commands. This was aided by the development of the Adventure Game Interpreter, a virtual machine that used a high-level language to control. This game became known as *King's Quest I*. It initially had poor sales due to its tie-in to the PCjr, but when IBM later abandoned the system, the Williamses were free to port the game to other systems, where it became highlight successful. Sierra began to expand, producing more games in the *King's Quest* series, which prompted thematic spinoffs in the *Space Quest* series by Mark Crowe and Scott Murphy, the *Police Quest* series by Jim Walls. The company would also produce other adventure games including the *Leisure Suit Larry* series by Al Lowe, *Quest for*

Glory by Corey and Lori Ann Cole, and *Gabriel Knight* by Jane Jensen. As games featuring point-and-click interfaces began to become popular in the mid-1990s, Sierra also began to produce these types of games, including the forementioned *Gabriel Knight* series, *Phantasmagoria*, and *Shivers*.

Sierra would develop new games and push the boundaries of adventure gaming until its purchase by Cendant in 1998. Then in 1998, Cendant sold off their entire interactive software branch for $1 billion to Havas Interactive, a subsidiary of Vivendi Universal. At that point, the adventure game market was starting to wane as other types of genres became more popular, partially enabled by more powerful home console hardware such as the PlayStation. Sierra exited the game development sector, and was rebranded as Sierra Entertainment to help with video game publishing. They would continue to publish titles through 2008; at that time, Vivendi has been acquired by Activision, who shut down Sierra though kept the name. Following the resurgence of adventure games in 2010, Activision reactivated Sierra Entertainment for the first of several projects, the 2015 *King's Quest* a new title in the series that was developed by The Odd Gentlemen.

LucasArts (1986–2000)

Maniac Mansion on the Commodore 64, the first game to use the SCUMM interface

Lucasfilm Games was a game-development division spun off from Lucasfilm in 1982, making a wide variety of titles; it eventually was renamed as LucasArts. LucasArts has made significant contributions to the adventure genre market in the 1980s and 1990s. Its initial foray was the text-adventure game *Labyrinth: The Computer Game* based on the film of the same name.

In 1987, LucasArts developers Ron Gilbert and Gary Winnick created the graphical adventure game *Maniac Mansion*. Gilbert was inspired to add graphics after seeing Sierra's *King's Quest*, having not been a fan of text-based adventure games. Gilbert created the SCUMM game engine (an initialism for "Simple Creation Utility for Maniac Mansion") that enabled for a point-and-click game interface, which would be expanded upon and used throughout most other LucasArts adventure games. Gilbert led the development of the comedic pirate adventure *The Secret of Monkey Island*, the first LucasArts game taking advantage of 256 color graphics, bringing along two new hires to LucasArts, Dave Grossman and Tim Schafer, to help in writing and programming. The team differentiated themselves from the Sierra games in that they eliminated any possibility of the player-character dying in the game, so that the player would never become stuck in a title. The game was highly successful, leading LucasArts to continue to develop titles in similar manner between Gilbert, Winnick, Grossman, and Schafer, including: the *Monkey Island* sequels *Monkey Island 2: LeChuck's Revenge* and *The Curse of Monkey Island*; *Day of the Tentacle*, a Chuck Jones-inspired sequel to *Maniac Mansion*; *Sam & Max Hit the Road* based on Steve Purcell's Sam & Max characters; *Full Throttle* which centered on biker gangs in the near-future; *The Dig*, a science-fiction themed title developed in collaboration with Steven Spielberg and Orson Scott Card; and the film noir-styled *Grim Fandango* that expanded the SCUMM engine to a three-dimensional canvas via the GrimE. Other adventure games developed by the LucasArts team included *Zak McKracken and the Alien Mindbenders*, *Loom*, *Indiana Jones and the Last Crusade: The Graphic Adventure*, and *Indiana Jones and the Fate of Atlantis*, These games would also integrate a fuller musical score through LucasArts' iMUSE system that was developed by music composers Peter McConnell and Michael Land.

At the time of *Grim Fandango*'s release around 2000, the computer game market was seeing a shift to more graphics-enabled games due to updated computer speeds. *Grim Fandango* sold poorly, and LucasArts' next adventure game release *Escape from Monkey Island* was panned. LucasArts cancelled two future adventure game projects, focusing more on action games, particularly those related to the *Star Wars* franchise which were better sellers. Gilbert, Winnick, Grossman, and Schafer would leave LucasArts for other pursuits. Though LucasArts did not make new adventure games from 2000 onward, they did help to develop remastered versions of *The Secret of Monkey Island* and *Monkey Island 2* in 2009 and 2010 respectively, and were reportedly working on a similar remaster of *Day of the Tentacle*. At that point in 2011, LucasArts was bought out and incorporated into Disney, and the division was eventually shuttered in 2013.

Most of LucasArts' adventure titles have been critically praised and still considered some of the best computer games over a decade from their initial release. Because of their popularity, fans have developed the ScummVM emulation engine that allows these titles to be played on modern systems, and since has been expanded to include other adventure game engines such as from Sierra Online, Revolution Software and Adventure Soft. Double Fine, a company founded by Schafer following his departure from LucasArts, has been able to secure the rights to some of the LucasArts adventure games and has been developing remastered versions for modern computer systems. Their remastered version of *Grim Fandango* was released in 2015 and *Day of the Tentacle* in 2016, with *Full Throttle* expected for a 2017 release.

Telltale Games (2004–present)

Telltale Games was founded in 2004 by a number of ex-LucasArts employees, including Grossman, following the cancellation of *Sam & Max: Freelance Police*. The company sought to continue the tradition of adventure games. Their initial games were standalone titles, including a two-game series based on Jeff Smith's *Bone* comics, and several games based on the *CSI: Crime Scene Investigation* television series.

Telltale hit upon success on creating episodic adventure games, with *Sam & Max: Season One* in 2006 as an unofficial sequel to LucasArts' *Sam & Max Hit the Road* and inspired by their existing work they had done on the cancelled *Freelance Police*. Two further seasons of *Sam &*

Max would follow, along with games based on other licensed properties, including *Homestar Runner*, *Wallace and Gromit*, *Monkey Island*, *Back to the Future* and *Jurassic Park*. In addition to home computers and consoles, Telltale would also develop these titles for mobile devices, a growing market at the time.

Telltale's *The Walking Dead* focused more on story and characters than puzzles and inventory, and was a critical success for both the studio and adventure games in general.

A subsequent licensing deal with Warner Bros. Entertainment brought the studio the rights to develop games based on Robert Kirkman's *The Walking Dead* and Bill Willingham's *Fables* comics. The first endeavor completed was the 2012 *The Walking Dead* video game, which had the same episodic nature as the studio's earlier games but was built more on developing characters and story over traditional puzzle elements. The game required the player to make significant game-changing decisions including the death of non-playable characters, sometimes with only a few seconds to deliberate which option to select through quick time events. Choices made would create determinants that would carry through the remaining episodes and into subsequent seasons, allowing players to come to feel as if the story they are presented was more personal due to the choices they made. The game was praised critically for its emotional story and use of the adventure genre, as well as designed its release around a timed episodic schedule. *The Walking Dead* was considered very successful, and one of the biggest surprises for the video game industry in 2012, and a "refresh" of the adventure game genre; Ron Gilbert noted that *The Walking Dead*'s approach to appear to the mass market can make adventure games as relevant as other genres to larger publishers. Following *The Walking Dead*, Telltale secures further deals to produce additional seasons of *The Walking Dead*, and seasons based on the *A Song of Ice and Fire/Game of Thrones* book series, and the *Borderlands* and *Minecraft* video games, among other deals. Telltale's episodic and deterministic narrative model has also been used by other developers, including *Life Is Strange* and *Dreamfall Chapters*.

Emulation

Many classic adventure games cannot run on modern operating systems. Early adventure games were developed for home computers that are not in use today. Emulators are available for modern computers that allow these old games to be played on the latest operating systems. One open-source software project called ScummVM provides a free engine for the LucasArts adventure games, the SCUMM-derived engine for Humongous Entertainment adventure games, early Sierra titles, Revolution Software 2D adventures, Coktel Vision adventure games and a few more assorted

2D adventures. ResidualVM is a sister project to ScummVM, aimed to emulate 3D-based adventure games such as *Grim Fandango* and *Myst III: Exile*. Another called VDMSound can emulate the old sound-cards which many of the games require.

One of the most popular emulators, DOSBox, is designed to emulate an IBM PC compatible computer running DOS, the native operating system (OS) of most older adventure games. Many companies, like Sierra Entertainment, have included DOSBox in their rereleases of older titles.

Text adventure games are more accessible. There are only a small number of standard formats, and nearly all the classics can be played on modern computers. A popular text adventure interpreter is Frotz, which can play all the old Infocom text adventures. Some modern text adventure games can even be played on very old computer systems. Text adventure games are also suitable for personal digital assistants (PDAs), because they have very small computer system requirements. Other text adventure games are fully playable via web browsers.

Dialog Tree

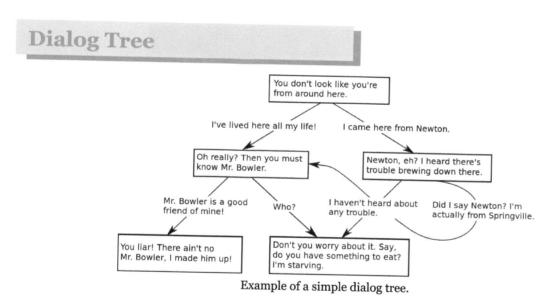

Example of a simple dialog tree.

A dialog tree or conversation tree is a gameplay mechanic that is used throughout many adventure games (including action-adventure games) and role-playing video games. When interacting with a non-player character, the player is given a choice of what to say and makes subsequent choices until the conversation ends. Certain video game genres, such as visual novels and dating sims, revolve almost entirely around these character interactions and branching dialogues.

History

The concept of a dialog tree has existed long before the advent of video games. The earliest known dialog tree is described in "The Garden of Forking Paths," a 1941 short story by Jorge Luis Borges, in which the combination book of Ts'ui Pên allows all major outcomes from an event branch into their own chapters. Much like the game counterparts this story reconvenes as it progresses (as possible outcomes would approach n^m where n is the number of options at each fork and m is the depth of the tree).

The first computer dialogue system was featured in ELIZA, a primitive natural language processing computer program written by Joseph Weizenbaum between 1964 and 1966. The program emulated interaction between the user and an artificial therapist. With the advent of video games, interactive entertainment have attempted to incorporate meaningful interactions with virtual characters. Branching dialogues have since become a common feature in visual novels, dating sims, adventure games, and role-playing video games.

Game Mechanics

The player typically enters the gameplay mode by choosing to speak with a non-player character (or when a non-player character chooses to speak to them), and then choosing a line of pre-written dialog from a menu. Upon choosing what to say, the non-player character responds to the player, and the player is given another choice of what to say. This cycle continues until the conversation ends. The conversation may end when the player selects a farewell message, the non-player character has nothing more to add and ends the conversation, or when the player makes a bad choice (perhaps angering the non-player to leave the conversation).

A dialog tree as implemented in the game *The Banner Saga*: the query from the non-player character appears at the bottom, and three possible player responses at the upper left.

Games often offer options to ask non-players to reiterate information about a topic, allowing players to replay parts of the conversation that they did not pay close enough attention to the first time. These conversations are said to be designed as a tree structure, with players deciding between each branch of dialog to pursue. Unlike a branching story, players may return to earlier parts of a conversation tree and repeat them. Each branch point (or node) is essentially a different menu of choices, and each choice that the player makes triggers a response from the non-player character followed by a new menu of choices.

In some genres such as role-playing video games, external factors such as charisma may influence the response of the non-player character or unlock options that would not be available to other characters. These conversations can have far-reaching consequences, such as deciding to disclose a valuable secret that has been entrusted to the player. However, these are usually not real tree data structure in programmers sense, because they contain cycles as can be seen on illustration on this page.

Certain game genres revolve almost entirely around character interactions, including visual novels such as *Ace Attorney* and dating sims such as *Tokimeki Memorial*, usually featuring complex branching dialogues and often presenting the player's possible responses word-for-word as the player character would say them. Games revolving around relationship-building, including visual novels, dating sims such as *Tokimeki Memorial*, and some role-playing games such as *Shin Megami Tensei: Persona*, often give choices that have a different number of associated "mood points" which influence a player character's relationship and future conversations with a non-player character. These games often feature a day-night cycle with a time scheduling system that provides context and relevance to character interactions, allowing players to choose when and if to interact with certain characters, which in turn influences their responses during later conversations. Some games use a real-time conversation system, giving the player only a few seconds to respond to a non-player character, such as Sega's *Sakura Wars* and *Alpha Protocol*.

Another variation of branching dialogues can be seen in the adventure game *Culpa Innata*, where the player chooses a tactic at the beginning of a conversation, such as using either a formal, casual or accusatory manner, that affects the tone of the conversation and the information gleaned from the interviewee.

Value and Impact

This mechanism allows game designers to provide interactive conversations with nonplayer characters without having to tackle the challenges of natural language processing in the field of artificial intelligence. In games such as *Monkey Island*, these conversations can help demonstrate the personality of certain characters.

Role-playing Video Game

A role-playing video game (commonly referred to as role-playing game or RPG, and in the past was also known as computer role-playing game or CRPG) is a video game genre where the player controls the actions of a character (and/or several party members) immersed in some well-defined world. Many role-playing video games have origins in pen-and-paper role-playing games (Including *Dungeons & Dragons*) and use much of the same terminology, settings and game mechanics. Other major similarities with pen-and-paper games include developed story-telling and narrative elements, player character development, complexity, as well as replayability and immersion. The electronic medium removes the necessity for a gamemaster and increases combat resolution speed. RPGs have evolved from simple text-based console-window games into visually rich 3D experiences.

Characteristics

Role-playing video games use much of the same terminology, settings and game mechanics as early pen-and-paper role-playing games such as *Dungeons & Dragons*. Players control a central game character, or multiple game characters, usually called a party, and attain victory by completing a series of quests or reaching the conclusion of a central storyline. Players explore a game world, while solving puzzles and engaging in tactical combat. A key feature of the genre is that characters grow in power and abilities, and characters are typically designed by the player. RPGs rarely challenge a player's physical coordination or reaction time, with the exception of action role-playing games.

Role-playing video games typically rely on a highly developed story and setting, which is divided into a number of quests. Players control one or several characters by issuing commands, which are performed by the character at an effectiveness determined by that character's numeric attributes. Often these attributes increase each time a character gains a level, and a character's level goes up each time the player accumulates a certain amount of experience.

Role-playing video games also typically attempt to offer more complex and dynamic character interaction than what is found in other video game genres. This usually involves additional focus on the artificial intelligence and scripted behavior of computer-controlled non-player characters.

Story and Setting

The premise of most role-playing games tasks the player with saving the world, or whichever level of society is threatened. There are often twists and turns as the story progresses, such as the surprise appearance of estranged relatives, or enemies who become friends or vice versa. The game world tends to be set in a fantasy or science fiction universe, which allows players to do things they cannot do in real life and helps players suspend their disbelief about the rapid character growth. To a lesser extent, settings closer to the present day or near future are possible.

The story often provides much of the entertainment in the game. Because these games have strong storylines, they can often make effective use of recorded dialog and voiceover narration. Players of these games tend to appreciate long cutscenes more than players of faster action games. While most games advance the plot when the player defeats an enemy or completes a level, role-playing games often progress the plot based on other important decisions. For example, a player may make the decision to join a guild, thus triggering a progression in the storyline that is usually irreversible. New elements in the story may also be triggered by mere arrival in an area, rather than completing a specific challenge. The plot is usually divided so that each game location is an opportunity to reveal a new chapter in the story.

Pen-and-paper role-playing games typically involve a player called the gamemaster (or GM for short) who can dynamically create the story, setting, and rules, and react to a player's choices. In role-playing video games, the computer performs the function of the gamemaster. This offers the player a smaller set of possible actions, since computers can't engage in imaginative acting comparable to a skilled human gamemaster. In exchange, the typical role-playing video game may have storyline branches, user interfaces, and stylized cutscenes and gameplay to offer a more direct storytelling mechanism. Characterization of non-player characters in video games is often handled using a dialog tree. Saying the right things to the right non-player characters will elicit useful information for the player, and may even result in other rewards such as items or experience, as well as opening up possible storyline branches. Multiplayer online role-playing games can offer an exception to this contrast by allowing human interaction among multiple players and in some cases enabling a player to perform the role of a gamemaster.

Exploration and Quests

Overworld map from the tactical RPG *The Battle for Wesnoth*.

Exploring the world is an important aspect of all RPGs. Players will walk through, talking to non-player characters, picking up objects, and avoiding traps. Some games such as *NetHack*, *Diablo*, and the *FATE* series randomize the structure of individual levels, increasing the game's variety and replayability. Role-playing games where players complete quests by exploring randomly generated dungeons and include the game mechanic "permadeath" are called roguelikes, named after the 1980 video game *Rogue*.

The game's story is often mapped onto exploration, where each chapter of the story is mapped onto a different location. RPGs usually allow players to return to previously visited locations. Usually, there is nothing left to do there, although some locations change throughout the story and offer the player new things to do in response. Players must acquire enough power to overcome a major challenge in order to progress to the next area, and this structure can be compared to the boss characters at the end of levels in action games.

The player typically must complete a linear sequence of certain quests in order to reach the end of the game's story, although quests in some games such as *Arcanum* or *Geneforge* can limit or enable certain choices later in the game. Many RPGs also often allow the player to seek out optional side-quests and character interactions. Quests of this sort can be found by talking to a non-player character, and there may be no penalty for abandoning or ignoring these quests other than a missed opportunity or reward. Quests may involve defeating one or many enemies, rescuing a non-player character, item fetch quests, or locational puzzles such as mysteriously locked doors.

Items and Inventory

Players can find loot (such as clothing, weapons, and armor) throughout the game world and collect it. Players can trade items for currency and better equipment. Trade takes place while interacting with certain friendly non-player characters, such as shopkeepers, and often uses a specialized trading screen. Purchased items go into the player's inventory. Some games turn inventory management into a logistical challenge by limiting the size of the player's inventory, thus forcing the player to decide what they must carry at the time. This can be done by limiting the maximum weight that a player can carry, by employing a system of arranging items in a virtual space, or by simply limiting the number of items that can be held.

Character Actions and Abilities

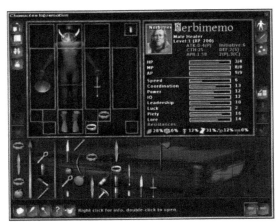

Character information and inventory screen in a typical computer role-playing game.
Pictured here is the roguelike *S.C.O.U.R.G.E.: Heroes of Lesser Renown*.

Most of the actions in an RPG are performed indirectly, with the player selecting an action and the character performing it by their own accord. Success at that action depends on the character's numeric attributes. Role-playing video games often simulate die-rolling mechanics from non-electronic role-playing games to determine success or failure. As a character's attributes improve, their chances of succeeding at a particular action will increase.

Many role-playing games allow players to play as an evil character. Although robbing and murdering indiscriminately may make it easier to get money, there are usually consequences in that other characters will become uncooperative or even hostile towards the player. Thus, these games allow players to make moral choices, but force players to live with the consequences of their actions. Games often let the player control an entire party of characters. However, if winning is contingent upon the survival of a single character, then that character effectively becomes the player's avatar. An example of this would be in *Baldur's Gate*, where if the character created by the player dies, the game ends and a previous save needs to be loaded.

Although some single-player role-playing games give the player an avatar that is largely predefined for the sake of telling a specific story, many role-playing games make use of a character creation screen. This allows players to choose their character's sex, their race or species, and their character class. Although many of theses traits are cosmetic, there are functional aspects as well. Character classes will have different abilities and strengths. Common classes include fighters, spellcasters, thieves with stealth abilities, and clerics with healing abilities, or a mixed class, such as a fighter who can cast simple spells. Characters will also have a range of physical attributes such as dexterity and strength, which affect a player's performance in combat. Mental attributes such as intelligence may affect a player's ability to perform and learn spells, while social attributes such as charisma may limit the player's choices while conversing with non-player characters. These attribute systems often strongly resemble the *Dungeons & Dragons* ruleset.

Some role-playing games make use of magical powers, or equivalents such as psychic powers or advanced technology. These abilities are confined to specific characters such as mages, spellcasters, or magic-users. In games where the player controls multiple characters, these magic-users usually complement the physical strength of other classes. Magic can be used to attack, to defend, or to temporarily change an enemy or ally's attributes. While some games allow players to gradually consume a spell, as ammunition is consumed by a gun, most games offer players a finite amount of mana which can be spent on any spell. Mana is restored by resting or by consuming potions. Characters can also gain other non-magical skills, which stay with the character as long as he lives.

Experience and Levels

Although the characterization of the game's avatar will develop through storytelling, characters may also become more functionally powerful by gaining new skills, weapons, and magic. This creates a positive-feedback cycle that is central to most role-playing games: The player grows in power, allowing them to overcome more difficult challenges, and gain even more power. This is part of the appeal of the genre, where players experience growing from an ordinary person into a superhero with amazing powers. Whereas other games give the player these powers immediately, the player in a role-playing game will choose their powers and skills as they gain experience.

Role-playing games usually measure progress by counting experience points and character levels. Experience is usually earned by defeating enemies in combat, with some games offering experience for completing certain quests or conversations. Experience becomes a form of score, and accumulating a certain amount of experience will cause the character's level to go up. This is called "levelling up", and gives the player an opportunity to raise one or more of his character's attributes. Many RPGs allow players to choose how to improve their character, by allocating a finite number of points into the attributes of their choice. Gaining experience will also unlock new magic spells for characters that use magic.

Some role-playing games also give the player specific skill points, which can be used to unlock a new skill or improve an existing one. This may sometimes be implemented as a skill tree. As with the technology trees seen in strategy video games, learning a particular skill in the tree will unlock more powerful skills deeper in the tree.

Three different systems of rewarding the player characters for solving the tasks in the game can be set apart: the *experience system* (also known as the "level-based" system), the *training system* (also known as the "skill-based" system) and the *skill-point system* (also known as "level-free" system)

- The experience system, by far the most common, was inherited from pen-and-paper role-playing games and emphasizes receiving "experience points" (often abbreviated "XP" or "EXP") by winning battles, performing class-specific activities, and completing quests. Once a certain amount of experience is gained, the character advances a level. In some games, level-up occurs automatically when the required amount of experience is reached; in others, the player can choose when and where to advance a level. Likewise, abilities and attributes may increase automatically or manually.

- The training system is similar to the way the Basic Role-Playing system works. The first video game to use this was *Dungeon Master*, and emphasizes developing the character's skills by using them—meaning that if a character wields a sword for some time, he or she will become proficient with it.

- Finally, in the skill-point system (as used in *Vampire: The Masquerade – Bloodlines* for example) the character is rewarded with "skill points" for completing quests, which then can be directly used to "buy" skills and/or attributes, without having to wait until the next "level up".

Combat

Older games often separated combat into its own mode of gameplay, distinct from exploring the game world. More recent games tend to maintain a consistent perspective for exploration and combat. Some games, especially earlier video games, generate battles from random encounters; more modern RPGs are more likely to have persistent wandering monsters that move about the game world independently of the player. Most RPGs also use stationary boss monsters in key positions, and automatically trigger battles with them when the PCs enter these locations or perform certain actions. Combat options typically involve positioning characters, selecting which enemy to attack, and exercising special skills such as casting spells.

In a classical turn-based system, only one character may act at a time; all other characters remain still, with a few exceptions that may involve the use of special abilities. The order in which the characters act is usually dependent on their attributes, such as speed or agility. This system rewards strategic planning more than quickness. It also points to the fact that realism in games is a means to the end of immersion in the game world, not an end in itself. A turn-based system makes it possible, for example, to run within range of an opponent and kill him before he gets a chance to act, or duck out from behind hard cover, fire, and retreat back without an opponent being able to fire, which are of course both impossibilities. However, tactical possibilities have been created by this unreality that did not exist before; the player determines whether the loss of immersion in the reality of the game is worth the satisfaction gained from the development of the tactic and its successful execution. *Fallout* has been praised as being "the shining example of a good turn-based Combat System [*sic*]".

Real-time combat can import features from action games, creating a hybrid action RPG game genre. But other RPG battle systems such as the Final Fantasy battle systems have imported real-time choices without emphasizing coordination or reflexes. Other systems combine real-time combat with the ability to pause the game and issue orders to all characters under his/her control; when the game is unpaused, all characters follow the orders they were given. This "real-time with pause" system (*RTwP*) has been particularly popular in games designed by BioWare. The most famous RTwP engine is the Infinity Engine. Other names for "real-time with pause" include "active pause" and "semi real-time". Tactical RPG maker Apeiron named their system Smart Pause Mode (SPM) because it would automatically pause based on a number of user-configurable settings.

Early *Ultima* games featured a RTwP system: they were strictly turn-based, but if the player waited more than a second or so to issue a command, the game would automatically issue a pass command, allowing the monsters to take a turn while the PCs did nothing. *Fallout Tactics: Brotherhood of Steel* is another game which used this system.

There is a further subdivision by the structure of the battle system; in many early games, such as *Wizardry*, monsters and the party are arrayed into ranks, and can only attack enemies in the front rank with melee weapons. Other games, such as most of the *Ultima* series, employed duplicates of the miniatures combat system traditionally used in the early role-playing games. Representations of the player characters and monsters would move around an arena modeled after the surrounding terrain, attacking any enemies that are sufficiently near.

Interface and Graphics

Players typically navigate the game world from a first or third-person perspective in 3D RPGs. However, an isometric or aerial top-down perspective is common in party-based RPGs, in order to give the player a clear view of their entire party and their surroundings. Role-playing games require the player to manage a large amount of information, and frequently make use of a windowed interface. For example, spell-casting characters will often have a menu of spells they can use. On the PC, players typically use the mouse to click on icons and menu options, while console games duplicate this functionality with the game controller. Older games often revealed calculations of the game as seen in *Dungeons & Dragons* games, although more recent games have removed this information to improve immersion.

History and Classification

The role-playing video game genre began in the mid-1970s on mainframe computers, inspired by pen-and-paper role-playing games such as *Dungeons & Dragons*. Several other sources of inspiration for early role-playing video games also included tabletop wargames, sports simulation games, adventure games such as *Colossal Cave Adventure*, fantasy writings by authors such as J. R. R. Tolkien, traditional strategy games such as chess, and ancient epic literature dating back to *Epic of Gilgamesh* which followed the same basic structure of setting off in various quests in order to accomplish goals.

After the success of role-playing video games such as *Ultima* and *Wizardry*, which in turn served as the blueprint for *Dragon Quest* and *Final Fantasy*, the role-playing genre eventually diverged into two styles, *Eastern role-playing games* and *Western role-playing games*, due to cultural differences, though roughly mirroring the platform divide between consoles and computers, respectively. Finally, while the first RPGs offered strictly a single player experience, the popularity of multiplayer modes rose sharply during the early to mid-1990s with action role-playing games such as *Secret of Mana* and *Diablo*. With the advent of the Internet, multiplayer games have grown to become massively multiplayer online role-playing games, including *Lineage*, *Final Fantasy XI*, and *World of Warcraft*.

Mainframe Computers

The role-playing video game genre began in the mid-1970s, as an offshoot of early university mainframe text-based RPGs on PDP-10 and Unix-based computers, such as *Dungeon*, pedit5 and dnd. In 1980, a very popular dungeon crawler, *Rogue* was released. Featuring ASCII graphics where the setting, monsters and items were represented by letters and a deep system of gameplay, it inspired a whole genre of similar clones on mainframe and home computers called "roguelikes".

Personal Computers

One of the earliest role-playing video game on a microcomputer was *Dungeon n Dragons*, written by Peter Trefonas and published by CLOAD (1980). This early game, published for a TRS-80

Model 1, was just 16K long and included a limited word parser command line, character generation, a store to purchase equipment, combat, traps to solve, and a dungeon to explore. Other contemporaneous CRPGs (Computer Role Playing Games) were *Temple of Apshai, Odyssey: The Compleat Apventure* and *Akalabeth: World of Doom*, the precursor to *Ultima*. Some early microcomputer RPGs (such as *Telengard* (1982) or *Sword of Fargoal*) were based on their mainframe counterparts, while others (such as *Ultima* or *Wizardry*, the most successful of the early CRPGs) were loose adaptations of *D&D*. They also included both first-person displays and overhead views, sometimes in the same game (*Akalabeth*, for example, used both perspectives). Most of the key features of RPGs were developed in this early period, prior to the release of *Ultima III: Exodus*, one of the prime influences on both computer and console RPG development. For example, Wizardry featured menu-driven combat, *Tunnels of Doom* featured tactical combat on a special "combat screen", and *Dungeons of Daggorath* featured real-time combat which took place on the main dungeon map.

Starting in 1984 with *Questron* and *50 Mission Crush*, SSI produced many series of CRPGs. Their 1985 game *Phantasie* is notable for introducing automapping and in-game scrolls providing hints and background information. They also released *Pool of Radiance* in 1988, the first of several "Gold Box" CRPGs based on the *Advanced Dungeons & Dragons rules*. These games featured a first-person display for movement, combined with an overhead tactical display for combat. One common feature of RPGs from this era, which Matt Barton calls the "Golden Age" of computer RPGs, is the use of numbered "paragraphs" printed in the manual or adjunct booklets, containing the game's lengthier texts; the player could be directed to read a certain paragraph, instead of being shown the text on screen. The ultimate exemplar of this approach was Sir-Tech's *Star Saga* trilogy (of which only two games were released); the first game contained 888 "textlets" (usually much longer than a single paragraph) spread across 13 booklets, while the second contained 50,000 paragraphs spread across 14 booklets. Most of the games from this era were turn-based, although *Dungeon Master* and its imitators had real-time combat. Other classic titles from this era include *The Bard's Tale* (1985), *Wasteland* (1988), the start of the *Might and Magic* (1986-2014) series and the continuing *Ultima* (1981-1999) series.

Later, in the middle to late 1990s, isometric, sprite-based RPGs became commonplace, with video game publishers Interplay Entertainment and Blizzard North playing a lead role with such titles as the *Baldur's Gate, Icewind Dale* and the action-RPG *Diablo* series, as well as the dialogue-heavy *Planescape: Torment* and cult classics *Fallout* and *Fallout 2*. This era also saw a move toward 3D game engines with such games as *Might and Magic VI: The Mandate of Heaven* and *The Elder Scrolls: Arena*. TSR, dissatisfied with SSI's later products, such as *Dark Sun: Wake of the Ravager* and *Menzoberranzan*, transferred the *AD&D* license to several different developers, and eventually gave it to BioWare, who used it in *Baldur's Gate* (1998) and several later games. By the 2000s, 3D engines had become dominant.

Video Game Consoles

The earliest RPG on a console was *Dragonstomper* on the Atari 2600 in 1982. Another early RPG on a console was *Bokosuka Wars*, originally released for the Sharp X1 computer in 1983 and later ported to the MSX in 1984, the NES in 1985 and the Sharp X68000 as *New Bokosuka Wars*. The game laid the foundations for the tactical role-playing game genre, or "simulation RPG" genre as it is known in Japan. It was also an early example of a real-time, action role-playing game. In 1986, Chunsoft created the NES title *Dragon Quest* (called *Dragon Warrior* in North America until the eighth game), which drew inspiration from computer RPG's Ultima and Wizardry and is regarded as the template for future Japanese role-playing video games released since then.

In 1987, the genre came into its own with the release of several highly influential console RPGs distinguishing themselves from computer RPGs, including the genre-defining Phantasy Star, released for the Master System. Shigeru Miyamoto's *Zelda II: The Adventure of Link* for the Famicom Disk System was one of the earliest action role-playing games, combining the action-adventure game framework of its predecessor *The Legend of Zelda* with the statistical elements of turn-based RPGs. Most RPGs at this time were turn-based. *Faxanadu* was another early action RPG for the NES, released as a side-story to the computer action RPG *Dragon Slayer II: Xanadu*. Square's *Final Fantasy* for the NES introduced side-view battles, with the player characters on the right and the enemies on the left, which soon became the norm for numerous console RPGs. In 1988, *Dragon Warrior III* introduced a character progression system allowing the player to change the party's character classes during the course of the game. Another "major innovation was the introduction of day/night cycles; certain items, characters, and quests are only accessible at certain times of day." In 1989, *Phantasy Star II* for the Genesis established many conventions of the genre, including an epic, dramatic, character-driven storyline dealing with serious themes and subject matter, and a strategy-based battle system.

Console RPGs distinguished themselves from computer RPGs to a greater degree in the early 1990s. As console RPGs became more heavily story-based than their computer counterparts, one of the major differences that emerged during this time was in the portrayal of the characters. Console RPGs often featured intricately related characters who had distinctive personalities and traits, with players assuming the roles of people who cared about each other, fell in love or even had families. Romance in particular was a theme that was common in most console RPGs at the time but absent from most computer RPGs. During the 1990s, console RPGs had become increasingly dominant, exerting a greater influence on computer RPGs than the other way around. Console RPGs had eclipsed computer RPGs for some time, though computer RPGs began making a comeback towards the end of the decade with interactive choice-filled adventures.

The next major revolution came in the late 1990s, which saw the rise of optical disks in fifth generation consoles. The implications for RPGs were enormous—longer, more involved quests, better audio, and full-motion video. This was first clearly demonstrated in 1997 by the phenomenal success of *Final Fantasy VII*, which is considered one of the most influential games of all time. With a record-breaking production budget of around $45 million, the ambitious scope of *Final Fantasy VII* raised the possibilities for the genre, with its dozens of minigames and much higher production values. The latter includes innovations such as the use of 3D characters on pre-rendered backgrounds, battles viewed from multiple different angles rather than a single angle, and for the first time full-motion CGI video seamlessly blended into the gameplay, effectively integrated throughout the game. The game was soon ported to the PC and gained much success there, as did several other originally console RPGs, blurring the line between the console and computer platforms.

Cultural Differences

After the success of console role-playing games in Japan, the role-playing genre eventually began being classified into two fairly distinct styles: *computer RPG* and *console RPG*, due to stylistic, gameplay and/or cultural reasons; with the latter having become popularized and heavily influenced by early Japanese video games such as *Dragon Quest* and *Final Fantasy*. In the early 2000s, however, as the platform differences began to blur, computer RPGs and console RPGs were eventually classified as *Western role-playing games* (or *WRPGs*) and *Japanese role-playing games* (or *JRPGs*), respectively.

Though sharing fundamental premises, Western RPGs tend to feature darker graphics, older characters, and a greater focus on roaming freedom, realism, and the underlying game mechanics (e.g. "rules-based" or "system-based"); whereas Eastern RPGs tend to feature brighter, anime-like graphics, younger characters, faster-paced gameplay, and a greater focus on tightly-orchestrated, linear storylines with intricate plots (e.g. "action-based" or "story-based"). Further, Western RPGs are more likely to allow players to create and customize characters from scratch, and since the late 1990s have had a stronger focus on extensive dialog tree systems (e.g. *Planescape: Torment*). On the other hand, Japanese RPGs tend to limit players to developing pre-defined player characters, and often do not allow the option to create or choose one's own playable characters or make decisions that alter the plot. In the early 1990s, Japanese RPGs were seen as being much closer to fantasy novels, but by the late 1990s had become more cinematic in style (e.g. *Final Fantasy* series), while at the same time Western RPGs started becoming more novelistic in style (e.g. *Planescape: Torment*); by the late 2000s, Western RPGs had also adopted a more cinematic style (e.g. *Mass Effect* series).

One reason given for these differences is that many early Japanese console RPGs can be seen as forms of interactive *manga* (Japanese comics) or anime wrapped around Western rule systems at the time, in addition to the influence of visual novel adventure games. As a result, Japanese console RPGs differentiated themselves with a stronger focus on scripted narratives and character drama, alongside streamlined gameplay. In recent years, these trends have in turn been adopted by Western RPGs, which have begun moving more towards tightly structured narratives, in addition to moving away from "numbers and rules" in favor of streamlined combat systems similar to action games. In addition, a large number of Western independent games are modelled after Japanese RPGs, especially those of the 16-bit era, partly due to the *RPG Maker* game development tools.

Example of *kawaii* art. "Cute" art such as this is unpopular with some players.

Another oft-cited difference is the prominence or absence of *kawaisa*, or "cuteness", in Japanese culture, and different approaches with respect to character aesthetics. Western RPGs tend to maintain a serious and gritty tone. JRPG protagonsists tend to be designed with an emphasis on aesthetic beauty, and even male characters are often young, androgynous, *shōnen* or *bishōnen* in appearance. JRPGs often have cute (and even comic-relief type) characters or animals, juxtaposed (or clashing) with more mature themes and situations; and many modern JRPGs feature characters designed in the same style as those in manga and anime. The stylistic differences are often due to differing target audiences: Western RPGs are usually geared primarily towards teenage to adult males, whereas Japanese RPGs are usually intended for a much larger demographic, including female audiences, who, for example, accounted for nearly a third of *Final Fantasy XIII*s fanbase.

Modern Japanese RPGs are more likely to feature turn-based battles; while modern Western RPGs are more likely to feature real-time combat. In the past, the reverse was often true: real-time action role-playing games were far more common among Japanese console RPGs than Western computer RPGs up until the late 1990s, due to gamepads usually being better suited to real-time action than the keyboard and mouse. There are of course exceptions, such as *Final Fantasy XII* (2006) and *Shin Megami Tensei: Devil Summoner* (1995 onwards), two modern Eastern RPGs that feature real-time combat; and *The Temple of Elemental Evil* (2003), a modern Western RPG that features turn-based combat.

Some journalists and video game designers have questioned this cultural classification, arguing that the differences between Eastern and Western games have been exaggerated. In an interview held at the American Electronic Entertainment Expo, Japanese video game developer Tetsuya Nomura (who worked on *Final Fantasy* and *Kingdom Hearts*) emphasized that RPGs should not be classified by country-of-origin, but rather described simply for what they are: role-playing games. Hironobu Sakaguchi, creator of *Final Fantasy* and *The Last Story*, noted that, while "users like to categorise" Japanese RPGs as "turn-based, traditional styles" and Western RPGs as "born from first-person shooters," there "are titles that don't fit the category," pointing to *Chrono Trigger* (which he also worked on) and the *Mana* games. He further noted that there have been "other games similar to the style of *Chrono Trigger*," but that "it's probably because the games weren't localised and didn't reach the Western audience." *Xeno* series director Tetsuya Takahashi, in reference to *Xenoblade Chronicles*, stated that "I don't know when exactly people started using the term 'JRPG,' but if this game makes people rethink the meaning of this term, I'll be satisfied." The writer Jeremy Parish of 1UP.com states that "*Xenoblade* throws into high relief the sheer artificiality of the gaming community's obsession over the differences between" Western and Japanese RPGs, pointing out that it "does things that don't really fit into either genre. Gamers do love their boundaries and barriers and neat little rules, I know, but just because you cram something into a little box doesn't mean it belongs there." Nick Doerr of Joystiq criticizes the claim that Japanese RPGs are "too linear," pointing out that non-linear Japanese RPGs are not uncommon—for instance, the *Romancing SaGa* series. Likewise, Rowan Kaiser of Joystiq points out that linear Western RPGs were common in the 1990s, and argues that many of the often mentioned differences between Eastern and Western games are stereotypes that are generally "not true" and "never was", pointing to classic examples like *Lands of Lore* and *Betrayal at Krondor* that were more narrative-focused than the typical Western-style RPGs of the time. In 2015, IGN noted in an interview with *Xenoblade Chronicles X*'s development team that the label "JRPG" is most commonly used to refer to RPGs "whose presentation mimics the design sensibilities" of anime and manga, that it's "typically the presentation and character archetypes" that signal "this is a JRPG."

Criticisms

Due to the cultural differences between Western and Japanese variations of role-playing games, both have often been compared and critiqued by those within the video games industry and press.

In the late 1980s, when traditional American computer RPGs such as *Ultima* and *Defender of the Crown* were ported to consoles, they received mixed reviews from console gamers, as they were "not perceived, by many of the players, to be as exciting as the Japanese imports," and lacked the arcade and action-adventure elements commonly found in Japanese console RPGs at the time. In the early 1990s, American computer RPGs also began facing criticism for their plots, where "the party sticks together through thick and thin" and always "act together as a group" rather than as individuals, and where non-player characters are "one-dimensional characters," in comparison to the more fantasy novel approach of Squaresoft console RPGs such as *Final Fantasy IV*. However in 1994, game designer Sandy Petersen noted that, among computer gamers, there was criticism against cartridge-based console JRPGs being "not role-playing at all" due to popular examples such as *Secret of Mana* and especially *The Legend of Zelda* using "direct" arcade-style action combat systems instead of the more "abstract" turn-based battle systems associated with computer RPGs. In response, he pointed out that not all console RPGs are action-based, pointing to *Final Fantasy* and *Lufia*. Another early criticism, dating back to the *Phantasy Star* games in the late 1980s, was the frequent use of defined player characters, in contrast to the *Wizardry* and Gold Box games where the player's avatars (such as knights, clerics, or thieves) were blank slates.

As Japanese console RPGs became increasingly more dominant in the 1990s, and became known for being more heavily story and character-based, American computer RPGs began to face criticism for having characters devoid of personality or background, due to representing avatars which the player uses to interact with the world, in contrast to Japanese console RPGs which depicted characters with distinctive personalities. American computer RPGs were thus criticized for lacking "more of the traditional role-playing" offered by Japanese console RPGs, which instead emphasized character interactions. In response, North American computer RPGs began making a comeback towards the end of the 1990s with interactive choice-filled adventures.

In more recent years, several writers have criticized JRPGs as not being "true" RPGs, for heavy usage of scripted cutscenes and dialogue, and a frequent lack of branching outcomes. Japanese RPGs are also sometimes criticized for having relatively simple battle systems in which players are able to win by repetitively mashing buttons, As a result, Japanese-style role-playing games are held in disdain by some Western gamers, leading to the term "JRPG" being held in the pejorative. Some observers have also speculated that Japanese RPGs are stagnating or declining in both quality and popularity, including remarks by BioWare co-founder Greg Zeschuk and writing director Daniel Erickson that JRPGs are stagnating—and that *Final Fantasy XIII* is not even really an RPG; criticisms regarding seemingly nebulous justifications by some Japanese designers for newly changed (or, alternately, newly un-changed) features of recent titles; calls among some gaming journalists to "fix" JRPGs' problems; as well as claims that some recent titles such as *Front Mission Evolved* are beginning to attempt—and failing to—imitate Western titles. In an article for *PSM3*, Brittany Vincent of RPGFan.com felt that "developers have mired the modern JRPG in unoriginality", citing Square Enix CEO Yoichi Wada who stated that "they're strictly catering to a particular audience", the article noting the difference in game sales between Japan and North America before going on to suggest JRPGs may need to "move forward". This criticism has also occurred in the wider media with an advertisement for *Fallout: New Vegas* (Obsidian Entertainment) in Japan openly mocked Japanese RPGs' traditional characteristics in favor of their own title. Nick Doerr of Joystiq noted that Bethesda felt that Japanese RPGs "are all the same" and "too linear," to which he responded that "most part, it's true" but noted there are also non-linear Japanese RPGs such as the *Romancing SaGa* series. Such criticisms have produced responses such as ones by Japanese video game developers, Shinji Mikami and Yuji Horii, to the effect that JRPGs were never as popular in the West to begin with, and that Western reviewers are biased against turn-based systems. Jeff Fleming of Gamasutra also states that Japanese RPGs on home consoles are generally showing signs of staleness, but notes that handheld consoles such as the Nintendo DS have had more original and experimental Japanese RPGs released in recent years.

Western RPGs have also received criticism in recent years. They remain less popular in Japan, where, until recently, Western games in general had a negative reputation. In Japan, where the vast majority of early console role-playing video games originate, Western RPGs remain largely unknown. The developer Motomu Toriyama criticized Western RPGs, stating that they "dump you in a big open world, and let you do whatever you like [which makes it] difficult to tell a compelling story." Hironobu Sakaguchi noted that "users like to categorise" Western RPGs as "a sort of different style, born from first person shooters." In recent years, some have also criticized Western RPGs for becoming less RPG-like, instead with further emphasis on action Christian Nutt of *GameSpy* states that, in contrast to Japanese RPGs, Western RPGs' greater control over the development and customization of playable characters has come at the expense of plot and gameplay, resulting in what he felt was generic dialogue, lack of character development within the narrative and weaker battle systems. He also states that Western RPGs tend to focus more on the underlying rules governing the battle system rather than on the experience itself. Tom Battey of *Edge Magazine* noted that the problems often cited against Japanese RPGs (mentioned above) also often apply to many Western RPGs as well as games outside of the RPG genre. BioWare games have been criticized for "lack of innovation, repetitive structure and lack of real choice." Western RPGs, such as Bethesda games, have also been criticized for lacking in "narrative strength" or "mechanical intricacy" due to the open-ended, sandbox structure of their games.

Despite the criticisms leveled at both variations, Rowan Kaiser of Joystiq argued that many of the often mentioned differences between Eastern and Western games are stereotypes that are generally not true, noting various similarities between several Western titles (such as *Lands of Lore, Betrayal at Krondor*, and *Dragon Age*) and several classic Eastern titles (such as *Final Fantasy* and *Phantasy Star*), noting that both these Western and Japanese titles share a similar emphasis on linear storytelling, pre-defined characters and "bright-colored" graphics. The developer Hironobu Sakaguchi also noted there are many games from both that don't fit such categorizations, such as his own *Chrono Trigger* as well as the *Mana* games, noting there have been many other such Japanese role-playing games that never released in Western markets.

Controversy

In what is viewed as the largely secular nature of Japanese culture has resulted in heavy usage of themes, symbols, and characters taken from a variety of religions, including Christianity and Japanese Shinto. This tends to be problematic when JRPGs are exported to Western countries where the topics of religion and blasphemy remain sensitive, such as the United States. It is not unusual for a JRPG to exhibit elements that would be controversial in the West, such as *Xenogears* or *Final Fantasy Tactics* featuring antagonists that bear similarities to the Abrahamic God and the Catholic Church, respectively; and Nintendo has made efforts in the past to remove references such as these prior to introducing their games into the North American market.

Relationship to other Genres

RPGs seldom test a player's physical skill. Combat is typically a tactical challenge rather than a physical one, and games involve other non-action gameplay such as choosing dialog options, inventory management, or buying and selling items.

Although RPGs share some combat rules with wargames, RPGs are often about a small group of individual characters. Wargames tend to have large groups of identical units, as well as non-humanoid units such as tanks and airplanes. Role-playing games do not normally allow the player to produce more units. However, the *Heroes of Might and Magic* series crosses these genres by combining individual heroes with large amounts of troops in large battles.

RPGs rival adventure games in terms of their rich storylines, in contrast to genres that do not rely upon storytelling such as sports games or puzzle games. Both genres also feature highly detailed characters, and a great deal of exploration. However, adventure games usually have a well-defined character, whereas while RPGs may do so, many allow the player to design their characters. Adventure games usually focus on one character, whereas RPGs often feature an entire party. RPGs also feature a combat system, which adventure games usually lack. Whereas both adventure games and RPGs may focus on the personal or psychological growth of characters, RPGs tend to emphasize a complex eternal economy where characters are defined by increasing numerical attributes.

Gameplay elements strongly associated with this genre, such as statistical character development, have been widely adapted to other video game genres. For example, *Grand Theft Auto: San Andreas*, an action-adventure game, uses resource statistics (abbreviated as "stats") to define a wide range of attributes including stamina, weapon proficiency, driving, lung capacity, and muscle tone, and uses numerous cutscenes and quests to advance the story. *Warcraft III: Reign of Chaos*, a real-time strategy game, features heroes that can complete quests, obtain new equipment, and "learn" new abilities as they advance in level.

According to Satoru Iwata, former president of Nintendo, turn-based RPGs have been unfairly criticized as being outdated, and action-based RPGs can frustrate players who are unable to keep up with the battles. According to Yuji Horii, creator of the popular *Dragon Quest* series and Ryutaro Ichimura, producer of Square Enix, turn-based RPGs allow the player time to make decisions without feeling rushed or worry about real-life distractions.

Roguelikes

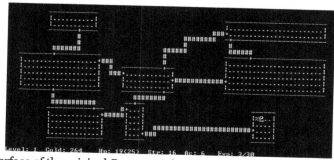

The interface of the original *Rogue* as it looked on an ASCII computer terminal

Roguelike is a subgenre of role-playing video games, characterized by procedural generation of game levels, turn-based gameplay, tile-based graphics, permanent death of the player-character, and typically based on a high fantasy narrative setting. Roguelikes descend from the 1980 game *Rogue*, particularly mirroring *Rogue*'s character- or sprite-based graphics. Some of the factors used in this definition include: These games were popularized among college students and computer programmers of the 1980s and 1990s, leading to a large number of variants but adhering to these common gameplay elements. Some of the more well-known variants include *Hack*, *NetHack*, *Ancient Domains of Mystery*, *Moria*, *Angband*, and *Tales of Maj'Eyal*. The Japanese series of *Mystery Dungeon* games by Chunsoft, inspired by *Rogue*, also fall within the concept of roguelike games.

More recently, with more powerful home computers and gaming systems, new variations of roguelikes incorporating other gameplay genres, thematic elements and graphical styles have become popular, typically retaining the notion of procedural generation. These titles are sometimes labeled as "roguelike-like", "rogue-lite", or "procedural death labyrinths" to reflect the variation from titles which mimic the gameplay of traditional roguelikes more faithfully. Other games, like *Diablo* and *UnReal World*, took inspiration from roguelikes.

Action RPGs

Video showing basic gameplay of point-and-click action RPGs.

Typically action RPGs feature each player directly controlling a single character in real time, and feature a strong focus on combat and action with plot and character interaction kept to a minimum. Early action RPGs tended to follow the template set by 1980s Nihon Falcom titles such as the *Dragon Slayer* and *Ys* series, which feature hack and slash combat where the player character's movements and actions are controlled directly, using a keyboard or game controller, rather than using menus. This formula was refined by the action-adventure game, *The Legend of Zelda* (1986), which set the template used by many subsequent action RPGs, including innovations such as an open world, nonlinear gameplay, battery backup saving, and an attack button that animates a sword swing or projectile attack on the screen. The game was largely responsible for the surge of action-oriented RPGs released since the late 1980s, both in Japan and North America. *The Legend of Zelda* series would continue to exert an influence on the transition of both console and computer RPGs from stat-heavy, turn-based combat towards real-time action combat in the following decades.

A different variation of the action RPG formula was popularized by *Diablo* (1996), where the majority of commands—such as moving and attacking—are executed using mouse clicks rather than via menus, though learned spells can also be assigned to hotkeys. In many action RPGs, non-player characters serve only one purpose, be it to buy or sell items or upgrade the player's abilities, or issue them with combat-centric quests. Problems players face also often have an action-based solution, such as breaking a wooden door open with an axe rather than finding the key needed to unlock it, though some games place greater emphasis on character attributes such as a "lockpicking" skill and puzzle-solving.

One common challenge in developing action RPGs is including content beyond that of killing enemies. With the sheer number of items, locations and monsters found in many such games, it can be difficult to create the needed depth to offer players a unique experience tailored to his or her beliefs, choices or actions. This is doubly true if a game makes use of randomization, as is common. One notable example of a game which went beyond this is *Deus Ex* (2000) which offered multiple solutions to problems using intricately layered story options and individually constructed environments. Instead of simply bashing their way through levels, players were challenged to act in character by choosing dialog options appropriately, and by using the surrounding environment intelligently. This produced an experience that was unique and tailored to each situation as opposed to one that repeated itself endlessly.

At one time, action RPGs were much more common on consoles than on computers. Though there had been attempts at creating action-oriented computer RPGs during the late 1980s and early 1990s, often in the vein of *Zelda*, very few saw any success, with the 1992 game *Ultima VII* being one of the more successful exceptions in North America. On the PC, *Diablo*'s effect on the market was significant: it had many imitators and its style of combat went on to be used by many games that came after. For many years afterwards, games that closely mimicked the *Diablo* formula were referred to as "*Diablo* clones". Three of the four titles in the series were still sold together as part of the *Diablo Battle Chest* over a decade after *Diablo*'s release. Other examples of action RPGs for the PC include *Dungeon Siege*, *Sacred*, *Torchlight* and *Hellgate: London*—the last of which was developed by a team headed by former Blizzard employees, some of whom had participated in the creation of the *Diablo* series. Like *Diablo* and *Rogue* before it, *Torchlight* and *Hellgate: London* made use of procedural generation to generate game levels.

Also included within this subgenre are role-playing shooters—games that incorporate elements of role-playing games and shooter games (including first-person and third-person). Recent examples include the *Mass Effect* series, *Borderlands 2* and *The 3rd Birthday*.

Tactical RPGs

This subgenre of role-playing game principally refers to games which incorporate elements from strategy games as an alternative to traditional role-playing game (RPG) systems. Tactical RPGs are descendents of traditional strategy games, such as chess, and table-top role-playing and strategic war games, such as *Chainmail*, which were mainly tactical in their original form. The format of a tactical CRPG is also like a traditional RPG in its appearance, pacing and rule structure. Like standard RPGs, the player controls a finite party and battles a similar number of enemies. And like other RPGs, death is usually temporary. But this genre incorporates strategic gameplay such as tactical movement on an isometric grid. Tactical RPGs tend not to feature multiplayer play.

A number of early Western role-playing video games used a highly tactical form of combat, including parts of the *Ultima* series, which introduced party-based, tiled combat in *Ultima III: Exodus* (1983). *Ultima III* would go on to be ported to many other platforms and influence the development of later titles, as would *Bokosuka Wars* (1983), considered a pioneer in the strategy/simulation RPG genre, according to Nintendo. Conventionally, however, the term tactical RPG (known as *simulation RPG* in Japan) refers to the distinct subgenre that was born in Japan; as the early origins of tactical RPGs are difficult to trace from the American side of the Pacific, where much of the early RPG genre developed.

Many tactical RPGs can be both extremely time-consuming and extremely difficult. Hence, the appeal of most tactical RPGs is to the hardcore, not casual, computer and video game player. Traditionally, tactical RPGs have been quite popular in Japan but have not enjoyed the same degree of success in North America and elsewhere. However, the audience for Japanese tactical RPGs has grown substantially since the mid-90s, with PS1 and PS2 titles such as *Final Fantasy Tactics*, *Suikoden Tactics*, *Vanguard Bandits*, and *Disgaea* enjoying a surprising measure of popularity, as well as hand-held war games like *Fire Emblem*. (*Final Fantasy Tactics* for the PS1 is often considered the breakthrough title outside Japan.) Older TRPGs are also being re-released via software emulation—such as on the Wii Virtual Console—and on handheld game consoles, giving games a new lease on life and exposure to new audiences. Japanese video games such as these are as a result no longer nearly as rare a commodity in North America as they were during the 1990s.

Western video games have utilized similar mechanics for years, as well, and were largely defined by *X-COM: UFO Defense* (1994) in much the same way as Eastern video games were by *Fire Emblem*. Titles such as *X-COM* have generally allowed greater freedom of movement when interacting with the surrounding environment than their Eastern counterparts. Other similar examples include the *Jagged Alliance* (1994–2013) and *Silent Storm* (2003–2005) series. According to a few developers, it became increasingly difficult during the 2000s to develop games of this type for the PC in the West (though several had been developed in Eastern Europe with mixed results); and even some Japanese console RPG developers began to complain about a bias against turn-based systems. Reasons cited include Western publishers' focus on developing real-time and action-oriented games instead.

Lastly, there are a number of "full-fledged" CRPGs which could be described as having "tactical combat". Examples from the classic era of CRPGs include parts of the aforementioned *Ultima* series; SSI's *Wizard's Crown* (1985) and *The Eternal Dagger* (1987); the *Gold Box* games of the late '80s and early '90s, many of which were later ported to Japanese video game systems; and the *Realms of Arkania* (1992-1996) series based on the German *The Dark Eye* pen-and-paper system. More recent examples include *Wasteland 2*, *Shadowrun: Dragonfall* and *Divinity: Original Sin*—all released in 2014. Partly due to the release of these games 2014 has been called "The CRPG Renaissance".

MMORPGs

Though many of the original RPGs for the PLATO mainframe system in the late 1970s also supported multiple, simultaneous players, the popularity of multiplayer modes in mainstream RPGs did not begin to rise sharply until the early to mid-1990s. For instance, *Secret of Mana* (1993), an early action role-playing game by Square, was one of the first commercial RPGs to feature cooperative multiplayer gameplay, offering two-player and three-player action once the main character had acquired his party members. Later, *Diablo* (1996) would combine CRPG and action game elements with an Internet multiplayer mode that allowed up to four players to enter the same world and fight monsters, trade items, or fight against each other.

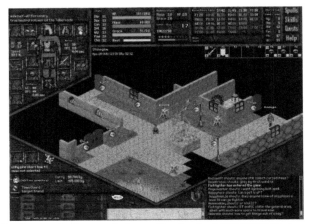

Multiple people chat and play online in the MMORPG *Daimonin*.

Also during this time period, the MUD genre that had been spawned by MUD1 in 1978 was undergoing a tremendous expansion phase due to the release and spread of LPMud (1989) and DikuMUD (1991). Soon, driven by the mainstream adoption of the Internet, these parallel trends merged in the popularization of graphical MUDs, which would soon become known as massively multiplayer online role-playing games or MMORPGs, beginning with games like *Meridian 59* (1995), *Nexus: The Kingdom of the Winds* (1996), *Ultima Online* (1997), *Lineage* (1998), and *EverQuest* (1999), and leading to modern phenomena such as *RuneScape* (2001), *Final Fantasy XI* (2003), *Eve Online* (2003) and *World of Warcraft* (2004).

Though superficially similar, MMORPGs lend their appeal more to the socializing influences of being online with hundreds or even thousands of other players at a time, and trace their origins more from MUDs than from CRPGs like *Ultima* and *Wizardry*. Rather than focusing on the "old school" considerations of memorizing huge numbers of stats and esoterica and battling it out in complex, tactical environments, players instead spend much of their time forming and maintaining guilds and clans. The distinction between CRPGs and MMORPGs and MUDs can as a result be very sharp, likenable to the difference between "attending a renaissance fair and reading a good fantasy novel".

Further, MMORPGs have been criticized for diluting the "epic" feeling of single-player RPGs and related media among thousands of concurrent adventurers. Stated simply: every player wants to be "The Hero", slay "The Monster", rescue "The Princess", or obtain "The Magic Sword". But when there are thousands of players all playing the same game, clearly not everyone can be *the* hero. This problem became obvious to some in the game *EverQuest*, where groups of players would compete and sometimes harass each other in order to get monsters in the same dungeon to drop valuable items, leading to several undesirable behaviors such as kill stealing, spawn camping, and ninja looting. In response—for instance by Richard Garriott in *Tabula Rasa*—developers began turning to instance dungeons as a means of reducing competition over limited resources, as well as preserving the gaming experience—though this mechanic has its own set of detractors.

Single-player games are great, and I love them. They have a great feature. Your life is very special. You are *the* hero and you get to save the *whole* world. (...) [*Tabula Rasa*] is like Disney World... You can go to shops and get food, but when you get on the boat for the pirate ride, you're in your own version of reality. Once the ride starts, you are blissfully unaware of the boats in front of you and behind you.

—*Richard Garriott, regarding the use of instancing in Tabula Rasa*

Lastly, there exist markets such as Korea and China that, while saturated with MMORPGs, have so far proved relatively unreceptive to single-player RPGs. For instance, Internet-connected personal computers are relatively common in Korea when compared to other regions—particularly in the numerous "PC bangs" scattered around the country where patrons are able to pay to play multiplayer video games—possibly due to historical bans on Japanese imports, as well as a culture that traditionally sees video games as "frivolous toys" and computers as educational. As a result, some wonder whether the stand-alone, single-player RPG is still viable commercially—especially on the personal computer—when there are competing pressures such as big-name publishers' marketing needs, video game piracy, a change in culture, and the competitive price-point-to-processing-power ratio (at least initially) of modern console systems.

Hybrid Genres

Finally, a steadily increasing number of other non-RP video games have adopted aspects traditionally seen in RPGs, such as experience point systems, equipment management, and choices in dialogue, as developers push to fill the demand for role-playing elements in non-RPGs. The blending of these elements with a number of different game engines and gameplay styles have created a myriad of hybrid game categories formed by mixing popular gameplay elements featured in other genres such as first-person shooters, platformers, and turn-based and real-time strategy games. Examples include first-person shooters such as parts of the *Deus Ex* (starting in 2000) and *S.T.A.L.K.E.R.* (starting in 2007) series; real-time strategy games such as *SpellForce: The Order of Dawn* (2003) and *Warhammer 40,000: Dawn of War II* (2009); puzzle video games such as *Castlevania Puzzle* (2010) and *Puzzle Quest: Challenge of the Warlords* (2007);

and turn-based strategy games like the *Steel Panthers* (1995–2006) series, which combined tactical military combat with RPG-derived unit advancement. As a group, hybrid games have been both praised and criticized; being referred to by one critic as the "poor man's" RPG for omitting the dialogue choices and story-driven character development of major AAA titles in order to cut costs, and by another critic as "promising" for shedding the conventions of more established franchises in an attempt to innovate.

Popularity and Notable Developers

The vast majority of RPG games that were successful were made from Japanese companies, making Japan a dominant country in an entertainment genre in East Asia, along with the Cinema of Hong Kong and the Korean wave, further increasing the prophecy that East Asian products are superior to those of the West. Notable RPG developers include Don Daglow for creating the first role-playing video game, *Dungeon*, in 1975; Yuji Horii for creating the *Dragon Quest* series; Hironobu Sakaguchi for creating the *Final Fantasy* series; Richard Garriott for creating the *Ultima* series; Brenda Romero for writing and design work on the entire Wizardry series, and Ray Muzyka and Greg Zeschuk for founding BioWare. Ryozo Tsujimoto (*Monster Hunter* series) and Katsura Hashino (*Persona* series) were also cited as "Japanese Game Developers You Should Know" by *1UP.com* in 2010. Oter notable RPG developers are Bethesda Game Studios, creators of *Fallout 3", "Fallout 4", and* The Elder Scrolls *series, and CD Projekt, creators of The Witcher series and Cyberpunk 2077.*

Hironobu Sakaguchi at the Game Developers Conference in San Francisco, California in 2007

The best-selling RPG series worldwide is *Pokémon*, which has sold over 260 million units as of March 2014. The second and third best-selling RPG franchises worldwide are Square Enix's *Final Fantasy* and *Dragon Quest* series, with over 110 million units and over 64 million units sold as of March 31, 2014, respectively. *Pokémon Red*, *Blue*, and *Green* alone sold approximately 23.64 million copies (10.23 million in Japan, 9.85 million in US, 3.56 million in UK). Nearly all the games in the main *Final Fantasy* series and all the games in the main *Dragon Quest* series (as well as many of the spin-off games) have sold over a million copies each, with some games selling more than four million copies. Square Enix's best-selling title is *Final Fantasy VII*, which has sold over 10 million copies worldwide.

Among the best-selling PC RPGs overall is the massively multiplayer online game *World of Warcraft* with 11.5 million subscribers as of May 2010. Among single player PC RPGs, *Diablo II* has sold the largest amount, with the most recently cited number being over 4 million copies as of 2001. However, copies of the *Diablo: Battle Chest* continued to be sold in retail stores, with the compilation appearing on the NPD Group's top 10 PC games sales, list as recently as 2010. Further, *Diablo: Battle Chest* was the 19th best selling PC game of 2008—a full seven years after the game's initial release; and 11 million users still play *Diablo II* and *StarCraft* over Battle.net. As a franchise, the *Diablo* series has sold over 20 million copies. *Diablo III* was released for Windows and OS X on May 15, 2012. It was also released for PlayStation 3 and Xbox 360 on September 3, 2013, and it will also be released for both PlayStation 4 and Xbox One on August 19, 2014.

The *Dragon Quest* series was awarded with six world records in the 2008 Gamer's Edition of the Guinness Book of World Records, including "Best Selling Role Playing Game on the Super Famicom", "Fastest Selling Game in Japan", and "First Video Game Series to Inspire a Ballet". Likewise, the *Pokémon* series received eight records, including "Most Successful RPG Series of All Time". *Diablo II* was recognized in the 2000 standard edition for being the fastest selling computer game ever sold, with more than 1 million units sold in the first two weeks of availability; though this number has been surpassed several times since. A number of RPGs are also being exhibited in the Barbican Art Gallery's "Game On" exhibition (starting in 2002) and the Smithsonian's "The Art of Video Games" exhibit (starting in 2012); and video game developers are now finally able to apply for grants from the US National Endowment of the Arts.

Bethesda Softworks' *Fallout 3* booth at the Games Convention 2008

According to Metacritic, as of May 2011, the highest-rated game is the Xbox 360 version of *Mass Effect 2*, with an average metascore of 96 out of 100. According to GameRankings, the four top-rated video game RPGs, as of May 2010, are *Mass Effect 2* with an average rating of 95.70% for the Xbox 360 version and 94.24% for the PC version; *Fallout 3: Game of the Year Edition* with an average rating of 95.40% for the PlayStation 3 version; *Chrono Trigger* with an average rating of 95.10%; and *Star Wars: Knights of the Old Republic* with an average rating of 94.18% for the Xbox version. Sales numbers for these six aforementioned titles are 10 million units sold worldwide for *Final Fantasy VII* as of May 2010; 161,161 units of *Xenoblade Chronicles* sold in Japan as of December 2010; 1.6 million units sold worldwide for *Mass Effect 2* as of March 2010, just three months after release; 4.7 million units for *Fallout 3* on all three platforms as of November 2008, also only a few months after publication; 3 million units for both the Xbox and PC versions of *Star Wars: Knights of the Old Republic* as of November 2004; and more than 2.65 million units for the SNES and PlayStation versions of *Chrono Trigger* as of March 2003, along with 790,000 copies for the Nintendo DS version as of March 31, 2009. Among these titles, none were PC-exclusives, three were North American multi-platform titles released for consoles like the Xbox and Xbox 360 within the past decade, and three were Japanese titles released for consoles like the SNES, PlayStation and Wii.

Final Fantasy VII topped *GamePro's* "26 Best RPGs of All Time" list, IGN's 2000 "Reader's Choice Game of the Century" poll, and the GameFAQs "Best Game Ever" audience polls in 2004 and 2005. It was also selected in *Empire* magazine's "100 Greatest Games of All Time" list as the highest-ranking RPG, at #2 on the list. On IGN's "Top 100 Games Of All Time" list in 2007, the highest ranking RPG is *Final Fantasy VI* at 9th place; and in both the 2006 and 2008 IGN Readers' Choice polls, *Chrono Trigger* is the top ranked RPG, in 2nd place. *Final Fantasy VI* is also the top ranked RPG in *Game Informer's* list of its 200 best games of all time list, in 8th place; and is also one of the eight games to get a cover for the magazine's 200th issue. The 2006 *Famitsu* readers' poll is dominated by RPGs, with nearly a dozen titles appearing in the top twenty; while most were Japanese, a few Western titles also made a showing. The highest-ranking games on the list were *Final Fantasy X*, followed by *Final Fantasy VII* and *Dragon Warrior III*. For the past decade, the *Megami Tensei* series topped several "RPGs of the Decade" lists. RPGFan's "Top 20 RPGs of the Past Decade" list was topped by *Shin Megami Tensei: Digital Devil Saga & Digital Devil Saga 2* followed by *Shin Megami Tensei: Persona 3*, while RPGamer's "Top RPGs of the Decade" list was topped by *Shin Megami Tensei: Persona 3*, followed by *Final Fantasy X* and *World of Warcraft*.

Lastly, in recent years, Western RPGs have consistently been released on consoles such as the Xbox and Xbox 360. However, systems like the Xbox and Xbox 360 have not shown as much market dominance in Eastern markets such as Japan, and only a few Western RPG titles have been localized to Japanese. Further, RPGs were not the dominant genre on the most popular of the seventh generation video game consoles, the Nintendo Wii, although their presence among handheld systems such as the Nintendo DS is considerably greater.

Simulation Video Game

A simulation video game describes a diverse super-category of video games, generally designed to closely simulate aspects of a real or fictional reality.

A simulation game attempts to copy various activities from real life in the form of a game for various purposes such as training, analysis, or prediction. Usually there are no strictly defined goals in the game, with players instead allowed to freely control a character. Well-known examples are war games, business games, and role play simulation.

From three basic types of strategic, planning, and learning exercises: games, simulations, and case studies, a number of hybrids may be considered, including simulation games that are used as case studies.

Comparisons of the merits of simulation games versus other teaching techniques have been carried out by many researchers and a number of comprehensive reviews have been published.

History

While many credit simulation games beginning with Will Wright and SimCity in 1989, the true progenitor of the genre was "Fortune Builder", released in 1984 on Colecovision. Certain games such as SimLife and SimEarth were subsequently created and are capable of teaching players the basics of genetics and global ecosystems.

In a study where adolescents played SimCity 2000, the study found that those participants who played the game had a greater appreciation and expectation of their government officials after playing.

Subgenres

Construction and Management Simulation

Construction and management simulation (CMS) is a type of simulation game in which players build, expand or manage fictional communities or projects with limited resources. Strategy games sometimes incorporate CMS aspects into their game economy, as players must manage resources while expanding their project. But pure CMS games differ from strategy games in that "the player's goal is not to defeat an enemy, but to build something within the context of an ongoing process." Games in this category are sometimes also called "management games".

Life Simulation

Life simulation games (or artificial life games) is a subgenre of simulation video games in which the player lives or controls one or more artificial lifeforms. A life simulation game can revolve around "individuals and relationships, or it could be a simulation of an ecosystem".

Sports

A sports game is a video game that simulates the playing of sports. Most sports have been recreated with a game, including team sports, athletics and extreme sports. Some games emphasize actually playing the sport (such as the *Madden NFL* series), whilst others emphasize strategy and organization (such as *Championship Manager*). Some, such as *Arch Rivals*, satirize the sport for comic effect. This genre has been popular throughout the history of video games and is competitive, just like real-world sports. A number of game series feature the names and characteristics of real teams and players, and are updated annually to reflect real-world changes.

Other Types

FlightGear, a flight simulator video game.

- Dating sims focuses on dating as the principal theme.

- In medical simulation games, players take the role of a surgeon. This includes the *Trauma Center* and *LifeSigns* series.

- In photography simulation games, players take photographs of animals or people. This includes games such as *Pokémon Snap* and *Afrika*.

- Certain wargames with higher degrees of realism than other wargames set in a fantasy or science fiction environment. These attempt to simulate real warfare at either a tactical or strategic level.

- Certain tactical shooters with higher degrees of realism than other shooters. Sometimes called "soldier sims", these games try to simulate the feeling of actually being in combat. This includes games such as *Arma*.

- Some simulators, like Geocommander by Intelligence Gaming, are designed for the US Military to help new officers learn how to handle situations in a game setting before actually having to take command in the field.

- "Sim" games marketed by companies such as Maxis. These games have simulated many kinds of experiences.

- Social simulation game.

- Vehicle simulation game.

  o Flight simulators, including combat flight simulators and space flight simulator games

  o Racing video games, including sim racing

  o Vehicular combat games

  o Train simulator games

- Digital card games simulating blackjack and poker (including video poker).

- Video games which are designed to simulate mechanical or other real-world games. These could include simulations of pinball games and casino games such as slot machines, pachinko, and roulette.

Massively Multiplayer Online Game

A massively multiplayer online game (MMOG or MMO) is an online game which is capable of supporting large numbers of players simultaneously in the same instance (or world). MMOs usually feature a huge, persistent open world, although some games differ. These games can be found for most network-capable platforms, including the personal computer, video game console, or smartphones and other mobile devices.

MMOs can enable players to cooperate and compete with each other on a large scale, and sometimes to interact meaningfully with people around the world. They include a variety of gameplay types, representing many video game genres.

History

The most popular type of MMOG, and the subgenre that pioneered the category, is the massively multiplayer online role-playing game (MMORPG), which descended from university mainframe computer MUD and adventure games such as *Rogue* and *Dungeon* on the PDP-10. These games predate the commercial gaming industry and the Internet, but still featured persistent worlds and other elements of MMOGs still used today.

The first graphical MMOG, and a major milestone in the creation of the genre, was the multiplayer flight combat simulation game *Air Warrior* by Kesmai on the GEnie online service, which first appeared in 1986. Kesmai later added 3D graphics to the game, making it the first 3D MMO.

Commercial MMORPGs gained acceptance in the late 1980s and early 1990s. The genre was pioneered by the GemStone series on GEnie, also created by Kesmai, and *Neverwinter Nights*, the first such game to include graphics, which debuted on AOL in 1991.

As video game developers applied MMOG ideas to other computer and video game genres, new acronyms started to develop, such as MMORTS. *MMOG* emerged as a generic term to cover this growing class of games.

The debuts of *The Realm Online*, *Meridian 59* (the first 3D MMORPG), *Ultima Online*, *Underlight* and *EverQuest* in the late 1990s popularized the MMORPG genre. The growth in technology meant that where Neverwinter Nights in 1991 had been limited to 50 simultaneous players (a number that grew to 500 by 1995), by the year 2000 a multitude of MMORPGs were each serving thousands of simultaneous players and led the way for games such as World of Warcraft and *EVE Online*.

Despite the genre's focus on multiplayer gaming, AI-controlled characters are still common. NPCs and mobs who give out quests or serve as opponents are typical in MMORPGs. AI-controlled characters are not as common in action-based MMOGs.

The popularity of MMOGs was mostly restricted to the computer game market until the sixth-generation consoles, with the launch of *Phantasy Star Online* on *Dreamcast* and the emergence and growth of online service Xbox Live. There have been a number of console MMOGs, including *EverQuest Online Adventures* (PlayStation 2), and the multiconsole *Final Fantasy XI*. On PCs, the MMOG market has always been dominated by successful fantasy MMORPGs.

MMOGs have only recently begun to break into the mobile phone market. The first, Samurai Romanesque set in feudal Japan, was released in 2001 on NTT DoCoMo's iMode network in Japan. More recent developments are CipSoft's TibiaME and Biting Bit's *MicroMonster* which features online and bluetooth multiplayer gaming. SmartCell Technology is in development of Shadow of Legend, which will allow gamers to continue their game on their mobile device when away from their PC.

Science fiction has also been a popular theme, featuring games such as *Mankind, Anarchy Online, Eve Online, Star Wars Galaxies* and *The Matrix Online.*

MMOGs emerged from the hard-core gamer community to the mainstream strongly in December 2003 with an analysis in the *Financial Times* measuring the value of the virtual property in the then-largest MMOG, EverQuest, to result in a per-capita GDP of 2,266 dollars which would have placed the virtual world of EverQuest as the 77th wealthiest nation, on par with Croatia, Ecuador, Tunisia or Vietnam.

World of Warcraft is a dominant MMOG with 8-9 million monthly subscribers worldwide. The subscriber base dropped by 1 million after the expansion Wrath of the Lich King, bringing it to 9 million subscribers in 2010, though it remained the most popular Western title among MMOGs. In 2008, Western consumer spending on *World of Warcraft* represented a 58% share of the subscription MMOG market in 2009. The title has generated over $2.2 billion in cumulative consumer spending on subscriptions from 2005 through 2009.

Virtual Economies

Within a majority of the MMOGs created, there is virtual currency where the player can earn and accumulate money. The uses for such virtual currency are numerous and vary from game to game. The virtual economies created within MMOGs often blur the lines between real and virtual worlds. The result is often seen as an unwanted interaction between the real and virtual economies by the players and the provider of the virtual world. This practice (economy interaction) is mostly seen in this genre of games. The two seem to come hand in hand with even the earliest MMOGs such as *Ultima Online* having this kind of trade, real money for virtual things.

The importance of having a working virtual economy within an MMOG is increasing as they develop. A sign of this is CCP Games hiring the first real-life economist for its MMOG Eve Online to assist and analyze the virtual economy and production within this game.

The results of this interaction between the virtual economy, and our real economy, which is really the interaction between the company that created the game and the third-party companies that want to share in the profits and success of the game. This battle between companies is defended on both sides. The company originating the game and the intellectual property argue that this is in violation of the terms and agreements of the game as well as copyright violation since they own the rights to how the online currency is distributed and through what channels. The case that the third-party companies and their customers defend, is that they are selling and exchanging the time and effort put into the acquisition of the currency, not the digital information itself. They also express that the nature of many MMOGs is that they require time commitments not available to everyone. As a result, without external acquisition of virtual currency, some players are severely limited to being able to experience certain aspects of the game.

The practice of acquiring large volumes of virtual currency for the purpose of selling to other individuals for tangible and real currency is called gold farming. Many players who have poured in all of their personal effort resent that there is this exchange between real and virtual economies since it devalues their own efforts. As a result, the term 'gold farmer' now has a very negative connotation within the games and their communities. This slander has unfortunately also extended itself to racial profiling and to in-game and forum insulting.

The reaction from many of the game companies varies. In games that are substantially less popular and have a small player base, the enforcement of the elimination of 'gold farming' appears less often. Companies in this situation most likely are concerned with their personal sales and subscription revenue over the development of their virtual economy, as they most likely have a higher priority to the games viability via adequate funding. Games with an enormous player base, and consequently much higher sales and subscription income, can take more drastic actions more often and in much larger volumes. This account banning could also serve as an economic gain for these large games, since it is highly likely that, due to demand, these 'gold farming' accounts will be recreated with freshly bought copies of the game.

The virtual goods revenue from online games and social networking exceeded US$7 billion in 2010.

In 2011, it was estimated that up to 100,000 people in China and Vietnam are playing online games to gather gold and other items for sale to Western players.

However single player in MMOs is quite viable, especially in what is called 'player vs environment' gameplay. This may result in the player being unable to experience all content, as many of the most significant and potentially rewarding game experiences are events which require large and coordinated teams to complete.

Most MMOGs also share other characteristics that make them different from other multiplayer online games. MMOGs host a large number of players in a single game world, and all of those players can interact with each other at any given time. Popular MMOGs might have thousands of players online at any given time, usually on company owned servers. Non-MMOGs, such as *Battlefield 1942* or *Half-Life* usually have fewer than 50 players online (per server) and are usually played on private servers. Also, MMOGs usually do not have any significant mods since the game must work on company servers. There is some debate if a high head-count is a requirement to be an MMOG. Some say that it is the size of the game world and its capability to support a large number of players that should matter. For example, despite technology and content constraints, most MMOGs can fit up to a few thousand players on a single game server at a time.

To support all those players, MMOGs need large-scale game worlds, and servers to connect players to those worlds. Some games have all of their servers connected so all players are connected in a shared universe. Others have copies of their starting game world put on different servers, called "shards", for a sharded universe. Shards got their name from Ultima Online, where in the story, the shards of Mondain's gem created the duplicate worlds.

Still others will only use one part of the universe at any time. For example, *Tribes* (which is not an MMOG) comes with a number of large maps, which are played in rotation (one at a time). In contrast, the similar title *PlanetSide* allows all map-like areas of the game to be reached via flying, driving, or teleporting.

MMORPGs usually have sharded universes, as they provide the most flexible solution to the server load problem, but not always. For example, the space simulation *Eve Online* uses only one large cluster server peaking at over 60,000 simultaneous players.

Technical Aspect

It is challenging to develop the database engines that are needed to run a successful MMOG with millions of players. Many developers have created their own, but attempts have been made to create *middleware*, software that would help game developers concentrate on their games more than technical aspects. One such piece of middleware is called BigWorld.

An early, successful entry into the field was VR-1 Entertainment whose Conductor platform was adopted and endorsed by a variety of service providers around the world including Sony Communications Network in Japan; the Bertelsmann Game Channel in Germany; British Telecom's Wireplay in England; and DACOM and Samsung SDS in South Korea. Games that were powered by the Conductor platform included Fighter Wing, Air Attack, Fighter Ace, EverNight, Hasbro Em@ail Games (Clue, NASCAR and Soccer), Towers of Fallow, The SARAC Project, VR1 Crossroads and Rumble in the Void.

Typical MUDs and other predecessor games were limited to about 64 or 256 simultaneous player connections; this was a limit imposed by the underlying operating system, which was usually Unix-like. One of the bigger problems with the modern engines has been handling the vast number of players. Since a typical server can handle around 10,000–12,000 players, 4000–5000 active simultaneously, dividing the game into several servers has up until now been the solution. This approach has also helped with technical issues, such as lag, that many players experience. Another difficulty, especially relevant to real-time simulation games, is time synchronization across hundreds or thousands of players. Many games rely on time synchronization to drive their physics simulation as well as their scoring and damage detection.

Game Types

There are several types of massively multiplayer online games.

Role-playing

A group photo of a "Linkshell" guild in the roleplaying game *Final Fantasy XI*.

Massively multiplayer online role-playing games, known as MMORPGs, are the most common type of MMOG. Some MMORPGs are designed as a multiplayer browser game in order to reduce infrastructure costs and utilise a thin client that most users will already have installed. The acronym *BBMMORPGs* has sometimes been used to describe these as *browser-based*.

Bulletin Board Role-playing Games

A large number of games are categorized as MMOBBGs,, Massively Multiplayer Online Bulletin Board Games, also called MMOBBRPGs. These particular types of games are primarily made up of text and descriptions, although images are often used to enhance the game.

First-person Shooter

MMOFPS is an online gaming genre which features a large number of simultaneous players in a first-person shooter fashion. These games provide large-scale, sometimes team-based combat. The addition of persistence in the game world means that these games add elements typically found in RPGs, such as experience points. However, MMOFPS games emphasize player skill more than player statistics, as no number of in-game bonuses will compensate for a player's inability to aim and think tactically.

Real-time Strategy

Massively multiplayer online real-time strategy games, also known as "MMORTS", combine real-time strategy (RTS) with a persistent world. Players often assume the role of a general, king, or other type of figurehead leading an army into battle while maintaining the resources needed for such warfare. The titles are often based in a sci-fi or fantasy universe and are distinguished from single or small-scale multiplayer RTSes by the number of players and common use of a persistent world, generally hosted by the game's publisher, which continues to evolve even when the player is offline.

Turn-based Strategy

Steve Jackson Games' UltraCorps is an example of a MMO turn-based strategy game. Hundreds of players share the same playing field of conquest. In a "mega" game, each turn fleets are built and launched to expand one's personal empire. Turns are usually time-based, with a "tick" schedule usually daily. All orders are processed, and battles resolved, at the same time during the tick. Similarly, in *Darkwind: War on Wheels*, vehicle driving and combat orders are submitted simultaneously by all players and a "tick" occurs typically once per 30 seconds. This allows each player to accurately control multiple vehicles and pedestrians in racing or combat.

Simulations

Some MMOGs have been designed to accurately simulate certain aspects of the real world. They tend to be very specific to industries or activities of very large risk and huge potential loss, such as rocket science, airplanes, trucks, battle tanks, submarines etc. Gradually as simulation technology is getting more mainstream, so too various simulators arrive into more mundane industries.

The initial goal of *World War II Online* was to create a map (in north western Europe) that had real world physics (gravity, air/water resistance, etc.), and ability for players to have some strategic abilities to its basic FPS/RPG role. While the current version is not quite a true simulated world, it is very complex and contains a large persistent world.

World War II Online simulation game showing the numbers of players during a special event in June 2008. Some 400 people had spawned in for this gathering in this location in the game.

The MMOG genre of air traffic simulation is one example, with networks such as VATSIM and IVAO striving to provide rigorously authentic flight-simulation environments to players in both pilot and air traffic controller roles. In this category of MMOGs, the objective is to create duplicates of the real world for people who cannot or do not wish to undertake those experiences in real life. For example, flight simulation via an MMOG requires far less expenditure of time and money, is completely risk-free, and is far less restrictive (fewer regulations to adhere to, no medical exams to pass, and so on).

Another specialist area is mobile telecoms operator (carrier) business where billion-dollar investments in networks are needed but marketshares are won and lost on issues from segmentation to handset subsidies. A specialist simulation was developed by Nokia called Equilibrium/Arbitrage to have over a two-day period five teams of top management of one operator/carrier play a "war-game" against each other, under extremely realistic conditions, with one operator an incumbent fixed and mobile network operator, another a new entrant mobile operator, a third a fixed-line/internet operator etc. Each team is measured by outperforming their rivals by market expectations of that type of player. Thus each player has drastically different goals, but within the simulation, any one team can win. Also to ensure maximum intensity, only one team can win. Telecoms senior executives who have taken the Equilibrium/Arbitrage simulation say it is the most intense, and most useful training they have ever experienced. It is typical of business use of simulators, in very senior management training/retraining.

Other online simulation games include *War Thunder*, *Motor City Online*, *The Sims Online*, and *Jumpgate*.

Sports

A massively multiplayer online sports game is a title where players can compete in some of the more traditional major league sports, such as football (soccer), basketball, baseball, hockey, golf or American football. According to GameSpot.com, Baseball Mogul Online was "the world's first massively multiplayer online sports game". Other titles that qualify as MMOSG have been around since the early 2000s, but only after 2010 did they start to receive the endorsements of some of the official major league associations and players.

Racing

MMOR means massively multiplayer online racing. Currently there are only a small number of racing-based MMOGs, including *iRacing*, *Kart Rider*, *Test Drive Unlimited*, *Project Torque*, *Drift City* and *Race or Die*. Other notable MMORs included *Upshift Strikeracer* and *Need for Speed: World*, both of which have since shut down. The *Trackmania* series is the world's largest MMO racing game and holds the world record for "Most Players in a Single Online Race". Although *Darkwind: War on Wheels* is more combat-based than racing, it is also considered an MMOR.

Casual

Many types of MMO games can be classified as casual, because they are designed to appeal to all computer users (as opposed to subgroup of frequent game buyers), or to fans of another game genre (such as collectible card games). Such games are easy to learn and require a smaller time commitment than other game types. Other popular casual games include simple management games such as *The Sims Online, Monopoly City Streets*, Roblox or *Kung Fu Panda World*.

MMOPGs, or massively multiplayer online puzzle games, are based entirely on puzzle elements. They are usually set in a world where the players can access the puzzles around the world. Most games that are MMOPGs are hybrids with other genres. *Castle Infinity* was the first MMOG developed for children. Its gameplay falls somewhere between puzzle and adventure.

There are also massively multiplayer collectible card games: *Alteil, Astral Masters* and *Astral Tournament*. Other MMOCCGs might exist (*Neopets* has some CCG elements) but are not as well known.

Alternate reality games (ARGs) can be massively multiplayer, allowing thousands of players worldwide to co-operate in puzzle trails and mystery solving. ARGs take place in a unique mixture of online and real-world play that usually does not involve a persistent world, and are not necessarily multiplayer, making them different from MMOGs.

Music/Rhythm

Massively multiplayer online music/rhythm games (MMORGs), sometimes called massively multiplayer online dance games (MMODGs), are MMOGs that are also music video games. This idea was influenced by *Dance Dance Revolution*. *Audition Online* is another casual massively multiplayer online game and it is produced by T3 Entertainment.

Just Dance 2014 has a game mode called World Dance Floor, which also structures like a MMORPG.

Social

Massively multiplayer online social games focus on socialization instead of objective-based gameplay. There is a great deal of overlap in terminology with "online communities" and "virtual worlds". One example that has garnered widespread media attention is Linden Lab's *Second Life*, emphasizing socializing, world-building and an in-world virtual economy that depends on the sale and purchase of user-created content. It is technically an MMOSG or Casual Multiplayer Online

(CMO) by definition, though its stated goal was to realize the concept of the Metaverse from Neal Stephenson's novel *Snow Crash*. Instead of being based around combat, one could say that it was based around the creation of virtual objects, including models and scripts. In practice, it has more in common with *Club Caribe* than *EverQuest*. It was the first MMO of its kind to achieve widespread success (including attention from mainstream media); however, it was not the first (as *Club Caribe* was released in 1988). Competitors in this subgenre (non-combat-based MMORPG) include *Active Worlds*, *There*, *SmallWorlds*, *Furcadia*, *Whirled* and *IMVU*.

Many browser based Casual MMOs have begun to spring up. This has been made easier because of maturing of *Adobe Flash* and the popularity of *Club Penguin*, *Growtopia*, and *The Sims Online*.

Combat

Massively multiplayer online combat games are realtime objective, strategy and capture the flag style modes.

Infantry Online is an example multiplayer combat video game with sprite animation graphics, using complex soldier, ground vehicle and space-ship models on typically complex terrains developed by Sony online entertainment.

Research

Some recent attempts to build peer-to-peer (P2P) MMOGs have been made. *Outback Online* may be the first commercial one, however, so far most of the efforts have been academic studies. A P2P MMOG may potentially be more scalable and cheaper to build, but notable issues with P2P MMOGs include security and consistency control, which can be difficult to address given that clients are easily hacked. Some MMOGs such as Vindictus use P2P networking and client-server networking together.

In April 2004, the United States Army announced that it was developing a massively multiplayer training simulation called *AWE* (asymmetric warfare environment). The purpose of *AWE* is to train soldiers for urban warfare and there are no plans for a public commercial release. Forterra Systems is developing it for the Army based on the *There* engine.

In 2010, Bonnie Nardi published an ethnographic study on World of Warcraft examined with Lev Vygotsky's activity theory.

As the field of MMOs grows larger each year, research has also begun to investigate the socio-informatic bind the games create for their users. In 2006, researchers Constance A. Steinkuehler and Dmitri Williams initiated research on such topics. The topic most intriguing to the pair was to further understand the gameplay, as well as the virtual world serving as a social meeting place, of popular MMOs.

To further explore the effects of social capital and social relationships on MMOs, Steinkuehler and Williams combined conclusions from two different MMO research projects: sociocultural perspective on culture and cognition, and the other on media effects of MMOs. The conclusions of the two studies explained how MMOs function as a new form of a "third place" for informal social interactions much like coffee shops, pubs, and other typical hangouts. Many scholars, however, such as Oldenburg (1999), refute the idea of a MMOs serving as a "third place" due to inadequate bridging social capital. His argument is challenged by Putnam (2000) who concluded that MMOs are well suited for the formation of bridging social capital, tentative relationships that lack in depth, because it is inclusive and serves as a sociological lubricant that is shown across the data collected in both of the research studies.

MMOs can also move past the "lubricant" stage and into the "superglue" stage known as bonding social capital, a closer relationship that is characterized by stronger connections and emotional support. The study concludes that MMOs function best as a bridging mechanism rather than a bonding one, similar to a "third place". Therefore, MMOs have the capacity and the ability to serve as a community that effectively socializes users just like a coffee shop or pub, but conveniently in the comfort of their own home.

Spending

British online gamers are outspending their German and French counterparts according to a recently released study commissioned by Gamesindustry.com and TNS. The UK MMO-market is now worth £195 million in 2009 compared to the £165 million and £145 million spent by German and French online gamers.

The US gamers spend more, however, spending about $3.8 billion overall on MMO games. $1.8 billion of that money is spent on monthly subscription fees. The money spent averages out to $15.10 between both subscription and free-to-play MMO gamers. The study also found that 46% of 46 million players in the US pay real money to play MMO games.

Today's Gamers MMO Focus Report, published in March 2010, was commissioned by TNS and gamesindustry.com. A similar study for the UK market-only (*UK National Gamers Survey Report*) was released in February 2010 by the same groups.

Strategy Video Game

Strategy video games are a video game genre that focuses on skillful thinking and planning to achieve victory. It emphasizes strategic, tactical, and sometimes logistical challenges. Many games also offer economic challenges and exploration. They are generally categorized into four sub-types, depending on whether the game is turn-based or real-time, and whether the game focuses on strategy or tactics.

Definition

Strategy video games are a genre of video game that emphasize skillful thinking and planning to achieve victory. Specifically, a player must plan a series of actions against one or more opponents, and the reduction of enemy forces is usually a goal. Victory is achieved through superior planning, and the element of chance takes a smaller role. In most strategy video games, the player is given a godlike view of the game world, and indirectly controls game units under their command. Thus, most strategy games involve elements of warfare to varying degrees, and feature a combination of tactical and strategic considerations. In addition to combat, these games often challenge the player's ability to explore, or manage an economy.

Relationship to other Genres

Even though there are many action games that involve strategic thinking, they are seldom classified as strategy games. A strategy game is typically larger in scope, and their main emphasis is on the player's ability to outthink their opponent. Strategy games rarely involve a physical challenge, and tend to annoy strategically minded players when they do. Compared to other genres such as action or adventure games where one player takes on many enemies, strategy games usually involve some level of symmetry between sides. Each side generally has access to similar resources and actions, with the strengths and weaknesses of each side being generally balanced.

Although strategy games involve strategic, tactical, and sometimes logistical challenges, they are distinct from puzzle games. A strategy game calls for planning around a conflict between players, whereas puzzle games call for planning in isolation. Strategy games are also distinct from construction and management simulations, which include economic challenges without any fighting. These games may incorporate some amount of conflict, but are different from strategy games because they do not emphasize the need for direct action upon an opponent.

Although strategy games are similar to role-playing video games in that the player must manage units with a variety of numeric attributes, RPGs tend to be about a smaller number of unique characters, while strategy games focus on larger numbers of fairly similar units.

Game Design

Units and Conflict

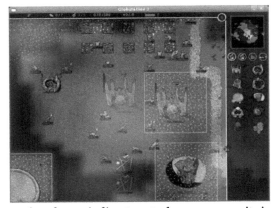

Strategy games give players indirect control over many units in a battlefield.
Many games, for example *Globulation 2*, include other challenges such as building construction.

Conflict in strategy games takes place between groups or singular combatants, usually called units. Games vary in how many types of units a player can use, but each unit has specific strengths and weaknesses. Units vary in their movement and speed, as well as the amount of health or damage they can withstand. Units may also have different levels of attack strength or range. Although units are typically used for combat, they may also be used for other purposes such as transport and scouting. Units that cannot move such as fixed turrets are often still treated as units. If a unit is destroyed, the player loses the benefit of that unit. Most strategy games allow players to construct new units in buildings or factories.

The player commands their forces by selecting a unit, usually by clicking it with the mouse, and issuing an order from a menu. Keyboard shortcuts become important for advanced players. Units can typically move, attack, stop, hold a position, although other strategy games offer more complex orders. Units may even have specialized abilities, such as the ability to become invisible to other units, usually balanced with abilities that detect otherwise invisible things. Some strategy games even offer special leader units that provide a bonus to other units. Units may also have the ability to sail or fly over otherwise impassable terrain, or provide transport for other units. Non-combat abilities often include the ability to repair or construct other units or buildings.

Even in imaginary or fantastic conflicts, strategy games try to reproduce important tactical situations throughout history. Techniques such as flanking, making diversions, or cutting supply lines may become integral parts of managing combat. Terrain becomes an important part of strategy, since units may gain or lose advantages based on the landscape. Some strategy games such as *Civilization III* and *Medieval 2: Total War* involve other forms of conflict such as diplomacy and espionage. However, warfare is the most common form of conflict, as game designers have found it difficult to make non-violent forms of conflict as appealing.

Economy, Resources and Upgrades

Strategy games often involve other economic challenges. These can include building construction, population maintenance, and resource management. Strategy games frequently make use of a windowed interface to manage these complex challenges.

Most strategy games allow players to accumulate resources which can be converted to units, or converted to buildings such as factories that produce more units. The quantity and types of resources vary from game to game. Some games will emphasize resource acquisition by scattering large quantities throughout the map, while other games will put more emphasis on how resources are managed and applied by balancing the availability of resources between players. To a lesser extent, some strategy games give players a fixed quantity of units at the start of the game.

Strategy games often allow the player to spend resources on upgrades or research. Some of these upgrades enhance the player's entire economy. Other upgrades apply to a unit or class of units, and unlock or enhance certain combat abilities. Sometimes enhancements are enabled by building a structure that enables more advanced structures. Games with a large number of upgrades often feature a technology tree, which is a series of advancements that players can research to unlock new units, buildings, and other capabilities. Technology trees are quite large in some games, and 4X strategy games are known for having the largest.

A build order is a linear pattern of production, research, and resource management aimed at achieving a specific and specialized goal. They are analogous to chess openings, in that a player will have a specific order of play in mind, however the amount the build order, the strategy around which the build order is built or even which build order is then used varies on the skill, ability and other factors such as how aggressive or defensive each player is.

Map and Exploration

Early strategy games featured a top-down perspective, similar in nature to a board game or paper map. Many later games adopted an isometric perspective. Even with the rise of 3D graphics and the potential to manipulate the camera, games usually feature some kind of aerial view. Very rarely do strategy games show the world from the perspective from an avatar on the ground. This is to provide the player with a big picture view of the game world, and form more effective strategies.

Exploration is a key element in most strategy games. The landscape is often shrouded in darkness, and this darkness is lifted as a player's units enters the area. The ability to explore may be inhibited by different kinds of terrain, such as hills, water, or other obstructions. Even after an area is explored, that area may become dim if the player does not patrol it. This design technique is called the fog of war, where the player can see the terrain but not the units within the explored area. This makes it possible for enemies to attack unexpectedly from otherwise explored areas.

Real-time Versus Turn-based

Strategy video games are categorized based on whether they offer the continuous gameplay of real-time strategy, or the discrete phases of turn-based strategy. These differences in time-keeping lead to several other differences. Typically, turn-based strategy games have stronger artificial intelligence than real-time strategy games, since the turn-based pace allows more time for complex calculations. But a real-time artificial intelligence makes up for this disadvantage with its ability to manage multiple units more quickly than a human. Overall, real-time strategy games are more action-oriented, as opposed to the abstract planning emphasized in turn-based strategy.

Bos Wars is a real-time strategy game, where events unfold continuously.

The relative popularity of real-time strategy has led some critics to conclude that more gamers prefer action-oriented games. Fans of real-time strategy have criticized the wait times associated with turn-based games, and praised the challenge and realism associated with making quick decisions in real-time. In contrast, turn-based strategy fans have criticized real-time strategy games because most units do not behave appropriately without orders, and thus a turn-based pace allows players to input more realistic and detailed plans. Game theorists have noted that strategic thinking does not lend itself well to real-time action, and turn-based strategy purists have criticized real-time strategy games for replacing "true strategy" with gameplay that rewards "rapid mouse-clicking". Overall, reviewers have been able to recognize the advantages associated with both of the main types of strategy games.

Strategy Versus Tactics

Most strategy video games involve a mix of both strategy and tactics. "Tactics" usually refer how troops are utilized in a given battle, whereas "strategy" describes the mix of troops, the location of the battle, and the commander's larger goals or military doctrine. However, there is also a growing subgenre of purely tactical games, which are referred to as real-time tactics, and turn-based tactics. Game reviewers and scholars sometimes debate whether they are using terminology such as "tactics" or "strategy" appropriately. Chris Taylor, the designer of *Total Annihilation* and *Supreme Commander*, has gone so far as to suggest that real-time strategy titles are more about tactics than strategy. But releases that are considered pure tactical games usually provide players with a fixed set of units, and downplay other strategic considerations such as manufacturing, and resource management. Tactical games are strictly about combat, and typically focus on individual battles, or other small sections in a larger conflict.

Settings and Themes

Strategy games can take place in a number of settings. Depending on the theatre of warfare, releases may be noted as naval strategy games, or space strategy games. A title may be noted for its grand strategic scale, whether the game is real-time, or turn-based. Strategy games also draw on a number of historical periods, including World War II, the medieval era, or the Napoleonic era. Some strategy games are even based in an alternate history, by manipulating and rewriting certain historical facts. It is also common to see games based in science fiction or futuristic settings, as well as fantasy settings.

Some strategy games are abstract, and do not try to represent a world with high fidelity. Although many of these may still involve combat in the sense that units can capture or destroy each other, these games sometimes offer non-combat challenges such as arranging units in specific patterns. However, the vast majority of computerized strategy games are representational, with more complex game mechanics.

Single Player, Multiplayer, and Massively Multiplayer

Strategy games include single-player gameplay, multiplayer gameplay, or both. Single player games will sometimes feature a campaign mode, which involves a series of matches against several artificial intelligence opponents. Finishing each match or mission will advance the game's plot, often with cut scenes, and some games will reward a completed mission with new abilities or upgrades. Hardcore strategy gamers tend to prefer multiplayer competition, where human opponents provide more challenging competition than the artificial intelligence. Artificial intelligence opponents often need hidden information or bonuses to provide a challenge to players.

More recently, massively multiplayer online strategy games have appeared such as *Shattered Galaxy* from 2001. However, these games are relatively difficult to design and implement compared to other massively multiplayer online games, as the numerous player-controlled units create a larger volume of online data. By 2006, reviewers expressed disappointment with the titles produced thus far. Critics argued that strategy games are not conducive to massively multiplayer gameplay. A single victory cannot have much impact in a large persistent world, and this makes it hard for a player to care about a small victory, especially if they are fighting for a faction that is losing an overall war. However, more recent developers have tried to learn from past mistakes, resulting in *Dreamlords* from 2007, and *Saga* from 2008. In 2012, Supercell released Clash of Clans, a mobile strategy video game.

History

The origin of strategy video games is rooted in traditional tabletop strategy games like Chess and Go, as well as board and miniature wargaming. The first console strategy game was a *Risk*-like game called *Invasion,* released in 1972 for the Magnavox Odyssey. Strategic Simulations (SSI)'s *Computer Bismarck*, released in 1980, was the first historical computer wargame. Companies such as SSI, Avalon Hill, MicroProse, and Strategic Studies Group released many strategy titles throughout the 1980s. *Reach for the Stars* from 1983 was one of the first 4X strategy games, which expanded upon the relationship between economic growth, technological progress, and conquest. That same year, *Nobunaga's Ambition* was a conquest-oriented grand strategy wargame with historical simulation elements. *The Lords of Midnight* combined elements of adventure, strategy and wargames, and won the Crash magazine award for Best Adventure game of 1984, as well as Best Strategy Game of the Year at the Golden Joystick Awards

1989's *Herzog Zwei* is often considered the first real-time strategy game, although real-time strategy elements can be found in several earlier games, such as Dan Bunten's *Cytron Masters* and Don Daglow's *Utopia* in 1982; Kōji Sumii's *Bokosuka Wars* in 1983; D. H. Lawson and John Gibson's *Stonkers* and Steven Faber's *Epidemic!* in 1983; and Evryware's *The Ancient Art of War* in 1984.

The genre was popularized by *Dune II* three years later in 1992. Brett Sperry, the creator of *Dune II*, coined the name "real-time strategy" to help market the new game genre he helped popularize. Real-time strategy games changed the strategy genre by emphasizing the importance of time management, with less time to plan. Real-time strategy games eventually began to outsell turn-based strategy games.

Since its first title was released in 2000, the *Total War* series by the *Creative Assembly* has become the most successful series of strategy games of all time, with sales of copies of *Empire: Total War* numbering in the millions.

Subgenres

4X

4X games are a genre of strategy video game in which players control an empire and "explore, expand, exploit, and exterminate". The term was first coined by Alan Emrich in his September 1993 preview of *Master of Orion* for *Computer Gaming World*. Since then, others have adopted the term to describe games of similar scope and design.

4X games are noted for their deep, complex gameplay. Emphasis is placed upon economic and technological development, as well as a range of non-military routes to supremacy. Games can take a long time to complete since the amount of micromanagement needed to sustain an empire scales as the empire grows. 4X games are sometimes criticized for becoming tedious for these reasons, and several games have attempted to address these concerns by limiting micromanagement.

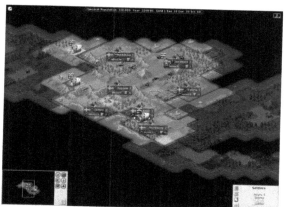

Freeciv is an open source implementation of the Civilization series

The earliest 4X games borrowed ideas from board games and 1970s text-based computer games. The first 4X games were turn-based, but real-time 4X games are also not uncommon. Many 4X games were published in the mid-1990s, but were later outsold by other types of strategy games. Sid Meier's *Civilization* and the Total War series are important examples from this formative era, and popularized the level of detail that would later become a staple of the genre. In the new 2000 millennium, several 4X releases have become critically and commercially successful.

Artillery

Artillery is the generic name for either early two- or three-player (usually turn-based) computer games involving tanks fighting each other in combat or similar derivative games. Artillery games are among the earliest computer games developed; the theme of such games is an extension of the original uses of computer themselves, which were once used to calculate the trajectories of rockets and other related military-based calculations. Artillery games have been typically described as a type of turn-based strategy game, though they have also been described as a type of "shooting game." Examples of this genre are Pocket Tanks, Hogs of War, Scorched 3D and the Worms series.

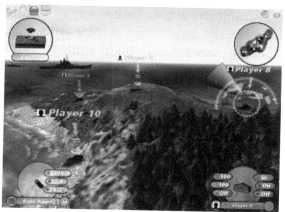

Scorched 3D is an artillery game.

Early precursors to the modern artillery-type games were text-only games that simulated artillery entirely with input data values. A BASIC game known simply as *Artillery* was written by Mike Forman and was published in *Creative Computing* magazine in 1976. This seminal home computer version of the game was revised in 1977 by M. E. Lyon and Brian West and was known as *War 3*; *War 3* was revised further in 1979 and published as *Artillery-3*. These early versions of turn-based tank combat games interpreted human-entered data such as the distance between the tanks, the velocity or "power" of the shot fired and the angle of the tanks' turrets.

Real-Time Strategy (RTS)

Usually applied only to certain computer strategy games, the moniker real-time strategy (RTS) indicates that the action in the game is continuous, and players will have to make their decisions and actions within the backdrop of a constantly changing game state, and computer real-time strategy gameplay is characterised by obtaining resources, building bases, researching technologies and producing units. Very few non-computer strategy games are real-time; one example is Icehouse.

Some players dispute the importance of strategy in real-time strategy games, as skill and manual dexterity are often seen as the deciding factor in this genre of game. According to Troy Dunniway, "A player controls hundreds of units, dozens of buildings and many different events that are all happening simultaneously. There is only one player, and he can only pay attention to one thing at a time. Expert players can quickly flip between many different tasks, while casual gamers have more problems with this." Ernest Adams goes so far as to suggest that real-time gameplay interferes with strategy. "Strategic thinking, at least in the arena of gameplay, does not lend itself well to real-time action".

Many strategy players claim that many RTS games really should be labeled as "real-time tactical" (RTT) games since the game play revolves entirely around tactics, with little or even no strategy involved. Massively Multiplayer Online Games (MMOG or MMO) in particular have had a difficult time implementing strategy since having strategy implies some mechanism for "winning". MMO games, by their nature, are typically designed to be never-ending. Nevertheless, some games are attempting to "crack the code," so-to-speak, of the true real-time strategy MMOG. One method by which they are doing so is by making defenses stronger than the weapons, thereby slowing down combat considerably and making it possible for players to more carefully consider their actions during a confrontation. Customizable units are another way of adding strategic elements, as long as players are truly able to influence the capabilities of their units. The industry is seeking to present new candidates worthy of being known for "thought strategy" rather than "dexterity strategy".

While *Herzog Zwei* is regarded as the first true RTS game, the defining title for the genre was Westwood Studios's *Dune II*, which was followed by their seminal *Command & Conquer* games. Cavedog's *Total Annihilation* (1997), Blizzard's *Warcraft* (1994) series, *StarCraft* (1998) series, and Ensemble Studios' *Age of Empires* (1997) series are some of the most popular RTS games. In addition, online games such as NukeZone can be considered belonging in this genre as well.

Real-Time Tactics (RTT)

Real-time tactics (abbreviated RTT and less commonly referred to as fixed-unit real-time strategy) is a subgenre of tactical wargames played in real-time simulating the considerations and circumstances of operational warfare and military tactics. It is also sometimes considered a subgenre of real-time strategy, and thus may in this context exist as an element of gameplay or as a basis for the whole game. It is differentiated from real-time strategy gameplay by the lack of resource micromanagement and base or unit building, as well as the greater importance of individual units and a focus on complex battlefield tactics. Example titles include *Warhammer: Dark Omen*, *World In Conflict*, the *Close Combat* series, and early tactical role-playing games such as *Bokosuka Wars*, *Silver Ghost*, and *First Queen*.

MMORTS

Massively multiplayer online real-time strategy games, also known as MMORTS, combine real-time strategy (RTS) with a persistent world. Players often assume the role of a general, king, or other type of figurehead leading an army into battle while maintaining the resources needed for such warfare. The titles are often based in a sci-fi or fantasy universe and are distinguished from single or small-scale multiplayer RTS games by the number of players and common use of a persistent world, generally hosted by the game's publisher, which continues to evolve even when the player is offline.

Multiplayer Online Battle Arena (MOBA)

Vainglory is a multiplayer online battle arena game designed for smartphones and tablets.

Multiplayer online battle arena (MOBA), also known as action real-time strategy (ARTS), is a genre of strategy video games that originated as a subgenre of real-time strategy, in which a player controls a single character in one of two teams. The objective is to destroy the opposing team's main structure with the assistance of periodically spawned computer-controlled units that march forward along set paths. Player characters typically have various abilities and advantages that improve over the course of a game and that contribute to a team's overall strategy. A fusion of action games, role-playing games and real-time strategy games, players usually do not construct either buildings or units.

The genre traces its roots to *Aeon of Strife*, a custom map for *StarCraft* where four players each controlling a single powerful unit and aided by weak computer-controlled units were put against a stronger computer-controlled faction. *Defense of the Ancients (DotA)*, a map based on *Aeon of Strife* for *Warcraft III: Reign of Chaos* and *The Frozen Throne*, was one of the first major titles of its genre and the first MOBA for which has been held sponsored tournaments. It was followed by the two spiritual successors *League of Legends* and *Heroes of Newerth*, and eventually a sequel, *Dota 2*, as well as numerous other games in the genre.

Tower Defense

Tower defense games have a very simple layout. Usually, computer-controlled monsters called *creeps* move along a set path, and the player must place, or "build" towers along this path to kill the creeps. In some games, towers are placed along a set path for creeps, while in others towers can interrupt creep movement and change their path. In most tower defense games different towers have different abilities such as poisoning enemies or slowing them down. The player is awarded money for killing creeps, and this money can be used to buy more towers, or buy upgrades for a tower such as increased power or range.

Turn-based Strategy (TBS)

The Battle for Wesnoth is a turn-based strategy game.

The term turn-based strategy (TBS) is usually reserved for certain computer strategy games, to distinguish them from real-time computer strategy games. A player of a turn-based game is allowed a period of analysis before committing to a game action. Examples of this genre are the *Civilization*, *Heroes of Might and Magic*, *Making History*, *Advance Wars*, *Master of Orion* and AtWar.

TBS games come in two flavors, differentiated by whether players make their plays simultaneously or take turns. The former types of games are called simultaneously executed TBS games, with *Diplomacy* a notable example. The latter games fall into the player-alternated TBS games category, and are subsequently subdivided into (a) ranked, (b) round-robin start, and (c) random, the difference being the order under which players take their turns. With (a), ranked, the players take their turns in the same order every time. With (b), the first player is selected according to a round-robin policy. With (c), random, the first player is, of course, randomly selected.

Almost all non-computer strategy games are turn-based; however, the personal computer game market trend has lately inclined more towards real-time games. Some recent games feature a mix of both real-time and turn-based elements thrown together.

Turn-based Tactics (TBT)

Turn-based tactics (TBT), or tactical turn-based (TTB), is a genre of strategy video games that through stop-action simulates the considerations and circumstances of operational warfare and military tactics in generally small-scale confrontations as opposed to more strategic considerations of turn-based strategy (TBS) games.

Turn-based tactical gameplay is characterized by the expectation of players to complete their tasks using only the combat forces provided to them, and usually by the provision of a realistic (or at least believable) representation of military tactics and operations. Examples of this genre include the *Wars, Jagged Alliance* and *X-COM* series, as well as tactical role-playing games such as the *Fire Emblem* and *Final Fantasy Tactics*.

Wargames

Wargames are a subgenre of strategy video games that emphasize strategic or tactical warfare on a map, as well as historical (or near-historical) accuracy.

The primary gameplay mode in a wargame is usually tactical: fighting battles. Wargames sometimes have a strategic mode where players may plan their battle or choose an area to conquer, but players typically spend much less time in this mode and more time actually fighting. Because it is difficult to provide an intelligent way to delegate tasks to a subordinate, war games typically keep the number of units down to hundreds rather than hundreds of thousands.

Examples of wargames include Koei's *Nobunaga's Ambition* and *Romance of the Three Kingdoms* series, and several titles by Strategic Simulations, Inc. (SSI) and Strategic Studies Group (SSG).

Subtypes of Strategy Video Game

4X

4X is a genre of strategy-based video and board games in which players control an empire and "eXplore, eXpand, eXploit, and eXterminate". The term was first coined by Alan Emrich in his September 1993 preview of *Master of Orion* for *Computer Gaming World*. Since then, others have adopted the term to describe games of similar scope and design.

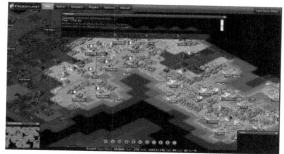

Detailed empire management, seen here in *Freeciv*, is a central aspect of 4X strategy games.

4X computer games are noted for their deep, complex gameplay. Emphasis is placed upon economic and technological development, as well as a range of non-military routes to supremacy. Games can take a long time to complete since the amount of micromanagement needed to sustain an empire increases as the empire grows. 4X games are sometimes criticized for becoming tedious for these reasons, and several games have attempted to address these concerns by limiting micromanagement, with varying degrees of success.

The earliest 4X games borrowed ideas from board games and 1970s text-based computer games. The first 4X computer games were turn-based, but real-time 4X games are not uncommon. Many 4X computer games were published in the mid-1990s, but were later outsold by other types of strategy games. Sid Meier's *Civilization* is an important example from this formative era, and popularized the level of detail that later became a staple of the genre. In the new millennium, several 4X releases have become critically and commercially successful.

In the board (and card) game domain, 4X is less of a distinct genre, in part because of the practical constraints of components and playing time. The *Civilization* board game that gave rise to Sid Meier's *Civilization* computer game, for instance, has no exploration and no extermination. Unless extermination is targeted at non-player entities, it tends to be either nearly impossible (because of play balance mechanisms, since player elimination is usually considered an undesirable feature) or certainly unachievable (because victory conditions are triggered before extermination can be completed) in board games.

Definition

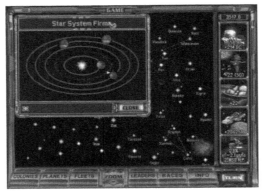

4X computer games such as *Master of Orion II* let empires explore the map, expanding by founding new colonies and exploiting their resources. The game can be won either by becoming an elected leader of the galaxy or by exterminating all opponents.

The term "4X" originates from a 1993 preview of *Master of Orion* in *Computer Gaming World* by Alan Emrich, in which he rated the game "XXXX" as a pun on the XXX rating for pornography. The four Xs were an abbreviation for "EXplore, EXpand, EXploit and EXterminate". Other game commentators adopted the "4X" label to describe a game genre with specific gameplay conventions:

- *Explore* means players send scouts across a map to reveal surrounding territories.

- *Expand* means players claim new territory by creating new settlements, or sometimes by extending the influence of existing settlements.

- *Exploit* means players gather and use resources in areas they control, and improve the efficiency of that usage.

- *Exterminate* means attacking and eliminating rival players. Since in some games all territory is eventually claimed, eliminating a rival's presence may be the only way to achieve further expansion.

These four elements of gameplay have been described as the four phases of a 4X computer game session. These phases often overlap with each other and vary in length depending on the game design. For example, the *Space Empires* series and *Galactic Civilizations II: Dark Avatar* have a long expansion phase, because players must make large investments in research to explore and expand into every area.

Difficulties in Definition

While many computer strategy games arguably contain a similar "explore, expand, exploit, exterminate" cycle, game journalists, developers and enthusiasts generally apply "4X" to a more specific class of games, and contrast 4X games with other strategy games such as *Command & Conquer*. Hence, writers have tried to show how 4X games are defined by more than just having each of the four Xs. Computer gaming sites have stated that 4X games are distinguished by their greater complexity and scale, and their intricate use of diplomacy beyond the standard "friend or foe" seen in other strategy games. Reviewers have also stated that 4X games feature a range of diplomatic options, and that they are well known for their large detailed empires and complex gameplay. In particular, 4X games offer detailed control over an empire's economy, while other computer strategy games simplify this in favor of combat-focused gameplay.

Game Design

4X computer games are a subgenre of strategy games, and include both turn-based and real-time strategy titles. The gameplay involves building an empire, which takes place in a setting such as Earth, a fantasy world, or in space. Each player takes control of a different civilization or race with unique characteristics and strengths. Most 4X games represent these racial differences with a collection of economic and military bonuses.

Research and Technology

4X games typically feature a technology tree, which represents a series of advancements that players can unlock to gain new units, buildings, and other capabilities. Technology trees in 4X games are typically larger than in other strategy games, featuring a larger selection of choices. Empires must generate research resources and invest them in new technology. In 4X games, the main prerequisite for researching an advanced technology is knowledge of earlier technology. This is in contrast to non-4X real-time strategy games, where technological progress is achieved by building structures that grant access to more advanced structures and units.

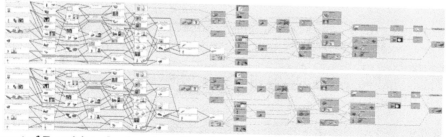

One part of *Freeciv*'s technology tree. Note the complex dependencies between technologies.

Research is important in 4X games because technological progress is an engine for conquest. Battles are often won by superior military technology or greater numbers, with battle tactics playing a smaller part. In contrast, military upgrades in non-4X games are sometimes small enough that technologically basic units remain important throughout the game.

Combat

Combat is an important part of 4X gameplay, because 4X games allow a player to win by exterminating all rival players, or by conquering a threshold amount of the game's universe. Some 4X games, such as *Galactic Civilizations*, resolve battles automatically, whenever two units from warring sides meet. This is in contrast to other 4X games, such as *Master of Orion*, that allow players to manage battles on a tactical battle screen. Even in 4X games with more detailed control over battles, victory is usually determined by superior numbers and technology, with battle tactics playing a smaller part. 4X games differ from other combat-focused strategy games by putting more emphasis on research and economics. Researching new technology will grant access to new combat units. Some 4X games even allow players to research different unit components. This is more typical of space 4X games, where players may assemble a ship from a variety of engines, shields, and weaponry.

Peaceful Competition

4X games allow rival players to engage in diplomacy. While some strategy games may offer shared victory and team play, diplomatic relations tend to be restricted to a binary choice between an ally or enemy. 4X games often allow more complex diplomatic relations between competitors who are not on the same team. Aside from making allies and enemies, players are also able to trade resources and information with rivals.

In addition to victory through conquest, 4X games often offer peaceful victory conditions or goals that involve no extermination of rival players (although war may be still be a necessary by-product of reaching said goal). For example, a 4X game may offer victory to a player who achieves a certain score or the highest score after a certain number of turns. Many 4X games award victory to the first player to master an advanced technology, accumulate a large amount of culture, or complete an awe-inspiring achievement. Several 4X games award "diplomatic victory" to anyone who can win an election decided by their rival players, or maintain peace for a specified number of turns. Galactic Civilizations has the diplomatic victory, which involves having at alliances with at least 4 factions and no other faction be out of your alliance, there are two ways to accomplish this, ally with all factions, or ally with the minimum number of factions then destroy the rest.

Complexity

4X games are known for their complex gameplay and strategic depth. Gameplay usually takes priority over elaborate graphics. Whereas other strategy games focus on combat, 4X games also offer more detailed control over diplomacy, economics, and research; creating opportunities for diverse strategies. This also challenges the player to manage several strategies simultaneously, and plan for long-term objectives.

To experience a detailed model of a large empire, 4X games are designed with a complex set of game rules. For example, the player's productivity may be limited by pollution. Players may need to balance a budget, such as managing debt, or paying down maintenance costs. 4X games often model political challenges such as civil disorder, or a senate that can oust the player's political party or force them to make peace.

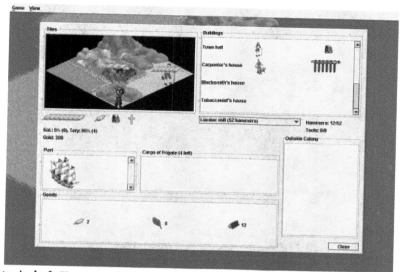

FreeCol is typical of 4X games where there is a separate interface for managing each settlement.

Such complexity requires players to manage a larger amount of information than other strategy games. Game designers often organize empire management into different interface screens and modes, such as a separate screen for diplomacy, managing individual settlements, and managing battle tactics. Sometimes systems are intricate enough to resemble a minigame. This is in contrast to most real-time strategy games. *Dune II*, which arguably established the conventions for the real-time strategy genre, was fundamentally designed to be a "flat interface", with no additional screens.

Gameplay

Since 4X games involve managing a large, detailed empire, game sessions usually last longer than other strategy games. Game sessions may require several hours of play-time, which can be particularly problematic for multiplayer matches. For example, a small-scale game in *Sins of a Solar Empire* can last for over 12 hours. However, fans of the genre often expect and embrace these long game sessions; Emrich wrote that "when the various parts are properly designed, other X's seem to follow. Words like EXcite, EXperiment and EXcuses (to one's significant others)". Turn-based 4X games typically divide these sessions into hundreds of turns of gameplay.

Because of repetitive actions and long-playing times, 4X games have been criticized for excessive micromanagement. In early stages of a game this is usually not a problem, but later in a game directing an empire's numerous settlements can demand several minutes to play a single turn. This increases playing-times, which are a particular burden in multiplayer games. 4X games began to offer AI governors that automate the micromanagement of a colony's build orders, but players criticized these governors for making poor decisions. In response, developers have tried other approaches to reduce micromanagement, and some approaches have been more well received than others. Commentators generally agree that *Galactic Civilizations* succeeds, which GamingNexus.com attributes to the game's use of programmable governors. *Sins of a Solar Empire* was designed to reduce the incentives for micromanagement, and reviewers found that the game's interface made empire management more elegant. On the other hand, *Master of Orion III* reduced micromanagement by limiting complete player control over their empire.

History

Origin

Sid Meier, the creator of the *Civilization* series of 4X games

Early 4X games were influenced by board games and text-based computer games from the 1970s. *Cosmic Balance II*, *Andromeda Conquest* and *Reach for the Stars* were published in 1983, and are now seen retrospectively as 4X games. Although *Andromeda Conquest* was only a simple game of empire expansion, *Reach for the Stars* introduced the relationship between economic growth, technological progress, and conquest.

Prior to Sid Meier, Robert T. Smith created the precursor of all 4X strategy video games: Armada 2525 (followed up by a version with enhanced graphics: Armada 2525 Deluxe). However, due to the financial problems of the publishing company Interstel Corporation, Armada 2525 never got enough marketing and attention from gamers. Future 4X space strategy games such as Master of Orion would go on to adopt the gameplay and concepts found in Armada 2525.

Armada 2526, the spiritual successor to Armada 2525 was released by Ntronium Games in 2009, 19 years after the original Armada 2525 was released in 1990.

In 1991, Sid Meier released *Civilization* and popularized the level of detail that has become a staple of the genre. *Sid Meier's Civilization* was influenced by board games such as *Risk* and the Avalon Hill board game also called *Civilization*. A notable similarity between the *Civilization* computer game and board game is the importance of diplomacy and technological advancement. Sid Meier's *Civilization* was also influenced by personal computer games such as the city management game *SimCity* and the wargame *Empire*. *Civilization* became widely successful and influenced many 4X games to come.

In 1991, two highly influential space games were released. *VGA Planets* was released for the PC, while *Spaceward Ho!* was released on the Macintosh. Although 4X space games were ultimately more influenced by the complexity of *VGA Planets*, *Spaceward Ho!* earned praise for its relatively simple yet challenging game design. *Spaceward Ho!* is notable for its similarity to the 1993 game *Master of*

Orion, with its simple yet deep gameplay. *Master of Orion* also drew upon earlier 4X games such as *Reach for the Stars*, and is considered a classic game that set a new standard for the genre. In a preview of *Master of Orion*, Emrich coined the term "XXXX" to describe the emerging genre. Eventually, the "4X" label was adopted by the game industry, and is now applied to several earlier game releases.

Peak

Following the success of *Civilization* and *Master of Orion*, other developers began releasing their own 4X games. In 1994, Stardock launched its first version of the *Galactic Civilizations* series for OS/2, and the long-standing *Space Empires* series began as shareware. *Ascendancy* and *Stars!* were released in 1995, and both continued the genre's emphasis on strategic depth and empire management. Meanwhile, the *Civilization* and *Master of Orion* franchises expanded their market with versions for the Macintosh. Sid Meier's team also produced *Colonization* in 1994 and *Civilization II* in 1996, while Simtex released *Master of Orion* in 1993, *Master of Magic* in 1994 and *Master of Orion II* in 1996.

By the late 1990s, real-time strategy games began outselling turn-based games. As they surged in popularity, major 4X developers fell into difficulties. Sid Meier's Firaxis Games released *Sid Meier's Alpha Centauri* in 1999 to critical acclaim, but the game fell short of commercial expectations. *Civilization III* encountered development problems followed by a rushed release in 2001. Despite the excitement over *Master of Orion III*, its release in 2003 was met with criticism for its lack of player control, poor interface, and weak AI. Game publishers eventually became risk-averse to financing the development of 4X games.

Real Time Hybrid 4X

Eventually real-time 4X games were released, such as *Imperium Galactica* in 1997, *Starships Unlimited* in 2001, and *Sword of the Stars* in 2006, featuring a combination of turn-based strategy and real-time tactical combat. The blend of 4X and real-time strategy gameplay led Ironclad Games to market their 2008 release *Sins of a Solar Empire* as a "RT4X" game. This combination of features earned the game a mention as one of the top games from 2008, including GameSpot's award for best strategy game, and IGN's award for best PC game.

Cross-fertilization between board games and video games continued. For example, some aspects of *Master of Orion III* were drawn from the first edition of the board game *Twilight Imperium*. Even *Sins of a Solar Empire* was inspired by the idea of adapting the board game *Buck Rogers Battle for the 25th Century* into a real-time video game. Going in the opposite direction, Eagle Games made a board game adaptation of *Sid Meier's Civilization* in 2002, completely different from the board game that had inspired the computer game in the first place.

Recent History

In 2003, Stardock released a remake of *Galactic Civilizations*, which was praised by reviewers who saw the game as a replacement for the *Master of Orion* series. In 2004 the Creative Assembly released the critically acclaimed *Rome: Total War*, which has spawned many sequels. *Civilization IV* was released at the end of 2005 and was considered the PC game of the year according to several reviewers, including GameSpot and GameSpy. It is now considered one of the greatest computer games in history, having been ranked the second-best PC game of all time by IGN. By 2008, the *Civilization* series had sold over eight million copies, followed the release of *Civilization Revolution* for game consoles soon after, Civilization V in 2010, and Civilization VI in 2016. Meanwhile, Stardock released *Galactic Civilizations II*, which was considered the sixth-best PC game of 2006 by GameSpy. Additionally, French developer Amplitude Studios released both Endless Space and Endless Legend. These successes have led Stardock's Brad Wardell to assert that 4X games have excellent growth potential, particularly among less hardcore players. This is in addition to the loyal base of 4X gamers who have supported free software releases such as *Freeciv, FreeCol, Freeorion, Golden Age of Civilizations.*, and *C-evo*.

Real-time Strategy

Real-time strategy (RTS) is a subgenre of strategy video games where the game does not progress incrementally in turns.

The term "Real-time strategy" appeared in *BYTE* magazine in 1982, but usually Brett Sperry is credited with coining the term to market *Dune II*.

In an RTS the participants position and maneuver units and structures under their control to secure areas of the map and/or destroy their opponents' assets. In a typical RTS, it is possible to create additional units and structures during the course of a game. This is generally limited by a requirement to expend accumulated resources. These resources are in turn garnered by controlling special points on the map and/or possessing certain types of units and structures devoted to this purpose. More specifically, the typical game of the RTS genre features resource gathering, base building, in-game technological development and indirect control of units.

The tasks a player must perform to succeed at an RTS can be very demanding, and complex user interfaces have evolved to cope with the challenge. Some features have been borrowed from desktop environments; for example, the technique of "clicking and dragging" to select all units under a given area.

Though some game genres share conceptual and gameplay similarities with the RTS template, recognized genres are generally not subsumed as RTS games. For instance, city-building games, construction and management simulations, and games of the real-time tactics variety are generally not considered to be "real-time strategy".

History

Origins

The genre that is recognized today as "real-time strategy" emerged as a result of an extended period of evolution and refinement. Games that are today sometimes perceived as ancestors of the real-time strategy genre were never marketed or designed as such at the original date of publication. As a result, designating "early real-time strategy" titles is problematic because such games are being held up to modern standards. The genre initially evolved separately in the United Kingdom, Japan, and North America, afterward gradually merging into a unified worldwide tradition.

The turn-based strategy game *Utopia* (1981), which featured timed turns, and Dani Bunten Berry's (of *M.U.L.E* fame) real-time tactics game *Cytron Masters* (1982), developed by Ozark Softscape and released by SSI, are considered precursors of the genre. *BYTE* in December 1982 published as an Apple II type-in program *Cosmic Conquest*. The winner of the magazine's annual Game Contest, the author described it as a "single-player game of real-time action and strategic decision making". The magazine described it as "a real-time space strategy game". The game has elements of resource management and wargaming. Another 1982 example is *Legionnaire* on the Atari 8-bit family, written by Chris Crawford for Avalon Hill. This was effectively the opposite of *Utopia* (1981), in that it offered a complete real-time tactical combat system with variable terrain and mutual-help concepts, but lacked any resource collection and economy/production concepts.

In the United Kingdom, the genre's roots can be traced to *Stonkers* by John Gibson, published in 1983 by Imagine Software for the ZX Spectrum, and *Nether Earth* published on ZX Spectrum in 1987. In North America, the oldest game retrospectively classified as real-time strategy by several sources is *The Ancient Art of War* (1984), designed by Evryware's Dave and Barry Murry, followed by the sequel *The Ancient Art of War at Sea* in 1987. Scott Sharkey of 1UP, however, considers *Cytron Masters* and other real-time examples prior to *Herzog Zwei* to be tactical rather than strategic, due to most lacking the ability to construct units or manage resources, and that the slower processors and modems "made for ticks so long that the games were practically turn based."

In Japan, the genre's roots can be traced to *Bokosuka Wars* (1983), an early strategy RPG (or "simulation RPG"); the game revolves around the player leading an army across a battlefield against enemy forces in real-time while recruiting/spawning soldiers along the way, for which it is considered by Ray Barnholt of 1UP.com to be an early prototype real-time strategy game. This led to several other games that combine role-playing and real-time strategy elements, such as the 1988 Kure Software Koubou computer strategy RPGs, *First Queen* and *Silver Ghost*, which featured an early example of a point-and-click interface, to control characters using a cursor. Another early title with real-time strategy elements was Sega's *Gain Ground* (1988), a strategy-action game that involved directing a set of troops across various enemy-filled levels. TechnoSoft's *Herzog* (1988) is regarded as a precursor to the real-time strategy genre, being the predecessor to *Herzog Zwei* and somewhat similar in nature, though primitive in comparison.

Herzog Zwei, released for the Sega Mega Drive/Genesis home console in 1989, is the earliest example of a game with a feature set that falls under the contemporary definition of modern real-time strategy. The game combined traditional strategy gameplay with fully real-time, fast-paced, arcade-style action gameplay, featuring a split-screen two-player mode where both players are in action simultaneously and there are no pauses while decisions are taken, forcing players to think quickly while on the move. In *Herzog Zwei*, though the player only controls one unit, the manner of control foreshadowed the point-and-click mechanic of later games. It introduced much of the genre conventions, including unit construction and resource management, with the control and destruction of bases being an important aspect of the game, as were the economic/production aspects of those bases. The game has been credited as a key influence on the creation of *Dune II*.

Notable as well are early games like *Mega Lo Mania* by Sensible Software (1991) and *Supremacy* (also called *Overlord* – 1990). Although these two lacked direct control of military units, they both offered considerable control of resource management and economic systems. In addition, *Mega Lo Mania* has advanced technology trees that determine offensive and defensive prowess. Another early (1988) game, *Carrier Command* by Realtime Games, involved real-time responses to events in the game, requiring management of resources and control of vehicles. The early game *Sim Ant* by Maxis (1991) had resource gathering, and controlling an attacking army by having them follow a lead unit. However, it was with the release of *Dune II* from Westwood Studios (1992) that real-time strategy became recognized as a distinct genre of video games.

1992–1998: Seminal Titles

Although real-time strategy games have an extensive history, some titles have served to define the popular perception of the genre and expectations of real-time strategy titles more than others, in particular the games released between 1992 and 1998 by Westwood Studios and Blizzard Entertainment.

Westwood's *Dune II: The Building of a Dynasty* (1992) featured all the core concepts and mechanics of modern real-time strategy games that are still used today, such as using the mouse to move units, and gathering resources, and as such served as the prototype for later real-time strategy games. According to its co-designer and lead programmer, Joe Bostic, a "benefit over *Herzog Zwei* is that we had the advantage of a mouse and keyboard. This greatly facilitated precise player control, which enabled the player to give orders to individual units. The mouse, and the direct control it allowed, was critical in making the RTS genre possible."

The success of *Dune II* encouraged several games which became influential in their own right. *Warcraft: Orcs & Humans* (1994) achieved great prominence upon its release, owing in part to its use of a fantasy setting and also to its depiction of a wide variety of buildings (such as farms) which approximated a full fictitious society, not just a military force. *Command & Conquer*, as well as *Command and Conquer: Red Alert*, became the most popular early RTS games. These two games contended with *Warcraft II: Tides of Darkness* after its release in late 1995.

Total Annihilation, released by Cavedog Entertainment in 1997, introduced 3D units and terrain and focused on huge battles that emphasized macromanagement over micromanagement. It featured a streamlined interface that would influence many RTS games in later years. *Age of Empires*, released by Ensemble Studios in 1997 tried to put a game in a slower pace, combining elements of *Civilization* with the real-time strategy concept by introducing ages of technologies. In 1998, Blizzard released the game *StarCraft*, which became an international phenomenon and is still played in large professional leagues to this day. Collectively, all of these games defined the genre, providing the *de facto* benchmark against which new real-time strategy games are measured.

Refinement and Transition to 3D

The real-time strategy genre has been relatively stable since 1995. Additions to the genre's concept in newer games tend to emphasize more of the basic RTS elements (higher unit caps, more unit types, larger maps, etc.). Rather than innovations to the game concept, new games generally focus on refining aspects of successful predecessors. As the paragon example of gameplay refinement, Cavedog's acclaimed *Total Annihilation* from 1997 distilled the core mechanics of *Command & Conquer*, and introduced the first 3D units and terrain in real-time strategy games. The Age of Empires idea was refined further by Stainless Steel Studios' *Empire Earth* in 2001. GSC Game World's *Cossacks: European Wars* series took the genre in a different direction, bringing population caps into the tens of thousands.

Dungeon Keeper (1997), *Populous: The Beginning* (1998), *Jeff Wayne's The War of the Worlds* (1998), *Warzone 2100* (1999), *Machines* (1999), *Homeworld* (1999), *Honour & Freedom* (1999), and *Dark Reign 2* (2000) were among the first completely 3D real-time strategy titles. *Homeworld* was notable in that it featured a 3D environment in space, therefore allowing movement in every direction, a feature which its semi-sequel, *Homeworld Cataclysm* (2000) continued to build upon adding features such as waypoints. *Homeworld 2*, released in 2003, streamlined movement in the 360° 3D environment. Furthermore, *Machines*, which was also released in 1999 and featured a nearly 100% 3D environment, attempted to combine the RTS genre with a first-person shooter (FPS) genre although it was not a particularly successful title. These games were followed by a short period of interest in experimental strategy games such as *Allegiance* (2000). *Jeff Wayne's The War of the Worlds* was notable for being one of the few completely non-linear RTS games ever.

It is only in approximately 2002 that 3D real-time strategy became the standard, with both *Warcraft III* (2002) and Ensemble Studio's *Age of Mythology* (2002) being built on a full 3D game engine. *Kohan: Immortal Sovereigns* introduced classic wargame elements, such as supply lines to the genre. *Battle Realms* (2001) was another full 3D game, but had limited camera views.

The move from 2D to 3D has been criticized in some cases. Issues with controlling the camera and placement of objects have been cited as problems.

Relatively few genres have emerged from or in competition with real-time strategy games, although real-time tactics, a superficially similar genre, emerged around 1995. In 1998, Activision attempted to combine the real-time strategy and first-person shooter genres in *Battlezone*, while in 2002 Rage Games Limited attempted this with the *Hostile Waters* games. Later variants have included *Natural Selection*, a game modification based on the Half-Life engine, and the free software *Tremulous/Unvanquished*. *Savage: The Battle for Newerth* combined the RPG and RTS elements in an online game.

Specialization and Evolution

A few games have experimented with diversifying map design, which continues to be largely two-dimensional even in 3D engines. *Earth 2150* allowed units to tunnel underground, effectively creating a dual-layer map; three-layer (orbit-surface-underground) maps were introduced in *Metal Fatigue*. In addition, units could even be transported to entirely separate maps, with each map having its own window in the user interface. *Three Kingdoms: Fate of the Dragon* (2001) offered a simpler model: the main map contains locations that expand into their own maps. In these examples, however, gameplay was essentially identical regardless of the map layer in question. *Dragonshard* (2005) emphasized its dual-layer maps by placing one of the game's two main resources in each map, making exploration and control of both maps fundamentally valuable.

Some games, borrowing from the real-time tactics (RTT) template, have moved toward an increased focus on tactics while downplaying traditional resource management, in which designated units collect the resources used for producing further units or buildings. Titles like *Warhammer 40,000: Dawn of War* (2004), *Star Wars: Empire at War* (2006), and *Company of Heroes* (2006) replace the traditional resource gathering model with a strategic control-point system, in which control over strategic points yields construction/reinforcement points. *Ground Control* was the first such game to replace individual units with "squads".

Others are moving away from the traditional real-time strategy game model with the addition of other genre elements. One example is *Sins of a Solar Empire*, released by Ironclad Games, which mixes elements of grand-scale stellar empire building games like *Master of Orion* with real-time strategy elements. Another example is indie game *Achron*, which incorporates time travel as a game mechanic, allowing a player to send units forward or backward in time.

A specific genre of strategy video games referred to as multiplayer online battle arena (MOBA), that originated as a subgenre of real-time strategy, gained popularity in the 2010s as a form of electronic sports, encompassing games such as the *Defense of the Ancients* mod for *Warcraft III*, its Valve-developed sequel *Dota 2*, *Heroes of the Storm* and *League of Legends*.

Gameplay

In a typical real-time strategy game, the screen is divided into a map area displaying the game world and terrain, units, and buildings, and an interface overlay containing command and production controls and often a "radar" or "minimap" overview of the entire map. The player is usually given an isometric perspective of the world, or a free-roaming camera from an aerial viewpoint for modern 3D games. Players mainly scroll the screen and issue commands with the mouse, and may also use keyboard shortcuts.

In most real-time strategy games, especially the earliest ones, the gameplay is generally fast-paced and requires very quick reflexes. For this reason, the amount of violence in some games makes RTS games close to action games in terms of gameplay.

Gameplay generally consists of the player being positioned somewhere in the map with a few units or a building that is capable of building other units/buildings. Often, but not always, the player must build specific structures to unlock more advanced units in the tech tree. Often, but not always, RTS games require the player to build an army (ranging from small squads of no more than 2 units, to literally hundreds of units) and using them to either defend themselves from a virtual form of Human wave attack or to eliminate enemies who possess bases with unit production capacities of their own. Occasionally, RTS games will have a preset number of units for the player to control and do not allow building of additional ones.

Resource gathering is commonly the main focus of the RTS games, but other titles of the genre place higher gameplay significance to the how units are used in combat (*Z: Steel Soldiers* for example, awards credits for territory captured rather than gathered resources), the extreme example of which are games of the real-time tactical genre. Some titles impose a ceiling on the number simultaneous troops, which becomes a key gameplay consideration, a significant example being *StarCraft*, while other titles have no such unit cap.

Micromanagement and Macromanagement

Micromanagement refers to when a player's attention is directed more toward the management and maintenance of his or her own individual units and resources. This creates an atmosphere in which the interaction of the player is constantly needed. On the other hand, macromanagement refers to when a player's focus is directed more toward economic development and large-scale strategic maneuvering, allowing time to think and consider possible solutions. Micromanagement frequently involves the use of combat tactics. Macromanagement tends to look to the future of the game, whereas micromanagement tends to the present.

Criticism of Gameplay

Because of their generally faster-paced nature (and in some cases a smaller learning curve), real-time strategy games have surpassed the popularity of turn-based strategy computer games. In the past, a common criticism was to regard real-time strategy games as "cheap imitations" of turn-based strategy games, arguing that real-time strategy games had a tendency to devolve into "click-fests" in which the player who was faster with the mouse generally won, because they could give orders to their units at a faster rate. The common retort is that success involves not just fast clicking, but also the ability to make sound decisions under time pressure. The "clickfest" argument is also often voiced alongside a "button babysitting" criticism, which pointed out that a great deal of game time is spent either waiting and watching for the next time a production button could be clicked, or rapidly alternating between different units and buildings, clicking their respective button.

A third common criticism is that real-time gameplay often degenerates into "rushes" where the players try to gain the advantage and subsequently defeat the opponent as quickly in the game as possible, preferably before the opposition is capable of successfully reacting. For example, the original *Command & Conquer* gave birth to the now-common "tank rush" tactic, where the game outcome is often decided very early on by one player gaining an initial advantage in resources and producing large amounts of a relatively powerful but still quite cheap unit—which is thrown at the opposition before they have had time to establish defenses or production. Although this strategy has been criticized for encouraging overwhelming force over strategy and tactics, defenders of the strategy argue that they're simply taking advantage of the strategies utilized, and some argue that it is a realistic representation of warfare. One of the most infamous versions of a rush is the "Zergling rush" from the real-time strategy game *StarCraft*; in fact, the term "zerging" has become synonymous with rushing.

A fourth criticism of the RTS genre is the importance of skill over strategy in real-time strategy games. The manual dexterity and ability to multitask and divide one's attention is often considered the most important aspect to succeeding at the RTS genre. According to Troy Dunniway, former Westwood developer who has also worked on *Command and Conquer 3: Tiberium Wars*, "A player controls hundreds of units, dozens of buildings and many different events that are all happening simultaneously. There is only one player, and he can only pay attention to one thing at a time. Expert players can quickly flip between many different tasks, while casual gamers have more problems with this."

Tactics vs. Strategy

Real-time strategy games have been criticized for an overabundance of tactical considerations when compared to the amount of strategic gameplay found in such games. According to Chris Taylor, lead designer of *Supreme Commander*, he said, "[My first attempt at visualizing RTSs in a fresh and interesting new way] was my realizing that although we call this genre 'Real-Time Strategy,' it should have been called 'Real-Time Tactics' with a dash of strategy thrown in." (Taylor then posits his own game as having surpassed this mold by including additional elements of broader strategic scope.)

In general terms, military strategy refers to the use of a broad arsenal of weapons including diplomatic, informational, military, and economic resources, whereas military tactics is more concerned with short-term goals such as winning an individual battle. In the context of strategy video games, however, the difference is often reduced to the more limited criteria of either a presence or absence of base building and unit production.

In an article for Gamasutra, Nathan Toronto criticizes real-time strategy games for too often having only one valid means of victory — attrition — comparing them unfavorably to real-time tactics games. Players' awareness that the only way for them to win or lose is militarily makes them unlikely to respond to gestures of diplomacy. The result is that the winner of a real-time strategy game is too often the best tactician rather than the best strategist. Troy Goodfellow counters this by saying that the problem is not that real-time strategy games are lacking in strategy (he says attrition is a form of strategy), rather it is that they too often have the *same* strategy: produce faster than you consume. He also states that building and managing armies is the conventional definition of real-time strategy, and that it is unfair to make comparisons with other genres.

In an article for Gamespy, Mark Walker criticizes real-time strategy games for their *lack* of combat tactics, suggesting real-time tactics games as a more suitable substitute. He also says that developers need to begin looking outside the genre for new ideas in order for strategy games to continue to be successful in the future.

Turn-based vs. Real-time

A debate has emerged between fans of real-time strategy and turn-based strategy (and related genres) based on the merits of the real-time and turn-based systems. Some titles attempt to merge the two systems: for example, the role-playing game *Fallout* uses turn-based combat and real-time gameplay, while the real-time strategy games *Homeworld*, *Rise of Nations*, and the games of the *Total War* series allow the player to pause the game and issue orders. Additionally, the *Total War* series has a combination of a turn-based strategy map with a real-time battle map. Another example of a game combining both turn-based game and real-time-strategy is *The Lord of the Rings: The Battle for Middle-Earth II* which allows players, in a 'War of the Ring' game, to play a turn-based strategy game, but also battle each other in real time.

On Consoles

Despite *Herzog Zwei*, a console game, laying the foundations for the real-time strategy genre, RTS games never gained popularity on consoles like they did on the PC platform. Real-time strategy games made for video game consoles have been consistently criticized due to their control schemes, as the PC's keyboard and mouse are generally considered to be superior to a console's gamepad for the genre. Thus, RTS games for home consoles have been met with mixed success. Scott Sharkey of 1UP notes that *Herzog Zwei* had already "offered a nearly perfect solution to the problem by giving the player direct control of a single powerful unit and near autonomy for everything else," and is surprised "that more console RTS games aren't designed with this kind of interface in mind from the ground up, rather than imitating" PC control schemes "that just doesn't work very well with a controller".

However, *Halo Wars*, which was released in 2009 for the Xbox 360, generated generally positive reviews, achieved an 82% critic average on aggregate web sites, and sold over 1 million copies. According to IGN, the gameplay lacks the traditional RTS concepts of limited resources and resource gathering and lacks multiple buildings.

Graphics

Total Annihilation (1997) was the first real-time strategy game to utilize true 3D units, terrain, and physics in both rendering and in gameplay. For instance, the missiles in *Total Annihilation* travel in real time in simulated 3D space, and they can miss their target by passing over or under it. Similarly, missile-armed units in *Earth 2150* are at a serious disadvantage when the opponent is on high ground because the missiles often hit the cliffside, even in the case when the attacker is a missile-armed helicopter. *Homeworld, Warzone 2100 and Machines* (all released in 1999) advanced the use of fully 3D environments in real-time strategy titles. In the case of *Homeworld*, the game is set in space, offering a uniquely exploitable 3D environment in which all units can move vertically in addition to the horizontal plane. However, the near-industry-wide switch to full 3D was very gradual and most real-time strategy titles, including the first sequels to *Command & Conquer*, initially used isometric 3D graphics made by pre-rendered 3D tiles. Only in later years did these games begin to use true 3D graphics and game-play, making it possible to rotate the view of the battlefield in real-time. *Spring* is a good example of the transformation from semi-3D to full-3D game simulations. It is an *open-source* project which aims to give a *Total Annihilation* game-play experience in three dimensions. The most ambitious use of full 3D graphics was realized in *Supreme Commander*, where all projectiles, units and terrain were simulated in real time, taking full advantage of the UI's zoom feature, which allowed cartographic style navigation of the 3D environment. This led to a number of unique gameplay elements, which were mostly obscured by the lack of computing power available in 2007, at the release date.

Japanese game developers Nippon Ichi and Vanillaware worked together on *Grim Grimoire*, a PlayStation 2 title released in 2007, which features hand-drawn animated 2D graphics.

From 2010, real-time strategy games more commonly incorporated physics engines, such as Havok, in order to increase realism experienced in gameplay. A modern real-time strategy game that uses a physics engine is Ensemble Studios' *Age of Empires III*, released on October 18, 2005, which used the Havok Game Dynamics SDK to power its real-time physics. *Company of Heroes* is another real-time strategy game that uses realistically modeled physics as a part of gameplay, including fully destructible environments.

Tournaments

RTS World tournaments have been held for both StarCraft, and *Warcraft III* since its release in 1998, and 2002. The games being that successful, that some players of *Warcraft III* playing *Warcraft III professional competition* have earned over $200,000 at the *Warcraft III World Championships*. In addition, hundreds of StarCraft II tournaments are held yearly, as it is becoming an increasingly popular branch of e-sports. Notable tournaments include MLG, GSL, and Dreamhack. RTS tournaments are especially popular in South Korea.

Real-time Tactics

Real-time tactics or RTT is a subgenre of tactical wargames played in real-time simulating the considerations and circumstances of operational warfare and military tactics. It is differentiated from real-time strategy gameplay by the lack of classic resource micromanagement and base or unit building, as well as the greater importance of individual units and a focus on complex battlefield tactics.

Characteristics

Typical real-time strategy titles encourage the player to focus on logistics and production as much as or more than combat, whereas real-time tactics games commonly do not feature resource-gathering, production, base-building or economic management, instead focusing on tactical and operational aspects of warfare such as unit formations or the exploitation of terrain for tactical advantage. Real-time tactical gameplay is also characterized by the expectation of players to complete their tasks using only the combat forces provided to them, and usually by the provision of a realistic (or at least believable) representation of military tactics and operations.

This contrasts with other current strategy game genres. For instance, in large-scale turn-based strategy games battles are generally abstracted and the gameplay close to that of related board games. Real-time strategy games de-emphasize realism and focus on the collection and conversion of resources into production capacities which manufacture combat units thereafter used in generally highly stylized confrontations. In contrast, real-time tactics games' military tactical and realistic focus and comparatively short risk/reward cycle usually provide a distinctly more immediate, intense and accessible experience of battlefield tactics and mêlée than strategy games of other genres.

As suggested by the genre's name, also fundamental to real-time tactics is real-time gameplay. The genre has its roots in tactical and miniature wargaming, where battle scenarios are recreated using miniatures or even simple paper chits. These board and table-top games were out of necessity turn-based. Only with computer support was turn-based play and strategy successfully transposed into real-time. Turn-based strategy and turn-based tactics were obvious first candidates for computer implementation; but as computer implementation eventually allowed for ever more complex rule sets, some games became less timeslice-focused and more continuous until eventually "real-time" play was achieved.

Genre Classification

While some publications do refer to "RTT" as a distinct subgenre of real-time strategy or strategy, not all publications do so. Further, precise terminology is inconsistent. Nonetheless, efforts have been made to distinguish RTT games from RTSs. For instance, GameSpy described *Axis & Allies* (the 2004 video game) as a "true RTS", but with a high level of military realism with such features as battlefield command organization and supply lines. A developer for *Close Combat* said their game never aspired to be an RTS in the "classic sense", but was rather a "real time tactical simulation", lacking such features as resource collection. A developer of *Nexus: The Jupiter Incident* remarked on his game being called a "tactical fleet simulator" rather than a "traditional RTS", citing its focus on tactical gameplay and fixed units at the start of each mission.

Comparison with Real-time Strategy

In general terms, military strategy refers to the use of a broad arsenal of weapons including diplomatic, informational, military, and economic resources, whereas military tactics is more concerned with short-term goals such as winning an individual battle. In the context of strategy video games, however, the difference often comes down to the more limited criteria of either a presence or absence of base building and unit production.

Real-time strategy games have been criticized for an overabundance of tactical considerations when compared to the amount of strategic gameplay found in such games. According to Chris Taylor, lead designer of *Supreme Commander*, *"[My first attempt at visualizing RTSs in a fresh and interesting new way] was my realizing that although we call this genre 'Real-Time Strategy,' it should have been called 'Real-Time Tactics' with a dash of strategy thrown in."* Taylor then went on to say that his own game featured added elements of a broader strategic level.

In an article for Gamespy, Mark Walker said that developers need to begin looking outside the genre for new ideas in order for strategy games to continue to be successful in the future.

In an article for Gamasutra, Nathan Toronto criticizes real-time strategy games for too often having only one valid means of victory—attrition—comparing them unfavorably to real-time tactics games. According to Toronto, players' awareness that their only way to win is militarily makes them unlikely to respond to gestures of diplomacy; the result being that the winner of a real-time strategy game is too often the best tactician rather than the best strategist. Troy Goodfellow counters this by saying that the problem is not that real-time strategy games are lacking in strategic elements (he calls attrition a form of strategy); rather, it is that they too often rely upon the *same* strategy: produce faster than you consume. He also says that building and managing armies is the conventional definition of real-time strategy, and that it is unfair to make comparisons with other genres when they break convention.

Brief History and Background

Wargaming with items or figurines representing soldiers or units for training or entertainment has been common for as long as organised conflicts. Chess, for example, is based on essentialised battlefield movements of medieval unit types and, beyond its entertainment value, is intended to instill in players a rudimentary sense of tactical considerations. Today, miniature wargaming, where players mount armies of miniature figurines to battle each other, has become popular (e.g., *Warhammer Fantasy Battle* and *Warhammer 40000*). Though similar to conventional modern board wargames (e.g. *Axis & Allies*), in the sense of simulating war and being turn-based, the rules for miniature wargames tend to lean heavily towards the minutiae of military combat rather than anything at a strategic scale.

Though popular as table-top games, tactical wargames were relatively late in coming to computers, largely due to game mechanics calling for large numbers of units and individual soldiers, as well as advanced rules that would have required hardware capacities and interface designs beyond the capabilities of older hardware and software. Since most established rule sets were for turn-based table-top games, the conceptual leap to translate these categories to real time was also a problem that needed to be overcome.

Avalon Hill's 1982 release *Legionaire* for the Atari 8-bit was a real-time wargame of Romans versus Barbarians with game play reminiscent of the current real-time tactics template, called by one review a "real-time simulation of tactical combat". Likewise, Free Fall Associates' 1983 title *Archon* can be considered an early real-time tactics game, built upon Chess but including real-time battle sequences. Archon was highly influential, and, for instance, Silicon Knights, Inc.'s 1994 game *Dark Legions* was virtually identical to it, adding only to *Archon*'s concept that the player, as in many table-top wargames, purchases his army before committing to battle. Another predecessor was Bits of Magic's *Centurion: Defender of Rome* (published for the PC by Electronic Arts in 1990), in which, similar to the recent *Rome: Total War* game, the game took place on a strategic map interspersed by battle sequences. However, though the battles were in real-time they were of small scope and player interaction was limited to deciding the initial troop disposition. *Lords of the Realm*, released in 1994 by Impressions Games, introduced real-time control of these real-time battles.

Establishing the Genre: The late-1990s Rise in Popularity

Around 1995, computer hardware and developer support systems had developed enough to facilitate the requirements of large-scale real-time tactical games. It was in 1995 that the regimentally focused wargame *Warhammer: Shadow of the Horned Rat* was released, groundbreaking not only in that it focused purely on the operational aspects of combat (with all aspects pertaining: regimental manoeuvring and formations, support tactics, terrain, etc.), nor only in that it was entirely real-time, but also that it introduced zoomable and rotatable 3D terrain. In 1997 Firaxis Games' released *Sid Meier's Gettysburg!*, a detailed and faithful recreation of some of the most significant battles of the American Civil War that introduced large scale tactical battlefield command using 3D.

Released in 1996 by Atomic Games, the *Close Combat series* is a simulation of squad- and platoon-type World War II combat tactics which introduced a higher degree of operational realism than seen before. *Combat Mission* went even further in this regard. Further, as *Warhammer: Shadow of the Horned Rat* was a translation of the *Warhammer Fantasy Battle* table-top system, so was 1998's FASA Studios' *MechCommander* a translation of the *BattleTech* boardgame into a 2D computer game format.

In 1997, Bungie released *Myth: The Fallen Lords*, which introduced radically larger battlefields than ever before and included a realistic (at the time) physics engine. In 2000, Creative Assembly created *Shogun: Total War*, taking map sizes to even greater levels, as well as introducing historical and tactical realism until then unheard of in real-time computer games. *Ground Control* was also released in 2000, gaining much attention for its luscious visuals but earning developers Massive Entertainment few sales. In 2007, *World in Conflict* was also released by Massive Entertainment.

Eastern Europe

The 2000s (decade) saw a number of tactical simulations developed in Eastern Europe. Examples include real-time tactics titles such as those belonging to the *Blitzkrieg*, *Sudden Strike* and *UFO* — not to be confused with *UFO: Enemy Unknown* by MicroProse — series; as well as stand-alone titles like *Nexus: The Jupiter Incident*, *Joint Task Force*, and *Codename: Panzers*.

Examples in Different Settings

Historical and Contemporary

Real-time tactics games with historical or contemporary settings generally try to recreate the tactical environment of their selected period, the most common eras and situations being the World War II, Napoleonic warfare or ancient warfare. Numerically they make up the bulk of the genre.

While the degree of realism is uniform, the scale of command and precise mechanics differ radically according to the period setting in keeping with the tactics of that period. So for instance, titles set in the Napoleonic Wars are often played at a company or battalion level, with players controlling groups of sometimes hundreds of soldiers as a single unit, whereas recreations of modern conflicts (such as the Iraq War) tend to offer control down to squad or even individual level.

- The *Total War* series by The Creative Assembly, as exemplified by the first title, *Shogun: Total War* (2000), is widely recognised for its large-scale tactical recreations of battles. Units are organised and controlled in regiments, frequently of fifty to a hundred soldiers, and the games are built to encourage the use of authentic tactics. Battles are freeform and generally take place in open country, and there are no plotted side-missions as in the *Warhammer* games (discussed below). *Rome: Total War* (2004) was praised for its impressive attention to detail and encouragement of tactical thought.

- *Sid Meier's Gettysburg!* (1997) and its sequel *Sid Meier's Antietam!* (1998) (by Firaxis Games), set in the American Civil War, are the best-known examples of Napoleonic style simulations directly after Napoleon Total War. Common to these games is the recreation in detail and scale of a particular set of significant or well-known battles. Using the same engine Firaxis and BreakAway Games also released *Waterloo: Napoleon's Last Battle* which recreates Napoleon Bonaparte's last and most famous battle of 1815. Also noteworthy is *Imperial Glory* (2005) by Pyro Studios which recreates the multi-polar conflicts of Europe between 1789 and 1830.

- The *Close Combat series* (1995–) (by Atomic Games) are tactical battle simulations set in WWII known for a very high degree of realism taking into account limited ammunition, severity of wounds and the psychology and mental welfare of individual soldiers.

- TalonSoft's *Age of Sail* (1996) and *Age of Sail II* (2001) are 3D naval real-time tactics games where you command sailing vessels in high sea and coastal battles. Beyond heading, aspects such as amount of sails and cannon ordnance can be ordered.

- *Sudden Strike* (2000) (by Fireglow Games). In contrast to the *Close Combat* series, this title focuses on larger-scale operations and mechanised tactics rather than low-level details, though individual units have ammunition supplies and gain experience.

- *Soldiers: Heroes of World War II* (2004) (Codemasters) is similar to *Close Combat*, also being set in WWII. It offers greater autonomy over individual units as well as 3D graphics.

- The *Full Spectrum Warrior* series (2004–) (by Pandemic Studios) is set in a fictional country similar to Iraq. The games revolve around a maximum of two fireteams of four soldiers each, and offer engagements at a far more intimate level than the *Total War* series, or indeed the genre at large. It also emphasises story more than most real-time tactics titles. Despite a visual appearance similar to first-person shooters, the player does not directly control any character, instead only issuing orders to his troops. As such it qualifies as a real-time tactical game, and is distinct from the subgenre of first-person shooters known as tactical shooters that incorporate some tactical aspects, such as Ubisoft's *Rainbow Six* series and Gearbox Software's *Brothers in Arms*.

- *Cossacks 2* (2005) is set during the Napoleonic Wars, and supports battles of up to 64000 soldiers. It has a high degree of realism with its morale system and damage model, as well as the fact that the player controls companies of certain number of individual units. Morale serves as a role similar to hit points, increasing or decreasing based upon certain events (such as soldiers being fired at, or soldiers firing upon the enemy). The player is thus deprived of control over the company whenever it falls under a certain level of danger. Soldiers in the Napoleonic wars carried muskets, which did little damage over long distances and took a lot of time to reload. This is reflected in the game, as it takes a long time for a company to reload before it can produce another volley. Further, reloading costs resources, and the food resource is constantly drained depending on how many soldiers the player controls.

- *Faces of War* (2006) (Ubisoft) is a sequel to Soldiers: Heroes of World War II.

- *World in Conflict* (2007) is set in an alternate 1989 as the Soviet Union invades Western Europe and the United States' West Coast in a last-ditch effort to hold onto power while economic troubles threaten to cripple the country.

- The Wargame series is another RTT Cold War type game which focuses on various Cold War scenarios between 1975 and 1995. There are currently three games in the series (*Wargame: European Escalation, Wargame: AirLand Battle*), with a third (*Wargame: Red Dragon*) released in 2014 offering new opportunities with the introduction of naval combat and amphibious operations. Wargame is characterized by its large maps, realistic feel and vast array of units and factions.

- *Tom Clancy's EndWar* (2008) is based on a fictional World War III in 2020 where nuclear weapons are obsolete and conventional warfare makes up the bulk of the gameplay.

- *XIII Century* (latest installment 2009) is set in the time of the Fourth to Ninth Crusades (1202–1272 CE) and features a complex battle resolution engine where each individual soldier is taken into account when determining the outcome.

- *Men of War* (2009) is a sequel to *Faces of War* and started the *Men of War* series.

Fantastical

While most *fantasy* titles bear some resemblance to a historical period (usually medieval), they also incorporate fictional creatures, areas, and/or magic, and are limited by few historical constraints.

The leading High Fantasy real-time tactics games belong to the *Warhammer Fantasy Battle* series. This loose series began with one of the earliest mainstream real-time tactics games, *Warhammer:*

Shadow of the Horned Rat (1995). While the game's depth of tactical simulation is comparable to that of *Total War*, it leans more toward skirmishes over epic battles, and features both unique hero characters and a tightly-authored story. The highly influential video game *Myth: The Fallen Lords* (1997) emphasised formation cohesion to a lesser degree than the *Warhammer* titles, but introduced more extensive maps. In 2006, *Warhammer: Mark of Chaos* was released. Similar in kind to the two preceding *Warhammer* titles, it however took gameplay away from the realistic focus and fidelity of the *Warhammer* rules toward a more arcade- and micromanagement-oriented form. *Kingdom Under Fire: The Crusaders* and its sequel were complex and difficult games made in Korea mixing both elements of RTT and *Dynasty Warriors*-like action. Recently released on PlayStation 3, Under Siege (2011 video game) is another example of tactical battles, where strategy is an interesting point to have in mind. The player is able to control a small group of heroes who fight against a huge invading army. It includes a single player campaign as well as local and online multiplayer content. The ingame editor enables the players to create and share their own maps with the world, taking advantage of the Player generated content .

Futuristic

A supply ship with destroyer escort in *Nexus: The Jupiter Incident*.

Games set in the future and combining elements of science fiction obviously are not constrained by historical accuracy or even the limitations of current technology and physics. Developers thus have a freer hand in determining a game's backstory and setting. Games that are set in outer space can also add a third, vertical movement axis, thereby freeing up new tactical dimensions.

- *Ground Control's* (2000) setting provided innovative new use of air units.

- *Starship Troopers: Terran Ascendancy* (2000) is an action-oriented game based on Robert A. Heinlein's book, *Starship Troopers*. It is characterised by smaller and more autonomous units.

- *MechCommander 2* (2001) is notable for implementing a lightweight resource acquisition system without turning into an RTS. Players could earn 'Resource Points' at the beginning of and during a mission, but they could only expend them upon support tasks. Save for repairs and plucky on-field salvage operations, the system did not affect the player's combat forces in any way.

- *Soldiers of Anarchy* (2002) is a post-apocalyptic, squad-level game which emphasised a realistic environment scale, vehicles, and scavenging in the aftermath of battles.

- *Nexus: The Jupiter Incident* (2004) is set in space and replaces as a result most genre conventions (not least of which is the use of terrain for cover and mobility) with its own.

- *Star Wolves* (2004) is focused on small-scale space fighter wing battles around fighter carriers. Notable for the distinct pilots under your command and for incorporating elements of role-playing games such as character attribute development with experience.

- *Ground Control II: Operation Exodus* (2004) is a sequel to Ground Control.

- *Warhammer 40,000: Dawn of War II* (2009) involves commanding four of six Space Marines squads in each mission, each of which can be customised through experience points and wargear upgrades. Its predecessor, *Dawn of War*, was a real-time strategy game.

- *Command & Conquer 4: Tiberian Twilight* (2010) is the final chapter in the Kane saga. It has changed the formula of a C&C RTS making it a full-fledged RTT.

- *End of Nations* (cancelled) combines the action and strategy of a traditional real-time tactics game (RTT) with the persistence, progression and social features of a massively multiplayer online game (MMO). It focuses on building squads consisting of different types of units and taking control points.

Multiplayer Online Battle Arena

Multiplayer online battle arena (MOBA), also known as action real-time strategy (ARTS), is a genre of strategy video games that originated as a subgenre of real-time strategy, in which a player controls a single character in one of two teams. The objective is to destroy the opposing team's main structure with the assistance of periodically spawned computer-controlled units that march forward along set paths. Player characters typically have various abilities and advantages that improve over the course of a game and that contribute to a team's overall strategy. MOBA games are a fusion of action games, role-playing games and real-time strategy games, in which players usually do not construct either buildings or units.

The genre largely began with *Aeon of Strife* (*AoS*), a custom map for *StarCraft* where four players each controlling a single powerful unit and aided by weak computer-controlled units were put against a stronger computer. *Defense of the Ancients* (*DotA*), a map based on *Aeon of Strife* for *Warcraft III: Reign of Chaos* and *The Frozen Throne*, was one of the first major titles of its genre and the first MOBA for which sponsored tournaments have been held. It was followed by the two spiritual successors *League of Legends* and *Heroes of Newerth*, and eventually a sequel, *Dota 2*, as well as numerous other games in the genre.

History

The roots of the genre can be traced back decades to one of the earliest real-time strategy titles, the 1989 Sega Mega Drive/Genesis game *Herzog Zwei*. It has been cited as a precursor to, or an early example of, the MOBA genre. It used a similar formula, where each player controls a single command unit in one of two opposing sides on a battlefield. In 1998, *Future Cop: LAPD* featured a strategic Precinct Assault mode similar to *Herzog Zwei*, where the players could actively fight alongside generated non-player units. *Herzog Zwei*'s influence is also apparent in several later MOBA games such as *Guilty Gear 2: Overture* (2007) and *AirMech* (2012).

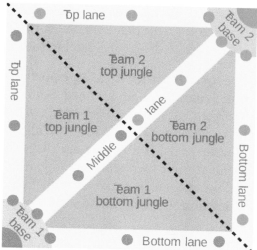

Typical map of a MOBA genre game. Yellow lines are the "lanes" where action is focused; blue and red dots are the defensive "towers/turrets" that defend them; light-colored quarter circles are the teams' bases; and blue and red corners are the structures whose destruction claims victory.

In 1998, computer game company Blizzard Entertainment released its best-selling real-time strategy game (RTS) *StarCraft* with a suite of game editing tools called *StarEdit*. The tools allowed members of the public to design and create custom maps that allowed play very different from the normal maps. A modder known as Aeon64 made a custom map named *Aeon of Strife* (AoS) that became very popular. Aeon64 stated that he was attempting to create gameplay similar to that of *Future Cop: LAPD's* Precinct Assault mode. In the Aeon of Strife map, players controlled a single powerful hero unit fighting amidst three lanes, though terrain outside these lanes was nearly vacant.

In 2002, Blizzard released *Warcraft III: Reign of Chaos* (WC3), with the accompanying *Warcraft III World Editor*. Both the MOBA and tower defense subgenres took substantive shape within the WC3 modding community. A modder named Eul began converting *Aeon of Strife* into the *Warcraft III* engine, calling the map *Defense of the Ancients (DotA)*. Eul substantially improved the complexity of play from the original Aeon of Strife mod. Shortly after creating the custom *DotA* map, Eul left the modding scene. With no clear successor, *Warcraft III* modders created a variety of maps based on *DotA* and featuring different heroes. In 2003, after the release of *Warcraft III: The Frozen Throne*, a map creator named Meian created a *DotA* variant closely modeled on Eul's map, but combining heroes from the many other versions of DotA that existed at the time. Called *DotA: Allstars*, it was inherited after a few months by a modder called Steve "Guinsoo" Feak, and under his guidance it became the dominant map of the genre. After more than a year of maintaining the *DotA: Allstars* map, with the impending release of an update that significantly changed the map layout, Guinsoo left the development to his adjutant Neichus in the year 2005. After some weeks of development and some versions released, the latter turned over responsibility to a modder named IceFrog, who initiated large changes to the mechanics that deepened its complexity and capacity for innovative gameplay. The changes conducted by IceFrog were well-received and the number of users on the *Dota: Allstars* forum is thought to have peaked at over one million.

By 2008, the popularity of *DotA* had attracted commercial attention. That year, The Casual Collective released *Minions*, a Flash web game. Gas Powered Games also released the first stand-alone commercial title in the genre, *Demigod*. In late 2009, Riot Games' debut title, *League of Legends* initially designed by Feak, was released. Riot began to refer to the game's genre as a multiplayer online battle arena (MOBA). Also in 2009, IceFrog, who had continued to develop *DotA: Allstars*, was hired by Valve Corporation, in order to design a sequel to the original map.

In 2010, S2 Games released *Heroes of Newerth*, with a large portion of its gameplay and aesthetics based on *DotA: Allstars*. The same year, Valve announced *Dota 2* and subsequently secured the franchise's intellectual property rights, after being contested by Riot Games for the DotA trademark. *Dota 2* was released in 2013, and was referred to by Valve as an "action real-time strategy" game. In 2012, Activision Blizzard settled a trademark dispute with Valve over the usage of the *DOTA* trademark and announced their own standalone game, which was eventually named *Heroes of the Storm*. Blizzard adopted their own personal dictation for their game's genre with "hero brawler", citing its focus on action. In 2014, Hi-Rez Studios released *Smite*, a MOBA with a third-person perspective.

Gameplay

There are two opposing teams whose goal collectively as a team is generally to destroy their enemy's base to win, though some games have the option of different victory conditions. Each team most typically consists of five players. Typically, there is one main structure which must be destroyed to win; destroying other structures within the opposing team's base may confer other benefits. Defensive structures are in place to prevent this, as well as relatively weak computer-controlled units which periodically spawn at each base and travel down predefined paths toward the opposing team's base. There are typically 3 "lanes" that are the main ways of getting from one base to another; in between the lanes is an uncharted area called the "jungle."

A player controls a single powerful in-game unit generally called a 'hero'. When a hero stands near a killed enemy unit or kills an enemy unit, it gains experience points which allow the hero to level up. When a hero levels up, it has the ability to strengthen its abilities, of which it typically has four. When a hero dies, it has to wait a designated time, which generally increases as it levels up, until it revives at the team's base.

Heroes typically fall into one of several roles, such as tanking, damage-dealing, or healing & support. Each individual hero is unique, with its own abilities that it does not share with any other character, even those which share its role(s). Also typically, there is a large starting pool of heroes; *League of Legends*, for instance, began with 40, and has added at least one new one every month for its entire lifespan, reaching 100 in 2012. This adds to the learning curve of the game, as players must not only learn the game's goals and strategies but also find at least one hero they excel at playing, not to mention familiarize themselves with the remaining roster. Additionally, each hero is deliberately limited in the roles they can fulfill. No one hero is ever (supposed to be) powerful enough to win the game without support from their team. This creates a strong emphasis on teamwork and cooperation.

Each player typically receives a small amount of gold per second during the course of the game. Moderate amounts of gold are rewarded for killing hostile computer-controlled units and larger amounts are rewarded for killing enemy heroes. Gold is used by heroes to buy a variety of different items that range in price and impact. For the most part, this involves improving the combat viability of the hero, although there may be other items that support the hero or team as a whole in different ways.

As the heroes of each team get stronger, they can use multiple strategies to gain an advantage. These strategies can include securing objectives, killing enemy heroes and farming gold by killing A.I. units. The stronger a team gets, the more capable they are at destroying the enemy team and their base.

Members of the genre do not generally feature several other elements traditionally found in real-time strategy games, notably base management, and army building. Some video games have certain heroes which control a few specialized units. The MOBA genre has more resemblance with role-playing games (RPG) in gameplay, though the MOBA genre focuses on multiplayer battle in an arena while RPG typically revolve around a single player story.

Tower Defense

Tower defense (or informally TD) is a subgenre of strategy video game where the goal is to defend a player's territories or possessions by obstructing enemy attackers, usually achieved by placing defensive structures on or along their path of attack. This typically means building a variety of different structures that serve to automatically block, impede, attack or destroy enemies. Tower defense is seen as a subgenre of real-time strategy video games, due to its real-time origins, though many modern tower defense games include aspects of turn-based strategy. Strategic choice and positioning of defensive elements is an essential strategy of the genre.

History

Precursors

The tower defense genre can trace its lineage back to the golden age of arcade video games in the 1980s. The object of the arcade game *Space Invaders* released in 1978 was to defend the player's territory (represented by the bottom of the screen) against waves of incoming enemies. The game featured shields which could be used to strategically, to obstruct enemy attacks on the player and assist the player to defend their territory, though not specifically to protect the territory. The 1980 game *Missile Command* changed that by introducing a strategy element. In the game, players could obstruct incoming missiles, and there were multiple attack paths in each attack wave. Missile Command was also the first of its kind to make use of a pointing device, a trackball, enabling players to use a crosshair. The innovation was ahead of its time and anticipated the genre's later boom, which was paved by the wide adoption of the computer mouse. Additionally, in Missile Command, the sole target of the attackers is the base, not a specific player character. For these reasons, some regard it as the first true game in the genre.

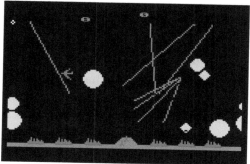

Missile Command (1980) (running on the Atari 5200) was the first popular game to include the key elements of tower defense strategy

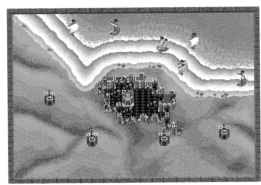

The 'battle' phase of Rampart (1990), considered by many to be the first true game of the genre

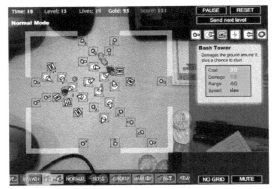

Desktop Tower Defense (running on PC) was one of a wave of popular
Flash-based tower defense games released in the late 2000s

While later arcade games like *Defender* (1981) and *Choplifter* (1982) lacked the strategy element of Missile Command, they began a trend of games that shifted the primary objective to defending non-player items. In these games, defending non-players from waves of attackers is key to progressing. Atari's 1982 title *Star Wars: The Empire Strikes Back* was one of the first tie-ins to popularize the base defense style. The concept of waves of enemies attacking the base in single file (in this case AT-ATs) proved a formula that was subsequently copied by many games as the shift from arcade to PC gaming began. Players were now able to choose from different methods of obstructing attackers' progress. By the mid 1980s, the strategy elements began to further evolve. Titles like Imagine Software's 1984 release *Pedro* mixed the player's abilities to actively defend and obstruct waves of different enemy types, including fixed obstructions, as well as the ability to build and repair a player's territory.

Modern Genre Emerges

Rampart, released in 1990 is generally considered to have established the prototypical tower defense. Rampart introduced player placed defenses that automatically attack incoming enemies. In addition, it has distinct phases of build, defend and repair. These are now staple gameplay elements of many games in the genre. It was also one of the first multiplayer video games of its kind.

While Rampart was popular, similar games were rarely seen until the widespread adoption of the computer mouse on the PC. The DOS title *Ambush at Sorinor* (1993) was a rare exception from this era. Tower defense gameplay was also rarely seen on consoles, a notable exception being the minigame Fort Condor from the popular 1997 title *Final Fantasy VII*, which was also one of the first to feature 3D graphics. As Real Time Strategy games gained popularity in PC gaming, many introduced tower defense modes in their gameplay, particularly in multiplayer modes. The 2006 mods *Element Tower Defense* (Element TD) and *Gem Tower Defense* released in February for the popular RTS title *Warcraft III: Reign of Chaos* almost single-handedly rekindled the genre. These titles would also bring Role Playing Game elements to the genre for the first time.

2007-2008 Boom

Between 2007 and 2008, the genre became a phenomenon, due in part to the popularity of the tower defense mode in real time strategy games, but mainly due to the rise of Adobe Flash independent developers as well as the emergence of major smartphone app stores from Apple and Google. The first stand-alone browser games emerged in 2007. Among them were the extremely popular titles *Flash Element Tower Defense* released in January and *Desktop Tower Defense* released in March. *Desktop Tower Defense* earned an Independent Games Festival award, and its success led to a version created for the mobile phone by a different developer. Another significant Flash title released in 2008 was *GemCraft*. Handheld game console were not ignored in the boom and titles included *Lock's Quest* and *Ninjatown* released in September and October respectively.

With the arrival of Apple's App Store tower defense developers adapted quickly to the touchscreen interface and the titles were among the most downloaded, many of them ported directly from Flash. Among the more notable include *Bloons TD 4* (2009) which sold more than a million copies on iOS.

The genre's success also led to new releases on PC and video game consoles. Popular 2008 titles included *PixelJunk Monsters* released in January, *Defense Grid: The Awakening* and *Savage Moon* in December. *Plants vs. Zombies* released in May 2009 was another highly popular tower defense which became a successful series on mobile devices.

A New Breed of 3D Games

Until 2010, most tower defense games used side scrolling, isometric, or top-down perspective graphics. *Dungeon Defenders*, released in October 2010, was one of the first tower defense games to bring the genre to the third person perspective. It sold over 250,000 copies in first two weeks of release and over 600,000 copies by the end of 2011.

In Anomaly: Warzone Earth, the tower defense formula is switched to "tower attack"

Anomaly: Warzone Earth released in 2011 introduced a variation of gameplay which has been described as "reverse tower defense", "tower attack", and "tower offense". In the game, the player must attack the enemy bases protected by numerous defenses. Sequels and other games have since experimented further with both styles of tower defense.

Sanctum released in May 2013, shifted to the first person perspective. It was followed by a string of similar titles such as the popular *Orcs Must Die!* series.

With the advent of social networking service applications, such as the Facebook Platform, tower defense has become a popular genre with titles such as *Bloons TD* and *Plants vs. Zombies Adventures* making the transition to turn-based play.

Gameplay

A screenshot of *Defenders of Ardania* showing the genre's characteristic
towers, as well as units and a castle that serves as an end point

The basic gameplay elements of tower defense are:

- territories or possessions (or collectively the "base") that must be defended by the player
- the base must survive waves of multiple incoming "enemy" attacks
- placement of "Tower" elements, or obstructions along the path of attacking enemies

What differentiates tower defense from other base defending games (such as Space Invaders) is the player's ability to strategically place or construct obstructions in the path of attacking enemies.

In Tower defense, unlike the base, the player's main character is usually, but not always, invincible, as the primary object is the survival of the base rather than the player.

Some features of modern tower defense:

- Player placed obstructions that can damage or kill enemy attackers before destroying the base
- Ability to repair obstructions
- Ability to upgrade obstructions
- Some sort of currency with which to purchase upgrades and repairs (this can be time, in game currency or experience points, such as being earned by the defeat of an attacking unit

- Enemies capable of traversing multiple paths

- Each wave usually have a set number and types of enemies

Many modern tower defense games evolved from real-time to turn based gameplay in which there is a cycle including distinct phases such as build, defend and repair. Many games, such as *Flash Element Tower Defense* feature enemies that run through a "maze", which allows the player to strategically place towers for optimal effectiveness. However, some versions of the genre force the user to create the maze out of their own towers, such as *Desktop Tower Defense*. Some versions are a hybrid of these two types, with preset paths that can be modified to some extent by tower placement, or towers that can be modified by path placement. Often an essential strategy is "mazing", which is the tactic of creating a long, winding path of towers to lengthen the distance the enemies must traverse to get past the defense. Sometimes "juggling" is possible by alternating between barricading an exit on one side and then the other side to cause the enemies to path back and forth until they are defeated. Some games also allow players to modify the attack strategy used by towers to be able to defend for an even more reasonable price.

The degree of the player's control (or lack thereof) in such games also varies from games where the player controls a unit within the game world, to games where the player has no direct control over units at all.

It is a common theme in tower defense games to have air units which do not pass through the layout of the maze, but rather fly over the towers directly to the end destination.

Some tower defense games or custom maps also require the player to send out enemies to their opponents' game boards respectively their controlled areas at a common game board. Such games are also known as tower wars games.

USPTO Trademark

On June 3, 2008, COM2US Corporation was awarded the trademark for the term "Tower Defense", filed on June 13, 2007 – serial number 3442002. The corporation is reported to have started enforcing the trademark: in early 2010, developers of games on Apple's App Store reported receiving messages requiring name changes for their games, citing trademark violation. Adding the phrase "Tower Defense" (in capital letters) to the description of an app submission to iTunesConnect and the app store automatically triggers a warning that the submission is likely to be rejected for use of the term; however, writing the phrase in lower case is still acceptable as "tower defense" is a valid description of a game style.

Artillery Game

Artillery games are early two or three-player (usually turn-based) video games involving tanks fighting each other in combat or similar. Artillery games are among the earliest computer games developed; the theme of such games is an extension of the original uses of computer themselves, which were once used to calculate the trajectories of rockets and other related military-based calculations. Artillery games have been described as a type of "shooting game", though they are more often classified as a type of strategy video game.

Early precursors to the modern artillery-type games were text-only games that simulated artillery entirely with input data values. A BASIC game known simply as *Artillery* was written by Mike Forman and was published in *Creative Computing* magazine in 1976. This seminal home computer version of the game was revised in 1977 by M. E. Lyon and Brian West and was known as *War 3*; *War 3* was revised further in 1979 and published as *Artillery-3*. These early versions of turn-based tank combat games interpreted human-entered data such as the distance between the tanks, the velocity or "power" of the shot fired and the angle of the tanks' turrets.

Emergence of Graphical Artillery

The Tektronix 4051 BASIC language desktop computer of the mid-1970s had a demo program called *Artillery* which used a storage-CRT for graphics. A similar program appeared on the HP 2647 graphics terminal demo tape in the late 1970s.

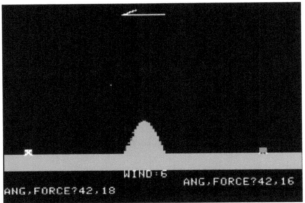

Artillery for the Apple II was among the earliest graphical versions of the turn-based artillery video game.

An early graphical version of the artillery game for personal computers emerged on the Apple II computer platform in 1980. Written in Applesoft BASIC, this variant, also called *Artillery*, built upon the earlier concepts of the artillery games published in *Creative Computing* but allowed the players to actually see a simple graphical representation of the tanks, battlefield, and terrain. The Apple II variant also took wind speed into account when calculating the eventual result of the fired shot. Lines on the screen showed the players the paths that previous shots had taken toward their target, allowing players to use visual data when considering future strategy. Similar games were made for home computers such as the Commodore PET by 1981. In 1983, Amoeba Software published a game called Tank Trax, which was very soon picked up and re-released by the early Mastertronic Games Company. This was again the classic version of the Artillery Game, however you could change the height of the hill in between the players to either a mountain or a foothill (However this sometimes made no difference in the actual gameplay as some foothills were as high as mountains and some mountains were low enough to be considered foothills). The players also had the default names of General Patton and Monty.

Video game console variants of the artillery game soon emerged after the first graphical home computer versions. A two-player game called *Smithereens!* was released in 1982 for the Magnavox Odyssey[2] console in which two catapults, each behind a castle fortress wall, launched rocks at each other. Although not turn-based, the game made use of the console's speech synthesis to emit sarcastic insults when one player fired at the other. The first widespread artillery-based video game was *Artillery Duel*. *Artillery Duel* was released in 1983 for the Atari 2600 and ColecoVision video game consoles as well as the Commodore 64 and VIC-20 home computer platforms. The game featured more elaborate background and terrain graphics as well as a simple graphical readout of wind speed and amount of munitions.

Around 1984 a game called Siege also appeared by publisher Melbourne House, this was released on many old computer systems such as the Commodore 16 (*the game was bundled with C16's on a compilation tape along with Zapp, Hangman and many other games*), VIC20 and several other comparable machines of that era, some variants for some reason were misspelled as Seige instead of Siege.

Artillery Games on the PC

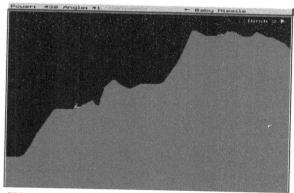

Scorched Earth for IBM-compatible PCs helped increase the popularity of the artillery game with its wide variety of weapons, numerous multi-player options and flexible configuration options.

With the increased presence of IBM-compatible PCs came the arrival of artillery games to the platform. In 1988, Artillery Combat, or EGAbomb, was released by Rad Delaroderie, written in Turbo BASIC, and was later distributed by RAD Software. Following in 1990, *Tank Wars* was released by Kenny Morse and published by Microforum for MS-DOS-based PCs. *Tank Wars* introduced the concept of buying weapons and multiple AI computer-player tanks to the artillery game. Gravity Wars was a conversion of the Amiga game of the same name that took the artillery game into space, introducing a 2D gravity field around planets, a format that has also inspired multiple re-makes.

In 1991, one artillery style game in particular got widespread attention when *Gorillas* was distributed as part of QBasic with MS-DOS 5.0, the Amiga also had a release at this time called *Amiga Tanx* distributed via Amiga Format magazine in the UK which included some digitized voices of the tank commanders, some quite amusing when shots got too close for comfort. That year also saw the release of the first version of *Scorched Earth* by Wendell Hicken. *Scorched Earth* was a popular shareware game for MS-DOS in which tanks do turn-based battle in two-dimensional terrain, with each player adjusting the angle and power of his or her tank turret before each shot. *Scorched Earth*, with numerous weapon types and power-ups, is considered the modern archetype of its format, on which the popular games *Worms, Atomic Cannon, Hogs of War, SpaceTanks, GunBound* and *Pocket Tanks* are based. *Scorched Earth* incorporates many of the features of previous graphical artillery games (including sarcastic comments by each player's tank before firing) while expanding the options available to each player in regard to the choice of weapons available, the ability to use shields, parachutes, and ability to move the player's tank (with the purchase of fuel tanks). The game is highly configurable and utilizes a simple mouse-driven graphical user interface.

Modern Derivatives of the Artillery Game

In 1994, Team17 Software released the first version of its successful *Worms* series of turn-based games on the Amiga computer platform. In *Worms*, players control a small platoon of worms (rather than tanks) across a deformable landscape, battling other computer- or player-controlled teams. The games feature bright and humorous cartoon-style animation and a varied arsenal of bizarre weapons. Subsequent games in the series have been released since 1995, including a 3D variant (*Worms 3D*) in 2003. This was later followed by *Worms Forts* and *Worms 4*. The game then went back to its 2D style gameplay in *Worms Open Warfare* (2006) and *Worms:Reloaded* (2010).

In 2001, Gavin Camp released a 3D artillery game called *Scorched 3D* that is loosely based on the earlier game *Scorched Earth*. *Scorched 3D* offers options such as multiplayer LAN and Internet play, player avatars and flexible camera views.

In 2003, Isotope244 released Atomic Cannon for Windows, Mac OS X, and Windows Mobile.

Other active projects include *Warmux* or *Hedgewars*, fully playable on many systems, including Windows, Linux or Mac OS X.

DDTank is a popular browser-based free-to-play mmorpg artillery game.

In December 2009, Finland-based Rovio Mobile released *Angry Birds*, a popular video game in which the player aims to find the most efficient way to destroy various structures by anticipating the trajectory and destructive effects of a bird fired from slingshot, which could be considered a version of an artillery game as it features a 2D limited world, angle/power input, passive missiles which follow gravity-driven trajectories, and the use of missile and/or landscape destruction to kill several non-vocal pigs in each level. It does, however, lack counterfire from the player's targets, as well as infinite ammo of at least one variety of projectile.

The March 2012 release of *Total War: Shogun 2: Fall of the Samurai* saw the inclusion of an in game variant of the artillery game. Players may manually control artillery pieces, firing, and subsequently adjusting, for each round.

References

- Harteveld, Casper (2011-02-26). Triadic Game Design: Balancing Reality, Meaning and Play. Springer Science & Business Media. p. 71. ISBN 1849961573. Retrieved 2014-12-19.
- Wolf, Mark J.P. (2008). The Video Game Explosion: A History from PONG to Playstation and Beyond. ABC-CLIO. p. 259. ISBN 031333868X. Retrieved 2014-12-03.
- Management Association, Information Resources (2010-11-30). Gaming and Simulations: Concepts, Methodologies, Tools and Applications. IGI Global. p. 503. ISBN 1609601963. Retrieved 2014-12-03.
- Lecky-Thompson, Guy W. (2008-01-01). Video Game Design Revealed. Cengage Learning. p. 23. ISBN 1584506075. Retrieved 2014-12-03.
- Egenfeldt-Nielson, Simon; Smith, Jonas Heide; Tosca, Susana Pajares (2013-04-27). Understanding Video Games: The Essential Introduction. Routledge. p. 46. ISBN 1136300422. Retrieved 2014-12-03.
- Konzack, Lars (2014-07-31). "Video Game Genres". " Encyclopedia of Information Science and Technology, Third Edition. IGI Global. ISBN 1466658894.
- van Eck, Richard (2010-03-31). Interdisciplinary Models and Tools for Serious Games: Emerging Concepts and

Future Directions. IGI Global. p. 56. ISBN 1615207201.

- Ashcraft, Brian, Arcade Mania! The Turbo-Charged World of Japan's Games Centers (Kodansha International, 2008) ISBN 978-4-7700-3078-8

- Craig Glenday, ed. (2008-03-11). "Record-Breaking Games". Guinness World Records Gamer's Edition 2008. Guinness World Records. Guinness. p. 84. ISBN 978-1-904994-21-3.

- Loguidice, Bill; Barton, Matt (2009), Vintage Games: An Insider Look at the History of Grand Theft Auto, Super Mario, and the Most Influential Games of All Time, Focal Press, ISBN 0-240-81146-1

- Barton, Matt (2008). Dungeons & Desktops: The History of Computer Role-Playing Games. A K Peters, Ltd. ISBN 1-56881-411-9. Retrieved September 8, 2010.

- King, Brad; Borland, John M. (2003). Dungeons and Dreamers: The Rise of Computer Game Culture from Geek to Chic. McGraw-Hill/Osborne. ISBN 0-07-222888-1. Retrieved September 25, 2010.

- Egenfeldt-Nielsen, Simon; Smith, Jonas Heide; Tosca, Susana Pajares (2008). Understanding Video Games: the Essential Introduction. Taylor & Francis. p. 48. ISBN 0-415-97721-5.

- Neal Hallford & Jana Hallford (2001), Swords & circuitry: a designer's guide to computer role-playing games, p. xxiv, Cengage Learning, ISBN 0-7615-3299-4

- Craddock, David L (August 5, 2015). Magrath, Andrew, ed. Dungeon Hacks: How NetHack, Angband, and Other Roguelikes Changed the Course of Video Games. Press Start Press. ISBN 069250186X.

- Barton, Matt (2008). Dungeons & Desktops: The History of Computer Role-Playing Games. A K Peters, Ltd. pp. 182 & 212. ISBN 1-56881-411-9. Retrieved 2010-09-08.

- Loguidice, Bill; Barton, Matt (2009), Vintage Games: An Insider Look at the History of Grand Theft Auto, Super Mario, and the Most Influential Games of All Time, Focal Press, p. 43, ISBN 0-240-81146-1

6

Diverse Aspects of Game Design

This chapter introduces the reader to game design jargon like nonlinear gameplay, virtual world, virtual economy, free-to-play, gold sink, time sink, gamification, game engine and gameplay micromanagement. Some concepts have been in use for many decades while challenging narration and story-arcs have led to the development of newer concepts of game design. The aspects elucidated in this chapter are of vital importance, and provide a better understanding of this field.

Nonlinear Gameplay

A video game with nonlinear gameplay presents players with challenges that can be completed in a number of different sequences. Each player sees only some of the challenges possible, and the same challenges may be played in a different order. Conversely, a video game with linear gameplay will confront a player with a fixed sequence of challenges: every player sees every challenge and sees them in the same order.

A nonlinear game will allow greater player freedom than a linear game. For example, a nonlinear game may permit multiple sequences to finish the game, a choice between paths to victory, or optional side-quests and subplots. Some games feature both linear and nonlinear elements, and some games offer a sandbox mode that allows players to explore an open world game environment independently from the game's main objectives, if any objectives are provided at all.

A game that is significantly nonlinear is sometimes described as being *open-ended* or a *sandbox*, though that term is used incorrectly in those cases, and is characterized by there being no "right way" of playing the game. Whether intentional or not, a common consequence of open-ended gameplay is emergent gameplay.

Classification

Branching Storylines

Games that employ linear stories are those where the player cannot change the story line or ending of the story. Many video games use a linear structure, thus making them more similar to other fiction. However, it is common for such games to use interactive narration in which a player needs to interact with something before the plot will advance, or nonlinear narratives in which events are portrayed in a non-chronological order. Many games have offered premature endings should the player fail to meet an objective, but these are usually just interruptions in a player's progress rather than actual endings. Even in games with a linear story, players interact with the game world by performing a variety of actions along the way.

More recently, some games have begun offering multiple endings to increase the dramatic effect of moral choices within the game, although early examples also exist. Still, some games have gone beyond small choices or special endings, offering a branching storyline, known as an interactive narrative, that players may control at critical points in the game. Sometimes the player is given a choice of which branch of the plot to follow, while sometimes the path will be based on the player's success or failure at a specific challenge. For example, Black Isle Studios' *Fallout* series of role-playing video games features numerous quests where player actions dictate the outcome of the story behind the objectives. Players can eliminate in-game characters permanently from the virtual world should they choose to do so, and by doing so may actually alter the number and type of quests that become available to them as the game progresses. The effects of such decisions may not be immediate. Branches of the story may merge or split at different points in the game, but seldom allow backtracking. Some games even allow for different starting points, and one way this is done is through a character selection screen.

Despite experimenting with several nonlinear storytelling mechanisms in the 1990s, the game industry has largely returned to the practice of linear storytelling. Linear stories cost less time and money to develop, since there is only one fixed sequence of events and no major decisions to keep track of. For example, several games from the *Wing Commander* series offered a branching storyline, but eventually they were abandoned as too expensive. Nonlinear stories increase the chances for bugs or absurdities if they are not tested properly, although they do provide greater player freedom. Some players have also responded negatively to branching stories because it is hard and tedious for them to experience the "full value" of all the game's content. As a compromise between linear and branching stories, there are also games where stories split into branches and then fold back into a single storyline. In these stories, the plot will branch, but then converge upon some inevitable event, giving the impression of a Nonlinear gameplay through the use of nonlinear narrative, without the use if interactive narratives. This is typically used in many graphic adventure games.

A truly nonlinear story would be written entirely by the actions of the player, and thus remains a difficult design challenge. As such, there is often little or no story in video games with a truly nonlinear gameplay. *Facade*, a video game often categorized as an interactive drama, features many branching paths that are dictated by the user's text input based on the current situation, but there is still a set number of outcomes as a result of the inherent limitations of programming, and as such, is non-linear, but not entirely so.

Visual Novels

Branching storylines are a common trend in visual novels, a subgenre of interactive narrative and adventure games. Visual novels frequently use multiple branching storylines to achieve multiple different endings, allowing non-linear freedom of choice along the way. Decision points within a visual novel often present players with the option of altering the course of events during the game, leading to many different possible outcomes. Visual novels are popular in East Asia, especially in Japan where they account for nearly 70% of personal computer games released there. A recent acclaimed example is *999: Nine Hours, Nine Persons, Nine Doors*, where nearly every action and dialogue choice can lead to entirely new branching paths and endings. Each path only reveals certain aspects of the overall storyline and it is only after uncovering all the possible different paths and outcomes through multiple playthroughs that everything comes together to form a coherent well-written story.

It is not uncommon for visual novels to have morality systems. A well-known example is the 2005 title *School Days*, an animated visual novel that Kotaku describes as going well beyond the usual "black and white choice systems" (referring to video games such as *Mass Effect*, *Fallout 3* and *Bio-Shock*) where you "pick a side and stick with it" while leaving "the expansive middle area between unexplored." *School Days* instead encourages players to explore the grey, neutral middle-ground in order to view the more interesting, "bad" endings.

It is also not uncommon for visual novels to have multiple protagonists giving different perspectives on the story. C's Ware's *EVE Burst Error* (1995) introduced a unique twist to the system by allowing the player to switch between both protagonists at any time during the game, instead of finishing one protagonist's scenario before playing the other. *EVE Burst Error* often requires the player to have both protagonists co-operate with each other at various points during the game, with choices in one scenario affecting the other. *Fate/stay night* is another example that features multiple perspectives. Chunsoft sound novels such as *Machi* (1998) and *428: Fūsa Sareta Shibuya de* (2008) develop this concept further, by allowing the player to alternate between the perspectives of several or more different characters, making choices with one character that have consequences for other characters. *428* in particular features up to 85 different possible endings.

Another approach to non-linear storytelling can be seen in *Cosmology of Kyoto*. The game lacks an overall plot, but it instead presents fragmented narratives and situations in a non-linear manner, as the player character encounters various non-player characters while wandering the city. These narratives are cross-referenced to an encyclopedia, providing background information as the narratives progress and as the player comes across various characters and locations, with various stories, situations and related information appearing at distinct locations. It provides enough freedom to allow for the player to experiment with the game, such as using it as a resource for their own role-playing game campaign, for example.

Role-playing Games

Branching storylines are also often used in role-playing video games (RPGs) to an extent. A successful recent example is Bioware's *Mass Effect*, where the player's decisions influence the gameplay. *Mass Effect* has a complex morality system that is measured in Paragon and Renegade. A good action will not make up for an evil one; therefore, being nice occasionally will not stop people from fearing a killer or remove the reputation of an unsympathetic heel, but nor will the occasional brutal action significantly damage the reputation of an otherwise upstanding soldier.

Another RPG example is tri-Ace's *Star Ocean* series, where instead of having the storyline affected by moral alignments like in other role-playing games, it instead uses a relationship system inspired by dating sims, with its storyline affected by the friendship points and relationship points between each of the characters. *Star Ocean: The Second Story* in particular offered as many as 86 different endings, with each of the possible permutations to these endings numbering in the hundreds, setting a benchmark for the amount of outcomes possible for a video game in its time. Another unique variation of this system is the *Sakura Wars* series, which features a real-time branching choice system where, during an event or conversation, the player must choose an action or dialogue choice within a time limit, or not to respond at all within that time; the player's choice, or lack thereof, affects the player character's relationship with other characters and in turn the direction and outcome of the storyline. Later games in the series added several variations, including an action gauge that can be raised up or down depending on the situation, and a gauge that the player can manipulate using the analog stick depending on the situation. A similar type of conversation system later appeared in a more recent action role-playing game also published by Sega, *Alpha Protocol*.

Another unique take on the concept is combining non-linear branching storytelling with the concepts of time travel and parallel universes. Early attempts at such an approach included Square-soft's *Chrono* role-playing game series (1995–1999) and ELF's visual novel *YU-NO: A girl who chants love at the bound of this world* (1996). *Radiant Historia* takes it further by giving players the freedom to travel backwards and forwards through a timeline to alter the course of history, with each of their choices and actions significantly affect the timeline. The player can return to certain points in history and live through certain events again to make different choices and see different possible outcomes on the timeline. The player can also travel back and forth between two parallel timelines, and can obtain many possible parallel endings. The PSP version of *Tactics Ogre* featured a "World" system that allows players to revisit key plot points and make different choices to see how the story unfolds differently. *Final Fantasy XIII-2* also features a similar non-linear time travel system to *Radiant Historia*.

Level Design

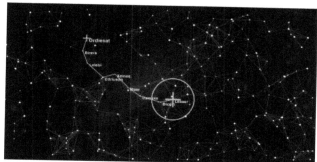

Galactic trade map of the space trading and combat simulator, *Oolite*.

A game level or world can be linear, nonlinear or interactive. In a game without nonlinear gameplay, there is only one plot that the player must take through the level, however, in games with nonlinear gameplay, players might have to revisit locations or choose from multiple paths to finish the level.

As with other game elements, linear level design is not absolute. While a nonlinear level can give the freedom to explore or backtrack, there can be a sequence of challenges that a player must solve to complete the level. If a player must confront the challenges in a fixed order nonlinear games will often give multiple approaches to achieve said objectives.

A more linear game requires a player to finish levels in a fixed sequence to win. The ability to skip, repeat, or choose between levels makes this type of game less linear. *Super Mario Bros.* is an early example of this, where the player had access to warp zones that skipped many levels of the game.

Open Worlds and Sandbox Modes

When a level is sufficiently large and open-ended, it may be described as an open world, or sandbox game, though this term is often used incorrectly. Open world game designs have existed in some form since the 1980s, such as the space trading game *Elite*, and often make use of procedurally generated environments.

In a game with a sandbox mode, a player may turn off or ignore game objectives, or have unlimited access to items. This can open up possibilities that were not intended by the game designer. A sandbox mode is an option in otherwise goal-oriented games and is distinguished from open-ended games which have no objectives such as *SimCity*. Another popular Sandbox Mode based modification is *Garry's Mod*, also known as Gmod, for Half Life 2.

Early Examples

The nonlinear style of gameplay has its roots in the 8-bit era, with early examples in the 1980s (showing a gradual progression in non-linearity) including:

- *TX-1* (1983)
- *Mega Zone* (1983)
- *Portopia Serial Murder Case* (1983)
- *Bega's Battle* (1983)
- *Elite* (1984),
- *Dragon Slayer* (1984)
- *The Battle-Road* (1984)
- *Brain Breaker* (1985)
- *Mercenary* (1985),
- *The Legend of Zelda* (1986)
- *Metroid* (1986)
- *Dragon Warrior* (1986)
- *Out Run* (1986)
- *Cholo* (1986),
- *Darius* (1986)
- *Vampire Killer* (1986)
- *Castlevania II: Simon's Quest* (1987)
- *Mega Man* (1987)
- *Megami Tensei* (1987)
- *Sid Meier's Pirates!* (1987)

- *The Goonies II* (1987)

- *War of the Dead* (1987)

Gamification

Gamification is the application of game-design elements and game principles in non-game contexts. Gamification commonly employs game design elements which are used in so called non-game contexts in attempts to improve user engagement, organizational productivity, flow, learning, crowdsourcing, employee recruitment and evaluation, ease of use and usefulness of systems, physical exercise, traffic violations, and voter apathy, among others. A review of research on gamification shows that a majority of studies on gamification find positive effects from gamification. However, individual and contextual differences exist. Gamification can also improve an individual's ability to comprehend digital content and understand a certain area of study such as music.

Techniques

Gamification techniques strive to leverage people's natural desires for socializing, learning, mastery, competition, achievement, status, self-expression, altruism, or closure. Early gamification strategies use rewards for players who accomplish desired tasks or competition to engage players. Types of rewards include points, achievement badges or levels, the filling of a progress bar, or providing the user with virtual currency. Making the rewards for accomplishing tasks visible to other players or providing leader boards are ways of encouraging players to compete. Potential consequences of competition can result from unethical behavior, low cooperation and collaboration, or from disadvantaging certain player demographics such as women. Best-practice gamification designs try to refrain from using this element.

Another approach to gamification is to make existing tasks feel more like games. Some techniques used in this approach include adding meaningful choice, onboarding with a tutorial, increasing challenge, and adding narrative.

Applications

Marketing

Gamification has been widely applied in marketing. Over 70% of Forbes Global 2000 companies surveyed in 2013 said they planned to use gamification for the purposes of marketing and customer retention. For example, in November 2011 Australian broadcast and online media partnership Yahoo!7 launched its Fango mobile app/SAP, which TV viewers use to interact with shows via techniques like check-ins and badges. As of February 2012, the app had been downloaded more than 200,000 times since its launch. Gamification has also been used in customer loyalty programmes. In 2010, Starbucks gave custom Foursquare badges to people who checked in at multiple locations and offered discounts to people who checked in most frequently at an individual store. There have also been proposals to use gamification for competitive intelligence, encouraging people to fill out surveys, and to do market research on brand recognition. Gamification has also been integrated into Help Desk software. In 2012, Freshdesk, a SaaS-based customer support product, integrated gamification features, allowing agents to earn badges based on performance. Gamification has also been used as a tool for customer engagement, and for encouraging desirable website usage behavior. Additionally, gamification is readily applicable to increasing engagement on sites built on social network services. For example, in August 2010, one site, DevHub, announced that they have increased the number of users who completed their online tasks from 10% to 80% after adding gamification elements. On the programming question-and-answer site Stack Overflow users receive points and/or badges for performing a variety of actions, including spreading links to questions and answers via Facebook and Twitter. A large number of different badges are available, and when a user's reputation points exceed various thresholds, he or she gains additional privileges, including at the higher end, the privilege of helping to moderate the site.

Inspiration

Gamification can be used for ideation (structured brainstorming to produce new ideas). A study at MIT Sloan found that ideation games helped participants generate more and better ideas, and compared it to gauging the influence of academic papers by the numbers of citations received in subsequent research.

Health

Applications like Fitocracy and QUENTIQ use gamification to encourage their users to exercise more effectively and improve their overall health. Users are awarded varying numbers of points for activities they perform in their workouts and gain levels based on points collected. Users can also complete quests (sets of related activities) and gain achievement badges for fitness milestones. Health Month adds aspects of social gaming by allowing successful users to restore points to users who have failed to meet certain goals.

In a first ever review of health apps, in the 2014 apple app store, over 100 apps showed a positive correlation between gamification elements used and high user ratings. Naming myfitnesspal as an app that used the highest amount of gamification elements.

Work

Gamification has been used in an attempt to improve employee productivity, health care, financial services, transportation, government, recruitment, and others. In general, enterprise gamification refers to work situations where" game thinking and game-based tools are used in a strategic manner to integrate with existing business processes or information systems, and these techniques are used to help drive positive employee and organizational outcomes."

Education

Crowdsourcing has been gamified in games like Foldit, a game designed by the University of Washington, in which players compete to manipulate proteins into more efficient structures. A 2010 paper in science journal Nature credited Foldit's 57,000 players with providing useful results that matched or outperformed algorithmically computed solutions. The ESP Game is a game that is used to generate image metadata. Google Image Labeler is a version of the ESP Game that Google has licensed to generate its own image metadata.

Education and training are areas where there has been interest in gamification. Microsoft released the game Ribbon Hero 2 as an add-on to their Office productivity suite to help train people to use it effectively, which was described by Microsoft as one of the most popular projects its Office Labs division ever released. The New York City Department of Education with funding from the MacArthur Foundation and the Bill and Melinda Gates Foundation has set up a school called Quest to Learn centred around game-based learning, with the intent to make education more engaging and relevant to modern kids. SAP has used games to educate their employees on sustainability. The US military and Unilever have also used gamification in their training. The Khan Academy is an example of the use of gamification techniques in online education. In August 2009, Gbanga launched the educational location-based game Gbanga Zooh for Zurich Zoo that asked participants to actively save endangered animals and physically bring them back to a zoo. Players maintained virtual habitats across the Canton of Zurich to attract and collect endangered species of animals. In 2014, the True Life Game project was initiated, with the main purpose of researching the best ways to apply concepts of gamification and crowdsourcing into lifelong learning. In 2015, Arizona State University added five interactive story based games to its environmental science curriculum. Within the game, students are placed in leadership roles and given the task of solving complicated environmental and sustainability issues. There is some indication that gamification can be particularly motivational for students with dyslexia in educational situations.

Politics and Terrorist Groups

Alix Levine, an American security consultant, described gamification as some techniques that a number of extremist websites such as Stormfront and various terrorism-related sites used to build loyalty and participation. As an example, Levine mentioned reputation scores.

Technology Design

Traditionally, researchers thought of motivations to use computer systems to be primarily driven by extrinsic purposes; however, many modern systems have their use driven primarily by intrinsic motivations. Examples of such systems used primarily to fulfill users' intrinsic motivations, include online gaming, virtual worlds, online shopping, learning/education, online dating, digital music repositories, social networking, online pornography, and so on. Such systems are excellent candidates for further 'gamification' in their design. Moreover, even traditional management information systems (e.g., ERP, CRM) are being 'gamified' such that both extrinsic and intrinsic motivations must increasingly be considered.

As illustration, Microsoft has announced plans to use gamification techniques for its Windows Phone 7 operating system design. While businesses face the challenges of creating motivating gameplay strategies, what makes for effective gamification is a key question.

Authentication

Gamification has also been applied to authentication. For example, the possibilities of using a game like Guitar Hero can help someone learn a password implicitly. Furthermore, games have been explored as a way to learn new and complicated passwords. It is suggested that these games could be used to "level up" a password, thereby improving its strength over time. Gamification has also been proposed as a way to select and manage archives. Recently, an Australian technology company called Wynbox has recorded success in the application of its gamification engine to the hotel booking process.

History

Though the term "gamification" was coined in 2002 by Nick Pelling, a British-born computer programmer and inventor, it did not gain popularity until 2010. Even prior to the term coming into use, other fields borrowing elements from videogames was common; for example, some work in learning disabilities and scientific visualization adapted elements from videogames. A Forbes blogger also retroactively labelled Charles Coonradt, who in 1973 founded the consultancy The Game of Work and in 1984 wrote a book by the same name, as the "Grandfather of Gamification."

The term "gamification" first gained widespread usage in 2010, in a more specific sense referring to incorporation of social/reward aspects of games into software. The technique captured the attention of venture capitalists, one of whom said he considered gamification the most promising area in gaming. Another observed that half of all companies seeking funding for consumer software applications mentioned game design in their presentations.

Several researchers consider gamification closely related to earlier work on adapting game-design elements and techniques to non-game contexts. Deterding *et al.* survey research in human–computer interaction that uses game-derived elements for motivation and interface design, and Nelson argues for a connection to both the Soviet concept of socialist competition, and the American management trend of "fun at work". Fuchs points out that gamification might be driven by new forms of ludic interfaces. Gamification conferences have also retroactively incorporated simulation; e.g. Will Wright, designer of the 1989 video game SimCity, was the keynote speaker at the gamification conference Gsummit 2013.

In addition to companies that use the technique, a number of businesses created gamification platforms. In October 2007, Bunchball, backed by Adobe Systems Incorporated, was the first company to provide game mechanics as a service, on Dunder Mifflin Infinity, the community site for the NBC TV show *The Office*. Bunchball customers have included Playboy, Chiquita, Bravo, and The USA Network. In June 2009 a Seattle-based startup called BigDoor was founded, providing gamification technology to non-gaming websites. Badgeville launched in late 2010, and raised $15 million in venture-capital funding in its first year of operation; it provides gamification services to a number of large customers. InsideSales.com provides a gamification solution targeted to sales representatives using the Charles Coonradt principles that are integrated into Salesforce.com platform. IActionable also launched a gamification platform aimed at integrating with Salesforce.com. In 2011, Playlyfe was launched which started offering gamification as a service to individual developers and enterprises.

Among established enterprise firms, SAP AG, Microsoft, IBM, SAP, LiveOps, Deloitte, and other companies have started using gamification in various applications and processes.

Gamification 2013, an event exploring the future of gamification, was held at the University of Waterloo Stratford Campus in October 2013.

The inaugural Loyalty Games 2014 Loyalty Gamification World Championship were held online with Live World Finals San Francisco.

Legal Restrictions

Through gamification's growing adoption and its nature as a data aggregator, multiple legal restrictions may apply to gamification. Some refer to the use of virtual currencies and virtual assets, data privacy laws and data protection, or labour laws.

The use of virtual currencies, in contrast to traditional payment systems, is not regulated. The legal uncertainty surrounding the virtual currency schemes might constitute a challenge for public authorities, as these schemes can be used by criminals, fraudsters and money launderers to perform their illegal activities.

Criticism

University of Hamburg researcher Sebastian Deterding has characterized the initial popular strategies for gamification as not being fun and creating an artificial sense of achievement. He also says that gamification can encourage unintended behaviours.

In the first comprehensive review of all health and fitness apps in the apple store, in 2014, using gamification as a method to modify behavior the authors concluded that "Despite the inclusion of at least some components of gamification, the mean scores of integration of gamification components were still below 50 percent. This was also true for the inclusion of game elements and the use of health behavior theory constructs, thus showing a lack of following any clear industry standard of effective gaming, gamification, or behavioral theory in health and fitness apps."

Concern was also expressed in a 2016 study analyzing outcome data from 1298 users who competed in gamified and incentivized exercise challenges while wearing wearable devices. In that study the authors conjectured that data may be highly skewed by cohorts of already healthy users, rather than the intended audiences of participants requiring behavioral intervention.

Game designers like Jon Radoff and Margaret Robertson have also criticized gamification as excluding elements like storytelling and experiences and using simple reward systems in place of true game mechanics.

Gamification practitioners have pointed out that while the initial popular designs were in fact mostly relying on simplistic reward approach, even those led to significant improvements in short term engagement. This was supported by the first comprehensive study in 2014, which concluded that an increase in gamification elements correlated with an increase in motivation score, but not with capacity or opportunity/trigger scores.

The same study called for standardization across the app industry on gamification principles to improve the effectiveness of health apps on the health outcomes of users.

MIT Professor Kevin Slavin has described business research into gamification as flawed and misleading for those unfamiliar with gaming. Heather Chaplin, writing in *Slate*, describes gamification as "an allegedly populist idea that actually benefits corporate interests over those of ordinary people". Jane McGonigal has distanced her work from the label "gamification", listing rewards outside of gameplay as the central idea of gamification and distinguishing game applications where the gameplay itself is the reward under the term "gameful design".

"Gamification" as a term has also been criticized. Ian Bogost has referred to the term as a marketing fad and suggested "exploitationware" as a more suitable name for the games used in marketing. Other opinions on the terminology criticism have made the case why the term gamification makes sense.

Fuchs et al. investigated historical predecessors to today's gamification that go back to the 18th century.

Game Engine

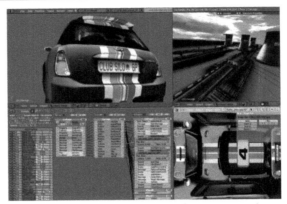

Creating a racing game in Blender Game Engine

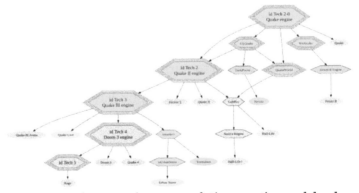

Some game engines experience an evolution over time and develop a
family tree, like for instance id's Quake engine which resulted in the id Tech family

A game engine is a software framework designed for the creation and development of video games. Developers use them to create games for consoles, mobile devices and personal computers. The core functionality typically provided by a game engine includes a rendering engine ("renderer") for 2D or 3D graphics, a physics engine or collision detection (and collision response), sound, scripting, animation, artificial intelligence, networking, streaming, memory management, threading, localization support, scene graph, and may include video support for cinematics. The process of game development is often economized, in large part, by reusing/adapting the same game engine to create different games, or to make it easier to "port" games to multiple platforms.

Purpose

In many cases game engines provide a suite of visual development tools in addition to reusable software components. These tools are generally provided in an integrated development environment to enable simplified, rapid development of games in a data-driven manner. Game engine developers attempt to "pre-invent the wheel" by developing robust software suites which include many elements a game developer may need to build a game. Most game engine suites provide facilities that ease development, such as graphics, sound, physics and AI functions. These game engines are sometimes called "middleware" because, as with the business sense of the term, they provide a flexible and reusable software platform which provides all the core functionality needed, right out of the box, to develop a game application while reducing costs, complexities, and time-to-market — all critical factors in the highly competitive video game industry. Gamebryo, JMonkey Engine and RenderWare are such widely used middleware programs.

Like other middleware solutions, game engines usually provide platform abstraction, allowing the same game to be run on various platforms including game consoles and personal computers with few, if any, changes made to the game source code. Often, game engines are designed with a component-based architecture that allows specific systems in the engine to be replaced or extended with more specialized (and often more expensive) game middleware components such as Havok for physics, Miles Sound System for sound, or Bink for video. Some game engines such as Render-Ware are even designed as a series of loosely connected game middleware components that can be selectively combined to create a custom engine, instead of the more common approach of extending or customizing a flexible integrated solution. However extensibility is achieved, it remains a high priority for game engines due to the wide variety of uses for which they are applied. Despite the specificity of the name, game engines are often used for other kinds of interactive applications with real-time graphical needs such as marketing demos, architectural visualizations, training simulations, and modeling environments.

Some game engines only provide real-time 3D rendering capabilities instead of the wide range of functionality needed by games. These engines rely upon the game developer to implement the rest of this functionality or assemble it from other game middleware components. These types of engines are generally referred to as a "graphics engine," "rendering engine," or "3D engine" instead of the more encompassing term "game engine." This terminology is inconsistently used as many full-featured 3D game engines are referred to simply as "3D engines." A few examples of graphics engines are: Crystal Space, Genesis3D, Irrlicht, OGRE, RealmForge, Truevision3D, and Vision Engine. Modern game or graphics engines generally provide a scene graph, which is an object-oriented representation of the 3D game world which often simplifies game design and can be used for more efficient rendering of vast virtual worlds.

As technology ages, the components of an engine may become outdated or insufficient for the requirements of a given project. Since the complexity of programming an entirely new engine may result in unwanted delays (or necessitate that the project be completely restarted), a development team may elect to update their existing engine with newer functionality or components.

Components

Such a framework is composed of a multitude of very different components.

Main Game Program

The actual game logic of course has to be implemented by some algorithms. It is distinct from any rendering, sound or input work.

Rendering Engine

The rendering engine generates 3D animated graphics by the chosen method (rasterization, ray-tracing or any different technique).

Instead of being programmed and compiled to be executed on the CPU or GPU directly, most often rendering engines are built upon one or multiple rendering application programming interfaces (APIs), such as Direct3D or OpenGL which provide a software abstraction of the graphics processing unit (GPU).

Low-level libraries such as DirectX, Simple DirectMedia Layer (SDL), and OpenGL are also commonly used in games as they provide hardware-independent access to other computer hardware such as input devices (mouse, keyboard, and joystick), network cards, and sound cards. Before hardware-accelerated 3D graphics, software renderers had been used. Software rendering is still used in some modeling tools or for still-rendered images when visual accuracy is valued over real-time performance (frames-per-second) or when the computer hardware does not meet needs such as shader support.

With the advent of hardware accelerated physics processing, various physics APIs such as PAL and the physics extensions of COLLADA became available to provide a software abstraction of the physics processing unit of different middleware providers and console platforms.

Game engines can be written in any programming language like C++, C or Java, though each language is structurally different and may provide different levels of access to specific functions.

Audio Engine

The audio engine is the component which consists of algorithms related to sound. It can calculate things on the CPU, or on a dedicated ASIC. Abstraction APIs, such as OpenAL, SDL audio, XAudio 2, Web Audio, etc. are available.

Physics Engine

The physics engine is responsible for emulating the laws of physics realistically within the application.

Artificial Intelligence

The AI is usually outsourced from the main game program into a special module to be designed and written by software engineers with specialist knowledge.

History

Before game engines, games were typically written as singular entities: a game for the Atari 2600, for example, had to be designed from the bottom up to make optimal use of the display hardware—this core display routine is today called the kernel by retro developers. Other platforms had more leeway, but even when the display was not a concern, memory constraints usually sabotaged attempts to create the data-heavy design that an engine needs. Even on more accommodating platforms, very little could be reused between games. The rapid advance of arcade hardware—which was the leading edge of the market at the time—meant that most of the code would have to be thrown out afterwards anyway, as later generations of games would use completely different game designs that took advantage of extra resources. Thus most game designs through the 1980s were designed through a hard-coded ruleset with a small number of levels and graphics data. Since the golden age of arcade video games, it became common for video game companies to develop in-house game engines for use with first party software.

While third-party game engines were not common up until the rise of 3D computer graphics in the 1990s, there were several 2D game creation systems produced in the 1980s for independent video game development. These include Pinball Construction Set (1983), ASCII's War Game Construction Kit (1983), Thunder Force Construction (1984), Adventure Construction Set (1984), Garry Kitchen's GameMaker (1985), Wargame Construction Set (1986), Shoot'Em-Up Construction Kit (1987), Arcade Game Construction Kit (1988), and most popularly ASCII's RPG Maker engines from 1988 onwards.

The term "game engine" arose in the mid-1990s, especially in connection with 3D games such as first-person shooters (FPS). Such was the popularity of Id Software's *Doom* and *Quake* games that, rather than work from scratch, other developers licensed the core portions of the software and designed their own graphics, characters, weapons and levels—the "game content" or "game assets." Separation of game-specific rules and data from basic concepts like collision detection and game entity meant that teams could grow and specialize.

Later games, such as id Software's *Quake III Arena* and Epic Games's 1998 *Unreal* were designed with this approach in mind, with the engine and content developed separately. The practice of licensing such technology has proved to be a useful auxiliary revenue stream for some game developers, as a one license for a high-end commercial game engine can range from US$10,000 to millions of dollars, and the number of licensees can reach several dozen companies, as seen with the Unreal Engine. At the very least, reusable engines make developing game sequels faster and easier, which is a valuable advantage in the competitive video game industry. While there was a strong rivalry between Epic and id around 2000, since then Epic's Unreal Engine has been far more popular than id Tech 4 and its successor id Tech 5.

Modern game engines are some of the most complex applications written, often featuring dozens of finely tuned systems interacting to ensure a precisely controlled user experience. The continued evolution of game engines has created a strong separation between rendering, scripting, artwork, and level design. It is now common, for example, for a typical game development team to have several times as many artists as actual programmers.

First-person shooter games remain the predominant users of third-party game engines, but they are now also being used in other genres. For example, the role-playing video game *The Elder Scrolls III: Morrowind* and the MMORPG *Dark Age of Camelot* are based on the Gamebryo engine, and the MMORPG *Lineage II* is based on the Unreal Engine. Game engines are used for games originally developed for home consoles as well; for example, the RenderWare engine is used in the *Grand Theft Auto* and *Burnout* franchises.

Threading is taking on more importance due to modern multi-core systems (e.g. Cell) and increased demands in realism. Typical threads involve rendering, streaming, audio, and physics. Racing games have typically been at the forefront of threading with the physics engine running in a separate thread long before other core subsystems were moved, partly because rendering and related tasks need updating at only 30–60 Hz. For example, on PlayStation 3, physics ran in *Need For Speed* at 100 Hz versus *Forza Motorsport 2* at 360 Hz.

Although the term was first used in the 1990s, there are a few earlier systems in the 1980s that are also considered to be game engines, such as Sierra's Adventure Game Interpreter (AGI) and SCI systems, LucasArts' SCUMM system and Incentive Software's Freescape engine. Unlike most modern game engines, these game engines were never used in any third-party products (except for the SCUMM system which was licensed to and used by Humongous Entertainment).

Recent Trends

As game engine technology matures and becomes more user-friendly, the application of game engines has broadened in scope. They are now being used for serious games: visualization, training, medical, and military simulation applications, with the CryEngine being one example. To facilitate this accessibility, new hardware platforms are now being targeted by game engines, including mobile phones (e.g. Android phones, iPhone) and web browsers (e.g. WebGL, Shockwave, Flash, Trinigy's WebVision, Silverlight, Unity Web Player, O3D and pure DHTML).

Additionally, more game engines are being built upon higher level languages such as Java and C#/.NET (e.g. TorqueX, and Visual3D.NET), Python (Panda3D), or Lua Script (Leadwerks). As most 3D rich games are now mostly GPU-limited (i.e. limited by the power of the graphics card), the potential slowdown due to translation overheads of higher level languages becomes negligible, while the productivity gains offered by these languages work to the game engine developers' benefit. These recent trends are being propelled by companies such as Microsoft to support Indie game development. Microsoft developed XNA as the SDK of choice for all video games released on Xbox and related products. This includes the Xbox Live Indie Games channel designed specifically for smaller developers who don't have the extensive resources necessary to box games for sale on retail shelves. It is becoming easier and cheaper than ever to develop game engines for platforms that support managed frameworks.

Game Middleware

In the broader sense of the term, game engines themselves can be described as middleware. In the context of video games, however, the term "middleware" is often used to refer to subsystems of functionality within a game engine. Some game middleware does only one thing but does it more convincingly or more efficiently than general purpose middleware. For example, *SpeedTree* was used to render the realistic trees and vegetation in the role-playing video game *The Elder Scrolls IV: Oblivion* and *Fork Particle* was used to simulate and render real time particle system visual effects or particle effects in Sid Meier's Civilization V.

The four most widely used middleware packages that provide subsystems of functionality include RAD Game Tools' Bink, Firelight FMOD, Havok, and Scaleform GFx. RAD Game Tools develops Bink for basic video rendering, along with Miles audio, and Granny 3D rendering. Firelight FMOD is a low cost robust audio library and toolset. Havok provides a robust physics simulation system, along with a suite of animation and behavior solutions. *Scaleform* provides GFx for high performance Flash UI, along with a high quality video playback solution, and an Input Method Editor (IME) add-on for in-game Asian chat support.

Other middleware is used for performance optimisation - for example 'Simplygon' helps to optimise and generate level of detail meshes, and 'Umbra' adds occlusion culling optimisations to 3d graphics.

Some middleware contains full source code, others just provide an API reference for a compiled binary library. Some middleware programs can be licensed either way, usually for a higher fee for full source code.

Massively Multiplayer Online Games

The Game Engine (or Middleware) for massively multiplayer online games (MMOs, MMOGs) is far more complex than for single-player video games. Technically every normal game engine can be used to implement an MMO game by combining it with MMO middleware. The increasing popularity of MMOGs is spurring development of MMO middleware packages. Some MMO middleware software packages already include a game engine, while others provide networking only and therefore must be combined with a game engine to create an MMO game.

First-person Shooter Engines

A well-known subset of game engines are 3D first-person shooter (FPS) game engines. Groundbreaking development in terms of visual quality is done in FPS games on the human scale. While flight and driving simulators and real-time strategy (RTS) games increasingly provide realism on a large scale, first-person shooters are at the forefront of computer graphics on these smaller scales.

The development of the FPS graphic engines that appear in games can be characterized by a steady increase in technologies, with some breakthroughs. Attempts at defining distinct generations lead to arbitrary choices of what constitutes a highly modified version of an "old engine" and what is a brand-new engine.

The classification is complicated as game engines blend old and new technologies. Features that were considered advanced in a new game one year become the expected standard the next year. Games with a mix of older generation and newer feature are the norm. For example, *Jurassic Park: Trespasser* (1998) introduced physics to the FPS games, but it did not become common until around 2002. *Red Faction* (2001) featured destructible walls and ground, something still not common in engines years later (for example in *Unreal Tournament 2004* there are still no destructible objects). *Battlezone* (1998) and *Battlezone II: Combat Commander* (1999) added vehicle based combat to the usual FPS mix, which did not hit the mainstream until later. *Tribes 2, Battlefield 1942, Halo: Combat Evolved*, and *Unreal Tournament 2004* fully realized the potential for vehicular-combat and first person shooter integration.

Micromanagement (Gameplay)

In gaming, micromanagement are minor, detailed gameplay elements that must be manually addressed by the player. It appears in a wide range of games including strategy video games, construction and management simulations and pet-raising simulations. Micromanagement has been perceived in different ways by game designers and players for many years: some perceive it as a useful addition to games that adds options and technique to the gameplay, something that is necessary if the game is to support top-level competitions; some enjoy opportunities to use tactical skill in strategic games; others regard it as an unwelcomed distraction from higher levels of strategic thinking and dislike having to do a lot of detailed work. Some developers attempt to minimize micromanagement in a game's interface for this reason.

In Strategy Games

Combat

Detailed management of units in combat aims to maximize damage given to enemy units and minimize damage to the player's units. For standard combat units the most common techniques are: grouping units into formations, for example to keep lightly armored shooters behind and protected by more heavily armored melee units; concentrating the fire of all ranged units on one target and then a second, etc., to destroy threats as fast as possible; withdrawing seriously damaged units from combat, if repairing / healing them is cheaper than replacing them; "dancing" units that have taken some damage out of enemy weapons range and then back into combat once the enemy have locked on to another target; using military tactics such as flanking and counterattacks; exploiting nontransitive ("circle of death" or "rock-paper-scissors") power relationships between units; using cheap units to draw the enemy's fire away from more expensive units, gameplay especially typical of games of the real-time tactics type. Micromanagement is even more necessary for units with special abilities, that can only be used infrequently. "Micromanagement" in this sense is often abbreviated to "micro", which can be used as a noun or a verb.

Versus Macromanagement

There is sometimes confusion regarding the difference between micromanagement and macromanagement, normally abbreviated as 'micro' and 'macro' respectively. Macro generally refers to managing large quantities of tasks at the same time. For example, building units from various structures throughout the game while also building more structures, scouting, creating new bases, etc. This is different from micro, which is generally controlling small amounts of units and giving them very specific orders.

Economic

The range of possible economic micromanagement techniques is much wider than for combat, because strategy games' economies work in so many different ways. If the game uses "worker" units to gather resources and / or build things (a common technique in real-time strategy games), one must make sure none are idle and that they are doing the right things, and must avoid letting enemy raiders destroy them (as is happening in the *Starcraft* image above). In some turn-based games one tells colonies what percentages of their efforts to put into various activities such as industrial growth, research, and building defenses or combat units; as colonies grow or the strategic situation changes, one has to check and adjust these ratios. In Sid Meier's *Civilization* series, it may be important for either economic or military reasons to build railroads as fast as possible, and doing this efficiently requires considerable micromanagement of Settler / Engineer units.

Twitch vs Trick

Some forms of micromanagement involve continuous input of a large number of commands over a short period of time. This is known as twitch micromanagement. For example, a micromanagement technique known as kiting requires continuous input from the player in order to keep their character at an optimum distance from a target. Another example of twitch micromanagement can be found in racing games whereby a player is required to keep making split second adjustments to the position of their vehicle.

In contrast to twitch micromanagement, some game elements need only occasional input from the player in order to exploit tricks in their behavior. In these situations, quick thinking is rewarded over continuous, quick reaction. This is known as trick micromanagement.

Other types of games are based entirely on micromanagement, such as pet-raising simulations and games like Cake Mania, where the player's ability to micromanage is often the only skill being tested by the game.

Policy-based

Some games are designed in such a way that players must constantly set or check strategic parameters to ensure that operations are proceeding smoothly and efficiently. A typical city-building game or 4X game, for example, requires the player to regulate taxation and production levels in order to keep their industries and commerce flowing. The amount of detail that goes into a simulation like this may necessitate spending a disproportionate amount of time in adjusting relatively minor parameters in order to achieve maximum efficiency.

Controversy

Micromanagement can divert the player's attention from grand strategy by overloading the player with repetitive and mechanical work. Some commentators think that "Strategy is irrelevant in today's real-time strategy games when you're playing against a fourteen-year-old who can click twice as fast as you." Games in which constant micromanagement is needed are often described as "micromanagement hell".

In turn-based games the need for economic micromanagement is generally regarded as a defect in the design, and more recent TBS games have tried to minimize it. But hands-on tactical combat is a feature of many turn-based games (e.g. *Master of Orion II*, *Space Empires III*, *Heroes of Might and Magic III*), and reviewers complained about the difficulty of controlling combat in *Master of Orion 3*.

There is controversy between fans of different RTS games about whether micromanagement is: (a) a skill which involves making decisions quickly while under pressure; or (b) a chore which degenerates into a "clickfest" where a player who is faster with the mouse usually beats a player who is better at grand strategy. As a result, RTS games vary widely from e.g. *Total Annihilation*, which eliminates most economic micromanagement and reduces tactical micromanagement, to *StarCraft*, in which both economic and tactical micromanagement are considered important skills. Software has been developed to analyze players' Actions Per Minute (commonly known as APM). Other games aim for differing levels of micromanagement of different types: for instance, the Relic Entertainment title Dawn of War 2 minimises economic micromanagement as much as possible, such that there is no base construction, all units are produced from a single source, and resources are accumulated automatically over time by controlling strategic battlefield locations, while on the other hand the game emphasises tactical micromanagement as its primary skill, with combat taking place principally between relatively small squads of highly effective and highly vulnerable units, with victory a function of the rapid deployment of special weapons and tactics in order to counter enemy manoeuvres and inflict maximum damage quickly while avoiding sustaining damage.

A Gamasutra article pointed out that micromanagement in Civilization III resulted in the game becoming "a chore more than a game," explaining: "Computers can now animate more units than any player could reasonably want to control, and the number will continue to increase exponentially."

Many role-playing video games and first-person shooters are developing more advanced hotkey layouts, allowing these genres to develop their own micromanagement skills.

In Popular Culture

- The popular Internet-distributed mockumentary series *Pure Pwnage* coined the term "über-micro", a term describing unusually superior levels of micromanagement. In one episode, it was claimed that micromanagement was discovered in "The Battle of 1974".

- In South Korea, the real-time strategy game *StarCraft* is highly popular as a professional sport. The need to micromanage efficiently and multitask under pressure are regarded as features that make it suitable for top-level competitions. The game is broadcast on Korean national television, showing professional players' micromanagement skills.

Virtual World

A yellow submarine created in *Second Life*

A virtual world or massively multiplayer online world (MMOW) is a computer-based simulated environment populated by many users who can create a personal avatar, and simultaneously and independently explore the virtual world, participate in its activities and communicate with others. These avatars can be textual, two or three-dimensional graphical representations, or live video avatars with auditory and touch sensations. In general, virtual worlds allow for multiple users.

The user accesses a computer-simulated world which presents perceptual stimuli to the user, who in turn can manipulate elements of the modeled world and thus experience a degree of presence. Such modeled worlds and their rules may draw from the reality or fantasy worlds. Example rules are gravity, topography, locomotion, real-time actions, and communication. Communication between users can range from text, graphical icons, visual gesture, sound, and rarely, forms using touch, voice command, and balance senses.

Massively multiplayer online games depict a wide range of worlds, including those based on science fiction, the real world, super heroes, sports, horror, and historical milieus. The most common form of such games are fantasy worlds, whereas those based on the real world are relatively rare. Most MMORPGs have real-time actions and communication. Players create a character who travels between buildings, towns, and worlds to carry out business or leisure activities. Communication is usually textual, but real-time voice communication is also possible. The form of communication used can substantially affect the experience of players in the game.

Virtual worlds are not limited to games but, depending on the degree of immediacy presented, can encompass computer conferencing and text based chatrooms. Sometimes, emoticons or 'smilies' are available to show feeling or facial expression. Emoticons often have a keyboard shortcut. Edward Castronova is an economist who has argued that "synthetic worlds" is a better term for these cyberspaces, but this term has not been widely adopted.

History

The concept of virtual worlds significantly predates computers. The Roman naturalist, Pliny the Elder, expressed an interest in perceptual illusion. In the twentieth century, the cinematographer Morton Heilig explored the creation of the Sensorama, a theatre experience designed to stimulate the senses of the audience—vision, sound, balance, smell, even touch (via wind)—and so draw them more effectively into the productions

Among the earliest virtual worlds implemented by computers were virtual reality simulators, such as the work of Ivan Sutherland. Such devices are characterized by bulky headsets and other types of sensory input simulation. Contemporary virtual worlds, in particular the multi-user online environments, emerged mostly independently of this research, fueled instead by the gaming industry but drawing on similar inspiration. While classic sensory-imitating virtual reality relies on tricking the perceptual system into experiencing an immersive environment, virtual worlds typically rely on mentally and emotionally engaging content which gives rise to an immersive experience.

Maze War was the first networked, 3D multi-user first person shooter game. Maze introduced the concept of online players in 1973-1974 as "eyeball 'avatars' chasing each other around in a maze." It was played on ARPANET, or Advanced Research Projects Agency Network, a precursor to the Internet funded by the United States Department of Defense for use in university and research laboratories. The initial game could only be played on an Imlac, as it was specifically designed for this type of computer.

The first virtual worlds presented on the Internet were communities and chat rooms, some of which evolved into MUDs and MUSHes. The first MUD, known as MUD1, was released in 1978. The acronym originally stood for Multi-User Dungeon, but later also came to mean Multi-User Dimension and Multi-User Domain. A MUD is a virtual world with many players interacting in real time. The early versions were text-based, offering only limited graphical representation and often using a Command Line Interface. Users interact in role-playing or competitive games by typing commands and can read or view descriptions of the world and other players. Such early worlds began the MUD heritage that eventually led to massively multiplayer online role-playing games, more commonly known as MMORPGs, a genre of role-playing games in which a large number of players interact within a virtual world.

Some prototype virtual worlds were *WorldsAway*, a two-dimensional chat environment where users designed their own avatars; *Dreamscape,* an interactive community featuring a virtual world by CompuServe; Cityspace, an educational networking and 3D computer graphics project for children; and *The Palace*, a 2-dimensional community driven virtual world. However, credit for the first online virtual world usually goes to *Habitat*, developed in 1987 by LucasFilm Games for the Commodore 64 computer, and running on the Quantum Link service (the precursor to America Online).

In 1996, the city of Helsinki, Finland with Helsinki Telephone Company (since Elisa Group) launched what was called the first online virtual 3D depiction intended to map an entire city. The Virtual Helsinki project was eventually renamed Helsinki Arena 2000 project and parts of the city in modern and historical context were rendered in 3D.

In 1999, Whyville.net the first virtual world specifically for children was launched with a base in game-based learning and one of the earliest virtual currency-based economies. Shortly after, in 2000, Habbo launched and grew to become one of the most popular and longest running virtual worlds with millions of users around the world.

Virtual World Concepts

Definitions for a "virtual world" include:

- a *"synchronous, persistent network of people, represented as avatars, facilitated by networked computers"*, by Mark W. Bell in 2008

- *"an automated, shared, persistent environment with and through which people can interact in real time by means of a virtual self"*, by Richard Bartle in 2010

- *"A persistent, simulated and immersive environment, facilitated by networked computers, providing multiple users with avatars and communication tools with which to act and interact in-world and in real-time."*, by Carina Girvan in 2013

There is no generally accepted definition of virtual world, but they do require that the world be persistent; in other words, the world must continue to exist even after a user exits the world, and user-made changes to the world should be preserved. While the interaction with other participants is done in real-time, time consistency is not always maintained in online virtual worlds. For example, *EverQuest* time passes faster than real-time despite using the same calendar and time units to present game time.

As *virtual world* is a general term, the virtual environment supports varying degrees of play and gaming. Some uses of the term include

- Massively multiplayer online games (MMOGs) games in which a large number of players interact within a virtual world. The concept of MMO has spread to other game types such as sports, real-time strategy and others. The persistence criterion is the only criterion that separates virtual worlds from video games, meaning that some MMO versions of RTS and FPS games resemble virtual worlds; *Destiny* is a video game that is such a pseudo virtual world. Emerging concepts include basing the terrain of such games on real satellite photos, such as those available through the Google Maps API or through a simple virtual geocaching of "easter eggs" on WikiMapia or similar mash-ups, where permitted; these concepts are virtual worlds making use of mixed reality.

- Collaborative virtual environments (CVEs) designed for collaborative work in a virtual environment.

- Massively multiplayer online real-life games (MMORLGs), also called virtual social worlds, where the user can edit and alter their avatar at will, allowing them to play a more dynamic role, or multiple roles.

Economy

A virtual economy is the emergent property of the interaction between participants in a virtual world. While the designers have a great deal of control over the economy by the encoded mechanics of trade, it is nonetheless the actions of players that define the economic conditions of a virtual world. The economy arises as a result of the choices that players make under the scarcity of real and virtual resources such as time or currency. Participants have a limited time in the virtual world, as in the real world, which they must divide between task such as collecting resources, practicing trade skills, or engaging in less productive fun play. The choices they make in their interaction with the virtual world, along with the mechanics of trade and wealth acquisition, dictate the relative values of items in the economy. The economy in virtual worlds is typically driven by in-game needs such as equipment, food, or trade goods. Virtual economies like that of Second Life, however, are almost entirely player-produced with very little link to in-game needs. While the relevance of virtual world economics to physical world economics has been questioned, it has been shown the users of virtual worlds respond to economic stimuli (such as the law of supply and demand) in the same way that people do in the physical world. In fact, there are often very direct corollaries between physical world economic decisions and virtual world economic decisions, such as the decision by prisoners of war in World War II to adopt cigarettes as currency and the adoption of Stones of Jordan as currency in *Diablo II*.

The value of objects in a virtual economy is usually linked to their usefulness and the difficulty of obtaining them. The investment of real world resources (time, membership fees, etc.) in acquisition of wealth in a virtual economy may contribute to the real world value of virtual objects. This real world value is made obvious by the trade of virtual items on online market sites like eBay,

PlayerUp, IGE for wow gold. Recent legal disputes also acknowledge the value of virtual property, even overriding the mandatory EULA which many software companies use to establish that virtual property has no value and/or that users of the virtual world have no legal claim to property therein.

Some industry analysts have moreover observed that there is a secondary industry growing behind the virtual worlds, made up by social networks, websites and other projects completely devoted to virtual worlds communities and gamers. Special websites such as GamerDNA, Koinup and others which serve as social networks for virtual worlds users are facing some crucial issues as the Data-Portability of avatars across many virtual worlds and MMORPGs.

Virtual worlds offer advertisers the potential for virtual advertisements, such as the in-game advertising already found in a number of video games.

Geography

The geography of virtual worlds can vary widely because the role of geography and space is an important design component over which the developers of virtual worlds have control and may choose to alter. Virtual worlds are, at least superficially, digital instantiations of three-dimensional space. As a result, considerations of geography in virtual worlds (such as World of Warcraft) often revolve around "spatial narratives" in which players act out a nomadic hero's journey along the lines of that present in *The Odyssey*. The creation of fantastic places is also a reoccurring theme in the geographic study of virtual worlds, although, perhaps counterintuitively, the heaviest users of virtual worlds often downgrade the sensory stimuli of the world's fantastic places in order to make themselves more efficient at core tasks in the world, such as killing monsters. However, the geographic component of some worlds may only be a geographic veneer atop an otherwise nonspatial core structure. For instance, while imposing geographic constraints upon users when they quest for items, these constraints may be removed when they sell items in a geographically unconstrained auction house. In this way, virtual worlds may provide a glimpse into what the future economic geography of the physical world may be like as more and more goods become digital.

Research

Virtual spaces can serve a variety of research and educational goals and may be useful for examining human behaviour. Offline- and virtual-world personalities differ from each other but are nevertheless significantly related which has a number of implications for self-verification, self-enhancement and other personality theories. Panic and agoraphobia have also been studied in a virtual world.

Given the large engagement, especially of young children in virtual worlds, there has been a steady growth in research studies involving the social, educational and even emotional impact of virtual worlds on children. The John D. and Catherine T. MacArthur Foundation for example have funded research into virtual worlds including, for example, how preteens explore and share information about reproductive health. A larger set of studies on children's social and political use of the virtual world Whyville.net has also been published in the book "Connected Play: Tweens in a Virtual World" Authored by Yasmin B. Kafai, Deborah A. Fields, and Mizuko Ito. Several other research publications now specifically address the use of virtual worlds for education.

Other research focused more on adults explores the reasons for indulging and the emotions of virtual world users. Many users seek an escape or a comfort zone in entering these virtual worlds, as well as a sense of acceptance and freedom. Virtual worlds allow users to freely explore many facets of their personalities in ways that are not easily available to them in real life. However, users may not be able to apply this new information outside of the virtual world. Thus, virtual worlds allow for users to flourish within the world and possibly become addicted to their new virtual life which may create a challenge as far as dealing with others and in emotionally surviving within their real lives. One reason for this freedom of exploration can be attributed to the anonymity that virtual worlds provide. It gives the individual the ability to be free from social norms, family pressures or expectations they may face in their personal real world lives. The avatar persona experiences an experience similar to an escape from reality like drug or alcohol usage for numbing pain or hiding behind it. The avatar no longer represents a simple tool or mechanism manipulated in cyberspace. Instead, it has become the individual's bridge between the physical and virtual world, a conduit through which to express oneself among other social actors. The avatar becomes the person's alter ego; the vehicle to which one utilizes to exist among others who are all seeking the same satisfaction.

While greatly facilitating ease of interaction across time and geographic boundaries, the virtual world presents an unreal environment with instant connection and gratification. Online encounters are employed as seemingly fulfilling alternatives to "live person" relationships (Toronto, 2009). When one is ashamed, insecure, lost or just looking for something different and stimulating to engage in, virtual worlds are the perfect environment for its users. A person has unlimited access to an infinite array of opportunities to fulfill every fantasy, grant every wish, or satisfy every desire. He or she can face any fear or conquer any enemy, all at the click of a mouse (Toronto, 2009). Ultimately, virtual worlds are the place to go when real life becomes overbearing or boring. While in real life individuals hesitate to communicate their true opinions, it is easier to do so online because they don't ever have to meet the people they are talking with (Toronto, 2009). Thus, virtual worlds are basically a psychological escape.

Another area of research related to virtual worlds is the field of navigation. Specifically, this research investigates whether or not virtual environments are adequate learning tools in regards to real-world navigation. Psychologists at Saint Michael's College found that video game experience corresponded with ability to navigate virtual environments and complete objectives; however, that experience did not correlate with an increased ability to navigate real, physical environments. An extensive study at the University of Washington conducted multiple experiments involving virtual navigation. One experiment had two groups of subjects, the first of which examined maps of a virtual environment, and the second of which navigated the virtual environment. The groups of subjects then completed an objective in the virtual environment. There was little difference between the two groups' performances, and what difference there was, it was in favor of the map-users. The test subjects, though, were generally unfamiliar with the virtual world interface, likely leading to some impaired navigation, and thus bias in the yielded analysis of the experiments. The study concluded that the interface objects made natural navigation movements impossible, and perhaps less intrusive controls for the virtual environment would reduce the effect of the impairment.

Virtual Worlds and Real Life

Some virtual worlds have off-line, real world components and applications. Handipoints, for example, is a children's virtual world that tracks chores via customizable chore charts and lets children get involved in their household duties offline. They complete chores and use the website and virtual world to keep track of their progress and daily tasks. There are also online platforms such as Uniiverse which are designed to re-connect people to the real world via virtual means. Users can post activities and services on-line and meet up off-line to share the experience.

Hardware

Unlike most video games, which are usually navigated using various free-ranging human interface devices (HIDs), virtual worlds are usually navigated (as of 2009) using HIDs which are designed and oriented around flat, 2-dimensional graphical user interfaces; as most comparatively-inexpensive computer mice are manufactured and distributed for 2-dimensional UI navigation, the lack of 3D-capable HID usage among most virtual world users is likely due to both the lack of penetration of 3D-capable devices into non-niche, non-gaming markets as well as the generally-higher pricing of such devices compared to 2-dimensional HIDs. Even those users who do make use of HIDs which provide such features as six degrees of freedom often have to switch between separate 3D and 2D devices in order to navigate their respectively-designed interfaces.

Like video gamers, some users of virtual world clients may also have a difficult experience with the necessity of proper graphics hardware (such as the more advanced graphics processing units distributed by Nvidia and AMD) for the sake of reducing the frequency of less-than-fluid graphics instances in the navigation of virtual worlds. However, in part for this reason, a growing number of virtual world engines, especially serving children, are entirely browser-based requiring no software down loads or specialized computer hardware. The first virtual world of this kind was Whyville.net, launched in 1999, built by Numedeon inc. which obtained an early patent for its browser-based implementation.

Application Domains

A film made in Second Life using machinima.

Social

Although the social interactions of participants in virtual worlds are often viewed in the context of 3D Games, other forms of interaction are common as well, including forums, blogs, wikis, chatrooms, instant messaging, and video-conferences. Communities are born in places which have their own rules, topics, jokes, and even language. Members of such communities can find like-minded people to interact with, whether this be through a shared passion, the wish to share information, or a desire to meet new people and experience new things. Users may develop personalities within the community adapted to the particular world they are interacting with, which can impact the way they think and act. Internet friendships and participation online communities tend to complement existing friendships and civic participation rather than replacing or diminishing such interactions.

Systems that have been designed for a social application include:

- Active Worlds

- Kaneva

- Habbo

- Onverse

- SmallWorlds

- There.com

- Twinity

- Whyville

The technological convergence of the mass media is the result of a long adaptation process of their communicative resources to the evolutionary changes of each historical moment. Thus, the new media became (plurally) an extension of the traditional media on the cyberspace, allowing to the public access information in a wide range of digital devices. In other words, it is a cultural virtualization of human reality as a result of the migration from physical to virtual space (mediated by the ICTs), ruled by codes, signs and particular social relationships. Forwards, arise instant ways of communication, interaction and possible quick access to information, in which we are no longer mere senders, but also producers, reproducers, co-workers and providers. New technologies also help to "connect" people from different cultures outside the virtual space, what was unthinkable fifty years ago. In this giant relationships web, we mutually absorb each other's beliefs, customs, values, laws and habits, cultural legacies perpetuated by a physical-virtual dynamics in constant metamorphosis (ibidem). In this sense, Professor Doctor Marcelo Mendonça Teixeira created, in 2014, a new model of communication to the virtual universe (The Communication Model of Virtual Universe), based on Claude Elwood Shannon's article "A Mathematical Theory of Communication" (1948).

Medical

Disabled or chronically invalided people of any age can benefit enormously from experiencing the mental and emotional freedom gained by temporarily leaving their disabilities behind and doing, through the medium of their avatars, things as simple and potentially accessible to able, healthy people as walking, running, dancing, sailing, fishing, swimming, surfing, flying, skiing, gardening, exploring and other physical activities which their illnesses or disabilities prevent them from doing in real life. They may also be able to socialize, form friendships and relationships much more easily and avoid the stigma and other obstacles which would normally be attached to their disabilities. This can be much more constructive, emotionally satisfying and mentally fulfilling than passive pastimes such as television watching, playing computer games, reading or more conventional types of internet use.

The Starlight Children's Foundation helps hospitalized children (suffering from painful diseases or autism for example) to create a comfortable and safe environment which can expand their situation, experience interactions (when the involvement of a multiple cultures and players from around the world is factored in) they may not have been able to experience without a virtual world, healthy or sick. Virtual worlds also enable them to experience and act beyond the restrictions of their illness and help to relieve stress.

Virtual worlds can help players become more familiar and comfortable with actions they may in real-life feel reluctant or embarrassed. For example, in World of Warcraft, /dance is the emote for a dance move which a player in the virtual world can "emote" quite simply. And a familiarization with said or similar "emotes" or social skills (such as, encouragement, gratitude, problem-solving, and even kissing) in the virtual world via avatar can make the assimilation to similar forms of expression, socialization, interaction in real life smooth. Interaction with humans through avatars in the virtual world has potential to seriously expand the mechanics of one's interaction with real-life interactions.

Commercial

As businesses compete in the real world, they also compete in virtual worlds. As there has been an increase in the buying and selling of products online (e-commerce) this twinned with the rise in the popularity of the internet, has forced businesses to adjust to accommodate the new market.

Many companies and organizations now incorporate virtual worlds as a new form of advertising. There are many advantages to using these methods of commercialization. An example of this would be Apple creating an online store within Second Life. This allows the users to browse the latest and innovative products. Players cannot actually purchase a product but having these "virtual stores" is a way of accessing a different clientele and customer demographic. The use of advertising within "virtual worlds" is a relatively new idea. This is because Virtual Worlds is a relatively new technology. Before companies would use an advertising company to promote their products. With the introduction of the prospect of commercial success within a Virtual World, companies can reduce cost and time constraints by keeping this "in-house". An obvious advantage is that it will reduce any costs and restrictions that could come into play in the real world.

Using virtual worlds gives companies the opportunity to gauge customer reaction and receive feedback. Feedback can be crucial to the development of a project as it will inform the creators exactly what users want.

Using virtual worlds as a tool allows companies to test user reaction and give them feedback on products. This can be crucial as it will give the companies an insight as to what the market and customers want from new products, which can give them a competitive edge. Competitive edge is crucial in the ruthless world that is today's business.

Another use of virtual worlds business is where players can create a gathering place. Many businesses can now be involved in business-to-business commercial activity and will create a specific area within a virtual world to carry out their business. Within this space all relevant information can be held. This can be useful for a variety of reasons. Players can conduct business with companies on the other side of the world, so there are no geographical limitations, it can increase company productivity. Knowing that there is an area where help is on hand can aid the employees. Sun Microsystems have created an island in Second Life dedicated for the sole use of their employees. This is a place where people can go and seek help, exchange new ideas or to advertise a new product.

Gronstedt identifies additional business applications, including: simulations, collaboration, role-playing, mentoring, and data-visualization.

According to trade media company Virtual Worlds Management, commercial investments in the "virtual worlds" sector were in excess of USD 425 million in Q4 2007, and totaled USD 184 million in Q1 2008. However, the selection process for defining a "virtual worlds" company in this context has been challenged by one industry blog.

E-commerce (Legal)

A number of virtual worlds have incorporated systems for sale of goods through virtual interfaces and using virtual currencies. Transfers of in-world credits typically are not bound by laws governing commerce. Such transactions may lack the oversight and protections associated with real-world commerce, and there is potential for fraudulent transactions. One example is that of Ginko Financial, a bank system featured in Second Life where avatars could deposit their real life currency after converted to Linden Dollars for a profit. In July 2007, residents of Second Life crowded around the ATM's in an unsuccessful attempt to withdraw their money. After a few days the ATM's along with the banks disappeared altogether. Around $700,000 in real world money was reported missing from residents in Second Life. An investigation was launched but nothing substantial ever came of finding and punishing the avatar known as Nicholas Portocarrero who was the head of Ginko Financial.

Civil and criminal laws exist in the real world and are put in place to govern people's behavior. Virtual Worlds such as *Eve Online* and *Second Life* also have people and systems that govern them.

Providers of online virtual spaces have more than one approach to the governing of their environments. *Second Life* for instance was designed with the expectation being on the residents to establish their own community rules for appropriate behaviour. On the other hand, some virtual worlds such as *Habbo* enforce clear rules for behaviour, as seen in their terms and conditions.

In some instances virtual worlds don't need established rules of conduct because actions such as 'killing' another avatar is impossible. However, if needed to, rule breakers can be punished with fines being payable through their virtual bank account, alternatively a players suspension may be put into effect.

Instances of real world theft from a virtual world do exist, Eve Online had an incident where a bank controller stole around 200bn credits and exchanged them for real world cash amounting to £3,115. The player in question has now been suspended as trading in-game cash for real money is against Eve Online's terms and conditions.

Entertainment

There are many MMORPG virtual worlds out on many platforms. Most notable are IMVU for Windows, PlayStation Home for PlayStation 3, and Second Life for Windows. Many Virtual worlds have shut down since launch however. Notable shutdowns are The Sims Online, The Sims Bustin Out Online Weekend Mode, and PlayStation Home.

Single-player Games

Some single-player video games contain virtual worlds populated by non-player characters (NPC). Many of these allow players to save the current state of this world instance to allow stopping and restarting the virtual world at a later date. (This can be done with some multiplayer environments as well.)

The virtual worlds found in video games are often split into discrete levels.

Single-player games such as Minecraft allow players to optionally create their own world without other players, and then combine skills from the game to work together with other players and create bigger and more intricate environments. These environments can then be accessed by other players, if the server is available to other players then they may be able to modify parts of it, such as the structure of the environment.

At one level, a more or less realistic rendered 3D space like the game world of Halo 3 or Grand Theft Auto is just as much a big database as Microsoft's Encarta encyclopedia.

Use in Education

Virtual worlds represent a powerful new medium for instruction and education that presents many opportunities but also some challenges. Persistence allows for continuing and growing social interactions, which themselves can serve as a basis for collaborative education. The use of virtual worlds can give teachers the opportunity to have a greater level of student participation. It allows users to be able to carry out tasks that could be difficult in the real world due to constraints and restrictions, such as cost, scheduling or location. Virtual worlds have the capability to adapt and grow to different user needs, for example, classroom teachers are able to use virtual worlds in their classroom leveraging their interactive whiteboard with the open source project Edusim. They can be a good source of user feedback, the typical paper-based resources have limitations that Virtual Worlds can overcome.

Multi-user virtual worlds with easy-to-use affordances for building are useful in project-based learning. For example, Active Worlds is used to support classroom teachers in Virginia Beach City Public Schools, the out-of-school NASA RealWorld-InWorld Engineering Design Challenge, and many after school and in school programs in EDUni-NY. Projects range from tightly scaffolded reflection spaces to open building based on student-centered designs. New York Museums AMNH and NYSci have used the medium to support STEM learning experiences for their program participants.

Virtual worlds can also be used with virtual learning environments, as in the case of what is done in the Sloodle project, which aims to merge Second Life with Moodle. Another project similar to Sloodle is Utherverse Academy.

Virtual worlds allow users with specific needs and requirements to access and use the same learning materials from home as they would receive if they were physically present. Virtual worlds can help users stay up to date with relevant information and needs while also feeling as they are involved. Having the option to be able to attend a presentation via a virtual world from home or from their workplace, can help the user to be more at ease and comfortable. Although virtual worlds are used as an alternative method of communicating and interacting with students and teachers, a sense of isolation can occur such as losing certain body language cues and other more personal aspects that one would achieve if they were face to face.

Some virtual worlds also offer an environment where simulation-based activities and games allow users to experiment various phenomenon and learn the underlying physics and principles. An example is Whyville launched in 1999, which targets kids and teenagers, offering them many opportunities to experiment, understand and learn. Topics covered in Whyville vary from physics to nutrition to ecology. Whyville also has a strong entrepreneurial structure based on user created virtual content sold in the internal virtual economy. VirBELA is a unity based virtual world that embeds business simulations as a way to assess and develop global leadership skills of students and professionals from around the world.

Some multi-user virtual worlds have become used for educational purposes and are thus called Multi-User Virtual Learning Environments (MUVLEs). Examples have included the use of Second Life for teaching English as a foreign languages (EFL) Many specialist types of MUVLE have particular pedagogies associated with them. For instance, George Siemens, Stephen Downes continue to promote the use of a type of MUVLE Dave Cormier coined called a 'MOOC'. Even though MOOCs were once seen as "next big thing" by universities and online education service providers such as Blackboard Inc, this was in fact what has been called a "stampede." By early 2013, serious questions emerged about whether MOOCs were simply part of a hype cycle and indeed following that hype whether academia was thus "MOOC'd out."

Language

Language learning is the most widespread type of education in virtual worlds.

Business

Online training overcomes constraints such as distance, infrastructure, accommodation costs and tight scheduling. Although video conferencing may be the most common tool, virtual worlds have been adopted by the business environment for training employees. For example, Second Life has been used in business schools.

Virtual training content resembles traditional tutorials and testing of user knowledge. Despite the lack of face to face contact and impaired social linking, learning efficiency may not be adversely affected as adults need autonomy in learning and are more self-directed than younger students.

Some companies and public places allow free virtual access to their facilities as an alternative to a video or picture.

In Fiction

Virtual worlds, virtual reality, and cyberspace are quite popular fictional motifs. A prominent example is the work of William Gibson. The first was probably John M. Ford's 1980 novel *Web of Angels*. Virtual worlds are integral to *Tron, Neuromancer, The Lawnmower Man, The Lawnmower Man 2, Ready Player One, Epic, Snow Crash, .hack//Sign, Real Drive*, Sword Art Online, *Summer Wars, The Matrix, Ghost in the Shell*, and the French animated television series *Code Lyoko* and *Code Lyoko Evolution*, and the Cyber World in the popular Viz Media series *MegaMan NT Warrior*. In *the Planiverse*, a 1984 novel by A.K. Dewdney, college students create a virtual world called 2DWorld, leading to contact with Arde, a two-dimensional parallel universe. In the cyberpunk, computers, psychological thirteen-episode anime entitled *Serial Experiments Lain*, the main focus is about the Wired, which is a virtual reality-world that governs the sum of all electronic communication and machines; outer receptors are used to mentally transport a person *into* the Wired itself as a uniquely different virtual avatar.

The fourth series of the New Zealand TV series *The Tribe* featured the birth of Reality Space and the Virtual World that was created by Ram, the computer genius-wizard leader of The Technos.

In 2009, BBC Radio 7 commissioned *Planet B*, set in a virtual world in which a man searches for his girlfriend, believed to be dead, but in fact still alive within the world, called "Planet B". The series is the biggest-ever commission for an original drama series.

In the novel *Holo.Wars: The Black Hats*, three virtual worlds overlap and are possibly a majority of the milieu in the book.

Future

Virtual worlds may lead to a "mobility" of labor that may impact national and organizational competitiveness in a manner similar to the changes seen with the mobility of goods and then the mobility of labor.

Virtual worlds may increasingly function as centers of commerce, trade, and business. With the increased growth of virtual asset trade being seen: In Second Life, revenue has reached approximately 7 million US Dollars per month. Real world brands such as Coca-Cola have used virtual worlds to advertise their brand.

Virtual Economy

A virtual economy (or sometimes synthetic economy) is an emergent economy existing in a virtual world, usually exchanging virtual goods in the context of an Internet game. People enter these virtual economies for recreation and entertainment rather than necessity, which means that virtual economies lack the aspects of a real economy that are not considered to be "fun" (for instance, avatars in a virtual economy often do not need to buy food in order to survive, and usually do not have any biological needs at all). However, some people do interact with virtual economies for "real" economic benefit.

Despite primarily dealing with in-game currencies, this term also encompasses the selling of virtual currency for real money.

Overview

Virtual economies are observed in MUDs and massively multi player online role-playing games (MMORPGs). The largest virtual economies are found in MMORPGs. Virtual economies also exist in life simulation games which may have taken the most radical steps toward linking a virtual economy with the real world. This can be seen, for example, in Second Life's recognition of intellectual property rights for assets created "in-world" by subscribers, and its laissez-faire policy on the buying and selling of Linden Dollars (the world's official currency) for real money on third party websites. Virtual economies can also exist in browser-based Internet games where "real" money can be spent and user-created shops opened, or as a kind of emergent gameplay.

Virtual property is a label that can refer to any resource that is controlled by the powers-that-be, including virtual objects, avatars, or user accounts. The following characteristics may be found in virtual resources in mimicry of tangible property. Note however that it is possible for virtual resources to lack one or more of these characteristics, and they should be interpreted with reasonable flexibility.

1. Rivalry: Possession of a resource is limited to one person or a small number of persons within the virtual world's game mechanics.

2. Persistence: Virtual resources persist across user sessions. In some cases, the resource exists for public view even when its owner is not logged into the virtual world.

3. Interconnectivity: Resources may affect or be affected by other people and other objects. The value of a resource varies according to a person's ability to use it for creating or experiencing some effect.

4. Secondary markets: Virtual resources may be created, traded, bought, and sold. Real-world assets (typically money) may be at stake.

5. Value added by users: Users may enhance the value of virtual resources by customizing and improving upon the resource.

The existence of these conditions create an economic system with properties similar to those seen in contemporary economies. Therefore, economic theory can often be used to study these virtual worlds.

Within the virtual worlds they inhabit, synthetic economies allow in-game items to be priced according to supply and demand rather than by the developer's estimate of the item's utility. These emergent economies are considered by most players to be an asset of the game, giving an extra dimension of reality to play. In classical synthetic economies, these goods were charged only for in-game currencies. These currencies are often sold for real world profit.

Marketplace

The release of Blizzard Entertainment's World of Warcraft in 2004 and its subsequent huge success across the globe has forced both MMORPGs and their secondary markets into mainstream consciousness, and many new market places have opened up during this time. A search for WoW Gold on Google will show a multitude of sites (more than 90 sponsored results as of June 2006) from which Gold can be purchased. Real money commerce in a virtual market has grown to become a multibillion-dollar industry. In 2001, EverQuest players Brock Pierce and Alan Debonneville founded *Internet Gaming Entertainment Ltd (IGE)*, a company that offered not only the virtual commodities in exchange for real money but also provided professional customer service. *IGE* had a trained staff that would handle financial issues, customer inquiries and technical support to ensure that gamers are satisfied with each real money purchase. It also took advantage of the global reach of synthetic worlds by setting up a shop in Hong Kong where a small army of technically savvy but low wage workers could field orders, load up avatars, retrieve store goods and deliver them wherever necessary. This lucrative market has opened a whole new type of economy where the border between the real and the virtual is obscure.

Hundreds of companies are enormously successful in this new found market, with some virtual items being sold for hundreds or even thousands of dollars. Some of these companies sell multiple virtual goods for multiple games, and others sell services for single games. Virtual real estate is earning real world money, with people like 43-year-old *Wonder Bread* deliveryman, John Dugger, purchasing a virtual real estate for $750, setting him back more than a weeks wages. This virtual property includes nine rooms, three stories, rooftop patio, wall of solid stonework in a prime location, nestled at the foot of a quiet coastal hillside. Dugger represents a group of gamers that are not in the market for a real house but instead to own a small piece of the vast computer database that was Ultima Online, the mythical world in which the venerable MMO Ultima Online unfolds. Such trading of real money for virtual goods simply represents the development of virtual economies where people come together where the real and the synthetic worlds are meeting within an economic sphere.

Although virtual markets may represent a growth area, it is unclear to what extent they can scale to supporting large numbers of businesses, due to the inherent substitutability of goods on these markets plus the lack of factors such as location to dispense demand. In spite of numerous famed examples of the economic growth of Second Life an amateur analyst in 2008 estimated the income inequity in Second Life's economy as worse than has ever been recorded in any real economy: a Gini coefficient of 90.2, a Hoover index of 77.8, and a Theil index of 91%. However, the application of these economic measures to a virtual world may be inappropriate where poverty is merely virtual and there is a direct relationship between in-game wealth and time spent playing.

The global secondary market - defined as real money trading between players - turnover was estimated at 880 million dollars in 2005 by the president of the, at the time, market leading company IGE. Before that, in 2004, the American economist Edward Castronova had estimated the turnover at over 100 million dollars based solely on sales figures from the two auction sites eBay and the Korean itemBay. A speculative extrapolation based on these quotes and other industry figures produced a global turnover figure of 2 billion dollars as of 2007.

However, the secondary market is unlikely to have followed the growth of the primary market since 2007 seeing as game companies have become better at monetizing on their games with microtransactions and many popular games such as World of Warcraft are sporting increased measures against player to player real money trading. Also hampering the turnover growth are the extreme price drops that has followed the increased competition from businesses in mainland China targeting the global secondary market. Furthermore, the global decline in consumption that followed the financial crisis of 2007–2008 would have affected the secondary market negatively as well. Post 2007 secondary market growth is likely localized to emerging markets such as Russia, eastern Europe, South America, and South East Asia - all of which are relatively inaccessible to international merchants due to payment systems, advertisement channels and language barrier. For example, South Korea is estimated to have the biggest share of the global real money trading market and it has there become an officially acknowledged and taxable part of the economy. In western countries the secondary market remains a black market with little to no social acceptance or official acknowledgement.

As for an actual economic model, secondary market turnover in popular player vs player oriented MMORPGs without trade restrictions such as Runescape, EVE Online and Ultima Online has been estimated at around 1.1 dollar per concurrent player and day. No model for more regulated MMORPGs such as World of Warcraft has been suggested. However, being a largely unregulated market and tax free market, any turnover figure or economic model remain speculative.

Latest Developments

Banks are increasingly interested in virtual economies as well, especially in new virtual currencies. JP Morgan Chase bank on December 10, 2013, filed for a patent in the U.S to develop a payment system utilizing "Virtual Cash". According to a document on the U.S. Patent & Trademark Office's website, ""The application is a renewal for intellectual property claims originally filed in 1999 covering a method and system for conducting financial transactions over a payment network." Similar to Bitcoin, JPMorgan's proposed system would enable users to make anonymous, electronic payments over the internet, without the requirement of revealing their name or account numbers or pay a fee, according to the patent application.

More Controlled Markets

An example of a much more controlled market is World of Tanks' "gold" currency which is only available from the vendor itself and typically only for cash payment. This has become a model for other freemium games. It does not allow for any vending of game goods or capabilities without the permission and direct participation and control of the game server/operator/vendor.

In this model, players are strictly forbidden from employing means or methods of maximizing gold availability (for instance bonuses for new accounts which are then shared). They can gift gold to each other but cannot solicit or ask for it. Gold sharing among game guilds is common and encouraged, but not among players who don't know each other for specific benefits. For instance, vehicles cannot be bought and sold within the game except to the server, for a fixed price ratio (selling earns back half the price paid).

Price Comparison

Information brokerages and other tools that aid in the valuation of virtual items on secondary markets have increased in number. This has occurred as a response to alleviate the labor involved in leveling that requires hours, days or weeks to achieve. Being able to exchange real money for virtual currency provides the player purchasing power for virtual commodities. As such, players are guaranteed opportunities, increased skills and a fine reputation, which is a definite advantage over others.

Taxation

Most scholars agree that the sale of virtual property for real currency or assets is taxable. However, there are significant legal and practical challenges to the taxation of income from the sale of virtual property. For example, uncertainty regarding the nature and conceptual location of virtual property makes it difficult to collect and apportion tax revenue when a sale occurs across multiple jurisdictions.

In addition to taxing income from transactions involving real currency or assets, there has been considerable discussion involving the taxation of transactions that take place entirely within a virtual economy. Theoretically, virtual world transactions could be treated as a form of barter, thus generating taxable income. However, for policy reasons, many commentators support some form of a "cash out" rule that would prevent in-game transactions from generating tax liabilities. Nevertheless, as one commentator notes, "the easier it is to buy real goods with virtual currency (e.g. order a real life pizza) the more likely the IRS will see exclusively in-world profits as taxable."

Gambling Regulation

Conversion between in-game and real-world currency has led to direct comparisons with other online *games of chance* as 'virtual winnings'. This is why gamers and companies engaged in this conversion, where it is permitted by a game, may fall under gambling legislation.

During an interview with Virtual World News, Alex Chapman of the British law firm Campbell Hooper stated: "Now we've spoken with the gambling commission, and they've said that MMOGs aren't the reason for the [Gambling Act 2005], but they won't say outright, and we've asked directly, that they won't be covered. You can see how these would be ignored at first, but very soon they could be in trouble. It's a risk, but a very easy risk to avoid." He suggested that compliance might require MMOGs and related traders to obtain a gambling license, which is not excessively difficult in the EU.

When queried about games where real-world transactions for in-game assets are *not* permitted, but there is an 'unofficial secondary market', Chapman responded: "Ultimately the point is whether the thing that you win has value in money or money's worth. If it does have value, it could be gambling." So to avoid regulation by these laws, the "operator would need to take reasonable steps to ensure that the rewards they give do not have a monetary value[,]" possibly by demonstrating enforcement of their Terms of Service prohibiting secondary markets.

Virtual Crime

Monetary issues can give a virtual world problems similar to those in the real world. In South Korea, where the number of video game players is massive, some have reported the emergence of gangs and mafia, where powerful players would threaten beginners to give money for their "protection", and actually steal and rob.

Other similar problems arise in other virtual economies. In the game *The Sims Online,* a 17-year-old boy going by the in-game name "Evangeline" was discovered to have built a cyber-brothel, where customers would pay sim-money for minutes of cybersex. Maxis canceled each of his accounts, but had he deposited his fortune in the Gaming Open Market he would have been able to keep a part of it.

A 2007 virtual heist has led to calls from some community members in *Second Life* to bring in external regulation of these markets: "In late July, a perpetrator with privileged information cracked a stock exchange's computers, made false deposits, then ran off with what appears to be the equivalent of US$10,000, disappearing into thin air. Despite the seemingly small haul, this heist left investors feeling outraged and vulnerable."

In *EVE Online* however, theft and scamming other players is perfectly allowed within the game's framework as long as no real world trading is committed. Players are allowed to loot all items from fallen victims in battle, but there is a disincentive in the form of NPC police intervention in higher-security space. Virtual possessions valued in the tens of thousands of USD have been destroyed or plundered through corporate espionage and piracy. This has resulted in widespread retributive warfare and crime between various player corporations.

Black Market

Many MMORPGS such as *RuneScape, World of Warcraft, Guild Wars, Warhammer Online, Lord of the Rings Online* and *Final Fantasy XI* strictly prohibit buying gold, items, or any other product linked with the game, with real world cash. *RuneScape* went as far as making this practice impossible by removing unbalanced trades and their traditional player vs. player fighting system (this was scrapped on February 1, 2011 after having been in place for 3 years), resulting in over 60,000 cancelled subscriptions in protest. *Final Fantasy XI* and *Warhammer Online* both have entire task forces dedicated to the removal of real money trading from the game. To control real money trading, *EVE Online* created an official and sanctioned method to convert real world cash to in-game currency; players can use real world money to buy a specific in-game item which can be redeemed for account subscription time or traded on the in-game market for in-game currency.

Stability

For a persistent world to maintain a stable economy, a balance must be struck between currency sources and sinks. Generally, games possess numerous sources of new currency for players to earn. However, some possess no effective "sinks", or methods of removing currency from circulation. If other factors remain constant, greater currency supply weakens the buying power of a given amount; a process known as inflation. In practice, this results in constantly rising prices for traded commodities. With the proper balance of growth in player base, currency sources, and sinks, a virtual economy could remain stable indefinitely.

As in the real world, actions by players can destabilize the economy. Gold farming creates currency within the game more rapidly than usual, exacerbating inflation. In extreme cases, a cracker may be able to exploit the system and create a large amount of money. This could result in hyperinflation.

In the real world entire institutions are devoted to maintaining desired level of inflation. This difficult task is a serious issue for serious MMORPG's, that often have to cope with mudflation. Episodes of hyperinflation have also been observed.

Capital

In these virtual economies, the value of in-game resources is frequently tied to the in-game power they confer upon the owner. This power allows the user, usually, to acquire more rare and valuable items. In this regard, in-game resources are not just tradable objects but can play the role of *capital*.

Players also acquire human capital as they become more powerful. Powerful guilds often recruit powerful players so that certain players can acquire better items which can only be acquired by the cooperation among many players.

Other Virtual Economies

Virtual economies have also been said to exist in the "metagame" worlds of live-action role-playing games and collectible card games. Other "metagame" currencies have cropped up in games such as *Everquest* and *World of Warcraft*. Dragon kill points or DKP are a semi-formal score-keeping system used by guilds in massively multiplayer online games. Players in these games are faced with large scale challenges, or raids, which may only be surmounted through the concerted effort of dozens of players at a time. Dragon kill points are not official currencies, but are created and managed by endgame guilds to manage distributions of rewards in those raids.

Virtual economies represented not only in mmorpg genre but also in online business simulation games (Virtonomics, Miniconomy). Simplified economy represented in almost all real-time strategies (StarCraft II: Heart of the Swarm, Red alert 2) in a form of gathering and spending resources. Diablo III has its virtual economy as well which is represented by online game auction.

Moderation on Social News and Networking Sites

On a number of discussion and networking sites, such as Slashdot, Reddit, care2 and Yahoo! Answers, points are gained through the garnering of trust evidenced in upward moderations of posted content; however, as stated by Slashdot co-founder CmdrTaco, his implementation of user moderation was not intended as a currency, even though it has evolved on other discussion-oriented sites into such a system. On some such sites, the accumulation of "karma points" can be redeemed in various ways for virtual services or objects, while most other sites do not contain a redemption system.

On some sites, points are gained for inviting new users to the site.

Controversy

A game's synthetic economy often results in interaction with a "real" economy; characters, currency, and items may be sold and bought on online auction websites or purchased from standalone webshops. Since January 2007 users are no longer allowed to sell virtual goods of online games on eBay due to the ambiguous legal status of real world trading.

While many game developers, such as Blizzard (creator of *World of Warcraft*), prohibit the practice, it is common that goods and services within virtual economies will be sold on online auction sites and traded for real currencies.

According to standard conceptions of economic value, the goods and services of virtual economies do have a demonstrable value. Since players of these games are willing to substitute real economic resources of time and money (monthly fees) in exchange for these resources, by definition they have demonstrated utility to the user.

In January 2010, Blizzard stepped up its offensive on account security scams with the launch of a new website. The new Battle.Net account security website hopes to highlight the importance of keeping it safe when it comes to subscribers' accounts.

These pages are part of a larger effort to provide you with the knowledge and tools necessary to identify and report threats to your account's safety, to spotlight ways in which we work to fulfill our security commitment, and to act as a helpful resource in case someone manages to steal account information from you.

Ongoing campaign by WoW fan sites to boycott gold ads on their sites is just one of several community efforts to raise awareness against crackers.

Gold sellers and leveling services are responsible for the vast majority of all account thefts, and they are the number-one source of World of Warcraft-related phishing attempts, spyware, and even credit card theft. Players who buy gold actively support spam, hacks, and keyloggers, and by doing so diminish the gameplay experience for everyone else.

On August 1, 2011, Blizzard Entertainment announced that their forthcoming MMORPG, Diablo III, will include a currency-based auction house, wherein players will be able to buy and sell in-game items for real money. Robert Bridenbecker, Vice President of Online Technologies at Blizzard, explained that the intent behind the effort is largely to reduce account thefts resulting from player interaction with third-party sites. An undisclosed fee structure including listing fees, sale fees, and cash-out fees will accompany the Auction House at launch, and all transactions will exist within the protected context of Blizzard's MMORPG. The "Real Money Auction House" (RMAH), as it is called by the Diablo III fanbase, will exist in the presence of a parallel auction house wherein items are exchanged for gold, the in-game currency. Accordingly, gold can be posted on the RMAH such that the two currencies may be exchanged for one another at the market rate less applicable fees.

Other virtual world developers officially sell virtual items and currency for real-world money. For example, the MMOG *There* has therebucks that sell for US dollars. If the currency in *Second Life*, the Linden Dollars, can be easily acquired with real money, the reverse is done through a market place owned by Linden Lab, but is not guaranteed, as the TOS of linden Lab explicitly says that Linden dollars are not redeemable. Rates would fluctuate based on supply and demand, but over the last few years they have remained fairly stable at around 265 Linden Dollars (L$) to the US Dollar, due to "money creation" by Linden Lab. The currency in *Entropia Universe*, Project Entropia Dollars (PED), could be bought and redeemed for real-world money at a rate of 10 PED for U.S\$. 1. On December 14, 2004, an island in *Project Entropia* sold for U.S. \$26,500 (£13,700). One gamer also purchased a virtual space station for U.S. \$100,000 (£56,200) and plans to use it as a virtual nightclub. Another example was recently cited on CNBC that one seller was selling a Pokémon Go account for \$999,999.

Many Korean virtual worlds (such as Flyff) and other worlds outside that country (such as Archlord and Achaea, Dreams of Divine Lands) operate entirely by selling items to players for real money. Such items generally cannot be transferred and are often used only as a means to represent a Premium subscription via a method which is easily integrated into the game engine.

These intersections with real economies remain controversial. Markets that capitalize in gaming are not widely accepted by the gaming industry. Reasons for this controversy are varied. Firstly, the developers of the games often consider themselves as trying to present a fantasy experience, so the involvement of real world transactions takes away from it. Further, in most games, it would be unacceptable to offer another player real currency in order to have them play a certain way (e.g., in a game of Monopoly between friends, offering another player a real dollar in exchange for a property on the board); and for this to be necessary or valuable may indicate a Kingmaker scenario within the game. However, such rules of etiquette need not apply, and in practice they often don't, to massive game worlds with thousands of players who know one another only through the game system.

Further and more involved issues revolve around the issue of how (or if) real-money trading subjects the virtual economy to laws relating to the real economy. Some argue that to allow in-game items to have monetary values makes these games, essentially, gambling venues, which would be subject to legal regulation as such. Another issue is the impact of taxation that may apply if in-game items are seen as having real value. If (for example) a magic sword is considered to have real-world value, a player who kills a powerful monster to earn such a sword could find himself being charged tax on the value of the sword, as would be normal for a "prize winning". This would make it impossible for any player of the game *not* to participate in real-money trading.

A third issue is the involvement of the world's developer or maintenance staff in such transactions. Since a developer may change the virtual world any time, ban a player, delete items, or even simply take the world down never to return, the issue of their responsibility in the case where real money investments are lost through items being lost or becoming inaccessible is significant. Richard Bartle argued that this aspect negates the whole idea of ownership in virtual worlds, and thus in the absence of real ownership no real trade may occur. Some developers have acted deliberately to delete items that have been traded for money, as in Final Fantasy XI, where a task force was set up to delete characters involved in selling in-game currency for real-world money.

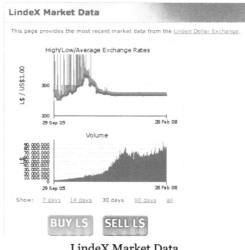

LindeX Market Data

However, Second Life has shown a legal example which may indicate that the developer can be in part held responsible for such losses. Second Life at one stage, offered and advertised the ability to "own virtual land", which was purchased for real money. In 2007, Marc Bragg, an attorney, was banned from Second Life; in response he sued the developers for thereby depriving him of his land, which he – based on the developers' own statements – "owned". The lawsuit ended with a settlement in which Bragg was re-admitted to Second Life. The details of the final settlement were not released, but the word "own" was removed from all advertising as a result. (Bragg purchased his land directly from the developers, and thus they were not an uninvolved third party in his transactions.)

Free-to-play

Free-to-play (F2P) refers to video games which give players access to a significant portion of their content without paying. There are several kinds of free-to-play games, but the most common is based on the freemium software model. For freemium games, users are granted access to a fully functional game, but must pay microtransactions to access additional content. Free-to-play can be contrasted with pay to play, in which payment is required before using a service for the first time.

The model was first popularly used in early massively multiplayer online games targeted towards casual gamers, before finding wider adoption among games released by major video game publishers to combat video game piracy and high system requirements. Without upfront payment, publishers may charge money for in-game items or integrate advertisements into the game.

Categories

There are several kinds of free-to-play games:

- Shareware refers to a trial of variable functionality intended to convince users to buy a full license of the pay-to-play game. Also known as game demos, shareware often gives free users severely limited functionality compared to the full game.

- Freemium games, such as *Star Wars: The Old Republic*, *Need for Speed: World*, and *Rift*, offer the "full version" of a product free of charge, while users are charged micropayments to access premium features and virtual goods, often in a piecemeal fashion.

Game Mechanics

In-game items can be purely cosmetic, enhance the power of the player, or accelerate progression speed. A common technique used by developers of these games is for the items purchased to have a time limit; after this expires, the item must be repurchased before use can continue. Another commonly seen mechanic is the use of two in-game currencies: one earned through normal gameplay, and another which can be purchased with real-world money. The second, "premium" currency is sometimes given out in small amounts to non-paying players at certain times, such as when they first start the game, or when they complete a quest or refer a friend to the game. Many browser games have an "energy bar" which depletes when the player takes actions. These games then sell items such as coffee or snacks to refill the bar.

Free-to-play games are free to install and play, but once the player enters the game, the player is able to purchase content such as items, maps, and expanded customization options. Some games, such as id Software's *Quake Live* also use in-game advertising to provide income for free-to-play games. In addition to making in-game items available for purchase, EA integrates in-game advertising into its games. In August 2007, EA completed a deal with Massive Incorporated, which lets Massive update and change in-game advertising in real-time within EA games. Independent game developer Edmund McMillen, has claimed that he makes most of his money from sponsors by placing advertisements into the introduction of a game and the game's title screen.

History

The free-to-play model originated in the late 1990s and early 2000s, coming from a series of highly successful MMOs targeted towards children and casual gamers, including *Furcadia, Neopets, RuneScape, MapleStory*, and text-based dungeons such as *Achaea, Dreams of Divine Lands*. Known for producing innovative titles, small independent developers also continue to release free-to-play games. The Internet has been cited as a primary influence on the increased usage of the free-to-play model, particularly among larger video game companies, and critics point to the ever-increasing need for free content that is available wherever and whenever as causes.

Particularly early on, free-to-play games caught on fastest in South Korea and Russia, where they took over 90% of the gaming market. There are free-to-play, pay-to-connect games where there is no charge for playing, but often the free servers are congested. Access to uncongested servers is reserved for fee-paying members. Free-to-play games are particularly prevalent in countries such as South Korea and the People's Republic of China. Microtransaction-based free-to-play mobile games and browser games such as *Puzzle & Dragons, Kantai Collection* and *The Idolmaster Cinderella Girls* also have large player populations in Japan. In particular, the *Nikkei Shimbun* reported that *Cinderella Girls* earns over 1 billion yen in revenue monthly from microtransactions. Electronic Arts first adopted the free-to-play concept in one of its games when it released *FIFA Online* in Korea.

In the late 2000s, many MMOs transitioned to the free-to-play model from subscriptions, including subscription-based games such as *The Lord of the Rings Online: Shadows of Angmar, Age of Conan: Hyborian Adventures, Dungeons & Dragons Online*, and *Champions Online*. This move from a subscription based model to a free-to-play one has proven very beneficial in some cases. Star Wars: The Old Republic is a good example of a game that transitioned from subscription to free-to-play. Turbine as of September 10, 2010 has given an F2P with Cash shop option to The Lord of the Rings Online which resulted in a tripling of profit. Sony Online Entertainment's move to transition EverQuest from a subscription model into a hybrid F2P/subscription game was followed by a 125% spike in item sales, a 150% up-tick in unique log-ins, and over three times as many account registrations.

The movement of free-to-play MMOs into the mainstream also coincided with experimentation with other genres as well. The model was picked up by larger developers and more diverse genres, with games such as *Battlefield Heroes, Free Realms, Quake Live* and *Team Fortress 2* appearing in the late 2000s. The experimentation was not successful in every genre, however. Traditional real time strategy franchises such as *Age of Empires* and *Command & Conquer* both attempted free-to-play titles. Age of Empires Online was shut down in the midst of a tiny player base and stagnant revenue, and Command & Conquer: Generals 2 was shut down in alpha due to negative reactions from players.

In 2011, revenue from free-to-play games overtook revenue from premium games in the top 100 games in Apple's App Store. The number of people that spend money on in-game items in these games ranges from 0.5% to 6%, depending on a game's quality and mechanics. Even though this means that a large number of people will never spend money in a game, it also means that the people that do spend money could amount to a sizeable number due to the fact that the game was given away for free. Indeed a report from mobile advertising company firm SWRV stated that only 1.5 percent of players opted to pay for in-game items, and that 50 percent of the revenue for such games often came from just ten percent of players. Nevertheless The Washington Post noted that the developers of two such games, Supercell (Clash of Clans) and Machine Zone (Game of War: Fire Age), were able to afford Super Bowl spots in 2015 featuring big-name celebrities (respectively Liam Neeson and Kate Upton). The latter, Game of War, was in fact, part of a roughly $40 million campaign starring Upton.

As of 2012, free-to-play MOBAs, such as League of Legends, Heroes of the Storm, Smite, and Dota 2 have become among the most popular PC games. The success in the genre has helped convince many video game publishers to copy the free-to-play MOBA model.

Comparison with Traditional Model

The free-to-play model has been described as a shift from the traditional model in the sense that previously, success was measured by multiplying the number of units of a game sold by the unit price, while with free-to-play, the most important factor is the number of players that a game can keep continuously engaged, followed by how many compelling spending opportunities the game offers its players. With free games that include in-game purchases, two particularly important things occur: first, more people will try out the game since there is zero cost to doing so and second, revenue will likely be more than a traditional game since different players can now spend different amounts of money that depend on their engagement with the game and their preferences towards it. It is likely that the vast majority of players "ride for free" and that a minority pay, and a very tiny minority pay the bulk of the income - 50% of revenue from 0.15% (15 in 10,000) of players in one report. It is not unlikely for a very few players to spend tens of thousands of dollars in a game that they enjoy.

On the PC in particular, two problems are video game piracy and high video game system requirements. The free-to-play model appears to solve both these problems, by providing a game that requires relatively low system requirements and no cost, and consequently provides a highly accessible experience funded by advertising and micropayments for extra content.

Free-to-play is much newer than the pay to play model, and the video game industry is still attempting to determine the best ways to maximize revenue from their games. Gamers have cited the fact that purchasing a game for a fixed price is still inherently satisfying because the consumer knows exactly what they will be receiving, compared to free-to-play which requires that the player pay for most new content that they wish to obtain. The term itself, "free-to-play", has been described as one with a negative connotation. One video game developer noted this, stating, "Our hope—and the basket we're putting our eggs in—is that 'free' will soon be disassociated with [sic] 'shallow' and 'cruddy'." However, another noted that developing freeware games gave developers the largest amount of creative freedom, especially when compared to developing console games, which requires that the game follow the criteria as laid out by the game's publisher. Many kinds of revenue are being experimented with. For example, with its *Free Realms* game targeted to children and casual gamers, Sony makes money from the product with advertisements on loading screens, free virtual goods sponsored by companies such as Best Buy, a subscription option to unlock extra content, a collectible card game, a comic book, and micropayment items that include character customization options.

Criticism

In some multiplayer free-to-play games, players who are willing to pay for special items or downloadable content may be able to gain a significant advantage over those playing for free. Critics of such games call them "pay-to-win" (p2w) games. A common suggestion for avoiding pay-to-win is that payments should only be used to broaden the experience without affecting gameplay. For example, Dota 2 only allows the purchase of cosmetic items, meaning that a "free-to-play player" will be on the same level as a player who has spent money on the game. Some suggest finding a balance between a game that encourages players to pay for extra content that enhances the game without making the free version feel limited by comparison. This theory is that players who do not pay for items would still increase awareness of it through word of mouth marketing, which ultimately benefits the game indirectly. In response to concerns about players using payments to gain an advantage in game, titles such as *World of Tanks* have explicitly committed to not giving paying players any advantages over their non-paying peers, while allowing the users buying the "gold" (premium) ammo and expendables without paying the real money. However, features helping to grind easier, such as purchasing a 100% training level or converting experience to free experience, remain available for the paying customers only.

In single player games, another concern is the tendency for free games to constantly request that the player buy extra content. Payment may be required in order to survive or continue in the game, annoying or distracting the player from the experience. Some psychologists, such as Mark D. Griffiths, have criticized the mechanics of freemium games as exploitative, drawing direct parallels to gambling addiction. Furthermore, the ubiquitous and often intrusive use of microtransactions in free-to-play games have sometimes caused children to either inadvertently or deliberately pay for large amounts of virtual goods, often for drastically high amounts of real money. In February 2013, Eurogamer reported that Apple had agreed to refund a British family £1700.41 after their son had racked up countless microtransactions whilst playing the F2P game *Zombies vs. Ninjas*. In February 2015 Apple began featuring popular non-freemium software on the App Store as "Pay Once & Play", describing them as "Great Games with No In-App Purchases ... hours of uninterrupted fun with complete experiences".

Outlook

Pointing to the disruptive effect of free-to-play on current models, IGN editor Charles Onyett has said "expensive, one-time purchases are facing extinction". He believes that the current method of paying a one-time fee for most games will eventually disappear completely. Greg Zeschuk, of BioWare believes there is a good possibility that free-to-play would become the dominant pricing plan for games, but that it was very unlikely that it would ever completely replace subscription-based games. Developers such as Electronic Arts have pointed to the success of freemium, saying that microtransactions will inevitably be part of every game. While noting the success of some developers with the model, companies such as Nintendo have remained skeptical of free-to-play, preferring to stick to more traditional models of game development and sales.

Gold Sink

Gold sink is an economic process by which a video game's ingame currency ('gold'), or any item that can be valued against it, is removed. This process is comparable to financial repression in real economies. Most commonly the genres are role-playing game or massively multiplayer online game. The term is comparable to timesink, but usually used in reference to game design and balance, commonly to reduce inflation when commodities and wealth are continually fed to players through sources such as quests, looting monsters, or minigames.

Overview

Gold sinks are commonly called drains or gold drains. They can also be associated with item drains. The intent of a sink is to remove added value from the overall economy. For example, in Ultima Online, items that were placed on the ground would be gathered by the server. This form is referred to as decay or garbage collection.

Economies in virtual worlds operate very differently from those in the real world. Passive gold sinks may be in operation at all times to slowly extract value from the game. Players are usually more willing to accept this method of sinking. Passive sinks would be item degradation, consistent taxes, or decay. Active sinks are aggressive actions by the programmers to remove excessive value. These can be changes in the severity of the passive sinks, such as higher taxes or faster decay. But more effectively, an active sink can be the selling of unique items whose intrinsic values are much lower than the selling price sold by NPC vendors. Zack Booth Simpson cites one example in Ultima Online when the NPC vendors carried blue tinted armor that couldn't be made by players. Blue armor prices could be much higher, but decayed and degraded just like any other piece of armor.

Another improvement to active sinking is to couple it to a feedback control system. Such systems can be designed to maintain a set of prices or asset ratios, and if properly set up can add a great deal of price stability to a virtual economy; one example of this can be found in the MMO MUD Alter Aeon. The feedback control system used in Alter Aeon works by tracking the total amount of money in the game in order to dynamically adjust drop rates and shop prices. Players with more than 1 million in currency are taxed for 2% of the money they own over that limit. This keeps the economy permanently stable. The peaks in the total amount of in-game currency do not vary more than 10% in a time period of 2 years.

Resource Flow

Depending on how resources are created and where resources go once destroyed, gold sinks are classified differently. There are two major types of resource management: linked and unlinked. Several aspects can be linked while others can be unlinked.

Linked

Linked resource flow means that the head is connected to the tail. All things have a resource intrinsic value. A deer may be worth three pieces of meat and two yards of leather. A sword can be worth three units of iron. When a resource such as a sword is destroyed through garbage collection, those three units of iron will go back into the mines of the virtual world for extraction. This is essentially no different from melting the sword down for the raw metal. A few steps of procurement are skipped, but essentially it's the same.

A strong linked system would have a governing equation for NPC vendors to follow. NPCs would be restricted to craft with the resources they have in stock. Player character Jake could sell the town vendor a sword for 10 gold. If Jake wanted to purchase gauntlets (let us assume gauntlets have a resource value of two units of iron), he could for 12 gold. The town vendor has made a 2 gold and 1 unit of iron profit off the transaction. Should another player character want to purchase something, the new character could only buy items that have a 1 unit of iron resource value or he could sell an item, let us say 1 leather and 1 iron, to now be able to purchase items that have a resource value equal to or less than 2 units of iron and 1 unit of leather.

To be a total linked system, NPCs would be programmed to break even or make small profits. Some virtual worlds may opt to leave NPCs unrestricted as to how much money they give out.

Examples

The intended purpose of gold sinks is to remove currency from the game, as excess currency leads to inflation of player driven prices. Game designers must balance between scarcity of currency and ease of acquiring currency.

Greater methods of currency spending can be implemented when players accumulate more wealth than intended. One example is Ultima Online; after the Renaissance expansion, players could earn money without fear of loss, due to the implementation of non-player versus player areas. As currency entered the economy at a greater pace, new "luxury" items were sold at high prices for the purpose of reducing large sums of money.

In *Kingdom of Loathing*, the massive acquisition of "meat" (the currency of the game) through exploitation of bugs led to the implementation of new high priced items that gave no in-game benefits (simply rare collectibles) to the player to eliminate excess currency.

In *RuneScape*, the Construction skill can be seen as a gold sink. This skill allows players to spend money on building a house. This way, money is taken out of the game, without players obtaining any tradeable items.

Other forms of gold sinks include:

- Quests requiring a certain amount to continue with the task at hand. This is offset by quest rewards and items that may be resold.

- Fees associated with NPC services and tasks.

- Fees associated with travel and convenience.

- Crafting, often requiring an initial investment and a continued chance of failure. Items may be crafted at a loss to increase crafting skill.

- Auction House Taxes

Time Sink

A time sink (or timesink) is an activity that consumes significant time. A variant of this term is "time drain." Although it is unknown when the term was coined, it makes an analogy with heat sink.

In massively multiplayer online role-playing games (MMORPGs), time sinks are a method of increasing the time needed by players to do certain tasks, hopefully causing them to subscribe for longer periods of time. Players may use the term disparagingly to describe a simplistic and time-consuming aspect of gameplay, possibly designed to keep players playing longer without significant benefit. Time sinks can also be used for other gameplay reasons, such as to help regenerate resources or monsters in the game world.

Negative Connotations

Many players consider time sinks to be an inherently poor design decision, only included so that game companies can increase profits. For example, one Slashdot article describes time sinks as "gameplay traps intended to waste your time and keep you playing longer". In most games, boring and lengthy parts of gameplay are merely an annoyance, but when used in subscription-based MMORPGs, where players are paying recurring fees for access to the game, they become a much more inflammatory issue. Game designers must be prudent in balancing efforts to produce both involving gameplay and the length of content that players expect.

Time sinks are often associated with hardcore games, though whether this is a positive or negative association depends on the context.

Trade-offs

Implementing time sinks in a video game is a delicate balancing act. Excessive use of time sinks may cause players to stop playing. However, if not enough time sinks are implemented, players may feel the game is too short or too easy, causing them to abandon the game much sooner out of boredom. A number of criteria can be used to evaluate use of time sinks, such as frequency, length, and variety (both of the nature of the time sink and the actions taken to overcome it). What is considered a good balance depends in part on the type of game in question. Casual games are often expected to have less in the way of time sinks, and hardcore games to have more, though this is not a hard and fast rule.

A good timesink has you interacting with the game on some level, earning some level of enjoyment or moving the story along. It might be "realistic", but keep in mind that you are trying to entertain people here and useless timesinks tend to do the opposite of entertain.

—*Matt Miller, MMODesigner.com*

Difference from Cooldowns

Time sinks are often confused with cooldowns. A cooldown is defined as set time limit between uses of an ability or other form of interaction, ranging in length from milliseconds (such as use of a weapon) to hours or even days (such as quests that can only be completed once a day) depending on the system in question. As soon as that timer is expired, the ability immediately becomes available. A time sink, on the other hand, requires a player to complete certain activities before it is completed. Additionally, cooldowns are front-loaded, in that they can be used once immediately, and then the player must wait until the timer has expired before it can be used again. Time sinks, on the other hand, are back-loaded, requiring the player to spend time and effort before the reward becomes available.

It is worth noting that activities may have both cooldowns and time sinks associated with them. For example, a quest that can only be done once every 10 hours and requires two hours of work to complete has a cooldown (10 hours between completions) and is also a time sink (in that it requires two hours to complete).

Examples

- Gaining levels through experience points (especially if grinding is involved).

- Lengthy travel times.

- Resource or item collecting (such as asteroid mining in space-themed MMORPGs).

- Frequent backtracking

References

- Dani Cavallaro (2010), Anime and the visual novel: narrative structure, design and play at the crossroads of animation and computer games, pp. 78–9, McFarland & Company, ISBN 0-7864-4427-4

- Mark J. P. Wolf (2008), The video game explosion: a history from PONG to Playstation and beyond, ABC-CLIO, p. 100, ISBN 0-313-33868-X, retrieved 2011-04-10

- Byron Reeves; J. Leighton Read (2009). Total Engagement: Using Games and Virtual Worlds to Change the Way People Work and Businesses Compete. Harvard Business Press. p. 177. ISBN 978-1-4221-4657-6.

- Jane McGonigal Read (2011). Reality Is Broken: Why Games Make Us Better and How They Can Change The World. Penguin Press. p. 122. ISBN 978-1-59420-285-8.

- Marczewski, Andrzej (April 2012). Gamification: A Simple Introduction (1st ed.). p. 3. ISBN 978-1-4717-9866-5. Retrieved 2012-11-25.

- Coonradt, Charles; Nelson, Lee (1985). The Game of Work: How to Enjoy Work as Much as Play (1st ed.). Deseret Book. p. 146. ISBN 0-87747-771-X. Retrieved 2012-11-25.

- Biocca, Frank; Levy, Mark R. (1995). Communication in the Age of Virtual Reality. Lawrence Erlbaum Associates. ISBN 0-8058-1550-3.

- Castronova, Edward (2005). Synthetic Worlds: The Business and Culture of Online Games. University of Chicago Press. ISBN 0-226-09626-2.

- Begault, Durand R. (1994). 3-D Sound for Virtual Reality and Multimedia (PDF). San Diego, CA, USA: Academic Press Professional, Inc. ISBN 0-12-084735-3.

- Biocca, Frank; Levy, Mark R. (1995). Communication in the Age of Virtual Reality. Lawrence Erlbaum Associates. ISBN 0-8058-1550-3.

- Castronova, Edward (2005). Synthetic Worlds: The Business and Culture of Online Games. Chicago: The University of Chicago Press. p. 164. ISBN 0-226-09626-2.

- Gilbert, Dan; Whitehead, James; Whitehead, James II (2007). Hacking World of Warcraft. John Wiley & Sons. pp. 183, 184. ISBN 978-0-470-11002-7.

Permissions

Index